P9-DFK-775

XQRQ-3D96-DXRU-4VAK-8966

IMPORTANT

HERE IS YOUR REGISTRATION CODE TO ACCESS MCGRAW-HILL
PREMIUM CONTENT AND MCGRAW-HILL ONLINE RESOURCES

For key premium online resources you need THIS CODE to
gain access. Once the code is entered, you will be able to
use the web resources for the length of your course.

Access is provided only if you have purchased a new book.

If the registration code is missing from this book, the registration screen on our
website, and within your WebCT or Blackboard course will tell you how to obtain
your new code. Your registration code can be used only once to establish
access. It is not transferable.

To gain access to these online resources

1. USE your web browser to go to: **www.mhhe.com/krysik1**

2. CLICK on "First Time User"

3. ENTER the Registration Code printed on the tear-off bookmark on the right

4. After you have entered your registration code, click on "Register"

5. FOLLOW the instructions to setup your personal UserID and Password

6. WRITE your UserID and Password down for future reference. Keep it in a safe place.

If your course is using WebCT or Blackboard, you'll be able to use this code to
access the McGraw-Hill content within your instructor's online course.

To gain access to the McGraw-Hill content in your instructor's WebCT or
Blackboard course simply log into the course with the user ID and Password
provided by your instructor. Enter the registration code exactly as it appears to
the right when prompted by the system. You will only need to use this code the
first time you click on McGraw-Hill content.

These instructions are specifically for student access. Instructors are not required
to register via the above instructions.

The McGraw-Hill Companies

McGraw Hill · Higher Education

Thank you, and welcome to your
McGraw-Hill Online Resources.

**ISBN-13: 978-0-07-320082-8
ISBN-10: 0-07-320082-4 t/a
Krysik/Finn
Research for Effective Social Work Practice, 1/e**

REGISTRATION CODE
REGISTRATION CODE

The McGraw-Hill Companies

Mc Graw Hill · Higher Education

This is a much-needed series for social work education and the social work profession...one of the best I have seen in decades!

Each title is the first of its kind to offer instructors and their students a multidimensional understanding and experience of the world of social work:

- **Each book in the series is accompanied by a custom Web site, updated weekly,** that allows students to examine events in the news and to think about and discuss those events in the context of what they are reading. The Web site also links students to a wealth of carefully selected Internet resources that are constantly updated and refreshed.

- **A specially designed online reader, *The Social Work Library,* is also available to students,** with over 100 articles and book chapters linked to the key ideas and principles covered in each volume in the series.

- ***Practicing Social Work™*, a CD-ROM packaged with each volume in the series,** offers complex, richly populated case exercises, with multiple options in text and video for analysis and intervention. The CD gives students a real-world sense of how social workers approach cases from micro, mezzo, and macro perspectives and trains them in the use of social work tools they will likely encounter in their professional lives.

- **A free booklet on social work ethics accompanies each text** in recognition of CSWE recommendations, and is authored by Kim Strom-Gottfried, University of North Carolina, who is nationally recognized for her educational workshops on the subject.

New Directions in Social Work is a comprehensive effort by a team of accomplished social work educators to move social work education forward. We want to help you enrich and deepen your students' learning experiences. And we want to know what you think! Please e-mail us with your feedback. In the meantime, we welcome your students to a most gratifying, heartbreaking, edifying profession: social work.

Judy L. Krysik
Arizona State University
e-mail: jkrysik@msn.com

Jerry Finn
University of Washington, Tacoma
e-mail: jfinn2@comcast.net

Research for Effective
Social Work Practice

NEW DIRECTIONS IN SOCIAL WORK: A McGRAW-HILL SERIES

Consulting editor, Alice A. Lieberman, University of Kansas

New Directions in Social Work is an innovative series of texts, software, and custom electronic content for the *foundations* courses in the Social Work curriculum. Each title is the first of its kind to offer instructors and their students a multidimensional experience and understanding of the world of social work. Each volume in the series includes a custom Web site, online reader, and *Practicing Social Work,* a unique collection of virtual case studies.

Books in the Series

Social Work and Social Welfare: An Invitation by Marla Berg-Weger

Contemporary Social Work Practice by Marty Dewees

Human Behavior in the Social Environment by Anissa Taun Rogers

Social Policy for Effective Practice: A Strengths Approach by Rosemary K. Chapin

Research for Effective Social Work Practice by Judy L. Krysik and Jerry Finn

Also from McGraw-Hill

Social Work Practice with a Difference: Stories, Essays, Cases, and Commentaries by Alice A. Lieberman and Cheryl B. Lester

The Social Work Experience: An Introduction to Social Work and Social Welfare, Fourth Edition by Mary Ann Suppes and Carolyn Cressy Wells

Research for Effective Social Work Practice

Judy L. Krysik, PhD
Arizona State University

Jerry Finn, PhD
University of Washington, Tacoma

Boston   Burr Ridge, IL   Dubuque, IA   Madison, WI   New York
San Francisco   St. Louis   Bangkok   Bogotá   Caracas   Kuala Lumpur
Lisbon   London   Madrid   Mexico City   Milan   Montreal   New Delhi
Santiago   Seoul   Singapore   Sydney   Taipei   Toronto

Published by McGraw-Hill, an imprint of The McGraw-Hill Companies, Inc., 1221 Avenue of the Americas, New York, NY 10020. Copyright © 2007 by The McGraw-Hill Companies. All rights reserved. No part of this publication may be reproduced or distributed in any form or by any means, or stored in a database or retrieval system, without the prior written consent of The McGraw-Hill Companies, Inc., including, but not limited to, in any network or other electronic storage or transmission, or broadcast for distance learning.

This book is printed on acid-free paper.

1 2 3 4 5 6 7 8 9 0 DOC/DOC 0 9 8 7 6

ISBN–13: 978-0-07-311226-8
ISBN–10: 0-07-311226-7

Editor in Chief: *Emily Barrosse*
Publisher and Sponsoring Editor: *Beth Mejia*
Special Projects Editor: *Rebecca Smith*
Developmental Editor: *Robert Weiss*
Editorial Coordinator: *Ann Helgerson*
Marketing Manager: *Dean Karampelas*
Media Producer: *Sean Crowley*
Media Project Manager: *Wendy Constantine*
Production Editor: *Leslie LaDow*
Manuscript Editor: *Judith Brown*

Designer: *Kim Menning*
Interior Designer: *Glenda King*
Cover Designer: *Marianna Kinigakis*
Photo Research Coordinator:
Natalia Peschiera
Production Supervisor: *Tandra Jorgensen*
Composition: *9.5/13 Stone Serif by Interactive Composition Corporation, India*
Printing: *50# Windsor Offset 92 Smooth by R.R. Donnelley & Sons*

Cover image: © Photodisc

Produced in association with NASW Press, a division of the National Association of Social Workers.

NASW PRESS

Library of Congress Cataloging-in-Publication Data

Krysik, Judy.
  Research for effective social work practice / Judy L. Krysik, Jerry Finn.
    p. cm. — (New direction in social work)
  Includes bibliographical references.
  ISBN-13: 978-0-07-311226-8 (alk. paper)
  ISBN-10: 0-07-311226-7 (alk. paper)
    1. Social service—Research. 2. Social service—Methodology. 3. Social workers—Professional ethics. 4. Qualitative research—Moral and ethical aspects. 5. Group work in research. 6. Sampling (Statistics) I. Finn, Jerry. II. Title. III. New directions in social work (Boston, Mass.)

HV11.K78 2007
361.3'2072—dc22

2005058408

The Internet addresses listed in the text were accurate at the time of publication. The inclusion of a Web site does not indicate an endorsement by the authors or McGraw-Hill, and McGraw-Hill does not guarantee the accuracy of the information presented at these sites.

www.mhhe.com

A B O U T   T H E   A U T H O R S

DR. JUDY KRYSIK is an associate professor in the School of Social Work at Arizona State University. A former faculty member of the University of Denver, Graduate School of Social Work, she received her doctorate from Arizona State University (1995) and her BSW (1988) and MSW (1991) from the University of Calgary, Alberta. Dr. Krysik has worked as a research and evaluation consultant for 16 years, primarily in the areas of child welfare and child abuse and neglect prevention. She has published numerous scholarly articles and book chapters and is co-author of *Social Policy and Social Work: Critical Essays on the Welfare State* (1998). She teaches in the areas of research, evaluation, social policy, and program planning.

DR. JERRY FINN is currently a professor in the Social Work Program, University of Washington, Tacoma. He received his doctorate from the University of Wisconsin–Madison in Social Welfare in 1980, MSW from the University of Hawaii in 1974, and BA in psychology from the University of California–Los Angeles in 1967. Dr. Finn has 26 years of teaching experience in social work that includes courses in human behavior, research, practice, and information technology and human services at the bachelor's and master's levels, and he has served on doctoral committees. In addition, he has published numerous scholarly articles and an edited book, primarily in areas related to the impact of information technology on human services. Dr. Finn has served as treasurer of the Council on Social Work Education (CSWE) and is currently on the Publications and Media Commission. He has also served with the Association of Baccalaureate Social Work Program Directors (BPD) as treasurer and registrar.

BRIEF CONTENTS

DETAILED CONTENTS

CHAPTER 8   *Describing the Data   219*

PREFACE

*Research is not exclusive to those who are so inclined;
research is for all social workers.*

Research for Effective Social Work Practice is written for undergraduate social work students. It covers the basics of using and conducting social work research in a user-friendly, practical way. The book provides many examples of social work research drawn from the literature, our colleagues, and our many years as social work educators, researchers, and evaluation consultants. The examples in this book relate to many populations and different levels of practice, and they span many areas, including substance abuse, corrections, gerontology, social work in an international context, child welfare, prevention research, community organizing, social policy, program planning, technology, and evaluation.

What sets this book apart from other social work research books is that it does not handle the research topics in a piecemeal approach. Like most social work research books, *Research for Effective Social Work Practice* has chapters devoted to basic topics such as formulating research questions, sampling, research design, measurement, and analysis. Unlike other textbooks, however, this book logically links the chapters so that based on the research question that the social worker selects, she or he will be able to (a) make a reasoned judgment about the best research methods to apply, (b) articulate the strengths and weaknesses of her or his choices, and (c) critique the research methods used in other studies. In addition, the critical thinking approach this book promotes and the examples and guidance it provides will help social workers avoid common errors in research and evaluation. Finally, as the name implies, the book will assist social workers in using and producing evidence-based knowledge that will lead to effective social work practice.

Some authors of social work research books maintain that research is too complex a task for undergraduate and even graduate social work students. Instead, these authors aspire to prepare social work students to read research and to have a greater appreciation for the role of research in social work. *Research for Effective Social Work Practice* goes beyond these limited objectives by helping you develop your own research skills. We are confident that if you read this book with the intent to learn and you engage in the exercises, not only will you be able to access, read, and critically evaluate research, but you also will develop valued research skills.

ORGANIZATION OF THE BOOK

Take a look inside, and you will see that each chapter follows a similar format. The chapters begin with a reflective quote, followed by an introduction to the chapter and a list of learning objectives. Many of the examples presented throughout the book are in the form of Case-in-Points that are easily distinguished from the rest of the content. Each chapter devotes attention to social work in a culturally diverse context, providing guidance to social workers striving for culturally proficient practice. In addition, as research terms are introduced, they are displayed in bold type and are supported by a glossary. Each chapter also uses graphics to illustrate points. The chapters encourage the use of technology in research by providing links to credible online sources of information and additional Internet-based learning opportunities, as well as exercises that require the use of different software for data management, analysis, and presentation. Finally, each chapter is summarized by a series of main points.

Three types of exercises are presented at the end of each chapter. The exercises under the heading "Practicing Social Work" ask you to apply newly acquired research knowledge and skills to the two case studies on the CD-ROM packaged with this book. These exercises illustrate how the information in each chapter is directly applicable to social work practice. The "Social Work Library" exercises ask you to read and critically analyze published research available at the online library. Each chapter contains references to articles published in social work journals that can be accessed from www.mhhe.com/krysik1. Finally, exercises presented under the heading "Other Exercises" ask general and applied questions related to the major points of each chapter. The Web site also contains links to valuable Internet resources such as job postings involving social work research, organizations that support and promote social work research, online research publications, and more.

To be consistent with the length of most social work research courses, we have organized this text into 12 chapters. Chapters 1 and 2 present an introduction to the context of social work research. Chapters 3–6 represent the design phase of research, and Chapters 7–11 discuss the implementation and analysis phases. Finally, Chapter 12 explains how to present your research for maximum impact.

- Chapter 1 sets the context for social work research and discusses the importance of research to the social work profession. The chapter presents social work research in its historical context, examining the challenges the profession has overcome and those it continues to face. As you prepare yourself for the job market, Chapter 1 introduces you to a world of opportunities to engage in social work research, both as a complement to practice and as a profession in itself.

- Chapter 2 reflects on the way politics shapes research agendas and the choice of research methods. It emphasizes the need for social workers to commit themselves to ethics in conducting and using research. Similar to the first chapter, Chapter 2 uses a historical approach, reflecting the belief that we should learn from the mistakes of our profession's past in order to move forward.

- Chapter 3 sets out the process of conducting research, and it provides a step-by-step approach to framing research problems and questions. After a research problem and question are identified, Chapters 4–9 present a how-to approach to answering the research question using either a quantitative, qualitative, or mixed-methods approach.

- Chapter 4 discusses research design in the context of answering the research question.

- Chapter 5 deals with sampling, that is, how to decide which people and how many people to include in the study. A sampling frame is available on the CD-ROM to use with the sampling exercises.

- Chapter 6 covers the basics of measurement, including how to design your own measures.

- Chapter 7 deals with the mechanics of collecting and safely storing data and preparing the data for analysis. The Web site provides step-by-step tutorials in SPSS and Excel to help you complete the exercises. The data for the exercises are from the Black Feather project and are on the CD-ROM.

- Chapter 8 presents a how-to approach to analyzing qualitative and quantitative data. As with Chapter 7, the Web site provides SPSS and Excel tutorials, and you can complete the chapter exercises using the Black Feather data provided on the CD-ROM in both Excel and SPSS formats. Qualitative data are provided on the Web site for practice with analysis.

- Chapter 9 examines the analysis of quantitative data, presents guidelines for selecting statistical tests, and describes how to interpret statistical output. The Web site provides tutorials on how to analyze the data using SPSS or Excel.

- Chapters 10 and 11 represent two contexts in which social workers apply the skills presented in Chapters 3–9. Chapter 10 addresses the evaluation of a single case through single subject and case study resarch.

- Chapter 11 discusses the evaluation of social programs, including evaluability assessment, needs assessment, process, outcome, and cost evaluation.

- The final chapter, Chapter 12, provides valuable tips on grant writing, publication, and presentation.

TO ONCE AND FUTURE RESEARCH STUDENTS

According to an old maxim, "What goes around comes around." In fact, this happened to me. I took my first policy class when I was a first-year MSW student. I wanted to be a therapist. After a week, I (foolishly) asked my professor, "Why do we need any of this?" He looked pained and proceeded to tell me that policy was "the rules" and that those rules would determine what services I could provide and to whom, as well as what funding and access would be available for my "therapy." I didn't "get it" at the time.

Now I am teaching research. One evening, one of my MSW students looked frustrated. I asked if there was something she didn't understand. "No," she answered, "I just don't see why I'll ever need this." I am sure I made the same pained expression that my policy professor had made 30 years earlier. For drama, I also clutched my heart. But she was serious and did not mean to induce cardiac arrest. In fact, she wasn't asking a question; she was honestly stating her feelings.

And so, I was sure I had failed her—not her grade, but her education. Hadn't I given the "Why you need research" lecture? Hadn't we examined fascinating research designs and crucial outcome studies? Hadn't we discussed research ethics, literature reviews, critical analyses, statistical testing, and outcome evaluation? We had . . . and yet the question had remained.

I came to realize that the student didn't doubt the importance of research. Rather, she doubted the relevance of research *for her*. She was sure that *she* would never knowingly do research, just as I was sure 30 years earlier that I would never (knowingly) do policy analysis (or teach research). Foolish me, and probably foolish her.

I guess I need to make my case again. How can you be a clinician, a therapist, an advocate for rape victims, a worker in a domestic violence shelter, a youth counselor, or any other direct service worker without developing research skills? It would be nice to think that we taught you everything you needed to know in the social work program. Too bad—we didn't. When I was a therapist, I was seeing a client for marital counseling. I had learned a lot about family systems and marital counseling. One day my client told me that his father had sexually abused him as a child. My first thought was, "My program never taught me about the sexual abuse of boys by their fathers. What should I do?" I needed to know the developmental impact of this kind of sexual abuse. What kinds of treatments were likely to be effective? How great was the risk of suicide? Should I explore and reflect the client's past feelings, or should I teach avoidance and compartmentalization? I was very glad—and relieved—that I knew how to use a library and access the research literature. Other people's

Adapted with permission, previously published in J. Finn, 2004, "To Once and Future Social work students, *The New Social Worker, 11*(4), 12.

research made my work a lot less anxiety provoking, for both my client and for me.

Good social workers care about what happens to their clients. Yes, using effective treatments and validating results are part of the NASW *Code of Ethics*. However, good social workers don't want to be effective just because their *Code of Ethics* demands it. Instead, they want to be effective because they *care*. Research helps you and your clients see what you are accomplishing (or not accomplishing) as a result of services provided. Also, it's fun to play "connect the dots" and interpret what they mean.

I recently heard about an exciting new treatment: rapid eyeball movement therapy. It really works. At least, that's what they tell me. Decisions, decisions, decisions . . . so many decisions to make as part of providing services to your clients. What exciting new services should you use? Is it better to use individual or group treatment? How many sessions does it take for a men's domestic violence group to effect change? Is a "climbing course" an effective way to promote group solidarity with teenagers? Should we encourage the school system to have a DARE program? Should we use e-mail with clients? Sometimes the research literature provides answers; sometimes it doesn't. You need to know how to get the evidence you need to make treatment decisions. You can be a force for evidence-based practice at your agency. We do things because it has been demonstrated that they work. OK, sometimes we try something innovative if there is enough theory or evidence to suggest it's worth it. However, we don't continue to spend money if it doesn't work. You have to know one way or another.

Money. Money. Money. Why does it always come down to money? You want money so you can continue your program. You want money so you can expand your services or offer new services. You can get the money, but you have to know how (and whom) to ask. These days, funders don't give money easily. You have to get it the old-fashioned way, by demonstrating that you need it and will use it wisely. Demonstrate that people want, need, and will use your service. Demonstrate that what you want to provide is effective. Demonstrate that you put the money already given you to good use. You demonstrate these things through program evaluation, aka research.

Sometimes people say some strange and hurtful things in the name of "truth." Sometimes they do this because they want to stop what you are doing. I'm referring to comments like, "Most people on welfare cheat the system" or "Almost 98 percent of men pay their child support." Going further, in some cases they actually come up with *research* to support it. You need to know enough about research to show them (or politicians/funders/your community) the error of their ways, or of their method of obtaining data, or of their statistical procedures, or of their (false) conclusions. First you have to "smell" it, then point it out, and then get rid of it.

OK, if you don't want to "walk the walk," at least learn to talk the talk. If not you, *someone* will do research at your agency. You can explain your program and objectives in language that a researcher understands, and you can understand the language of the researcher to be sure that what is being done is appropriate. Bilingual is good.

So, maybe you won't ever have to do research or policy analysis. But maybe you will. Maybe you think you'll be a case manager or a therapist for the rest of your life. I thought that. Funny, though, things change. You may become a supervisor, an advocate, an administrator, a program evaluator, or even a *research professor*. Who knows where life leads? In the meantime, I have a hammer in my garage. I rarely use it, but when I need one, it's incredibly handy. We wish you the best with your research tools.

ACKNOWLEDGMENTS

There are many people who have been instrumental in the completion of this book and deserving of our gratitude. First, thanks to our students who over the years have served as the inspiration for the ideas, content, and resources in the book. Second, thank you to Alice Lieberman, Series Editor whose vision gave this series life and who brought us together to collaborate on the writing of this research book. Third, thanks to Ann Helgerson, Editorial Coordinator from McGraw-Hill and Robert Weiss, Development Editor, who have been with us throughout this project and who have been diligent in keeping us on track and providing us with excellent feedback.

Special thanks to our social work colleagues who served as reviewers, we were extremely impressed by your thoroughness and benefited greatly from your helpful comments. Thank you as well to the authors of the other books in this series, Marla Berg-Weger, Rosemary Chapin, Anissa Rogers, and Marty Dewees for your ongoing encouragement and support. Finally, thank you to our families, who were always interested and committed to helping us see this through.

Quiero dar las gracias a mi esposo Alonso, a mi hijo Roberto y a mi hija Rosario. Thank you also to the rest of the Krysik Peralta family. J.K.

Thanks, Pat, for giving up on the basement project this summer so that this book could be written. J. F.

CHAPTER 1

The Context of Social Work Research

The continued growth and acceptance of social work knowledge depends not only on social workers' appreciation and support of research but also on their competence to engage in research and use research findings.

—PROCTOR, 2001, P. 3

PEOPLE GENERALLY BECOME SOCIAL WORKERS BECAUSE THEY want to have a positive impact on social conditions in order to improve the lives of other people. *Impact* comes from the commitment to make change and the knowledge and skills to put that commitment to use. Social work history is rich with examples of committed individuals informed by knowledge and skill. Case-in-Point 1.1 tells the story of Dorothea Dix, a pioneering social worker who used research to make an enormous impact in the area of mental health. It also describes how research continues to impact the approach to mental health.

This book was written to help social work students develop the research knowledge and skills that you as a social worker will need in order to have a positive impact on social work practice and social conditions. To accomplish this task, you will need to answer many fundamental questions: Did I help the individual, couple, or family I worked with? What types of interventions are most likely to lead to positive change? Who is not receiving social work services even though he or she is eligible for such services? What interventions are the most cost effective in this era of diminishing resources? What evidence do I need in order to obtain or maintain funding for a social program? What information do I need to give policy makers to promote change that will help people in the community? To answer these questions, you will need knowledge and skills in research. The realization that research is vital to social work practice is not new, and the need for research has been demonstrated over and over again, as illustrated in many of the Case-in-Points throughout this book.

Before we begin to develop research knowledge and skills, however, we must first address the one question that is on the minds of so many beginning social work students: Why do *I* need to learn research? To answer this question,

On Sunday, March 28, 1841, Dorothea Dix volunteered to teach a Sunday school class of 20 women inmates at the Cambridge, Massachusetts, jail. After the lesson was over, she went down to the lower level of the building—the dungeon cells. This was where the "insane" were sheltered. She saw miserable, wild, and dazed men and women chained to walls and locked in pens. They were naked, filthy, brutalized, underfed, given no heat, and sleeping on stone floors.

This visit moved Dix to commit her life's work to improve conditions for people with mental illness (Muckenhoupt, 2003). She started a campaign to have stoves placed in the cells and to have the inmates fully clothed. She also began to study firsthand the conditions for people with mental illness throughout the state. She traveled from county to county, gathering evidence to present to the Massachusetts legislature as the basis for laws to improve conditions. She eventually visited states all over the nation, systematically gathering evidence and making presentations to lobby for the establishment of state-supported institutions. The first state hospital built as a result of her efforts was located in Trenton, New Jersey. The construction of this hospital was the first step in the development of a national system of "asylums"—places of refuge (Viney & Zorich, 1982). Proponents argued that putting people in asylums would be more humane and cost effective than the existing system.

By 1955 there were 560,000 people in mental hospitals throughout the United States. The institutions themselves became overcrowded, abusive, and in need of reform. What was once a viable solution to the problem of mental illness became a problem over time. Social workers again used research, this time to convince state legislators that mental hospitals were ineffective treatment facilities. They used interviews with patients and family members to document abuses. They argued that releasing people from mental hospitals would be more humane and cost effective than the existing policy of institutionalization. As a result, beginning in the mid-1960s, many mental hospitals were closed in favor of community treatment models (Scott & Dixon, 1995; Stein & Test, 1980). Although community treatment is promising, it has also led to an increase in homelessness and incarceration among adults with mental illness (Lamb & Weinberger, 1998). Research continues today on the effectiveness of community-based treatment, and it promises to be a major factor in the establishment and funding of new programs.

we begin by briefly examining the function of research in social work. We also look at the history of research in social work, the struggles the profession has overcome, and the opportunities and challenges that lie ahead. Overall, this chapter is devoted to helping you to achieve an appreciation for the place of research in social work practice and to increase your knowledge of the infrastructure that has been developed to support social work research. The remaining chapters are geared toward helping you develop the research knowledge and skills that will enable you to fulfill your dream of making an impact. By the end of this chapter you should be able to:

- Articulate the role of research in social work.

- Discuss the alternatives to knowledge based on research.

- Summarize the positions of social work's professional organizations on the use of research in social work.

- Describe the concept of evidence-based practice.

- Identify the types of career opportunities that research skills afford the entry-level social worker.

- Describe how research can be used to empower both social workers and the people they endeavor to help.

THE FUNCTIONS OF RESEARCH IN SOCIAL WORK

At this point you may be wondering, "How can research make me a better social worker?" There are several answers to that question, and they all relate to the functions of research in social work. In this section we discuss research both as a method for providing the scientific basis of the social work profession and as a tool for improving social conditions. We focus on four basic functions of social work research:

- promoting science as a way of knowing

- increasing accountability

- improving communication

- enhancing access to scarce resources

Promoting Science as a Way of Knowing

Where do social workers obtain their knowledge? Social workers have many ways of acquiring knowledge, and they are all important (see Exhibit 1.1). One way of knowing is through direct experience. Social work education promotes knowing through experience by requiring students to complete a specified number of hours in an internship or a field placement. Through observation and direct experience, social workers develop a sense of what works and under what circumstances.

Intuition is another way of knowing. As social workers we are told to pay attention to our reactions or our "gut feelings." Sometimes our intuition causes us to explore certain lines of questioning or to make observations that lead to important insights in our work.

We also gain knowledge from authority. From infancy we are programmed to believe that what people in positions of authority tell us is true. For instance, we may seldom question what our parents, teachers, clergy, and political leaders tell us. In social work practice we gain knowledge from our supervisors

---

EXHIBIT 1.1

Many Ways of Knowing

Direct experience: *A caseload of 60 cases per worker will cause burnout.* I know because I experienced it. I know because I saw, smelled, touched, or tasted it.

Intuition: *I think the child is being abused. I don't know why exactly, but my intuition tells me so.* I know because I feel it to be so.

Authority: *Anger is depression turned against the self.* I know because my supervisor told me.

Tradition: *Our agency is open Monday through Friday from 9:00 a.m. to 5:30 p.m.* I know because it has always been that way.

Science: *On average, husbands and boyfriends murder more than three women in the United States every day. In 2000, 1,247 women were killed by an intimate partner compared to 440 men (Bureau of Justice Statistics, 2003).*

Two important characteristics of the scientific method are a defined approach and a skeptical attitude.

and our colleagues. We also acquire knowledge from our clients, who are authorities on their own lives.

Another source of knowledge is tradition. Knowing through tradition involves believing something because that is the way it has always been, because it is a part of who you are. Tradition is an important source of culturally specific knowledge. For instance, many indigenous cultures have folk healers; in Mexico they are called *curanderas* (or *curanderos*, masculine). The curanderos are a cornerstone of Mexican culture. Some people who seek the services of the curanderos are true believers; others are skeptical. In either case, however, their participation is a product of knowledge based on tradition.

Human service agencies may also have traditions, for instance, traditions about the best ways to deliver social services. The way it is done is because "that's how it has always been done." For example, an agency may pride itself on providing insight-oriented therapy to their clients. However, this "tradition" of service delivery may become outdated as changes within the community bring more people with severe and persistent mental illnesses to the agency.

One particularly important source of knowledge for social workers is **social work research,** a systematic way of developing knowledge that relies on the scientific method. The **scientific method** is a process of accumulating knowledge that involves five distinct steps:

- identifying a problem
- defining that problem in terms of a question that is capable of study
- developing a plan to answer the question
- gathering data according to prescribed practices
- drawing conclusions from the data

The knowledge and skills we learn in social work research—like those we learn in other social work courses, such as interviewing and assessment—change the ways we see, hear, and understand people and make us more effective social workers. An education in social work research leads us to question the knowledge claims of *all* sources. One of the most important reasons you are taking this course is to learn to question what you think you know and how you know it. Making judgments about what to believe is a part of everyday life for social workers. The danger of basing social work practice decisions on direct experience, intuition, authority, or tradition is that what you think you know may be no more than a few isolated observations, what we refer to as *anecdotal information*. For example, knowledge based on authority may be based on what feels right or comfortable for a particular person. It may be rooted in tradition or an untested fad.

To be effective as social workers, we must critically evaluate our ways of knowing and make judgments based on the best information available. We must learn to question basic values and claims, even those that are made on the basis of published scientific findings that we previously may have taken for granted. Social work research promotes a way of knowing that we as social workers as well as people outside the profession can have confidence in. This does not mean that social workers discount other ways of knowing or never use them. They are, however, keenly aware that much of their work, from understanding problems to selecting interventions and evaluating their effectiveness, should be based on science.

Increasing Accountability

A second function of social work research is to help us evaluate our own effectiveness. How do we know when our actions are working (or not working)? How will we know if something can be done better, faster, or less expensively? Through social work research we soon learn that our interventions are usually not entirely effective. We use research to help us determine when to stay the course and when to take corrective action. We learn to be curious about and question the effectiveness of what we, as social workers, do.

Through research, we also provide information to others about our effectiveness. We are accountable to our clients. They have a right to know the extent to which we have been successful in meeting their needs and goals. In addition, we must be accountable to those who fund social work services, whether that is through public funds, private donations, or fee for service. Indeed, the funding of social programs depends increasingly on providing evidence of success.

Improving Communication

A third basic function of social work research is communication. Social workers use research to communicate precisely and with confidence and to enhance their image as professionals. When social workers use research, they are not just talking; they are talking knowledgeably.

For example, Jeannie Jertson, a social worker in Arizona, is currently leading a workgroup to address what she perceives as inequity in the funding formula used by the federal Low-Income Home Energy Assistance Program (LIHEAP). Informed by her research, Jertson claims that Arizona receives enough LIHEAP funding to assist only 6 percent of its income-eligible population because the program favors cold-weather states over hot-weather states. In contrast, some states are able to assist almost 60 percent of their eligible population through the program. Jertson and her workgroup have sought assistance from national experts and advocates, as well as from the Arizona governor's office, in their fight to change the federal funding formula for the LIHEAP. Jertson, who began her social work career in 1974, claims that she has seen a lot of changes in the profession over time. One fundamental change is the way that social workers increasingly use research to communicate and advocate for better services. In her words: "The facts are where we have to start, not just talking" (personal communication, May 17, 2004).

Enhancing Access to Scarce Resources

A fourth basic function of social work research is to gain access to scarce resources. Research can make the difference between losing and maintaining the funding for vital social work services. Case-in-Point 1.2 illustrates this point.

CONTROVERSIES IN THE HISTORY OF SOCIAL WORK RESEARCH

So far we have taken the position that in order to have an impact, social workers need to acquire knowledge and skills in research. There have been many times since the days of Dorothea Dix, however, that the place of research in social work has been hotly debated. These historical controversies have called into question the status of social work as a profession, the very nature and value of research, and the roles of the social work practitioner and researcher in producing and using research. A brief history of these controversies is warranted because it allows us to appreciate where we are today and how we got here. Understanding our professional history is also part of the socialization process for social work students.

The Social Work Library

Read Flexner (1925) and a commentary on Flexner's statements by Austin online in the Social Work Library.

Historical Controversy 1: Is Social Work a Profession?

Of course social work is a profession. Isn't it? How do we know? In 1915 the National Conference of Charities and Correction in Baltimore invited an

In 1995 property taxes in Franklin County, Ohio, covered about 50 percent of the cost of mental health and substance abuse services. As the tax levy was set to expire, an initial attempt to pass a new levy failed. Suddenly, mental health and substance abuse services were on the chopping block. With only one more election left to pass the tax before it expired, a coalition consisting of the funding board and the agencies providing the services embarked on a mission to save the services.

At the outset, two opposing ideas regarding how to focus the campaign emerged among the coalition partners. The funding board wanted to broadcast messages about the mental health system, its structure, and its clients in order to give it more of a public identity. The providers' idea was to showcase their agencies as providers of services in the campaign. Research supported by the coalition to examine the opinions of the local residents on the suggested campaign strategies soon served to eliminate both ideas. The research revealed that there was very little awareness—and a great deal of confusion— among the voting public concerning the mental health system and the providers. It further showed that the clients of the mental health and substance abuse services were not people with whom most of the voters could identify. Many voters viewed alcohol or drug problems as the fault of the individual. Therefore, funding these services was a low priority.

Having rejected both proposed approaches, the coalition used research to develop a campaign message to pass the tax levy. The strategy was to test messages for their ability to move voters from a negative or neutral position to a positive one. The coalition employed paid consultants who polled voters and used focus groups to test potential messages. The messages found to work the best with voters were that (a) services were helping people to help themselves and (b) a large proportion of the budget would help children. What voters wanted to hear about was positive results with which they could identify, such as a client going back to work because of the services.

Had the coalition not used research to test the messages, they probably would have repeated the same mistakes that led to the defeat of the tax levy in 1995, including telling the story from the administrator and provider perspective as opposed to the voter's perspective (Allen & Boettcher, 2000). Instead, by using research, the coalition learned to stay away from messages like the average annual cost of the levy to the taxpayer and the quality of the local mental health system. Research also played a mediating role, reducing the tension between the administrators and providers, who were no longer placed in the position of arguing their differing ideas for the campaign. The group could move on together using research-based information.

The research provided information on the characteristics of people who were solidly in support of the tax levy, people who were solidly against the levy, and undecided people who might be persuaded. This information enabled the coalition to target most of the campaign resources toward the last group, a population that was essential to securing victory. The campaign moved from a 47 percent chance of winning in the June poll to a 62 percent victory in the election four months later. One of the most important lessons learned from this experience was "Pay attention to research, not instinct" (Allen & Boettcher, 2000, p. 30).

educational reformer named Abraham Flexner to speak. Flexner chose to focus his address on the question of whether social work was a profession. To answer this question, Flexner presented the defining criteria of a profession, applied them to social work, and concluded that social work did not measure up. In fact, Flexner publicly stated that social work *was not* a profession. Flexner's comments sent shock waves throughout the social work community.

Flexner's criteria to define professional status included the following:

- The work involves personally responsible intellectual activity.

- The work has a practical purpose.

- The work is teachable in a curriculum.

- The work pursues a broader social good.

- The content of the discipline is derived from science and learning and does not employ knowledge that is generally accessible to everyone (Kirk & Reid, 2002).

Although there is some controversy with regard to the criteria Flexner used to assign social work a failing grade, social work was most vulnerable to the criticism that it lacked a unique scientific body of knowledge. Does social work have a unique scientific knowledge base? If so, what makes it unique?

The **research methods** that social workers use—that is, the procedures for conducting research studies and gathering and interpreting data to get the most valid findings—are *not* unique to our profession. The same is true of the theories that social workers draw upon to guide their research. Perhaps the best explanation of what makes social work research unique is based on the idea that the identity of a profession depends more on the uniqueness of its goals than on its technology (Wakefield, 1988).

What makes social work research unique, then, is not the means used to conduct the research but the ends toward which the research is conducted. The ends to which social workers strive are defined in the preamble to the NASW *Code of Ethics.* The preamble defines social work's primary mission as "to enhance human well-being and help meet the basic human needs of all people, with particular attention to the needs and empowerment of people who are vulnerable, oppressed, and living in poverty" (NASW, 1999, p. 1). Social work research is needed to fulfill this mission. After all, the purpose of social work research is to create **applied knowledge;** that is, we use research to develop knowledge that will inform social work practice.

Social workers consider not only the usefulness of the research questions they ask to inform practice but also the ways that research findings may be misused. Social workers have been instrumental in expanding research to include problem areas that were little understood and populations that were largely ignored by research in other disciplines. They also study people and problems in a way that challenges stereotypes and focuses on strengths as well as problems. For instance, they tend to examine not only risk factors for problems but also protective factors, that is, factors that reduce the risk of certain problems.

Historical Controversy 2: Do Social Workers Use Research?

The next major area of controversy in social work research focused not on the production of research by social workers, or the lack thereof, but on the use of research. Aaron Rosenblatt (1968) was the first social work researcher to conduct a study on the use of research by social workers. Rosenblatt found that social workers rated research the least used or least valued activity in making treatment decisions. Other early studies of social workers' use of research found similar results. Specifically, they revealed that social workers (a) did not read many research articles, (b) seldom used research studies in their professional work, and (c) had difficulty accepting findings that challenged their beliefs (Casselman, 1972; Kirk & Fischer, 1976).

In response to the question of why social workers did not use research to a greater extent, some researchers offered the following explanations:

- Social workers were not appreciative of the work that researchers do.

- Social agencies were barely tolerant hosts of research.

- Agency administrators were interested only in research that supports the status quo. (For a discussion of this controversy, see Kirk & Reid, 2002.)

More recently, research has led to optimism that research use in social work is increasing (Reid & Fortune, 1992). The response to the claim that social workers did not use research to inform their practice served to shift the debate away from the shortcomings of the social worker to the nature of the research. If social workers were not using research to inform practice, perhaps it was because they failed to see the utility of much of the research.

Historical Controversy 3: Is Research Relevant to Social Work?

The third controversy in social work research involves the utility of research for social work practice (Kirk & Reid, 2002). Specifically, many social workers questioned whether research could improve their practice, while others insisted that the profession use knowledge that was research based. This issue and the preceding controversy on the use of research illustrate the division that existed between those who saw themselves as social work practitioners and those who saw themselves as social work researchers. To understand how this gap between research and practice occurred, we must briefly comment on the origins of modern-day science.

The Emergence of Logical Positivism.   The idea of applying science to the social world grew out of a period of European history known as the Enlightenment. Seventeenth-century thinkers moved away from religious and authoritarian explanations of human behavior toward an empirical analysis that relied on observation and measurement as the way of knowing. This new framework, or paradigm, was called **logical positivism.** It was seen as a way to replace the old ways of knowing with objective rationality. Essentially, logical positivism argued that scientists could understand the human experience in the same way as they do the physical world. Going further, social scientists who understood the human experience in this way could engineer individual and social problems just as physical scientists attempted to engineer the natural world. In order to remain objective, the expert scientist had to distance "himself" from the subjects of the research. (We use the gender-specific term *himself* because early social science was dominated by men.) Many social scientists embraced logical positivism as the path that would lead to objectivity and truth. For all its promise, however, logical positivism was not without its problems. For instance, it could consider only a limited number of variables at one time.

The idea of the objective scientist was criticized because, after all, scientists are human, and, like all humans, they are socialized to a set of values and beliefs that influence what they see and how they interpret it. The critics of logical positivism contended that, despite its claims of objectivity, logical positivism was biased and often served as a form of power rather than a source of truth. History provides us with numerous examples to support this position. One illustration is the following commentary by the late Stephen Jay Gould, an evolutionary biologist and science historian.

In his 1981 book *The Mismeasure of Man,* Gould presents numerous examples of bad science that was produced in the name of objectivity and has served to maintain the status quo. For example, during the 19th century, scientists involved in the field of craniometry compiled data on skull size to rank people by race and sex. Gould states that the proponents of craniometry regarded themselves as "servants of their numbers, apostles of objectivity" (p. 74). As an example he cites Paul Broca, an eminent French scientist of the time:

> We might ask if the small size of the female brain depends exclusively upon the small size of her body. Tiedemann has proposed this explanation. But we must not forget that women are, on the average, a little less intelligent than men, a difference which we should not exaggerate but which is, nonetheless, real. We are therefore permitted to suppose that the relatively small size of the female brain depends in part upon her physical inferiority, and in part upon her intellectual inferiority. (cited in Gould, 1981, p. 104)

Interpretivism: The Alternative to Positivism.   The claims that (1) research carried out in the tradition of logical positivism leads to the objective truth and (2) knowledge flows one way, from expert to nonexpert, have contributed to the division and distrust between researchers and social work practitioners. In the 1970s and 1980s, the debate in social work focused on the most appropriate paradigm for developing social work knowledge. As a scientific alternative to logical positivism, many researchers came to embrace a paradigm known as **interpretivism.** The interpretivist paradigm is concerned with understanding social conditions through the meaning individuals ascribe to their personal experiences. In essence, interpretivism maintains that (a) there may be several versions of the truth, and (b) the version that a researcher adopts will depend upon her or his vantage point. Given these assumptions, then, the meaning a researcher ascribes to an event or phenomenon should not be separated from the context in which the event occurs. The researcher's personal perceptions and experiences strongly influence the way she or he sees and interprets the world. This reality should always be acknowledged in the findings of the research.

Entire editions of journals and books have been devoted to arguing the relative merits of positivism and interpretivism for social work research (see, for example, Hudson & Nurius, 1994). The debate has revolved around philosophical questions such as What is truth? If there is such a thing as truth, how can we know it? Researchers who favor the interpretivist paradigm argue that the positivist paradigm is **reductionistic:** it oversimplifies life's complexities by reducing them to a set of observations, and it leaves out important aspects of the human experience. Proponents of the positivist framework respond that interpretivist research is subjective and cannot be generalized beyond the individuals or groups studied.

The differences in research conducted using either paradigm are reflected in the following example, which involves welfare reform. What is the best way to learn the "truth" about women's experiences as a result of welfare reform? One possibility is to investigate at great depth the experiences of individual women receiving Temporary Assistance for Needy Families (TANF) through interviews with these women, their children, their families, their neighbors, and other community members. We might even stay with a families receiving TANF for a period of time, observing how they live. We would be interested in their explanations of why they are on welfare, how they view the future, what they want for their children, how they spend their time, and what their everyday experience is like.

From our observations, we would then develop additional questions and hypotheses that would increase our understanding of their circumstances. Our goal would be to develop insight and perhaps a theory to explain the impact of welfare on a woman's life. We might better understand the forces that lead women either to leave welfare or to remain on it, while developing a sense of empathy at the same time. In-depth research focusing on extensive examination of a limited number of subjects conducted in the interpretivist tradition is

The Social Work Library

Read the Bloom article for a discussion of the debate over the best way to conduct research.

EXHIBIT 1.2

*Types of
Qualitative
Research*

Case study	Develops understanding of a phenomenon through in-depth analysis of one or a few single case examples. The case can be an individual, group, organization, or event. The focus is on understanding a single case rather than the entire population of cases.
Ethnography	A form of field research that focuses on understanding an entire culture or subculture through extensive participant observation. The ethnographer becomes immersed in the culture as an active participant and records extensive field notes. Development of explanatory theory as well as description of processes are the goals of the research.
Field research	A broad approach to qualitative research in which the researcher goes "into the field" to observe the phenomenon in its natural state. The field researcher typically takes extensive field notes that are subsequently coded and analyzed.
Grounded theory	A process of inductive theory development based on intensive observation. Theory development is *grounded* in observation. Grounded theory is an iterative process in which the researcher begins with raising broad questions and ends with construction of theoretical concepts and their relationships, clearly linked to the data.
Phenomenology	Emphasizes a focus on people's subjective experiences and interpretations of the world. The goal of the researcher is to describe the world from the point of view of the person(s) being studied.

known as **qualitative research.** Exhibit 1.2 presents a brief description of five types of qualitative research.

Another way to find the "truth" is to "count things" that we believe are important. Again using welfare as an example, how many women receive TANF? What is their age, race, education, employment status, income, number of children, number of years receiving TANF, number of job interviews, attitudes about work and child rearing, and so on? After we have accumulated these data, we can look for relationships among these variables. We might learn, for example, that women who never finished high school have a higher likelihood of remaining unemployed than women who have finished high school. This type of research conducted in the positivist tradition, which involves the use of numerical data, is known as **quantitative research.**

Although both qualitative and quantitative research approaches are valued for their unique contributions to social work research, there is a perceived hierarchy of research approaches. Quantitative research has been described as objective and scientific and has been equated with masculinity. To illustrate this type of thinking, in a discussion of the politics of research paradigms, one researcher recounted her surprise at learning that her manuscript, which reported a quantitative study on wife abuse, was rejected by a respected feminist journal (Yllo, 1988).

The reason she was offered for the rejection was that the positivist research paradigm was patriarchal and as a result could contribute no feminist insights. In contrast, qualitative research is often considered subjective and nonscientific and is equated with femininity. Quantitative research has been referred to as "hard science" and qualitative research as "soft science." There has also been a perception that social workers who wanted their research to be funded and published were better off pursuing a quantitative research approach.

In response to the debate on *epistemology*—how we know what we know—positivism has evolved considerably. As a result, we no longer use the term *logical positivism* to describe today's brand of positivism. We are more likely to use the terms *post-positivism* or *quantitative research*. Similarly, we often use the term *qualitative research* to refer to research conducted in the interpretivist paradigm. The evolution in positivism includes the recognition that scientists are not immune to values, political pressure, and ideologies, and that objectivity is something to strive for rather than a characteristic of a research approach. The contemporary positivist paradigm maintains that knowledge derived from observation is superior to knowledge based on authority, experience, tradition, or other forms of knowing. Through highly structured research methods and controls, positivism seeks to limit the influence of any type of bias that might threaten the validity or truthfulness of the findings.

The Social Work Library

Read the Davis article online for a discussion of male and female voices in social work.

Lessons Learned from the Controversies

The three historical controversies have provided opportunities for professional growth. As social workers have tackled each controversy with passion and debate, the profession has emerged with a stronger position on the place of research in social work and what the nature of that research should be. Social work as a profession has drawn several lessons from the controversies, including the following:

- The ends our research serves are as important as the methods we use to conduct our research.

- We must always be critical consumers of research-based knowledge, and we need to reliably evaluate the observations, facts, inferences, and assumptions stated in the research.

- When scientific claims depart radically from our professional experiences, we should not quickly discount our professional knowledge, and we should vigorously pursue the reasons for the discrepancy.

- Research benefits from popular participation, and it works best when knowledge flows in more than one direction—from expert in research to expert in the phenomenon being studied—rather than from expert researcher to nonexpert research object.

- As social workers, we must concern ourselves with the social consequences of our research findings, and we should divorce ourselves from the political and moral passivity that can result when we cloak ourselves in a veil of scientific objectivity.

Undoubtedly, there will always be social workers on either side of the research paradigm debate who fail to see the value in the other side. Contemporary social workers, however, need not choose one paradigm over the other. As social workers in search of knowledge, we now recognize that each paradigm provides useful and complementary knowledge and makes a unique contribution. Moreover, we sometimes combine the two approaches in which the limitations of one approach are offset by the benefits of the other. We call this approach a **mixed-methods approach.**

Finally, if social workers are going to use research-based knowledge, researchers need to consider the following priorities:

- Produce research that is relevant for social work practitioners, in part by collaborating with practitioners.

- Produce focused research in areas we know little about, such as the factors that influence the effectiveness of treatment with different ethnic and racial groups.

- Adopt better methods of sharing research methods and findings.

- Write for social work practitioners, producing succinct reports that state the core findings understandably and explain how the research can be applied to practice.

The controversies regarding the professional status of social work, research use, and research relevance have moved the profession forward to explicitly state a position on the value of research in social work and the types of research that are valued. In addition, they have prompted the development of an infrastructure to support research from within the profession. We examine these developments in the next section.

THE PROFESSIONAL MANDATE

The days of questioning the relevance of research to the social work profession are over. The current position is clear: Professional social workers are expected to understand and use research. Our professional organizations have made explicit statements concerning the importance of research to social work. To further the goal of widespread use of research, the profession has created an infrastructure to promote social work research and to create opportunities for social workers to engage in research. This next section briefly describes the professional mandate and the infrastructure.

The National Association of Social Workers (NASW) and the Council on Social Work Education (CSWE) are two bodies that represent and guide the social work profession. Support for social work research within these two institutions is strong and explicit.

NASW and CSWE

The **National Association of Social Workers (NASW)** is the largest organization of professional social workers in the world, having approximately 153,000 members (NASW, 2005). The NASW works to enhance the professional growth and development of its members and to create and maintain professional standards. The NASW *Code of Ethics* specifically states the following under Section 5, Social Workers' Ethical Responsibilities to the Social Work Profession, 5.02 Evaluation and Research:

(a) Social workers should monitor and evaluate policies, the implementation of programs, and practice interventions.

(b) Social workers should promote and facilitate evaluation and research to contribute to the development of knowledge.

(c) Social workers should critically examine and keep current with emerging knowledge relevant to social work and fully use evaluation and research evidence in their professional practice.

(d) Social workers engaged in evaluation or research should carefully consider possible consequences and should follow guidelines developed for the protection of evaluation and research participants. Appropriate institutional review boards should be consulted. (NASW, 1999)

The responsibility to conduct and use research is considered an ethical obligation of all professional social workers. This expectation has been formalized through its inclusion in the *Code of Ethics*.

Another major social work organization, the **Council on Social Work Education (CSWE),** develops educational policy and accreditation standards for social work programs on the baccalaureate and master's levels. In February 2004 the CSWE implemented new Educational Policy and Accreditation Standards (EPAS). Under Educational Policy 4.6 Research, the CSWE educational policy specifically states the following:

Qualitative and quantitative research content provides understanding of a scientific, analytic, and ethical approach to building knowledge for practice. The content prepares students to develop, use, and effectively communicate empirically based knowledge, including evidence-based interventions. Research knowledge is used by students to provide high-quality services; to initiate change; to improve practice, policy, and social service delivery; and to evaluate their own practice. (CSWE, 2004, p. 10)

CSWE has given all schools of social work a mandate to educate students in research in order to prepare them for careers in which they will produce and use research to make a positive impact.

The Infrastructure to Support Social Work Research

In 1988 the National Institute of Mental Health (NIMH) created the Task Force on Social Work Research. The task force was created in response to a recognition by NIMH that whereas 70 percent of mental health services were being provided by social workers, only about 1 percent of all research on mental health was being undertaken by social workers (Levy Zlotnik, Biegel, & Solt, 2002). A 1991 report from the task force reached this conclusion:

There is a crisis in the current development of research resources in social work. . . . This has serious consequences for individuals using social work services, for professional practitioners, for the credibility of the profession, and for the American society. Billions of dollars are being spent for services to deal with critical social problems, including services provided by social workers. Extremely little is being spent on research to improve the effectiveness of such services. (p. viii)

In reaction to this report, social workers developed an infrastructure to promote social work research. The infrastructure is made up of two entities: the **Institute for the Advancement of Social Work Research (IASWR)** and the **Society for Social Work Research (SSWR)** (Levy Zlotnik et al., 2002). Together these two entities work to promote a culture of research in social work.

Institute for the Advancement of Social Work Research (IASWR).   IASWR began in 1993 as a collaboration among five groups: NASW, CSWE, the Association of Baccalaureate Social Work Program Directors (BPD), the National Association of Deans and Directors of Schools of Social Work (NADD), and the Group for the Advancement of Doctoral Education (GADE). The mission of the IASWR is to "advance the scientific knowledge base of social work practice by building the research capacity of the profession, by increasing support and opportunities for social work research, and by promoting linkages among the social work practice, research, and education communities" (Levy Zlotnik et al., 2002, p. 322).

The IASWR promotes research that focuses on issues of serious social concern. It is rooted in the social work values of promoting social justice and enhancing the quality of life for all people. The IASWR disseminates information on funding opportunities, works with the executive branch of government to promote attention to social work research, serves as facilitator and catalyst to create a research culture in social work education programs, and hosts technical assistance workshops for faculty and students on research development.

Society for Social Work Research (SSWR). SSWR is a membership organization of individual researchers, faculty, practitioners, and students. Since 1994 the SSWR has worked to support individual researchers by hosting an annual conference and publishing the journal *Social Work Research* in addition to a newsletter.

TRENDS THAT SUPPORT RESEARCH UTILIZATION

Several trends have also converged to solidify the place of research utilization in the future of social work. For example, the Internet has promoted the development of communication networks such as Listservs and Web sites that connect researchers and practitioners who have similar interests and information needs. In addition, information technology has made electronic bibliographic databases, indexing services, and electronic journals widely available, thus making research more accessible to social workers. It has also given social work the means to bridge research and practice. This development has been encouraged by legislative changes such as the Government Performance and Results Act, as well as paradigm shifts in social work education such as evidence-based practice. We examine these trends in this section.

Government Performance and Results Act

A landmark piece of legislation, the Government Performance and Results Act (P.L. 103-62, or GPRA) has forced agencies and organizations receiving federal funds to become more accountable for their results. Enacted in 1993, the GPRA requires all federally funded agencies to become results oriented by setting program performance targets and reporting annually on the degree to which they met the previous year's targets. The GPRA shifted the federal government away from a focus on process—that is, which services the agency provided, in what context, at what cost, and how well these services matched what was planned—to

The Social Work Library

In 1995 the SSWR developed an awards program for outstanding social work research scholarship. You can find an analysis of the 299 journal articles nominated for SSWR outstanding research awards between 1996 and 2000 in the article by Craig, Cook, and Fraser (2004) in the Social Work Library.

Web Links

Links to the IASWR, the SSWR, and other organizations that support the development of a culture of research in social work can be found at www.mhhe.com/krysik1.

a focus on outcome, or what the agency actually accomplished with the use of resources. Outcome questions pertain to the effects of treatment on participants, the program and individual factors associated with the outcomes, and whether the effects can be maintained over time.

At the local level, the GPRA requires social workers who are applying for federal funds to demonstrate their ability to collect and report data. Moreover, if a worker is awarded a federal grant, the terms and conditions of the grant specify the data to be submitted and the schedule for submission.

Evidence-Based Practice

In the past, social workers were reluctant to use research-based knowledge, in part because it was not widely available and social workers had difficulty understanding how research applied to practice. Another reason for this reluctance, however, is that teaching students how to use research findings or even how to conduct research was not part of the broad culture of social work education in the past. Perhaps one of the newest and most promising developments in this area is the advent of **evidence-based practice (EBP).** In their simplest form, evidence-based practices are interventions that appear to be related to preferred client outcomes based on scientific evidence. For example, scientific studies have shown behavioral and cognitive-behavioral treatments to be effective in treating anxiety disorders (DeRubeis & Crits-Christoph, 1998). Thus, mental health practitioners should choose these treatments first over insight-oriented therapies that have not been supported by evidence of effectiveness. Increasingly, funding decisions are being tied to the use of EBPs and treatment outcomes.

In the context of social work education, EBP is much more than a set of interventions whose effectiveness has been documented by scientific evidence. By adopting EBP as a guiding pedagogical principle, schools of social work are attempting to produce professionals who are lifelong learners, who draw on practice-related research findings, and who involve clients as informed participants in intervention decisions (Gibbs & Gambrill, 2002). EBP involves "teaching students the values and skills they need to identify, critically appraise, and apply practice-relevant scientific evidence over the course of their professional careers" (Howard, McMillen, & Pollio, 2003, p. 234). Because information technology has given social workers greater access to research studies, schools of social work must now teach students the skills to use and produce research.

The challenges inherent in EBP extend the paradigm shift in social work education. How will evidence-based practices move from their establishment in research to broad awareness and wide-scale adoption in the practice community? Much remains to be discovered about the trajectory of EBP in social work, as Exhibit 1.3 illustrates.

 The Social Work Library

For a discussion of evidence-based practice in social work, read Gibbs and Gambrill (2002) and Howard, McMillen, and Pollio (2003) in the Social Work Library.

The need for more and better research is not an end in itself. The goal of all these efforts is to provide the best prevention and treatment services to those persons in need of social work services to promote individual, family, and community well-being. (Levy Zlotnik et al., 2002, p. 331)

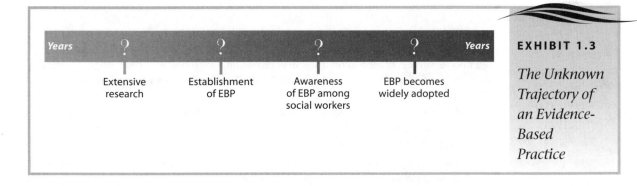

Years	?	?	?	?	Years
	Extensive research	Establishment of EBP	Awareness of EBP among social workers	EBP becomes widely adopted	

EXHIBIT 1.3

The Unknown Trajectory of an Evidence-Based Practice

PROFESSIONAL SOCIAL WORK PRACTICE

What does being a professional social worker mean to you? To answer this question, think for a moment about what you expect from other professionals whom you encounter. One of the first things you might look for is a degree hanging on the office wall. This degree will tell you where and when the individual received her or his professional education. Second, you might expect a certain professional demeanor, dress, and use of language. Third, you probably expect that the individual will act ethically, not violating her or his professional boundaries or your trust and safety. Fourth, you expect a professional to be aware of and use the most effective methods of practice—EBPs. Finally, you might expect a professional to know her or his limitations, to evaluate her or his work, and to be willing to refer you elsewhere if necessary. Empathy, warmth, and genuineness—three characteristics valued in any professional—are of limited value unless they are accompanied by attention to effective practice.

In March 2005 the NASW launched a multiyear awareness campaign to make the public aware that social work is a valuable service and that social workers are educated professionals. Case-in-Point 1.3 summarizes the findings of a study on the public's perception of social workers as professionals. The findings of this study are good news for us as social workers and for the NASW. There may be no better way, however, to promote the profession of social work than through research that demonstrates our accountability and makes a valued contribution to knowledge development.

 Web Links

Visit www.mhhe.com/krysik1 to locate the link for the NASW public awareness campaign.

Making a Commitment to Lifelong Learning

The expectations for producing and using research in professional social work practice are clear. The question that remains is How? Entry-level social work jobs can be demanding, leaving little time for consultation, research, or even reflection. A social worker is more likely to use research if the employing agency or organization has a culture that supports it and if the worker is committed to

CASE-IN-POINT 1.3

Public Perception of Social Work

Are social workers viewed as professionals in the public eye? The students in Craig LeCroy's social work research course tried to answer this question. They conducted a nationwide telephone survey of 386 randomly selected adult householders. Their findings were published in *Social Work* (LeCroy & Stinson, 2004). Their findings are summarized here:

- Most respondents believed that social workers require some level of postsecondary education. Specifically, 53% said social workers needed a bachelor's degree, and 33% believed that a master's degree was necessary.
- The majority of respondents recognized appropriate social work roles, such as agent of social change (59%), group therapist (67%), administrator (65%), mental health therapist (57%), community organizer (69%), and child protector (91%).
- The majority of respondents (59%) had a positive evaluation of social workers. Some were neutral (25%), and only a small percentage (16%) had a negative evaluation.
- A large majority (80%) agreed that social workers play an important role in addressing social problems. In addition, 85% disagreed with the statement that social workers don't make a difference in our community, and only 9% agreed.
- A strong majority (73%) concurred that more social workers are needed, with only 9% dissenting.

By and large these results suggest that the public views social workers as learned professionals who make a positive difference in a wide variety of roles.

---

making it happen. Will you commit yourself to a career of lifelong learning? If so, the first step is to develop an action plan to make it happen. Here are a few ideas that you might consider adopting.

- Join the NASW.
- Choose a conference that is relevant to your practice area, and make a commitment to attend every year.
- Ask your manager or supervisor to subscribe to a professional journal(s).
- Join a Listserv dedicated to critiquing knowledge in your area of practice.
- Join your local library, and spend at least one day a month in professional development reading about the latest research in your area.
- Initiate a brown-bag lunch session at your workplace at which you and your colleagues discuss research.
- Attend research-based training and workshops whenever possible.
- Continue your formal education by taking courses online or at a university or college.

- Make a presentation to share your research at a conference.

- Evaluate your practice.

- Collaborate with others to evaluate the services provided by your agency or organization.

- Seek employment in agencies and organizations whose culture supports using research and evaluating practice.

Research Opportunities for Entry-Level Social Workers

Virtually all social work positions present opportunities for research, even though research may not be the primary activity. Research opportunities may include assessment, deciding on an intervention strategy, evaluating success with a single case, evaluating a program of services, conducting a needs assessment, and writing grant proposals. Sometimes research involves helping communities to do their own research while offering guidance and added credibility. All of these activities require social workers to have a working knowledge of research.

Other employment opportunities for social workers have research as their primary focus. Careers in social work research can be personally rewarding. Social workers in research positions enjoy the opportunity to be influential in the creation, continuation, expansion, and sometimes termination of social programs and in the promotion of EBPs. Research conducted by social workers often influences whether legislative amendments will be made to government-funded programs.

Regardless of whether research is the focus of a social work position or a complement to some other form of social work practice, employing agencies often seek out and highly value graduates who are skilled in research. Marketable research skills include expertise with database development and management, data analysis, and presentation software. The exercises in this book and the tutorials included on the Student Study Guide will help you develop these marketable skills. In addition, many universities and colleges offer training workshops on these types of software programs that either are free of charge or cost far less than courses taught outside. In addition, software programs are often available at great discounts to students through campus bookstores and computing centers.

 Web Links

For further information on social work employment opportunities with a focus on research, visit www.mhhe.com/krysik1.

CONCLUSION

Social workers are employed in areas where difficult and life-changing decisions are made on a daily basis. Many of the problems social workers deal with are multidimensional and complex; some are chronic and relapsing. Some problems, such as HIV/AIDS, are major public health issues that affect millions of people and place an enormous social and financial burden on society. To make a positive impact, social workers require knowledge about how best to intervene in these problems—EBPs. In some cases, our knowledge of what is effective is still in the beginning stages. Social workers also need the skills to produce new, scientifically based knowledge about social problems and the most effective ways to address these problems.

The bright spot in a social worker's day comes when we know with confidence that something we did had a positive impact. To know something with confidence is empowering. Social workers must be confident in the knowledge they acquire, not only for themselves, but also to demonstrate accountability to and communicate with the people they serve and those who fund their services. In addition, social workers need to know when they are *not* effective so that they can either adopt a different approach or refer people elsewhere. Moreover, being able to demonstrate to a client—whether an individual, a couple, a family, an agency, an organization, or a community—that progress is being made is empowering to the client as well as the social worker. For example, to help a community group obtain funding for a teen center by providing accurate information on the impact of the teen center on juvenile delinquency rates is empowering. Social workers also empower organizations and policy makers when they use their knowledge to provide information to inform policy decisions and to understand the costs and benefits of policy changes.

Not knowing or not being able to demonstrate the positive impact of what you do as a social worker is disempowering, both to you and to your clients. Similarly, not being able to adequately assess the needs of a population or community or to advocate knowledgeably to change policy is disempowering. The research skills necessary for effective social work practice do not come naturally; rather, they are cultivated through learning and experience. The remainder of this book is devoted to helping you develop the research knowledge and skills you need to be an effective social worker with a lifelong commitment to learning.

MAIN POINTS

- As professionals, social workers are expected to use research to inform their practice and to contribute to the production of research.

- The purpose of social work research is applied, to better help those we aim to serve.

- Research helps us to critically evaluate information and make judgments on the best information available; to assess our own effectiveness; to communicate; and to gain additional resources.

- Research is a process that teaches social workers to question how they know what they think they know and to be skeptical of knowledge claims, even those based on the scientific method.

- The struggle over the primacy of qualitative versus quantitative research approaches has been more or less settled by an appreciation of the uniqueness of each approach and in the adoption of mixed-method approaches that recognize the strengths and limitations of each.

- There are many sources of organizational support for social workers engaged in research, including the NASW, CSWE, IASWR, and SSWR.

- Evidence-based practices (EBPs) are interventions that have shown consistent scientific evidence of being related to preferred client outcomes. A commitment to using EBPs is a commitment to lifelong learning.

- For most social workers, research will be a complement to their career. For those social workers who are interested, there are many employment opportunities with a research focus. Developing research skills gives all social work graduates an edge in the job market.

EXERCISES: PRACTICING SOCIAL WORK

1. After you have met the Sanchez family on the *Practicing Social Work* CD-ROM that accompanies this book, discuss the role of research in your work with the family.

2. In what ways would the role of research be the same or different if you were working with the Black Feather project, the second case study on your *Practicing Social Work* CD-ROM?

EXERCISES: SOCIAL WORK LIBRARY

1. Read the article by Franklin (1986) and describe how Mary Richmond and Jane Addams, two pioneering social workers, used research to create social change.

2. What are the objections to evidence-based practice described by Gibbs and Gambrill (2002), and how might you respond to these objections?

3. Read Davis (1985) and describe what is meant by "male" and "female" voices in social work. On what points do you agree with Davis? Where do you disagree with Davis?

OTHER EXERCISES

1. Search the Internet to find entry-level social work positions. List the research skills described in the ads.

2. Conduct an Internet or library search of the term *evidence-based practice*. How is the term defined? If various authors define evidence-based practice differently, explain the extent of the differences.

CHAPTER 2

The Politics and Ethics of Social Work Research

It is not we, a handful of social workers against a sea of human misery.
It is humanity itself, building a dike and we are helping in our
particularly useful way.
— BERTHA CAPEN REYNOLDS, 1885–1978

RESEARCH TAKES PLACE IN A SOCIAL AND POLITICAL CONTEXT. Unfortunately, many terrible and unethical things have been done in the name of research. For example, from 1940 to 1944 doctors performed "experiments" to test the effects of poisons and surgeries on prisoners in Nazi concentration camps. In the United States, our own record of research is far from clean. For example, from 1932 to 1972 the U.S. Public Health Service studied 600 African American men, of whom 399 had contracted syphilis and 201 had not, in order to observe the long-term effects of the disease. The men were not given penicillin even though the medical profession had known since the end of World War II that the drug could be used to treat syphilis. Forty men died during the experiment, and wives and children became infected. (We describe the study in more detail later in the chapter.)

In 1955 the Willowbrook School, a New York institution for children with developmental disabilities, conducted a study that involved more than 700 developmentally delayed children. Without giving consent, some children were intentionally infected with hepatitis so that researchers could follow the course of the disease and test the effectiveness of gamma globulin (Pence, 2000). As we will see in this chapter, these abuses and others have led to the creation of a strict code of ethics related to research procedures.

Social workers are often faced with ethical dilemmas when planning and conducting research. For example, can we pay low-income mothers to participate in a study of childhood sexual abuse experiences? Can we survey junior high school students about drug use without getting their parents' permission? Can we divide consumers of mental health services into an experimental group that receives a new treatment and a control group that receives no treatment? Can we research messages on a public online self-help group without telling members that we are copying their messages? In order to answer these questions, we must have a clear understanding of the principles that guide the ethical conduct of research.

Like research, the human services delivery system also exists within a social and political context. Which services get funded at what cost is a political issue, meaning that choices must be made, with interest groups advocating for their particular agenda. Where should we put our research dollars: HIV/AIDS or sudden infant death syndrome (SIDS)? Interventions for child abuse or for elder abuse? These value-laden questions raise the issue of the uneasy relationship among power, politics, and research.

A common maxim asserts that "knowledge is power." If this saying is true, research should play a major role in decision making about the funding and organization of human services. The social work researcher's role is, in part, to ensure that research findings influence decision making. To perform this role, researchers must consider the ends for which they engage in research and their ethical responsibilities to clients, colleagues, and the broader community. Chapter 1 discussed the context of social work research. This chapter extends that discussion by addressing the politics and ethics of social work research. By the end of this chapter you should be able to:

- Identify the mission and goals of the social work profession.
- Identify the social work skills needed to ensure that social work research is used to achieve the mission and goals of the profession.
- Discuss the interrelationship of politics and research.
- Discuss the implications of applying social work values to research with persons and groups who historically have suffered disadvantage.
- Describe what is meant by ethics and ethical conduct in research.

SOCIAL WORK RESEARCH: THE MEANS TO SOCIAL JUSTICE

Chapter 1 examined the relationship between social work research and practice and the advent of evidence-based practices. To pursue goals such as social justice, social work research must be used not only to inform direct practice but also to influence and inform policy practice. If we define social justice as access to basic social goods for all individuals and groups, the roles of case manager and therapist fall short of the social justice goal. Rather, progress toward social justice requires social workers to become directly involved in developing and modifying social policy (Figueira-McDonough, 1993). To perform this role, social workers often must conduct research that will influence policy makers and the general public to make changes in policies. Failing to attend to policy practice weakens the impact of social work research, as illustrated in Case-in-Point 2.1.

The true measure of any society is not what it knows but what it does with what it knows. —Warren Bennis, Professor, Author, Leadership Consultant

Healthy Families Arizona (HFAz) is a child abuse and neglect prevention program that provides supportive services and education through home visitation to parents of newborns who are considered at risk. The program is part of a national network of child abuse and neglect prevention programs that fall under the Healthy Families America umbrella. Initiated in 1991 as a pilot program in 3 sites, by 2005 HFAz had grown into a network of 50 sites statewide.

Initially, the state legislature appropriated funds for the HFAz program on an annual basis. Consequently, state legislators would debate the merits of the program each year during budget negotiations and decide whether to terminate the program, modify it, expand it, or leave it as is. To inform their decision-making process, the lawmakers had access to two annual evaluation reports. Evaluation research focuses on whether programs have met their goals and to what extent they are responsible for intended and sometimes unintended changes. (We discuss evaluation in detail in Chapter 11.) In 1998 the state auditor's department reported that HFAz parents who previously had been reported to Child Protective Services (CPS) had a higher rate of child abuse and neglect at follow-up (26.9 percent) than those parents who had no prior involvement with CPS (3.3 percent). Based on these data, the state auditor's report inferred that the HFAz program was not successful with families who had prior CPS involvement.

On the basis of these findings, the legislators announced that HFAz would no longer serve anyone who had ever been the subject of a substantiated CPS report. In addition, they ruled that any participant who became the subject of a substantiated CPS report while participating in HFAz would become ineligible for the program.

Unfortunately, the legislators who mandated these changes did not consider that percentages calculated on the basis of small numbers, such as the rates of child abuse and neglect among HFAz parents previously involved with CPS, can be very misleading. There was also no comparison group that included parents with prior CPS involvement who were not participating in the program. Finally, the legislators did not take into account the valuable monitoring function that the HFAz program performed in the early identification of child abuse and neglect. Once families with prior CPS involvement were denied participation, they were no longer subject to the monitoring provided by the HFAz program.

It would be easy to criticize the legislators for a lack of research knowledge, but the legislators did not consider these things because the evaluators did not clearly articulate them. Had the evaluators included parents with prior CPS involvement in the comparison group, they might have discovered that the HFAz program was actually successful at reducing subsequent incidents of substantiated child abuse and neglect among these parents. In the year following the change in eligibility criteria, about 37 parents with prior CPS involvement were denied participation in HFAz.

As a result of lobbying and advocacy efforts by human service providers and consumers informed by research, state legislators again changed the HFAz eligibility criteria in 2004 to allow families with prior CPS involvement to participate. It is encouraging that state legislators are using evaluation research to inform their decisions. This example demonstrates that in conducting evaluation research, social workers must not limit their role to acquiring and sharing knowledge. Instead, they must work to ensure that research findings are clearly reported and properly interpreted and evaluated. In some instances, they may also need to assist program personnel and advocates to integrate research with policy practice methods.

CASE-IN-POINT 2.1

Legislative Use of Evaluation

FUNDING FOR SOCIAL WORK RESEARCH

In most cases, before research can be conducted, it has to be funded. Research expenses include the costs of the researcher's time, materials such as paper, computers, transportation, telephone charges, and, in some instances, contracted expertise and incentives to participants such as movie tickets, food vouchers, and cash. Generally, the larger the research study and the longer its duration, the greater the expenses.

Who funds social work research? To begin with, the federal government provides a great deal of funding. The National Institutes of Health (NIH), for instance, has an annual budget of about $20 billion that is divided among competing interests in health and behavioral health. Additional sources of funding include federal, state, and local governments as well as private nonprofit and for-profit institutions. Sometimes research funding is provided by a partnership between government and private entities. Agencies and organizations that employ social workers also fund research and evaluation. Programs receiving government funds commonly set aside 10 percent of the program budget for research that is related to evaluation.

Search tools are available online and in the library or the research office of your academic institution that can help you identify funding sources and their priorities. Some research funding opportunities are specifically for students.

To receive funding for research or evaluation, the researcher generally must submit an application in response to a Request for Proposals (RFP). The RFP will typically include questions pertaining to the intent of the research or evaluation, the methods of collecting and analyzing data, a proposed timeline, qualifications of the researcher, and anticipated benefits of the research. In addition, it will specify a submission deadline, as well as any other pertinent instructions for the applicant.

What's Hot, What's Not

Research and research priorities are strongly influenced by funding, and funding in turn is strongly influenced by politics. As the old saying goes, "The one who pays the piper calls the tunes." Besides the applicant's qualifications and the strength of the proposal, perhaps the key factor that determines the likelihood of being funded is how well the proposal fits with the funder's current priorities. Two factors that can help determine research priorities are the extent of knowledge in the field and the amount of attention focused on a particular issue. Research priorities can also be influenced by what is considered politically popular or safe at a given time, as was the case with HIV/AIDS in the 1980s.

The death of former U.S. President Ronald Reagan in June 2004 sparked considerable debate about his presidential legacy. One issue on which former President Reagan has been criticized is his response, or lack thereof, to the growing AIDS pandemic. Although AIDS was reported as early as 1981—President Reagan's first year in office—it was not until October 1987 that he publicly addressed the issue. By that time, almost 28,000 Americans had died of the disease, and the numbers were multiplying each year. By the end of 1989, deaths due to AIDS had reached 70,000 in the United States alone. Globally the numbers were much higher.

Looking back at the Reagan administration's handling of the AIDS issue, Michael Bronski, a writer and activist, has written that the president's "appalling policies led to enormous setbacks for HIV/AIDS science and research, discrimination against people with AIDS, and the lack of any comprehensive outreach for prevention or education work, all adding to the already staggering amount of mounting deaths" (2004, p. 1). Bronski points out that between June 1981 and May 1982, the Centers for Disease Control (CDC)—the federal agency responsible for combating preventable diseases—spent less than $1 million on AIDS, compared to $9 million on Legionnaires' disease, a bacterial form of pneumonia. At that point more than 1,000 people in the United States had already died of AIDS, in contrast to fewer than 50 from Legionnaires' disease. When researchers at the CDC and the NIH requested more funding from the Reagan administration for treatment and research on AIDS, they were routinely denied.

What factors influenced the lack of early attention to AIDS? First, it is not unusual for presidents to maintain a low profile when a new public health hazard is identified, because addressing these hazards can involve many political risks, especially when the outcomes of the intervention are not known. Second, Reagan was new to the presidency in 1981. In addition, as a presidential candidate he had promised to reduce the size and role of the federal government and to promote morality and family in issues of social policy. The Reagan administration's vision of morality and family did not fit well with AIDS, which was branded by certain spokespersons for the Religious Right as God's revenge on homosexuals. Politically, AIDS could not have struck at a worse time.

The Politics of Intervention

Political priorities and political inaction are not the only problems confronting advocates of a research-based approach to creating and changing social policy. Sometimes the research itself is used to support an ideology rather than to determine the most effective course of action. This problem occurs when selective findings from a few methodologically weak research studies are used to support the conclusions of individuals and institutions in positions of power. The result is that politics prevails, and policy responses gather public support and become justified regardless of whether they are designed to address the roots of the problem. An example of this is found in the welfare reform policies of the 1990s.

A familiar mantra of the White House during the presidency of Bill Clinton (1993–2000) was the promise to "end welfare as we know it." Following his election in 1992, Clinton appointed several welfare research experts to high-level policy positions. These experts soon created a vision for welfare reform (Bane, 1997; Ellwood, 1996). The resulting welfare reform legislation, the Personal Responsibility and Work Opportunity Reconciliation Act (PRWORA) of 1996, did end welfare as we knew it, but the changes were based more on ideology than on research (Zuckerman, 2000).

In the ideological struggle over welfare reform, research became more of a weapon to support conflicting points of view than a tool to guide policy formulation. For instance, the same research was used by both proponents and opponents of welfare expenditures to prove that government intervention had or had not been effective in promoting individual self-sufficiency and social well-being.

To illustrate this process, consider how a research study that was intended to show that "welfare mothers" were not lazy and dependent was actually used to support the negative stereotypes it sought to counteract. Specifically, critics of federal welfare programs interpreted the finding that 4 out of every 10 welfare mothers worked at paid jobs during a two-year period while receiving welfare benefits as evidence that most (60 percent) of the women did not earn any money. Among other things, they criticized the researchers' definition of work because it was based on a minimum of 600 hours over a two-year period, the equivalent of less than two months of full-time work per year (Zuckerman, 2000). Critics of the existing welfare system also used anecdotal evidence to support their position that the system had failed. For example, the *Washington Post* published a Pulitzer Prize–winning series about three generations of a welfare-dependent family who were plagued by drug addiction and crime (Dash, 1994). This case, regardless of how isolated or common it was, created the perception that the system was broken and that any change was therefore better than no change.

In the conservative political climate that prevailed, progressive organizations had difficulty making their case, especially in the absence of credible research to predict what would happen if the conservative welfare reform bill were passed (Zuckerman, 2000). The result was that Congress passed a more punitive welfare reform plan than the Clinton administration had intended, as reflected in the focus on marriage in the introduction of the PRWORA. The resulting welfare reform legislation has since been softened through regulations. For example, states have been allowed to provide assistance longer than 60 months for up to 20 percent of the welfare caseload based on hardship or domestic violence.

Is it possible that new research on the impact of the PRWORA will inform the welfare reform efforts of the future? Unfortunately the prospects for such reforms have become less likely because the PRWORA devolved considerable responsibility for income support from the federal government to the states. Consequently, decisions that once were made in Washington are now made in 50 different states.

CASE-IN-POINT 2.2

The Tuskegee Syphilis Study

In 1932 the U.S. Public Health Service began a study of untreated syphilis in African American males that eventually became the longest-running, nontherapeutic experiment conducted on human beings in medical history. As mentioned at the beginning of the chapter, the Tuskegee Study, as it became known, recruited almost 400 African American men who were infected with syphilis. The original design was intended to look at the results of untreated syphilis over a period of six to nine months.

Deception was built into the study from the start. The participants were never informed that they were part of an experiment. An African American public health nurse was hired to form trusting relationships with the men and to arrange for their medical care. The participants were extremely poor and had no other access to health care. They were deliberately not informed about the dangers of syphilis and how it could be transmitted. Instead, they were told that they were being tested for "bad blood." The Public Health Service gave incentives such as free medical tests, food, transportation, and burial stipends to families in return for permission to conduct autopsies. When penicillin was introduced as a treatment for syphilis in 1947, the Public Health Service deliberately withheld treatment. During World War II, when the military identified 50 of the subjects as positive for syphilis and told them to come in for treatment, the Public Health Service intervened with the draft board to prevent them from receiving treatment. In 1969 a federal review panel made the decision to continue the study. The study was finally ended when public health workers leaked information to a journalist in 1972 (Jones, 1992).

THE ETHICS OF RESEARCH

Thus far, we have observed that politics influences the subject matter of research, the amount of attention a particular issue receives, and the likelihood that research will be considered when policies are developed to address a problem. Chapter 1 addressed the production and use of research among social workers as an ethical obligation. Social workers also have an ethical responsibility to ensure that research is conducted in a way that does not violate the trust or well-being of those involved.

Due to their life circumstances, some groups of people are particularly vulnerable to abuse by researchers. Vulnerability is not always a result of poverty and disadvantage. It can also stem from age—including both very old and young people—and disability. In addition, ethnic and racial minority groups have often been subject to research abuse. A classic example of this is the Tuskegee syphilis study described in Case-in-Point 2.2.

Rules of Ethical Conduct

In response to research abuses such as the Nazi experiments in World War II and the Tuskegee Study, the United States and the international community have established rules of ethical conduct specifically for research. **Ethics** is a set of moral principles or values to guide behavior in certain contexts. The ethical standards for research and evaluation articulated in the NASW *Code of Ethics* and the Belmont Report—discussed in the next paragraph—represent a proactive attempt to educate researchers concerning their ethical responsibilities to research participants and the broader society.

In 1974 Congress passed the National Research Act, which led to the creation of the National Commission for the Protection of Human Subjects of Biomedical and Behavioral Research. One of the responsibilities of the commission was to identify the basic ethical principles that should underlie the conduct of medical and social research. The document detailing these principles is called the Belmont Report.

The Belmont Report does not make specific recommendations. However, it outlines the three basic ethical principles that should guide ethical decision making in research: (1) respect for persons, (2) beneficence, and (3) justice. The first principle, respect for persons, implies that people should be treated as autonomous individuals, capable of making informed decisions when provided the information to do so. This principle also recognizes that due to some circumstances such as age or disability, some persons have diminished autonomy and therefore require additional protection in research. The extent of this protection should depend on the risk of harm and the likelihood of benefit.

The principle of **beneficence** is reflected in two general rules: (1) do no harm and (2) maximize benefits while minimizing risks. Researchers need to weigh the potential risks and the benefits of the research, including the benefits extended directly to participants. Participants should not be asked to subject themselves to potential harm when they are unlikely to receive any direct benefit from their participation.

The third principle, justice, pertains to who should pay the price for participation and who benefits. The principle of justice implies that it is unfair to expect one group to take the majority of the risk when a different group will likely realize the benefit. For instance, in the Tuskegee Study, the burden of the research fell to poor, rural, African American families, whereas the disease knew no boundaries, including geography, color, or income. In this study, one group assumed all the risk, whereas the entire society would benefit from any knowledge about the disease that emerged from the study.

Being knowledgeable about ethical principles and standards can help social workers avoid hurting the very people they endeavor to help. The current version of the NASW *Code of Ethics*, revised in 1999, sets out 16 ethical standards relevant to evaluation and research. All 16 standards are reproduced in Exhibit 2.1. The first three guidelines speak to the conduct, promotion, and use of research as an ethical responsibility—a position consistent with the one we adopted in Chapter 1.

(a) Social workers should monitor and evaluate policies, the implementation of programs, and practice interventions.

(b) Social workers should promote and facilitate evaluation and research to contribute to the development of knowledge.

(c) Social workers should critically examine and keep current with emerging knowledge relevant to social work and fully use evaluation and research evidence in their professional practice.

(d) Social workers engaged in evaluation or research should carefully consider possible consequences and should follow guidelines developed for the protection of evaluation and research participants. Appropriate institutional review boards should be consulted.

(e) Social workers engaged in evaluation or research should obtain voluntary and written informed consent from participants, when appropriate, without any implied or actual deprivation or penalty for refusal to participate; without undue inducement to participate; and with due regard for participants' well-being, privacy, and dignity. Informed consent should include information about the nature, extent, and duration of the participation requested and disclosure of the risks and benefits of participation in the research.

(f) When evaluation or research participants are incapable of giving informed consent, social workers should provide an appropriate explanation to the participants, obtain the participants' assent to the extent they are able, and obtain written consent from an appropriate proxy.

(g) Social workers should never design or conduct evaluation or research that does not use consent procedures, such as certain forms of naturalistic observation and archival research, unless rigorous and responsible review of the research has found it to be justified because of its prospective scientific, educational, or applied value and unless equally effective alternative procedures that do not involve waiver of consent are not feasible.

(h) Social workers should inform participants of their right to withdraw from evaluation and research at any time without penalty.

(i) Social workers should take appropriate steps to ensure that participants in evaluation and research have access to appropriate supportive services.

(j) Social workers engaged in evaluation or research should protect participants from unwarranted physical or mental distress, harm, danger, or deprivation.

(k) Social workers engaged in the evaluation of services should discuss collected information only for professional purposes and only with people professionally concerned with this information.

(l) Social workers engaged in evaluation or research should ensure the anonymity or confidentiality of participants and of the data obtained from them. Social workers should inform participants of any limits of confidentiality, the measures that will be

EXHIBIT 2.1

NASW Ethical Guidelines for Research and Evaluation

continued

EXHIBIT 2.1

*NASW
Ethical
Guidelines
for Research
and
Evaluation*
continued

taken to ensure confidentiality, and when any records containing research data will be destroyed.

(m) Social workers who report evaluation and research results should protect participants' confidentiality by omitting identifying information unless proper consent has been obtained authorizing disclosure.

(n) Social workers should report evaluation and research findings accurately. They should not fabricate or falsify results and should take steps to correct any error later found in published data using standard publication methods.

(o) Social workers engaged in evaluation or research should be alert to and avoid conflicts of interest and dual relationships with participants, should inform participants when a real or potential conflict of interest arises, and should take steps to resolve the issue in a manner that makes participants' interests primary.

(p) Social workers should educate themselves, their students, and their colleagues about responsible research practices.

Source: NASW, 1999. Reprinted with permission from NASW.

Institutional Review Boards (IRBs). The fourth guideline in the NASW *Code of Ethics* deals with complying with the guidelines developed for protecting evaluation and research participants and consulting appropriate institutional review boards. An **institutional review board (IRB)** is a peer/community review committee of five or more individuals who volunteer their time to review research proposals and monitor ongoing research studies to ensure that the people participating in the research are being adequately protected. Participants in research studies are sometimes referred to as **human subjects.**

IRBs may be associated with an academic institution, a hospital, or a social worker's employing or contracting agency or organization. Since 1991 federal law has required all research conducted at institutions receiving federal funds to be reviewed by an IRB. Some privately funded agencies and organizations are not required to submit to an IRB process, but they voluntarily do so to protect both themselves and their research participants.

Some research may be exempt from an IRB review or qualify for an expedited review because it poses no more than minimal risk. In contrast, certain types of research require a full IRB review. For example, research that poses more than minimal risk or that involves vulnerable human participants is never exempt because of the potential for coercion and harm. Vulnerable participants include children under 18 years of age, prisoners, pregnant women, people with mental disabilities, economically disadvantaged people, persons not proficient in the language of the research study, and any participants likely to be vulnerable to coercion or undue influence.

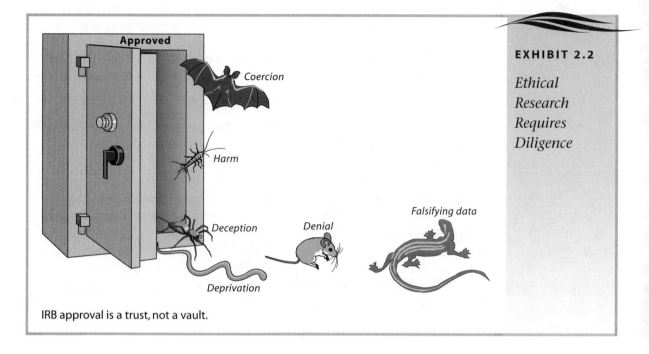

EXHIBIT 2.2

*Ethical
Research
Requires
Diligence*

Approved

Coercion

Harm

Deception

Denial

Falsifying data

Deprivation

IRB approval is a trust, not a vault.

It is usually best either to confirm with the IRB administrator that a proposed study is exempt or to submit an application and then let the IRB committee decide. IRB committees typically meet monthly during the regular academic session, and they often are overwhelmed with research proposals. Consequently, the IRB approval process can be a lengthy affair. To minimize the waiting period, most IRB committees have a fast-track review process called "expedited review" that they can apply to research proposals that pose only minimal risk or that involve only minor changes in previously approved research protocols (Oakes, 2002).

The IRB has the power to deny permission for a research study to begin or to stop a study in midstream. IRBs typically are not obstructionist, and they often work with researchers by requesting further details and by providing valuable suggestions on revisions to ensure that research participants are protected. Despite these actions and precautions, however, all of the ethical standards and review boards in the world cannot guarantee that research will be conducted ethically. As illustrated in Exhibit 2.2, IRB approval is a trust, not a guarantee that ethical violations will not occur. Ultimately, ethical conduct is the responsibility of the individual social work researcher.

Informed Consent. NASW guidelines *e* through *h* deal with **informed consent,** a procedure whereby subjects agree in writing or verbally, using audio

 Web Links

For free online access to the Journal of Social Work Values and Ethics, visit www.mhhe.com/krysik1.

or video recording, to participate in research under the following conditions:

(a) They are informed of the foreseeable risks and potential benefits of participation.

(b) Participation is voluntary and does not reflect mere acquiescence.

(c) Consent is rendered only by an intellectually competent and mature individual (Kuther, 2003).

Depending on the duration of participation required by the research, informed consent can be an ongoing process. The purpose of informed consent is to ensure that those participating in research are doing so under voluntary and informed circumstances; it is *not* to protect the researcher. Unfortunately, that is how informed consent is sometimes approached, apologetically and regretfully and as an unnecessary nuisance that merely involves signing a document.

The words *informed consent* imply that the potential participant fully understands all of the following:

- The purpose of the research.

- The auspices, that is, who is funding and who is conducting the research.

- Risks and benefits that may occur as a result of the research.

- Services that will be provided, such as transportation, food, child care, and incentives to participate.

- Procedures in place to deal with any risks that may occur, for instance, emotional distress that may arise as a result of the subject matter.

- The nature of participation, including what is expected, when, and where.

- How and when the information will be recorded, stored, and destroyed.

- Who will have access to the information.

- How the information will be published and used, including procedures to protect the identity of participants.

In addition to these safeguards, participants must be assured that (a) they will not be coerced into participating and (b) if they decline to participate, they will not be punished in any way. Moreover, they may ask for more information at any time. To facilitate this process, they should be given the name and contact information for an appropriate person or persons. Participants also understand that they can withdraw their consent to participate at any time and for any reason, without consequence. Finally, informed consent requires an agreement as to what exactly participants are consenting to, as illustrated by Case-in-Point 2.3.

In February and March 2004, the Havasupai tribe of Arizona and some of its members filed two federal lawsuits seeking a total of $75 million in damages from Arizona State University (Fehr-Snyder, Nichols, & Slivka, 2004). The lawsuits claim that genetic information contained in various blood and handprint samples taken from tribal members was used for studies of which they were not advised and would not have approved. The tribal members claim that they gave their consent to participate only in a study on diabetes. The researchers, however, used the data to study a broad range of issues including inbreeding, schizophrenia, and population migration. This last topic in particular is in stark contrast to traditional Havasupai cultural beliefs of how the tribe originated.

The alleged breach came to light when tribal members read some of the published findings and recognized that the study was referring to their tribe. This incident is tragic given the fact that American Indians die from chronic liver disease and cirrhosis, diabetes, and tuberculosis at rates that are higher than those of other Americans and therefore could greatly benefit from health-related research (Barnes, Adams, & Powell-Griner, 2005).

CASE-IN-POINT 2.3

Havasupai Indians Sue Arizona State University

NASW guidelines provide a useful outline for developing an informed consent form. While developing the form the researcher must make a special effort to avoid jargon and to write at a level that is understandable to the lowest level of reading ability found among potential participants. Researchers can use the checklist in Exhibit 2.3 to evaluate the sample letter of informed consent in Exhibit 2.4.

The informed consent letter should include the following information:

- ❏ Introduction of the researcher, the research project, and sponsorship.
- ❏ Purpose of the research.
- ❏ How and why the participant was selected.
- ❏ Statement of benefits of the research to the participant and larger community.
- ❏ Statement of possible harm or risk and procedures to deal with it.
- ❏ Expectations of the participant: time, place, procedures.
- ❏ Ways that the researcher will maintain privacy and confidentiality.
- ❏ Promise of confidentiality.
- ❏ Rights regarding refusal and dropping out of the study.
- ❏ An appeal for help/cooperation.
- ❏ Name and contact information of the researcher and the person in charge if questions or concerns arise.

EXHIBIT 2.3

Checklist for Evaluating Informed Consent

EXHIBIT 2.4

*Sample
Informed
Consent
Letter*

INFORMED CONSENT FORM—PARENT

The Casey Family Services Building Skills–Building Futures Information Technology Pilot Project (BSBF) seeks to evaluate the usefulness of providing information technology resources to foster families. As a current foster family with Casey Family Services, you have been selected to participate in the project and the evaluation. The University of New Hampshire has been chosen to conduct the evaluation of the project. We are requesting your assistance by providing information about foster family needs, foster family learning, and your use of information technology.

Families agree to participate in the program and the entire evaluation by:

a. Filling out several information forms at the beginning of the project and at one-year and two-year intervals. These forms will assess your use of information technology, your satisfaction with the program, and the impact of the program on family life.

b. Participating in a telephone interview about the program after three months.

c. Participating in a two-hour discussion group at 12-month and 24-month intervals to provide feedback to the program.

d. Participating in an e-mail survey by answering a monthly e-mail question about your use of and satisfaction with the program.

e. Reviewing and providing feedback about Web sites and other Internet resources related to parenting and foster care.

The researchers will protect the confidentiality of the information you provide by:

a. Using code numbers instead of names in keeping or reporting any information.

b. Reporting the summary of group information rather than any individual responses.

c. Keeping all information in a secure place.

d. Having a signed confidentiality oath from all program staff and evaluators.

e. Assuring that you have the right to see your evaluation information at any time.

Benefits
Families will receive hardware, software, training, and Internet connection. (Please see the Casey Family Service Contract with Families Form for an explanation of resources.) It is expected that this will provide families with greater access to information, greater interaction with CFS staff, and increased social support.

Risks
The risks and/or discomforts of participating in this evaluation are minimal. As with any new experience, learning to use the Internet can, at times, be a frustrating experience. In addition, a very small number of people that use the Internet experience difficulties such as receiving unwanted e-mail, development of inappropriate relationships, loss of privacy, and accessing unwanted Web sites (for example, pornography). CFS will facilitate training and technical support to minimize these risks.

In addition, efforts have been made to reduce the risk of discomfort:

EXHIBIT 2.4

*Sample
Informed
Consent
Letter*
continued

a. No one is required to participate in this evaluation of the project. Your participation is completely voluntary.

b. You may withdraw from the evaluation at any time and continue to receive standard Casey services.

c. No family will be refused or denied standard services at Casey Family Services because they do not participate in this evaluation.

d. You may skip any question at any time, with no penalty.

e. All information collected by the University of New Hampshire is confidential and securely stored as described above.

f. Evaluation information will NOT be available to Casey Family Services for personnel evaluation.

If you have any questions about the evaluation process or your rights as a participant in the project, please call Dr. Jerry Finn, University of New Hampshire, (603) XXX-XXXX (e-mail: research@unh.edu), or Julie Simpson, Office of Sponsored Research, UNH, (603) XXX-XXXX (e-mail: OSR@unh.edu).

I have read and understand this Informed Consent form and agree to participate in the Casey Family Services Building Skills–Building Futures Information Technology Pilot Project.

Signed:

_____ / _____
BSBF Family Participant   / Date

_____ / _____
Jerry Finn, Project Evaluator   / Date
University of New Hampshire

Assent.   Due to age or developmental capacity, some individuals may not be able to legally or reasonably provide informed consent. In such cases a parent or legal guardian may be asked to provide consent on their behalf. Nevertheless, these individuals may be asked to sign an **assent** form stating that they are aware that their parent or guardian has consented to their participation and that they voluntarily agree to participate. This procedure is intended as a sign of respect for their rights as individuals. Exhibit 2.5 presents a sample assent form.

Researchers who recruit children through schools and communities can face considerable challenges in obtaining parental consent. This challenge becomes particularly acute when only a select group of children who are not representative of the population as a whole return the signed consent forms. Research has demonstrated that parents from lower socioeconomic backgrounds are less

---

EXHIBIT 2.5

Sample Assent Form

INFORMED ASSENT FOR MINORS

If there is something you don't understand on these pages, please ask your parents for help.

The Casey Family Services Building Skills–Building Futures Information Technology Pilot Project (BSBF) wishes to learn the usefulness of providing computers and Internet to foster families. As a member of a foster family with Casey Family Services, you have been selected to be in the project, if you choose to do so. In this project, you would use the computer and Internet and answer questions about what you are doing.

Children agree to help by:

a. Filling out several information forms at the beginning of the project and at one-year and two-year intervals. These forms will ask about how you use computers and how much you like the program.

b. Participating in a two-hour discussion group at 12-month and 24-month intervals to talk about the program.

c. Reviewing and providing information about Web sites for foster families.

All of your answers will be private, and your name will never be on any reports. The University of New Hampshire will protect the confidentiality of the information you provide by:

a. Removing your name from any data that are collected or reported.

b. Keeping all information in a secure place.

c. Having a signed confidentiality oath from all program staff and evaluators.

d. Assuring that you have the right to see your evaluation information at any time.

EXHIBIT 2.5

Sample Assent Form
continued

Benefits

Families will receive hardware, software, training, and Internet connection. You will also be able to communicate with others over the Internet.

Risks

There are very few risks in participating in this evaluation. As with any new experience, learning to use the Internet can, at times, be a frustrating experience. In addition, a very small number of people that use the Internet have problems such as receiving unwanted e-mail and meeting people or finding information on the Internet that can upset you. CFS will give you training and help to minimize these risks.

In addition, efforts have been made to reduce the risk of discomfort:

a. No one has to be in the project. Your participation is voluntary.

b. You may leave the evaluation at any time and still receive standard Casey services.

c. No family will be refused or denied standard services at Casey Family Services because they do not participate in this project.

d. You may skip any question at any time, with no penalty.

e. All information collected by the University of New Hampshire is confidential and securely stored as described above.

If you have any questions about the project, please call Dr. Jerry Finn, University of New Hampshire, (603) XXX-XXXX (e-mail: research@unh.edu), or Julie Simpson, Office of Sponsored Research, UNH, (603) XXX-XXXX (e-mail: OSP@unh.edu).

I have read and understand this Informed Assent form and agree to be in the Casey Family Services Building Skills–Building Futures Information Technology Pilot Project.

Signed:

_____ / _____
BSBF Family Youth   / Date

_____ / _____
Jerry Finn, Project Evaluator / Date
University of New Hampshire

likely to return parental consent forms and are less likely to allow their children to participate when they do return the forms (Dent et al., 1993). This pattern is problematic because successful research requires that the study include participants who are representative of the entire group.

To deal with this issue of nonparticipation, some researchers have developed passive consent procedures. **Passive consent** requires that parents or legal guardians provide written notice only if they *refuse* to allow their children to participate. Otherwise, the children decide for themselves whether they want to participate at the time the study is conducted. Passive consent thus differs from **active consent,** which requires the parent or legal guardian to sign an informed consent form under all circumstances. The argument for passive consent is that the failure of parents or legal guardians to respond to active consent procedures does not always indicate a refusal to participate. Rather, it may be due to nonreceipt—that is, the child never took the consent form home—lost or misplaced forms, or confusion regarding the consent procedures. Passive consent procedures typically yield participation rates that far exceed those attained through active consent. However, passive consent may be objectionable to the IRB, as it violates principles of informed consent and infringes on parental rights (Fletcher & Hunter, 2003). Case-in-Point 2.4 describes a method of obtaining a high rate of participation using active consent.

"Informed consent is more than a legality; it is a moral responsibility on the part of healthcare providers, based on the recognition of individual autonomy, dignity, and the capacity for self-determination" (Kuther, 2003, p. 344).

Privacy.   NASW guidelines *k* through *m* deal with protecting participants' privacy by not revealing identifying information. Identifying information goes beyond names and addresses and can include demographic characteristics such as race or ethnicity, age, position or title, membership in various organizations, and details of an event or circumstance. Researchers must be extremely careful not to violate privacy by identifying an individual by his or her demographic information. Some research studies can put a participant at risk of harm through embarrassment, retaliation, penalty, or discrimination if her or his identity is revealed. For example, in a worker satisfaction survey, a social worker who is critical of the administration may worry that providing honest answers could affect his or her relationships with supervisors.

As social workers we should always consider privacy from the point of view of the participant, not the researcher. In some cultural groups, certain information is considered sacred, and having that information shared outside the group would be considered a breach of confidentiality. Indeed, our overriding concern as social work researchers is to do no harm.

The perception of possible harm, real or imagined, is a great disincentive to participation and therefore must be dealt with before recruiting participants.

Citing ethical concerns and IRB objections to the use of passive consent, researchers Fletcher and Hunter (2003) outline a tested strategy for obtaining a high participation rate using active parental consent procedures for school-based research. Their study involved children's friendships and parental involvement in these friendships. Potential participants were third-grade students enrolled in nine schools in a single county. Fletcher and Hunter used the following strategy to obtain a return rate of 95 percent for parental consent forms.

1. The researchers engaged the support of key school personnel, beginning with the highest office and working to the classroom level. They asked principals to designate a contact person for the duration of the project to serve as an intermediary between the research staff and the teachers. Often the contact person was the counselor who knew teachers and students and was able to elicit a high level of enthusiasm for the research. In addition, they informed teachers in writing and via the school contact person about the importance of obtaining the participation of a representative group of children. They further declared that no research would be conducted in any classroom that did not have a 90 percent rate of returned forms, regardless of whether consent was granted. Teachers who had a rate of return of 90 percent or better received $5 gift certificates from a local educational supply store for each consent form returned. These certificates were given to the teachers on the day of data collection from their class, thereby providing immediate reinforcement.

2. Research assistants were assigned to specific schools and were encouraged to become personally invested in the consent process. Teachers appreciated the consistent communication and attention they received from a familiar research assistant.

3. The informed consent forms were designed to be clear and easy to read and to catch the parents' attention. A cover page with large bold print stated a set of instructions for completing the forms. The instructions informed parents that the child's class would receive a donation for each form returned, regardless of whether they checked yes or no. Areas that had to be filled out were highlighted. Any information that could be filled out in advance, like the school name and address and child's grade, was completed to reduce the burden on the parent. Different colors of paper were used to indicate different schools. Significantly, the researchers discovered that the brightest paper yielded the quickest and most complete responses. Parents commented that they liked receiving the bright paper.

4. The researchers provided consent forms multiple times to those children who had not returned the form on the first round. They gave out the forms one week apart. Moreover, they personalized the second and third waves by writing the child's name on the top of each form. The fourth time the forms were given out, a teacher or school official called the parent to ask if she or he had received the form and, if so, to request her or him to return it the next day.

For example, in the research on the Havasupai described in Case-in-Point 2.3, the use of data to examine population migration represents an infringement on the privacy of the tribe from a tribal perspective as opposed to a researcher perspective.

Because social work research is concerned with reflecting reality as accurately as possible, we must work creatively and strategically to encourage and enable a representative group of participants to participate safely. One method of encouraging participation is through the use of incentives.

Incentives.   It is common and useful in research projects to provide small incentives for participants. For example, the researcher might give a small stipend or gift certificate to subjects to cover the costs of transportation to the research site or to compensate them for their time. Incentives, however, can be considered coercion when the value is such that people who would not ordinarily participate in a study feel that they must participate because they need the incentive. For example, from 1963 to 1971, a study involving testicular radiation and vasectomy was conducted in the Oregon prison system. Participants were paid $25 per session for up to five sessions. This incentive was offered at a time when prisoners generally earned 25 cents a day for their labor. In this case, the incentive may have "coerced" men to participate in the study when they otherwise would not have chosen to do so (Goliszek, 2003). Similarly in social work, a mother receiving TANF may feel that she "must" participate in a study of childhood sexual abuse experiences that offers a $500 incentive because the money would greatly benefit her children. Social work researchers often conduct research with vulnerable and needy populations. Therefore, they should carefully consider the use of incentives when they design their projects. In Chapter 7 we discuss further the use of incentives to encourage participation.

Confidentiality and Anonymity

The promise of confidentiality that we so often make to a potential participant during the informed consent process is a promise not to reveal identifying information that the participant has provided. Fulfilling the promise of confidentiality can be especially problematic in some forms of qualitative research, in which (1) the intent is to obtain as much detailed information as possible, (2) everything about the participant has the potential to become data, and (3) the participant's words are used in the publication and presentation of the findings.

One research scenario in which confidentiality becomes highly problematic is the case study. The **case study** is a qualitative research strategy that seeks to examine a single unit of analysis, be it an event, a person, a family, a group, an organization, or a company, in order to generate an in-depth understanding of that unit. (We examine case studies in greater detail in Chapter 10.) Frequently, researchers engaged in case studies either cannot protect or do not desire confidentiality because of the level of detail that participants report. In such cases, the researcher must negotiate with the participants concerning which information they wish to reveal to other individuals and which information they wish to withhold.

Large quantitative studies can also put participants at risk of identification. This risk is especially prevalent in cases that involve a small number of participants who possess particular characteristics that might enable anyone reading the study to identify them. This is particularly true of participants whose demographic characteristics are rare within the sample. For example, in the Midwest, a 59-year-old male Pacific Islander may be the only individual in the sample who fits those demographic characteristics. Therefore, he may be relatively easy to identify. In such studies the researcher should not report results by category.

The promise of **anonymity**—the agreement not to record a participant's name or other identifying information such as address or Social Security number—does not guarantee confidentiality. Although a promise of anonymity can make research participants more comfortable and more willing to participate, it does not guarantee that they cannot be identified by other revealing characteristics after the study is published. For example, a direct quotation from a participant in a research study may allow someone to identify the participant even if the name is not given. In one study, a social worker was quoted as saying, "Someone should just slap the management. They should check with the workers before changing policy." Although no name was given, many people at the agency knew who regularly used the expression "should just slap." Social work researchers must carefully consider issues of privacy and confidentiality when they are designing research projects.

CONCLUSION

The uniqueness of social work research is not in its research methods, theory, statistical analysis, or technology. Social work research can be distinguished from research in other disciplines by its purpose—the ends to which the research is conducted. In brief, the mission of social work is the enhancement of human well-being with attention to the vulnerable, oppressed, and poor. Historically, these groups are the most likely to be the victims of ethical misconduct through research studies. They may also feel especially powerless to refuse requests to participate in research studies since they may feel that their access to needed resources and services is at stake. The social work researcher must be more than a technician. The social work researcher must be able to explain, promote, and use social work research in direct and policy practice. At the same time, social workers must have as their highest concern the protection of all those who participate in research and their ethical responsibilities to their clients. This requires a clear understanding of research ethics before engaging in the research methods described in the remainder of the text.

MAIN POINTS

- In working to achieve the mission of social work, researchers must pay attention to research and evaluation quality as well as clarity in reporting and interpretation. In addition, they must assist program personnel and advocates in using data to influence social policy.

- Research and research priorities are strongly influenced by funding, and funding is strongly influenced by politics. Research priorities can also be affected by the extent of knowledge in the field and the degree of advocacy for a particular issue.

- All social workers should be familiar with the ethical standards of the profession. The current version of the NASW *Code of Ethics,* revised in 1999, sets out 16 ethical standards relevant to evaluation and research. The NASW ethical guidelines and local IRBs are resources to aid in the conduct of ethical research.

- The principle of informed consent requires that potential research participants thoroughly understand the nature of their involvement in the research as well as the risks and potential benefits of the research. Moreover, participants must possess the legal and mental capacity to consent, and they must be given a free choice as to whether to participate without fear of consequence.

- Privacy should be viewed from the perspective of the research participant and not from the perspective of the researcher. Protecting the identity of research participants goes beyond promises of anonymity and confidentiality in data collection and safe data storage. The researcher must be vigilant not to reveal a participant's identity through publication or presentation of information that is particularly revealing.

EXERCISES: PRACTICING SOCIAL WORK

1. You have been awarded a research grant to examine domestic violence in the Black Feather community. List the ethical, cultural, and gender considerations involved in your research.

2. How might the ethical, cultural, and gender considerations change if your research is focused on the Hispanic community in the town where the Sanchez family lives?

EXERCISES: SOCIAL WORK LIBRARY

1. After reading Fletcher and Hunter (2003), describe the differences between passive and active consent strategies for conducting research with children. What are the ethical issues involved in either method? On what basis would you make a decision between the two methods of obtaining parental consent?

2. Read Drumm and Pittman (2003). What do you consider the major ethical issues in this study?

OTHER EXERCISES

1. Discuss the ethical issues in the following research projects:

    a. You want to see if counseling of batterers by social workers, arrest by police officers, or doing nothing is more effective in reducing spouse abuse.

    b. You want to survey students about bullying. You give all students in grades 5–8 a questionnaire asking about the types of in-school bullying they have experienced. The questionnaire is anonymous.

    c. You want to see how agency staff in child protective services feels about supervisors. You hire a researcher to pose as new staff to learn the true feelings of line workers.

    d. You want to see if megavitamin therapy is helpful to prisoner mental health. You offer prisoners a cash payment and extra health checkups if they will participate in the study.

e. You want to see if sexual abuse experiences impact grade point average. You do a questionnaire of college students about their experiences with childhood sexual abuse.

f. You want to see if children of color are more likely to have learning disabilities. You will check school and medical records to find out.

2. Research the IRB guidelines and procedures at your university or college. Obtain a copy of the application form for ethics review. What ethical principles and guidelines are emphasized?

CHAPTER 3

The Research Process: From Problems to Research Questions

Human understanding evolves through a process of critiquing
existing knowledge and consequently expanding and refining
the state of knowledge.
—FISCHER, 1991

A T THIS POINT IN YOUR SOCIAL WORK EDUCATION, YOU MAY feel more comfortable, or at least more familiar, with social work practice than with social work research. Social work practice, like research, is a systematic process. That is, social workers use a practice framework to guide their actions. Therefore, an effective strategy to become familiar with the steps in social work research is to relate them to your practice framework. When you are conducting research in a social work context, the steps of the **research process** serve as the framework for your actions. Exhibit 3.1 presents the research process as a series of eight steps. It also illustrates how the steps in the research process parallel those in generalist social work practice. Both social work practice and social work research use existing information to identify a problem, create a plan of action, seek valid and reliable measurement, collect data, and analyze and interpret the data to direct further action.

Good social work practice, at any level, begins with an **assessment,** defined as a thorough understanding of the problem area. For instance, a professional social work counselor or case manager begins with an assessment before she or he considers an intervention. Similarly, a social work manager writing a proposal for a new social program would be required to include an assessment of need before specifying the overall purpose of the proposed program—its **goal**—and measurable statements of its intent, or **objectives.** The social worker engaged in policy practice would not lobby for new legislation without first becoming familiar with the problem that the proposed legislation is intended to alleviate. So too, social work research begins with identifying a problem.

The first two chapters dealt with the need to base social work practice on knowledge and the ethics and the politics involved in generating knowledge.

EXHIBIT 3.1

The Relationship between Social Work Research and Practice

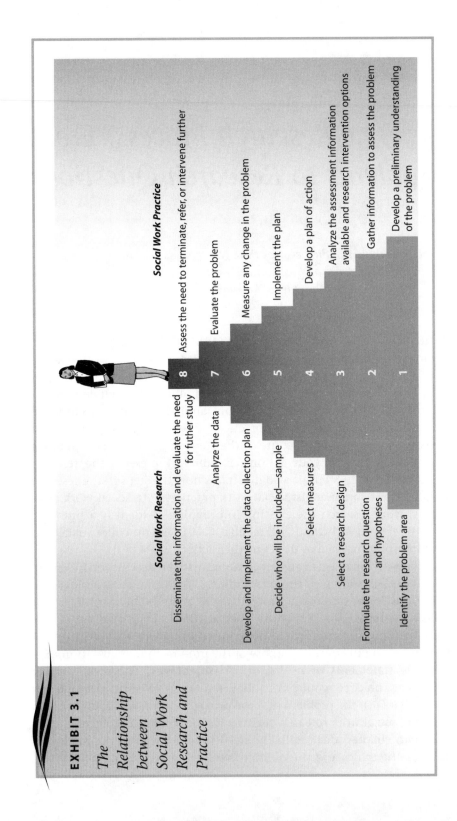

Social Work Practice

8 — Assess the need to terminate, refer, or intervene further

7 — Evaluate the problem

6 — Measure any change in the problem

5 — Implement the plan

4 — Develop a plan of action

3 — Analyze the assessment information available and research intervention options

2 — Gather information to assess the problem

1 — Develop a preliminary understanding of the problem

Social Work Research

Disseminate the information and evaluate the need for futher study

Analyze the data

Develop and implement the data collection plan

Decide who will be included—sample

Select measures

Select a research design

Formulate the research question and hypotheses

Identify the problem area

This chapter begins our journey into the *how to* of conducting social work research. As Enola Proctor, editor of the premier journal *Social Work Research,* wrote, "The advancement of social work knowledge requires not only that we pose significant questions, but also that we answer them well" (2001, p. 3). This chapter provides you with the knowledge and skills you will need in order to pose relevant and researchable questions. The remaining chapters deal with the knowledge and skills you will need in order to answer these questions with confidence.

By the end of this chapter you should be able to:

- Explain how a working knowledge of the research process is important to all social workers.

- List and briefly describe the first two steps in the social work research process.

- Explain the parallel between social work research and social work practice.

- Apply criteria to critically evaluate a research problem and research question in a published research study.

- Describe the concept of operationalization and provide an example of its relevance to social work research.

- Discuss how sensitivity to culture at each step in the research process will produce better information.

OVERVIEW OF THE RESEARCH PROCESS

The research process consists of all the steps that must be considered in planning and carrying out research in a social work context. The word *process* implies that order is involved in conducting social work research. When social workers ignore that order or fail to make a connection between the steps in the research process, they waste a lot of time and resources producing information that is likely to be flawed and misleading. Worst of all, despite their good intentions, they will not benefit and may even harm the very people they aim to help—their clients, communities, programs, and organizations.

Conducting research to produce useful information for social work requires careful planning, sound design, adequate resources, and a step-by-step process that begins with a definition of the problem. Case-in-Point 3.1 illustrates the importance of focusing on accurate problem identification.

What if you are not planning to be a social work researcher or an evaluator? Why should you spend time learning the research process? The answer is that, regardless of your role as a social worker, possessing a working knowledge of the

CASE-IN-POINT 3.1

Prevention Program Fails to Address the Target Problem

A social worker was asked to consult with the administrator of a school-based substance abuse prevention program that targets children in grades 3–8. The program was designed around a standardized curriculum to discourage students in these grades from using alcohol, drugs, and tobacco. The administrator reported that for the second year in a row the evaluation of the program revealed no significant change in students' attitudes or behavior regarding these substances. What did this mean? Was the prevention program not working?

By examining the data and talking to groups of parents, the administrator determined that the vast majority of students in the program had not experimented with alcohol, drugs, or tobacco. They didn't need a substance abuse prevention program. Rather, the major problem in the school, as perceived by groups of students and teachers, was aggressive behavior. On the basis of this feedback, in the third year of the program the administrator decided to use the scarce prevention funds to target aggression rather than substance use. This case illustrates a basic principle of social work research, namely, that all of the steps in the research process should logically flow from an accurate identification of the problem.

research process will serve you well. Using the research process as a framework for evaluating existing information will help you become more critical in your thinking. In addition, knowledge of the research process is essential for the evaluation of social work practice, whether it involves work with a single client or an entire program of services. Further, social work administrators attempting to raise funds to support a new or existing program are more likely to succeed when they use the research process as a framework for deciding what information to include in their proposals. Finally, policy makers, lobbyists, and advocates will appear more credible when they debate issues and create arguments using their knowledge of the research process.

IDENTIFYING THE RESEARCH PROBLEM

To say that something is "problematic" in a research context is to mean that something is unknown and we would be better off if we knew about it. Research, the process of searching for an answer to the unknown, is a problem-driven enterprise. Problems become recognized in the public domain not because they exist but because they are identified and defined as problems. In other words, problems are socially constructed. For example, people sometimes claim that poverty was discovered in the 1960s, sexual abuse in the 1970s, and domestic violence in the 1980s. In reality, of course, all of these phenomena existed before these times. However, they did not receive sufficient attention to be defined as social problems.

FIGURE 3.1   Children make up approximately 40 percent of the homeless population in the United States. Moreover, families with children are among the fastest-growing segments of the homeless population. Homelessness results from a complex set of circumstances that include a lack of affordable housing, low wages, a decline in public assistance, domestic violence, mental illness, addiction disorders, and insufficient health care coverage.

Source: Copyright © Tony Freeman/PhotoEdit.

Because social workers encounter social problems on a daily basis, they are in a unique position to bring their knowledge of these problems to the public's attention. In addition, they can help dispel popular myths and stereotypes by giving the affected populations a face and a voice through research. For instance, many social workers practicing in the area of homelessness have noticed that the clients of homeless shelters and soup kitchens are increasingly single mothers with children. Figure 3.1 reflects the new face of homelessness in the United States.

The federal government has undertaken an enormous data collection effort to increase our understanding of the problem of homelessness in the United States. In 2001 Congress directed the U.S. Department of Housing and Urban Development (HUD) to collect data on the extent of homelessness at the local level (H.B. 106-988; Senate Report 106-410). As a result, jurisdictions that receive HUD funds are busily implementing management information systems to answer four questions: (1) How many individuals are homeless? (2) What are the characteristics of homeless individuals? (3) What services do homeless individuals need? (4) What services do homeless individuals receive? Some data collection efforts are statewide, and others are limited to cities and counties.

 Web Links

To learn more about the Homeless Management Information System (HMIS) mandate, visit the HUD Web site at www.mhhe.com/krysik1. While there, you can also view the Los Angeles Homeless Services Authority Web site to learn how a coalition of cities and counties in the Los Angeles area have implemented the HMIS.

It is highly unlikely that a social worker will need to go looking for a problem that needs to be researched. Just the opposite, practicing social workers consistently encounter situations for which they need more information. For example, assume that your internship is in a middle school and a child who is being picked on by other children has been brought to your attention. Suddenly you are full of questions. Is this abuse an isolated incident? If not, how long has it been occurring? How many other children are encountering the same problem? Are the teachers and administrators aware of the problem? If so, how have they responded? Is the problem limited to this school setting? What are the characteristics of the children being picked on and of the perpetrating children? What are the long-term consequences for the victims? What do the parents of the victims and the perpetrators know about the situation? How have they reacted? Are there any verified strategies for dealing with this problem? In your search for answers to these questions, you find that school bullying has received a lot of recent attention in the research literature. You also find that some of your initial questions have been answered, but others require further research.

Based on opportunity, personal interest, and experience, make a quick list of potential research problem areas. You might be surprised at how many research problems you can identify.

Although work-related opportunity is probably the most common way a social worker will identify problems for research, personal interest and experience can also play a role. Many social workers, for example, are personally committed to the social problems of developing countries, such as economic development in the face of transitional economies, child poverty, and the spread of HIV/AIDS. Other social workers commit themselves to advancing knowledge in specific problem areas as a result of personal, and sometimes tragic, experiences. A social worker who has lost a teenage child or sibling, for example, might feel a responsibility to expand the base of knowledge associated with that social problem. One of the most exciting aspects of social work is the breadth of populations and problem areas it addresses. This observation applies to social work research as well as to social work practice.

Making the Case to Study a Research Problem

Identifying a research problem can be quite easy. Unfortunately, there are more problems that merit research than there are resources for studying them. What factors, then, determine that one problem area warrants the time and resources associated with research more than another? Possible answers to this question include the frequency with which the problem occurs, the extent of human suffering the problem produces, the costs of the problem to society, the lack of attention the problem has received in the past, and the belief that the problem can and should be addressed at the current time. Through an initial exploration of a problem area, social workers come to understand the magnitude, extent of suffering, and costs associated with a social problem, as well as the attention, or lack thereof, it has already received. Social workers seek answers to such questions as How many people are affected, and in what ways?

Finding Relevant Information Sources.   There are several useful resources for conducting an initial exploration of a problem area. For instance, conducting a key word search at the library, reading agency case files, and browsing the annual program evaluation reports of agencies and organizations can give us a sense of the magnitude and nature of a problem area. Talking with social work colleagues and professors can also be helpful, particularly if they can suggest valuable sources of information. The World Wide Web will likely contain information related to your problem area. The Web has the added advantages of speed and convenience. A key word search on the Internet may produce information from a wide variety of sources, including university-based projects, archives of government agencies, electronic journals, interest groups, magazines, and Web pages from companies and individuals.

 Web Links

Visit www.mhhe.com/krysik1 for a number of Web sites containing information on research problem areas.

Evaluating the Credibility of Information Sources.   Sometimes when we are searching for information, something leads us to question the credibility of a particular source. Although we should approach all information sources with a healthy amount of skepticism, information from the Internet is especially prone to error and bias because there are no controls on its publication. Consequently, we must carefully evaluate which Internet sources are credible and which are not using accepted principles of critical analysis. One way to manage this process is to use a framework such as the one presented in Exhibit 3.2.

The information found in the initial exploration of the problem area will help social workers decide whether further research is warranted. To demonstrate the worth of a problem area for research, the social worker must be able to convincingly answer the question Why is this important? It is likely that a social worker will be interested in more than one compelling problem area. In such cases, she or he must select one area based on some combination of personal interest and expressed agency or organizational need for the research.

Striving for Cultural Proficiency

When social workers consider which research to undertake, they must take into account the cultural context in which the research will take place. There is a broad agreement within the social work literature on the need for social workers to be proficient in issues of culture. **Cultural competence** is the ability to perform effectively in multicultural settings based on an understanding of one's own and others' language, customs, values, and beliefs. **Cultural proficiency** is the culmination or endpoint on the continuum of cultural competence. It is characterized by knowledge, attitudes, and behavior that hold culture in high esteem (Cross, Bazron, Dennis, & Isaacs, 1989).

Culturally proficient social workers seek to do more than provide unbiased services. Rather, they value the positive role that culture can play in their

EXHIBIT 3.2

Framework for Evaluating the Credibility of Information Sources

CRITERIA	SOURCE 1	SOURCE 2	SOURCE 3
1. Authority			
2. Intent			
3. Currency			
4. Reliability			
5. Fairness			
Total Score			

DIRECTIONS FOR USE

Create a table similar to the one presented here. List each source of existing information you have gathered by title or author in the top row. Next, for each of the five criteria, rate each source on a scale of 0 to 5. A score of 0 represents a failing grade, and a score of 5 represents excellence. When you have rated all five criteria, add up the total score for each source and record it in the bottom row. A total score close to 25 indicates a credible source; a low score suggests that the source should not be used.

EXPLANATION OF THE CRITERIA

Authority: Is the source of the information identified by name? Is there a way to verify the legitimacy of the source, such as an address or telephone number? Does the source have a bias or reason to distort its information? What credentials does the source have to provide this information? Have experts subjected the information to a process of review?

Intent: Is the motivation for providing the information clear? Is the intent informational, that is, to provide facts and figures? Is the intent advocacy, meaning that the source is sponsored by an organization attempting to influence public opinion? Is the intent advertising, meaning that the purpose of the source is to promote or sell something?

Currency: How recent are the facts and figures? Is there a date to indicate when the source was first published or last updated? Might things have changed considerably since this information was gathered?

Reliability: How did the authors derive the information? Do they cite their sources? Are the data consistent with other known sources? Did the authors follow accepted research procedures? Do they provide enough detail? Do they address the limitations of the information? Is the information well presented and free of grammatical, spelling, and typographical errors?

Fairness: Do the authors present the material in a balanced manner, or do they focus only on the positive or negative aspects?

Source: Adapted with permission from Janet Alexander and Marsha Ann Tate.

clients' health and well-being. Training for social work practitioners on cultural proficiency generally includes self-awareness, knowledge of different cultures, and intervention strategies that are tailored for specific cultures (Lum, 1999; Sue, Arredondo, & McDavis, 1995). When applied to social work research, cultural proficiency involves adding to the knowledge base of culturally competent practices by conducting original research, tailoring research approaches so that they are appropriate for the client's culture, and publishing and disseminating the results of research in ways that are accessible to varied cultural groups that may be interested in the research.

To achieve cultural proficiency in research—to produce knowledge that is respectful of culture and as error free as possible—social workers must be sensitive to culture during each step of the research process. Culturally proficient research begins with being sensitive to culture in identifying the research problem. Cultural proficiency in research is a developing domain, and it is imperative that social workers continue to advance this area. The following guidelines are a useful beginning in achieving culturally proficient research.

Acknowledge Personal Biases.   People are separated socially, economically, and educationally on the basis of ethnicity, race, gender, sexual orientation, and age. This separation frequently generates myths, stereotypes, attitudes, and assumptions regarding diverse groups and their cultures. Heightened self-awareness is necessary for the researcher to identify his or her personal biases.

Assess Bias in the Literature.   The presence of bias in the existing literature can limit the generation of culturally competent research problems in three ways. First, certain cultural groups might not be represented in the literature because researchers simply have failed to study them. For example, researchers have paid a lot of attention to teenage mothers but very little to teenage fathers. Second, a study of a subset of people can overgeneralize to the entire group. For example, researchers might make inferences about Hispanic immigrants in general based solely on a study of undocumented immigrants from Mexico.

Finally, researchers can focus on the negative attributes associated with particular cultures at the expense of acknowledging positive features. Over time, this negative focus can lead to the development and reinforcement of destructive stereotypes, particularly the tendency to define differences as pathological. For example, a great deal of research on American Indians focuses on alcohol and drug use (Padilla & Salgado de Snyder, 1992). In contrast, the concept of kinship care has been central to the American Indian culture for generations, but it has taken researchers decades to frame it as a positive practice that has conceptual relevance to the field of child welfare (Duer Berrick & Barth, 1994).

Assess Bias in Agencies and Organizations.   Bias in social service agencies can lead to the study of diverse populations in only limited contexts (Reinharz, 1992).

For example, research may focus on poor African Americans but not on middle-class African Americans. Studying populations in limited contexts promotes stereotypes and masks within-group diversity. Bias within an agency can also lead to a narrow view of culturally diverse groups and the difficulties they face. For example, social service practitioners have tended to emphasize individual parenting deficits and to ignore external and institutional factors such as poverty, poor education and health care, and loss of culture that make parenting even more of a challenge for particular groups.

Acquire Prerequisite Knowledge.   Social workers need to invest time and effort in learning about the cultural groups of interest. At the very minimum, social work researchers should acquire knowledge of the cultural group's history, communication norms, language preferences, religion or spiritual beliefs, and attitudes toward gender and age.

Differentiate "Research For" from "Research On."   Research *for* can be conceptualized as an altruistic activity, pursued out of an unselfish concern for the welfare of others that promotes the expressed needs and perspectives of the group being studied (Bowman, 1983). Research *on*, in contrast, can be perceived as an opportunistic activity, viewing the cultural group as merely a subject of study.

What guidelines can you add to help achieve the goal of cultural proficiency in identifying the research problem?

Involve Members of the Cultural Group.   Members of the identified group to be involved in the research should be consulted about decision making related to research (Bowman, 1983). Research problems identified through involvement of participants may have a very different focus from research problems identified independent of such consultation.

Final Checklist for Evaluating Identification of the Research Problem.   After you have identified a problem area for study, you should evaluate it according to these five criteria:

1. The problem area is relevant to social work.

2. The need for research on the problem area is compelling.

3. The claim that the problem area warrants research is supported by credible sources of information.

4. Various sources of bias have been considered in identifying the research problem.

5. Potential participants in the study agree that research on the problem is needed and view it as potentially beneficial.

FORMULATING THE RESEARCH QUESTION AND HYPOTHESES

After you identify the research problem, the next step in the research process is to formulate a research question and possibly one or more hypotheses. The process of moving from general problem area to more narrow research question, sometimes referred to as the *funnel approach*, is essential to making the research process manageable.

Formulating the General Research Question

One useful approach to formulating the general research question is to begin with a brainstorming session. Brainstorming involves writing down as many general research questions related to the problem area as you can think of, without being overly concerned about their wording. To expand your list of questions, engage your classmates and colleagues in brainstorming with you; after all, social work research is seldom a solitary activity. The rationale for beginning the process of formulating the research question by brainstorming is to avoid being limited to the ideas published in the literature.

Value-Laden Questions.   Some of the questions produced in a brainstorming session are likely to involve values. Value-laden questions cannot be answered through research; their answers are purely a matter of personal opinion. Examples of value-laden questions are Should same-sex couples be allowed to legally marry? Should abortion be legal? Is euthanasia morally acceptable? Is capital punishment moral? These questions cannot be answered by research. Social workers may, however, be concerned with related questions, such as What is the range of public opinion on same-sex marriage? How do women who have experienced an abortion view the procedure one year later? What are the psychological consequences of euthanasia for surviving family members? Does capital punishment deter violent crime? These questions differ from value-laden questions in that they can be answered through research.

Categorizing Research Questions by Their Purpose.   Once you have compiled a list of potential research questions, you can place each question into one of three categories of inquiry, depending on the purpose of the question. The three categories are exploratory, descriptive, and explanatory questions. The rationale for classifying research questions according to purpose is to help identify which category of questioning is most appropriate for the problem area. We determine the most appropriate category of questioning by reviewing the literature to identify what we already know about the problem area and what we still need to learn.

- *Exploratory research:* The purpose of **exploratory research** is to gain an initial understanding of the problem area. This type of research is especially important when we know very little about the problem.

- *Descriptive research:* As the name suggests, the purpose of **descriptive research** is to describe. Descriptive research questions pertain to the characteristics of the problem and the characteristics of those affected by the problem. This involves questions such as How many people are affected, and with what consequences? How does the problem differ by demographic and cultural characteristics?

- *Explanatory research:* As you have probably deduced, the purpose of **explanatory research** is to explain how and why things happen. Explanatory research questions are designed to generate an in-depth understanding of the problem area. They often seek to establish cause-and-effect relationships that enable us to predict future events. We can use explanatory research to test such aspects of a problem as (a) the factors related to the presence or absence of the problem, (b) a common order or sequence in how the problem develops, and (c) the effectiveness of intervention strategies aimed at alleviating the problem.

To illustrate the question categorization process, we will refer to a current issue that has relevance to social work: same-sex marriage. In February 2004 San Francisco began issuing marriage licenses to same-sex couples (Murphy, 2004). In the ensuing month, more than 4,000 gay and lesbian couples from 46 states and 8 countries were legally married in the city. Then, in March, the California Supreme Court prohibited the city from issuing any more marriage licenses to same-sex couples. A flurry of legislative activity followed around the country as state legislators worked to ban same-sex marriages through constitutional amendments.

The controversies surrounding same-sex marriage raise a number of potential research questions. We can classify these questions by their primary purpose: to explore, to describe, or to explain.

The following are examples of exploratory research questions:

1. How has marriage affected same-sex couples?

2. What significance does marriage have for the children of same-sex unions?

3. How does the advent of same-sex marriage influence the process of coming out, whereby gays and lesbians publicly proclaim their sexual orientation?

The following are examples of descriptive research questions:

1. What are the demographic characteristics of the gay and lesbian couples who were married in San Francisco?

2. How many same-sex unions are there in the United States, and what forms do they take?

3. What employee-related benefits are currently available to the spouses of same-sex unions?

The following are examples of explanatory research questions:

1. What factors predict whether a same-sex couple will choose legal marriage when it is available?

2. How will legal marriage impact the quality of same-sex relationships?

3. What types of interventions support healthy parental adjustment to a child's disclosure of homosexuality?

Conducting the Literature Review

A significant step in formulating a research problem is to review the research that has already been conducted. A **literature review** is an account of what has been published on a problem area by scholars and researchers. The purpose of the literature review in social work research is fourfold:

1. To gain an understanding of the knowledge and ideas that have been established in a problem area.

2. To identify the strengths and weaknesses of our existing knowledge.

3. To identify the controversies that exist in the literature.

4. To identify questions that require further research.

To achieve its purpose, the literature review may examine issues of theory, methodology, policy, and evaluation that relate to the effectiveness of a policy or intervention. The review can include information from a variety of disciplines other than social work, including health, psychology, sociology, medicine, law, political science, and women's studies, as long as the information is directly related to the problem area.

One way to begin the literature review is to conduct an electronic search of a library database for relevant books, journal articles, theses, dissertations, and conference proceedings. In addition, government documents may provide valuable statistical information on the problem, including the numbers and demographic characteristics of the people affected by it. Reference librarians can be particularly helpful in locating government documents and other unpublished sources of information such as evaluation reports. The Internet is an increasingly valuable source of information, and it also might identify relevant printed resources, sometimes in the form of an annotated bibliography and online publications.

Familiarity with the literature on the problem area will likely help you reword some of your original research questions and generate ideas for additional questions. When conducting the literature review, remember to perform the following activities:

- Look for information on the scope, severity, and relevance of the problem area.

- Assess the relationship between the theory related to the problem area and the available research.

- Note the problematic issues that the literature raises, and assess how these issues have been addressed in prior research.

- Identify areas of controversy related to the problem.

- Synthesize the literature review into a summary of what is and is not known.

- Identify questions that require further research.

- Make the literature search wide enough to ensure that you have included the relevant material yet narrow enough to exclude irrelevant material.

- Relate the study you propose to do to the previous literature.

Case-in-Point 3.2 describes the use of theory as a basis for generating research questions.

How to Select the Right Research Question for the Study.   A literature review that fails to produce any reference to the problem area or very little information would indicate that exploratory research questions are the most appropriate avenue of inquiry. The purpose of exploratory research is to generate an initial understanding of the problem area and to identify relevant concepts. If the literature describes important concepts and variations of the problem but contains little information about the extent or costs of the problem or the people affected by it, descriptive research questions are warranted. If exploratory and descriptive information is available, the most appropriate category of inquiry is explanatory. Explanatory questions could involve replicating existing studies, clarifying controversies, evaluating intervention strategies, and advancing relevant theories.

In the simplest of terms, **theory** is an explanation for why things are the way they are; it is an explanation of the relationships among phenomena. When we are developing research questions, theory can lead us to ask certain research questions or to word our questions in a specific way. When we are explicit about the theory or theories we use to help guide our study, we make clear our rationale for asking the specific research questions that we do.

Hawlin Tina Liu, a doctoral student in social work at Arizona State University, was interested in how elderly immigrants from Taiwan adjust to life in the United States (Liu, 1998). As a gerontological social worker—someone who works with elderly populations—she wanted to know what problems these immigrants encounter and what strategies they employ to solve their problems. By reviewing the literature, she discovered that little was known about recent immigrants. Instead, prior research had focused on elderly immigrants who had arrived years before as young laborers, students, or professionals. These groups differed substantially from recent immigrants, many of whom were the parents of former student immigrants and followed their children to the United States.

Liu selected three theories to help her formulate her research questions. First, she chose ecological theory to identify the different levels of systems—micro, meso, exo, and macro—that both impact and help resolve individual need (Bronfenbrenner, 1979). Liu incorporated these four levels of systems into her inquiry into the behaviors of the elderly immigrants.

Second, Liu used dual perspective theory, developed by Delores G. Norton (1978). *Dual perspective theory* suggests that all people are linked to at least two interrelated social systems, the nurturing system (family and community) and the sustaining system (the general social and political systems). The idea of dualism developed from the belief that the family and community environments of ethnic minorities may be very different from those of the larger society. Differences between the nurturing and sustaining systems can sometimes cause conflicts in the lives of minority-group individuals. Liu used the dual perspective theory to look at the ways in which the two systems both complemented and conflicted with each other as the elderly Taiwanese immigrants tried to maintain their traditional beliefs while meeting their needs in a new culture.

Third, Liu used the help-seeking behavior model developed by James Green (1995). This model describes the major processes that individuals use in obtaining resources, including recognizing problems, labeling and diagnosing problems, using help providers, and employing client-based goals for problem resolution. Using this model required Liu to view problems through the eyes of the immigrants, to consider how cultural norms influence their evaluation of problems, and to examine their strategies for overcoming their problems. Her search for prior research and theory led her to formulate these general exploratory research questions: What are the needs of the elderly Taiwanese recent immigrants? Are these immigrants aware of resources that exist to meet their needs? Do they use available human services? If yes, what factors influence their use? If not, why not?

CASE-IN-POINT 3.2

Using Theory as a Guide

After you have determined the most appropriate avenue of inquiry—exploratory, descriptive, or explanatory—you should review the list of potential research questions one by one to establish their relevance to social work. For each question ask the following:

- Will the answer to this question inform social work practice?
- Will the answer to this question influence social policy?
- Will the answer to this question lead to a better understanding of the populations affected by the problem?

You should continue this process until you have identified the most useful question. As social workers we are far too busy—and our resources are far too limited—to pursue answers to research questions that are not going to make a valuable contribution.

Final Checklist for Evaluating the General Research Question.   After you have developed a general research question, your next step is to evaluate it according to these five criteria:

1. The question is logically related to the identification of the problem area.
2. The question can be answered through research; it is not value laden.
3. The question has not been answered. If it has been, what related questions might you ask?
4. Answering the question will be useful for informing social work practice, developing social policy, or advancing theory.
5. The question is sensitive to issues of culture.

Specifying the General Research Question

General research questions need to be specified before they can be answered. The question needs to be put into a format that makes it researchable. The challenge is to make the question specific enough so that it can be answered but not so narrow that it loses its relevance. The following section describes the many tasks involved in this process.

Identifying and Defining Concepts.   The first task in specifying the general research question is to identify the major concepts contained in the question. A **concept** is an abstract or a general idea, a symbol for some observable attribute or phenomenon. For example, if our general research question is What is the recidivism rate of juvenile girls? three concepts are readily identified: recidivism, juvenile, and girl. Some concepts leave less room for interpretation than others. For instance, the concept *girl* is not at all ambiguous and requires no formal definition. The concepts of *recidivism*—whether delinquency is repeated—and *juvenile,* however, are subject to various interpretations.

Defining the major concepts contained in the research question is necessary so that (1) the social work researcher is clear about what she or he plans to study and (2) the study participants and eventual consumers of the research will define the concepts the same way the researcher does. Concepts are usually defined with both a nominal definition and an operational definition. A **nominal definition** is one that describes a concept in ways similar to a dictionary definition. An **operational definition** defines concepts in ways that can be measured. To **operationalize** a concept means to define it in a measurable way. Operationalizing a concept provides conceptual clarity and removes all ambiguity about the meaning of the concept. Social workers can draw on prior research to help them identify the options for operationalizing a concept.

Using *juvenile* as an example, a nominal definition might be "a young person not fully grown or developed." This definition, however, makes it hard to know exactly who should be considered a juvenile. For instance, should we consider someone who is two years old a juvenile? What about a "late bloomer" who is 21 and has not yet reached full physical maturity? In order to avoid this ambiguity, we use operational definitions to specify exactly what should be included. At times, operationalizing a concept is easy because an official definition already exists. Juvenile status, for example, will likely be determined by the state where the research is being conducted. The Arizona justice system, for instance, considers children as young as eight years to be juveniles. Thus, one possible operational definition of juvenile is "any child between the ages of 8 and 17."

Many times, more than one official definition for a particular concept exists. In these cases, the researcher must select the most appropriate one. For example, *recidivism* is often operationalized according to a legal definition. In a study involving risk prediction, recidivism was defined as "any delinquent complaint, regardless of the final disposition, occurring within 365 days of the initial referral." Although using this definition of recidivism included more juveniles than were eventually judged to be delinquent, the definition represented the legal status that the Supreme Court was interested in predicting (Krysik & LeCroy, 2002). In contrast, other researchers have used a different definition of recidivism that includes re-arrest, adjudication, and incarceration (Carney & Buttell, 2003). More important than the operational definition we choose is the reasoning behind the choices we make. We must specify and provide reasons for the operational definitions we use. When it comes to social work research, our mantra is "justify, justify, justify!" Case-in-Point 3.3 highlights the importance of specifying the definition of concepts.

Feasibility.   Many times the operationalization of a concept will be determined largely by what is feasible. The concept of recidivism, for instance, can be

CASE-IN-POINT 3.3

Poverty: An Outdated Definition of a Concept

At times an official definition does such a poor job of representing a concept that we intentionally avoid using it. This can be true no matter how popular or embedded its use may be. As an example, consider the official definition of poverty used in the United States. This definition dates back to the 1960s when Mollie Orshansky, a worker in the Social Security Administration, developed what became known as the *poverty threshold* (Glennester, 2002). Orshansky created this measure by multiplying the cost of a minimum food basket by three, based on the assumption that the average family at that time spent one-third of its income on food. Poverty thresholds are recalculated annually and vary according to the number of adults and children in a family and for some family types. Thus, the official definition of poverty is an economic measure based on a family's annual before-tax cash income and the cost of food. The poverty thresholds are used to determine eligibility for a host of federal, state, and local government programs as well as private-sector programs, including assistance with utility bills.

Since its development, the poverty threshold has been adjusted only for inflation. It has never been updated to account for changes in the consumption patterns of U.S. households. For example, expenditures for food accounted for about one-third of family income in the 1950s, but they now account for as little as one-seventh. Therefore, the current threshold might be unrealistically low and might not include many families whose income is too low for them to meet their expenses. Additionally, the official threshold ignores many costs associated with maintaining a job, such as child care and travel costs, as well as unavailable income such as child support payments that the wage earner must send to other households. It also disregards regional variations in the cost of living, especially the cost of housing, and it ignores differences in health insurance coverage and medical needs. From a different perspective, the official poverty measure has been criticized for excluding in-kind benefits such as food stamps and housing assistance when counting family income.

Due to the deficiencies in the official definition of poverty, some researchers have decided to use alternative standards. One alternative is to use a consumption-based rather than an economic measure of poverty. A consumption-based poverty measure defines as poor any household whose actual consumption fails to meet accepted conventions of minimum need. One such measure uses five indicators to operationalize poverty: food insufficiency, eviction for not paying rent or mortgage, utility disconnection for nonpayment, telephone disconnection due to missed payment, and inability to obtain needed medical care (Beverly, 2001).

The Social Work Library

Read the article by Beverly (2001) online at the Social Work Library.

operationalized behaviorally as well as by legal status. To measure recidivism behaviorally, offenders self-report their criminal involvement. Proponents of a behavioral definition argue that self-reports capture more variability in behaviors and yield higher occurrence rates than official crime records do (Herrenkohl et al., 2003). In contrast, official records are at least in part a measure of how vigilant officials are in catching offenders. They do not include people who committed subsequent offenses but were not caught (Cullen, Wright, & Applegate, 1996). Despite these arguments, researchers commonly use legal definitions of recidivism because the data that are consistent with these definitions are readily available.

Feasibility, then, is a primary consideration when we make choices about how to operationalize the major concepts contained in our research question.

Unit of Analysis.   The **unit of analysis** refers to the system level that will be studied. It is common for the unit of analysis in social work research to be people, including individuals, couples, and families. Sometimes the unit of analysis is made up of an aggregation of people like a household, tribe, community, city, county, state, school, school district, hospital, organization, or agency. In other cases, the units of analysis are **social artifacts,** the products of social beings and their behavior (Rubin & Babbie, 1997). Examples of social artifacts are suicide notes, stories and poems, drawings, newspapers, and agency case files. For instance, it is possible to study childhood trauma by examining children's drawings as the unit of analysis. Whatever the system level, however, the unit of analysis should be explicitly stated in the research question.

One reason that researchers must clearly identify the unit of analysis is to avoid committing an **ecological fallacy.** This occurs when a researcher makes a statement related to one unit of analysis on the basis of data collected from a different unit of analysis. For example, we might find that cities with high percentages of Hispanics have higher rates of violent crime than cities with low percentages of Hispanics. In this case, the unit of analysis is cities, and we can draw conclusions about cities. On the basis of this information, we might be tempted to conclude that Hispanics commit violent crimes at higher rates than other ethnic and racial groups. This would be an ecological fallacy, because we did not make this statement on the basis of knowing the ethnic or racial characteristics of the individuals who committed the violent crimes. It is possible that in cities with large Hispanic populations, another racial or ethnic group is committing the majority of the crimes. We can't identify the actual criminals by examining general data such as the crime rate per capita.

Anchoring the Question in Time and Place.   After you identify and define the concepts contained in the research question and decide upon a unit of analysis, you need to anchor the question in time and place. When the research question implies one observation at one point in time, the research is referred to as a **cross-sectional study.** For instance, a study of the impact of marital status on the poverty rates of elderly women at one point in time would be a cross-sectional study. Cross-sectional studies exist in contrast to **longitudinal studies,** which examine some phenomenon at multiple points in time.

There are three different types of longitudinal studies: panel, cohort, and trend studies. Studies that follow the same individuals over time are called **panel studies.** A panel study of the economic well-being of elderly women would follow the same group of women as they age. Alternatively, a study that follows a group of individuals over time but is not concerned that they be the same individuals from one time to the next is called a **cohort study.** A cohort study of the economic well-being of elderly women would make multiple observations but would observe different groups of progressively older women over time. One advantage of using cohort studies is that the researcher doesn't have to deal with the problem of participants leaving the study through the years since each group involves a different sample of people. The disadvantage is that the researcher cannot be certain that each cohort is actually similar. Finally, a **trend study** compares individuals with the same defining characteristics at different points in time. For example, it might compare the income composition of elderly women in the 1970s with that of elderly women in the 1980s and 1990s.

At first glance, some research questions that are cross-sectional may appear to be longitudinal. Consider the question "What factors are predictive of recidivism within 12 months of the first juvenile offense?" The term "12 months" may lead to the erroneous conclusion that the study is longitudinal. The key to deciding whether a study is cross-sectional or longitudinal is to determine how many observations are involved. In this instance, one observation is required, occurring 12 months after the first offense. The research question, therefore, is cross-sectional.

The final consideration in specifying the research question is to anchor it in a geographic area. Is the research concerned with juvenile offenders in a particular county, with children in a particular school or school district, or with families living within the geographic boundaries of a particular community? Many of the choices that we make in anchoring the question in time and place will be influenced by feasibility. Specifically, we must consider the time and expense involved in relation to the resources available for conducting the study. For example, we might want to conduct a national study of recidivism among juvenile offenders, but due to limited resources, we can study only a single state.

Final Checklist for Evaluating the Specific Research Question. After you specify the research question, you should evaluate it according to these six criteria:

1. The major concepts contained in the research question have been defined in a way that will ensure a common understanding.

2. Choices made in the operationalization of major concepts have been well justified.

3. The research question clearly specifies a unit of analysis.

4. The research question specifies a time frame.

5. The research question is grounded in a specific geographic area.

6. Answering the research question is feasible.

Case-in-Point 3.4 provides a critique of the first two steps of the research process based on a social work research article titled "Social Work Interventions

The authors—Drumm, Pittman, and Perry—set the stage for their study by claiming that the number of refugees around the globe is growing rapidly (*prevalence*). They move on to discuss the extent of emotional problems refugees face compared with the general population (*magnitude of the problem in terms of human suffering*). The authors state that the *existing literature* on refugees is primarily prescriptive, that is, a set of guidelines for working with refugees. Little has been written using a comprehensive theoretical model as a framework for understanding the emotional needs of refugees, especially from the refugees' perspective. The choice of the problem is *culturally sensitive*, as it focuses on a disadvantaged ethnic minority. The authors also demonstrate cultural sensitivity by insisting that perceived need be defined from the perspective of the refugees as well as of the people who serve them in the camps.

The *general research question*, "What are the emotional needs of recent refugees?" is implied rather than explicitly stated in the article. The research question is *logically related* to the authors' conceptualization of the problem. The authors discuss the *relevance* of this research question to social work in both the short and long terms. They cite the current lack of theoretical modeling as an obstacle to developing sound intervention strategies for refugees. To address this problem, they propose to construct a theory on the emotional needs of recent refugees based on an ecological framework. In addition, they promise to provide suggestions for intervention at the micro, meso, exo, and macro levels. In the long term, the authors suggest that the research will contribute to the implementation of carefully defined interventions that can be clearly evaluated.

The authors explicitly state the specified research question as "What are Kosovar refugees' concerns soon (within one month) after their arrival in a refugee camp?" The *unit of analysis* is individuals, that is, Kosovar Albanian refugees. The authors again demonstrated sensitivity by defining refugees broadly as ranging from children through elderly people, thereby including a wide range of perspectives. The *time frame* was restricted to refugees who had been at the refugee camps approximately one month before data collection. The study is *cross-sectional*, as it does not follow the refugees' changing perceptions of need over the course of their internment. The research question is also anchored in a *geographic area*. The authors selected four southwestern Albanian refugee camps because these camps had reasonable food and water supplies. The *justification* for the choice of camps was based on Maslow's hierarchy of need (Maslow, 1970). The authors made the assumption that crucial unmet physical needs would make it difficult to find out about refugees' emotional needs.

The degree of difficulty involved in this research was extensive, especially given the cultural and language differences between the researchers and the participants. Specifying the research question in time and geographic area helped make the research *feasible*.

Consistent with the nature of *exploratory research*, the authors did not operationalize concepts such as emotional need before conducting the study. The specified research question used the term *concern* rather than *emotional need*, thereby leaving room for a discussion of a broad range of expressed needs. The authors intended to operationalize concepts such as emotional need based on the actual research.

CASE-IN-POINT 3.4

Exploratory Research: The Emotional Needs of Refugees

The Social Work Library

Read the article by Drumm, Pittman, and Perry (2003) online at the Social Work Library.

in Refugee Camps: An Ecosystems Approach" (Drumm, Pittman, & Perry, 2003). The article explores the problems encountered by Kosovar Albanian refugees in four refugee camps in Albania. The purpose of this critique is to illustrate the use of the evaluative criteria and research terminology introduced throughout this chapter with an exploratory research study. Reading the critique should increase your familiarity with the research terms.

Developing Research Hypotheses

In addition to specifying the research questions, a researcher may also specify one or more **hypotheses**—tentative answers to a research question. Hypotheses are written as statements, not questions. For example, in a study of juvenile recidivism, a researcher may ask, "What factors influence whether a juvenile becomes an offender?" A related hypothesis is "The higher a juvenile's self-esteem, the less likely he or she will become an offender." How do you decide whether your research study warrants a hypothesis? In general, when the theory pertaining to a problem area or prior research suggests with confidence what the answer to a research question should be, that is an indication that a hypothesis is appropriate. In contrast, where the state of knowledge on a problem area is not well developed and there is more speculation than research findings, a hypothesis is not justified. This is why a hypothesis sometimes is referred to as an "educated guess." For this reason, it would be uncommon to specify a hypothesis if the research question were exploratory or descriptive. Hypotheses are more likely to be developed in conjunction with explanatory research questions.

Variables and Constants.   In order to discuss how to develop hypotheses, we must first understand two research terms: variable and constant. A **variable** is simply a concept that can vary. For instance, the concept of recidivism is a variable because offenders can either commit another offense or not. The concept of sexual orientation can also be considered a variable, as individuals can identify themselves as heterosexual, gay, lesbian, bisexual, or transgendered.

In contrast, a **constant** is something that does not vary. For instance, in a research study that is concerned only with females, gender would be a constant rather than a variable. The research question should make clear which concepts are being considered as variables and which ones are being considered as constants.

All research is concerned with studying how concepts vary; that is, all research is concerned with studying variables. A hypothesis, then, is essentially a statement about the relationship between two or more variables. For example, a hypothesis related to juvenile offenders might be "The younger the girls are at the time of their first offense, the more likely they are to commit a subsequent delinquent offense." Note that this hypothesis is written as a statement, not a question. The variables implied in this hypothesis are age and recidivism. Gender, in this instance, is a constant, as only females are being considered.

Types of Hypotheses.   There are important distinctions in the way hypotheses are stated. A **null hypothesis** asserts that no relationship exists between two or more variables. The null hypothesis for the previous example would be "There is no relationship between age at first offense and recidivism for female delinquents." The null hypothesis suggests that any apparent relationship between two or more variables is simply due to chance and does not exist in a true sense. The null hypothesis is the hypothesis that is tested in the subsequent analysis of the data. If the analysis fails to support the null hypothesis, in research terms we claim that the null hypothesis is refuted and support is provided for the research hypothesis. The **research hypothesis,** or **alternative hypothesis,** is the opposite of the null hypothesis. It proposes that a relationship exists between two or more variables.

Hypotheses may also be specified as directional or nondirectional. A **directional (one-tailed) hypothesis** specifies the nature of the relationship, either positive or negative. Our previous example hypothesized that age is negatively related to recidivism. That is, girls who are younger at the time of first offense are more likely to commit a subsequent offense than girls who are older at the time of first offense. Thus, as age *decreases,* recidivism *increases.* A hypothesis that does not specify the proposed direction of a relationship is a **nondirectional (two-tailed) hypothesis.** For example, "There is a relationship between age at first offense and recidivism." In this case, the researcher does not predict whether younger or older girls are more likely to experience recidivism. A directional hypothesis should be specified if prior research or theory reasonably suggests a direction. The more specifically a hypothesis is written, the more easily it can be tested and—when it is not valid—refuted. We explore hypotheses testing in Chapter 9.

Final Checklist for Evaluating Research Hypotheses.   After you carefully state the null and research hypotheses, you should evaluate them according to the following five criteria.

1. The hypotheses are in the form of a tentative answer to the research question and are not phrased as questions.

2. The hypotheses are specifically stated.

3. The hypotheses are justified either by theory or by prior research.

4. Statement of a directional hypothesis is justified on the basis of existing theory or research.

5. The hypotheses can be tested through research and are capable of being refuted.

Sensitivity to Culture in Formulating the Research Question

The seven guidelines presented below will assist you in achieving cultural proficiency in formulating the research question and hypotheses. These guidelines are not intended as a definitive list, but they are fundamental to becoming culturally proficient.

Explore Culturally Specific Meanings.   Always remember that concepts do not necessarily have equivalent meaning across all cultures. The concept of wealth, for instance, has a variety of meanings across culturally diverse populations. To one culture, wealth may mean money; to another culture, the presence of children; and to yet another, spirituality. For this reason, the researcher should always explore culturally specific meanings of concepts with the relevant group.

Determine Measures of Success.   Measures of success and what is valued also differ across cultures. The concept of independence, for instance, is generally valued as a healthy developmental task for adolescents in North American families. To a traditional Hindi family, however, adolescent independence is not only irrelevant but also undesirable. What a social worker with a Western perspective might describe as an enmeshed and undifferentiated parent-child relationship may be considered healthy in the context of another culture.

Anticipate Potential Consequences.   Consider how the collected data might be misused, and anticipate any harm, physical or psychological, that such misuse could inflict on the research participants or members of their cultural group. Research that relates race to intelligence is one of the most blatant examples of cultural destructiveness. As a general rule, the researcher should anticipate both the positive and negative potential consequences of conducting the research.

Prevent Exploitation.   The study regarding the Havasupai Indian tribe of Arizona cited in Chapter 2 is an example of research that was perceived as exploitative by the participants. Groups that already feel marginalized or stigmatized are at increased risk for feeling that they are being exploited through research. To avoid generating these feelings, as researchers we must show members of marginalized cultural groups how the benefits of the research will outweigh any efforts or sacrifices on their part. In addition, we should always define exploitation based on the participants' perspective, not ours.

Consider Issues of Privacy.   All research is intrusive to some degree. As with exploitation, we should evaluate whether the research is overly intrusive from the perspective of the research participants and not our own. Using the same example, the question of whether the Havasupai originated from Asia was in direct opposition to the Havasupai's cultural beliefs of creation. Research should only be done and reported with the permission of the participants.

Seek and Use Feedback.   Research participants should be directly involved throughout all phases of the research process. Ensuring that research participants have input at the question/hypothesis formulation stage will help avoid feelings of surprise or exploitation on their part when the findings are reported. The review process should be continued until consensus on the research questions and hypotheses is reached.

Use Precise and Sensitive Language.   Culturally proficient researchers avoid using generic variable labels to indicate specific subgroups. For instance, a research question that refers to parents but studies only women, or a research study that refers to Hispanics but studies only Hispanics of Mexican origin, is neither precise nor sensitive with regard to language. Sometimes the myriad labels associated with cultural groups can be confusing. For instance, is the appropriate term *Hispanic*, *Latino/Latina*, or *Chicano/Chicana*? When in doubt, consult the research participants for their preference.

Case-in-Point 3.5 illustrates the first two steps of the research process by examining a research article titled "Protective Factors against Serious Violent Behavior in Adolescence: A Prospective Study of Aggressive Children" (Herrenkohl et al., 2003). The purpose of providing this critique is to demonstrate the use of the evaluative criteria and research terminology introduced throughout this chapter with a research study that is explanatory.

BUILDING CONFIDENCE THROUGH CRITICAL ANALYSIS

One way to learn a new skill is to practice it. Practice in social work research is not limited to conducting original research. In fact, practice should begin with a critical review of the published research. Many social work journals publish research-based articles. In addition, social workers publish research articles in the journals of related disciplines. When searching for research articles to critique, be aware that just because an article is published in a journal does not mean that it is based on research. Some journal articles are conceptual in nature; others describe a practice approach or a specific practice skill; still others examine a statistical technique and its application; yet others provide a summary of the research studies in one problem area. One way to identify a

CASE-IN-POINT 3.5

Explanatory Research: Serious Violent Behavior

The authors identify the problem area by citing research to support the relationship between aggressive behavior in childhood and later violence. They report that the existing research supports this relationship regardless of whether self-reported behaviors or official arrest data are used to *operationalize* violence. The authors frame their study in the context of extensive research and theory. They present the intent of their study as *objectives* rather than research questions. The objectives are (1) to identify the factors in adolescence that either decrease or increase the probability for later violence among aggressive children; (2) to assess whether the identified factors differ for boys or girls and by race/ethnicity; and (3) to examine whether exposure to multiple protective factors during adolescence could offset the influence of co-occurring risks shown to increase the probability of later violence. The purpose of the study is consistent with *explanatory research*. The objectives of the study might have been stated as hypotheses. For example, the null hypothesis might have been "There is no difference by gender in factors that increase the probability for violence," or "There is no relationship between exposure to protective factors and the probability for later violence."

The *relevance* of the study to social work practice and theory advancement is clear from the authors' articulation of the study's objectives. In the area of *cultural proficiency*, the authors' efforts to examine differences between girls and boys and among different racial and ethnic groups are important to establish the degree to which the findings are applicable to various subgroups.

The authors use data from a *longitudinal panel study*. This study followed the same children from fifth grade in 1985 until they reached age 18 in 1993. The *unit of analysis* is the individual child. Data for the study were collected from the children, their teachers, and their parents. The participants were purposively recruited from 18 public elementary schools in high-crime neighborhoods in Seattle. Thus, the authors anchor the study in a *time frame* and an appropriate *geographic area*.

The authors *operationalize* the major concepts included in the objectives of the research, that is, childhood aggression and violence at age 18. They provide a *justification* for their choice in operationalizing the major *variable* of interest—violence at age 18. The authors include six categories of risk and protective factors, based on theory and prior research: socialization, community, family, school, peer, and individual.

The Social Work Library

Read Herrenkohl, et al. (2003) online at the Social Work Library.

research-based article is to read the abstract, located at the beginning of the article. The **abstract** is a brief statement of approximately 100 words that summarizes the objectives, methods, results, and conclusions of the article. If the abstract mentions a research question or hypothesis, research participants, a method of collecting or analyzing data, or findings, you can be certain that the article is research based.

As you review research-based articles, you will quickly observe that the authors follow a similar format. The introductory or first section of the article consists of a discussion of the problem area addressed by the research study, including information on its relevance to social work. This discussion is followed by a critical analysis of the existing knowledge based on a review of existing research and theory. This analysis also considers which issues are contested and what is yet to be discerned. The justification for the research study is customarily framed within the context of prior published work. The research question is not always explicitly stated, but it may be implied or labeled as objectives of the research. Hypotheses customarily follow the statement of the research question. The operationalization of major concepts is usually found under the heading "Method."

Now it is your turn. Locate a social work research article online or at your local library and critique the authors' efforts at identifying the problem and formulating questions and hypotheses. Use the criteria presented in this chapter to guide your critique.

CONCLUSION

Good social work research, like good social work practice, has to be built on a strong foundation that begins with identification of the problem area. Specifying research questions makes the study of a problem area feasible and facilitates the work of others who wish to replicate the study. As with social work practice, in research, the use and meaning of words is important. Asking the right question(s) and providing clear and measurable definitions of terms are essential to obtaining useful information. Careful consideration of cultural factors should be included when conceptualizing the research and defining variables. Once the research problem has been identified, a research question has been specified, and maybe a hypothesis has been presented, it is time to move on to answering the research question.

The remaining steps in the research process must be logically consistent with the conceptualization of the research problem and the specification of the research question and hypotheses. The research design—the blueprint for how the research will be conducted—must allow us to answer our research question with confidence. How to choose a research design that you can use to answer the research question with confidence is the subject of the next chapter.

MAIN POINTS

- A working knowledge of the research process empowers social workers to be better practitioners, evaluators, administrators, advocates, and policy makers.

- Social work research and practice are complementary activities, such that through practice the social worker identifies problem areas that require research, and through research the social worker provides knowledge for practice.

- Social workers are expected to base their practice on knowledge, and yet not all sources of existing information are equally valid. The research process can be used as a framework for critically evaluating existing information.

- Culturally proficient research practices are necessary to dispel destructive myths and stereotypes and to avoid exploiting and harming those whom social workers aim to help through research. Cultural sensitivity should be considered at each step of the research process.

- To demonstrate the worth of a problem area for research, the social worker must be able to credibly answer the question Why is this important?

- The research process begins with a broad conceptualization of the problem and narrows as a general research question is developed, followed by increasing specification as concepts are operationalized and the research is grounded in a time and a geographic area. Increasing specification makes the research problem researchable.

- Research questions can be categorized into one of three types: exploratory, descriptive, or explanatory. Through a thorough literature review of the problem area, the social work researcher will determine what avenue of inquiry is most appropriate for the problem area.

- There is no one correct way to do research. The social worker engaged in research must make many choices and must be able to justify those choices within the context of the research study.

EXERCISES: PRACTICING SOCIAL WORK

1. Working with the Black Feather community, how might you go about developing the research problem?

2. From the information presented on the Black Feather project, develop one research question that fits for each level of knowledge: exploratory, descriptive, and explanatory. Describe how the questions differ.

EXERCISES: SOCIAL WORK LIBRARY

1. Read Herrenkohl et al. (2003) and then describe the research problem and the research question. State a hypothesis that could have been tested in this study.

2. Read Nichols-Casebolt and McGrath Morris (2002). Is there logical consistency between the way the research problem was framed and the way the research question is specified? Explain.

OTHER EXERCISES

1. Propose a research problem, research question, and hypothesis that involve the key concepts of gender and social work. How might the research problem, question, and hypothesis change if you were to substitute the term *sex* for *gender*? Discuss the difference between the two concepts of gender and sex.

2. Make a list of research problems that would be relevant to your personal life. Now make a list of research problems that would be relevant to a close family member of a different generation. What are the similarities and differences?

CHAPTER 4

Group Research Design

A research design should be selected for its ability to answer the research question and test the research hypothesis.

THIS CHAPTER COULD ALTERNATIVELY HAVE BEEN TITLED "Now that I have a research question, what do I do with it?" The previous chapter stated that social work research is about asking good research questions and answering them with confidence. The choice of a research design, which serves as the blueprint for answering the research question, should always be guided by what the research question requires.

There is an important distinction to be made in research designs. Basically, there are two classes of research design: group research design and case-level research design. **Group research designs** are appropriate for answering research questions that deal with groups of elements, such as people, organizations, and agencies. **Case-level research designs,** in contrast, are appropriate for answering research questions about a single element: one person, one family, one organization, one community, and so on. Case-level research designs include single-subject research designs and case studies. We examine case-level designs in Chapter 10.

This chapter is about group research designs. It addresses such topics as how to select a research design based on the research question, how many groups to study, how groups are formed, the number and timing of measurements, and the exposure of groups to an experimental condition, also known as the **independent variable. Experimental conditions** in social work are the interventions used to produce positive changes. There are many possible experimental conditions. Interventions such as cognitive behavioral therapy, a change in the eligibility criteria for the Free and Reduced Price Lunch Program, and the implementation in a middle school of an abstinence-based curriculum aimed at preventing sexual behavior are examples of experimental conditions.

Mastering the material in this chapter and the two following chapters on sampling and measurement is critical to planning, conducting, and critiquing research. Although mistakes in the analysis of data at the end of a research study can be corrected, errors in specifying the study's research design, how many subjects to study, or the data to be collected are costly. Moreover, once they are made, they cannot be undone. Decisions related to the choice of group research design, sampling, and measurement will impact how the evidence generated by the research study will be accepted and, ultimately, whether the results will be used to affect practice. By the end of this chapter you should be able to:

- Describe the difference between group research design and case-level research design.

- Suggest an appropriate group research design based on what the research question requires.

- Describe the strengths and weaknesses of the different types of group research designs.

- Understand group research design notation as the building block of research design.

- Explain what is meant by internal validity and how threats to internal validity vary with the choice of group research design.

- Explain what is meant by external validity and how threats to external validity vary with the choice of group research design.

Beware of those who are so enamored with the technicalities of research that the purpose of conducting the research gets lost.

A PURPOSE-DRIVEN APPROACH TO SELECTING A RESEARCH DESIGN

Different group research designs are appropriate for generating different kinds of information or knowledge. The previous chapter presented three different types of knowledge: exploratory, descriptive, and explanatory. Before selecting a group research design, you need to decide where on the knowledge continuum the research question fits. You must then purposively select a research design capable of producing that type of knowledge.

The research question drives the research methodology, not the reverse.

Exploratory Research Questions

To determine whether a particular research question is exploratory, we can ask several questions. If the answer to any of these questions is yes, a group research design capable of producing exploratory knowledge is required.

- Does the research question pertain to an area of research that is new or that has not been investigated in depth?

- Is the research question designed to help us acquire a preliminary understanding of a phenomenon?

- Is the intent of the research question to determine what variables and concepts are important in relation to a certain phenomenon?

- Is the purpose of the research to discover what the research questions should be, or to derive working hypotheses and theories?

- Is the intent of the research to study some phenomenon as it is, without trying to alter it?

The following are examples of exploratory research questions:

- How does culture influence medical outcomes among people with HIV?

- What are the reasons that families seek help from private food assistance programs?

- How does adolescent disclosure of a gay or lesbian sexual orientation affect the parent-child relationship?

The Social Work Library

Visit the Social Work Library to access exploratory research studies that deal with each of these three research questions.

These questions are exploratory because they have been subject to very little investigation until this point. The important variables and concepts related to the cultural influences on medical treatment for HIV, help-seeking from private food assistance programs, and the parental experience of learning that an adolescent child is gay or lesbian have yet to be identified.

Exploratory research questions often call for an **inductive approach** to research. In this approach, researchers collect and analyze observations and then reach tentative conclusions based on those observations.

Descriptive Research Questions

All research is descriptive to some extent. A descriptive research question, however, is concerned with describing some phenomenon in a holistic way, for example:

- How prevalent is a certain condition in a set geographic area?

- What is the relationship between two or more variables?

- What demographic characteristics are associated with the condition?

- How much change has occurred in knowledge, skills, behaviors, or attitudes after the administration of an independent variable?

- What is the trajectory of a developmental process such as dying, a behavior disorder, or a stage of maturation?

- Has some minimum standard of outcome been achieved at a specified point in time?

If the research question calls for description, a research design capable of producing descriptive knowledge is required. The following are examples of descriptive research questions:

- What is the return rate of parental consent forms when a specified set of procedures is used to obtain active parental consent for child participation in research?

- How does the prevalence of material hardship (food, housing, and medical care security) in the United States differ among ethnic/racial subgroups?

- What factors in adolescence are associated with the presence of serious violent behavior at age 18?

It may be difficult to differentiate a descriptive research question from an exploratory one. For instance, what makes the previous question on youth violence descriptive rather than exploratory? The answer is based on the amount of theory and research that already exists in the area. In the study of serious violent behavior in adolescence, a great deal of research has already been conducted, theories have been postulated, and important variables have been identified.

The Social Work Library

Visit the Social Work Library to access descriptive research studies that deal with each of these three descriptive research questions.

Explanatory Research Questions

Explanatory research questions are difficult to answer, and yet they are crucial in terms of accountability and furthering our social work knowledge base. Explanatory research questions focus on understanding the relationship between variables, especially on cause-and-effect relationships, for example:

- What is the **etiology** of a problem, that is, the causal chain of events?

- How effective is a program in making specified changes?

- Which approaches are the most effective means to produce specified changes?

- How will altering an intervention (independent variable) change the outcome (dependent variable) of the intervention?

The following rule can help you determine whether a research question is explanatory or descriptive: If the question addresses effectiveness, it is explanatory. If it describes the outcomes observed in a social program or demonstration project, it is descriptive. If the research question is related to cause and effect, a group research design capable of producing explanatory knowledge is required. The following are examples of explanatory research questions:

The Social Work Library

Visit the Social Work Library to access explanatory research studies that deal with each of these three explanatory research questions.

- Does home visitation prevent child abuse and neglect for children born to at-risk parents?

- How do parents' characteristics influence their methods of disciplining young children?

- How effective are paraprofessional home visitors compared with nurse home visitors in preventing child abuse and neglect?

Explanatory research questions are answered through **deductive reasoning,** which involves first developing hypotheses and then collecting observations. The hypotheses are then either accepted as probable or rejected on the basis of the evidence produced by the observations. Note that hypotheses are never proved one way or the other. Rather, the cumulative evidence leads to their support or rejection. (See Chapter 9 for an explanation of hypothesis testing.)

TYPES OF GROUP RESEARCH DESIGNS

Once we are clear about the type of research question to be answered, it is time to select a group research design. Similar to research questions, group research designs have also been classified into a threefold system that includes pre-experimental, quasi-experimental, and experimental designs (Campbell & Stanley, 1963). Differentiating experimental designs from the other two classes of research design is easy. Most sources, however, fail to present criteria on how to differentiate pre-experimental from quasi-experimental designs. The exception is William Trochim (2002), and the decision tree for classifying research designs presented in Exhibit 4.1 is based on his work.

As you can see in Exhibit 4.1, if the research design involves random assignment to two or more groups, it is an **experimental design. In random assignment,** all elements—people, communities, organizations, and so on—have an equal chance of being assigned to each group. If there is no random assignment to groups but there is more than one group or more than one round of measurement, the research design is **quasi-experimental.** If the research design involves only one group or one round of observation and there is no random assignment to groups, it is considered **pre-experimental.**

The usefulness of classifying research questions and group research designs is in matching the type of knowledge sought with the class of group research design that is able to produce that type of knowledge. For instance, if the

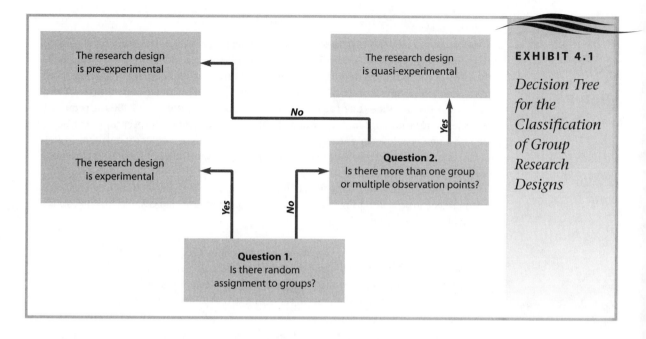

EXHIBIT 4.1

Decision Tree for the Classification of Group Research Designs

research question calls for explanatory knowledge, an experimental group research design is required to answer the research question with confidence. If the research question calls for exploratory knowledge, a pre-experimental group research design is likely sufficient. Although it is possible to answer exploratory and descriptive research questions with an experimental research design, it would be a great misuse of resources, comparable to using a sledgehammer to pound a tack. Similarly, you could not expect to answer an explanatory research question with a pre-experimental research design.

The type of research design needed to answer a descriptive research question is a little less straightforward. Some descriptive research questions can be answered well with a pre-experimental research design. However, other questions that inquire about change over time or a comparison of outcomes achieved using different methods will require a quasi-experimental research design.

There will be times, however, when the research question is explanatory and an experimental design is not feasible. Similarly, there will be times when the only option is a pre-experimental design. In these instances, it is helpful to be aware of the limitations of the group research design used to answer the research question and to be explicit about them when you present the research findings. Descriptive and exploratory research designs can produce findings that are suggestive of causation. In such cases, if it is warranted, they can be tested with experimental designs. The research examples presented in Case-in-Point 4.1 show that all three classes of group research designs have value in social work research.

Communities across the United States have become increasingly invested in preventing child abuse and neglect and enriching early childhood experiences. Significantly, more than 500 of the programs developed to prevent child abuse and neglect in the past three decades involve home visitation by paraprofessionals or professionals trained to teach and support new parents identified as at risk for child abuse and neglect. In 2000 the total cost of these home visitation programs was estimated at $170 million, representing a considerable and growing investment in preventing child abuse and neglect (Leventhal, 2001). Given the substantial investment in home visitation programs, it is not surprising that there is a great need for research in this area.

Social workers involved in the field of home visitation rely on exploratory research studies to provide insight into the experiences of new parents considered at risk for child abuse and neglect (Paris & Dubus, 2005).

- Exploratory studies using pre-experimental designs have also helped us to understand the nature of the relationship between the home visitor and the parent (Hebbeler & Gerlach-Downie, 2002), and they have examined the problem of early termination from home visitation services (Daro, McCurdy, Falconnier, & Stonjanovic, 2003).

- Descriptive studies in home visitation using quasi-experimental designs are used largely to evaluate program outcomes and to identify risk and protective factors associated with child abuse and neglect. Quasi-experimental research designs are implemented to describe changes in parents' stress levels over time, to document improvements in the home environment that are conducive to healthy child development, and to determine whether prevention targets involving substantiated incidents of child abuse and neglect are met (see, for example, McDonald Culp et al., 2004).

- Explanatory studies using experimental research in home visitation, although rare, are highly valued by program personnel, child advocates, and state government officials responsible for funding decisions. These studies provide evidence as to whether home visitation works to prevent child abuse and neglect and to improve child development outcomes in both the short and the long term (Olds et al., 1997, 2004a, 2004b).

The Social Work Library

Visit the Social Work Library to access the Olds (2004a–b) article referenced in Case-in-Point 4.1.

Whereas pre-experimental and quasi-experimental research studies lead to improvements in program theory and practice, experimental studies play a vital role in deciding the future of home visitation.

Notation and Terminology of Group Research Design

Before addressing the issue of how to select a group research design, you need to learn some basic notation and terminology. The basic notation of group research design involves four symbols: the letters O, X, R, and N. These symbols can be thought of as building blocks that researchers put together in different ways to enable them to address the research questions.

Although there are some standard group research designs, there is no limit to the number of ways that we can put the building blocks together. In the following sections, we will describe the four symbols used in group research design.

Observation (O).   The first symbol, O, denotes an observation or measurement of the **dependent variable**—the condition or behavior to be changed by our interventions. Examples of dependent variables include substance abuse, sexual behavior, income, and child abuse.

All group research designs involve at least one O. If there is more than one O, numeric subscripts (for example, O_1 O_2 O_3) are used to identify the sequence of observations. The subscript 1 represents the first observation, 2 the second observation, and so on. We read design notation the same way that we read the text in a book, from left to right. The activities represented by the notation to the left precede the activities represented by the notation to the right. In addition, we can use a key or a legend, similar to that found on a map, to describe the subscripts. For example, if our interest is in prenatal care during pregnancy, O_1 might be the number of prenatal visits completed at the end of the first trimester, O_2 at the end of the second trimester, and O_3 in the third trimester until the pregnancy ends. The purpose of repeated observations is to examine variation in the dependent variable over time. When there is only one observation, there is no need to use a subscript after the O.

When we are considering a group research design, it is important to justify the timing and number of observations. One key factor in determining the number of observations is feasibility: "How many observations are possible given the type and amount of resources available?" Research budgets are usually limited, and each observation point requires additional resources for collecting, entering, and processing data, as well as incentives to participants when appropriate.

Multiple observations over an extended period are especially difficult to implement with transient and unstable populations. Examples of such populations are graduating high school students, individuals who are homeless, victims of domestic violence, frail elders, and people afflicted with chronic diseases such as AIDS.

The Intervention, or Experimental Condition (X).   The second symbol used in group research design notation, X, denotes the introduction of an experimental condition, also known as the independent variable. Although all group research designs have an O, not all have an X. The absence of X denotes the absence of an experimental condition or an independent variable. This is the case when we want to observe a phenomenon as it naturally exists or evolves. For example, we might want to understand the meaning of social support in a rural community or the prevalence of breast cancer screening on a reservation.

Some friends recently gave my two young children some wooden stacking blocks shaped like kiwi birds from New Zealand. Included in the box was a card illustrating 20 different stacking configurations that could be made from the blocks. Ignoring the card, my daughter and son enthusiastically set about making their own designs. Group research designs are a lot like stacking blocks. Although there are some standard ways of putting them together, the possibilities depend on our own creativity.

Numeric subscripts placed after an X (X_1 X_2 X_3) are used to denote variations when more than one independent variable is being studied. For example, X_1 might be a targeted marketing campaign designed to motivate low-income minority women to access breast cancer screening. In contrast, X_2 might represent a general advertising campaign for breast cancer screening that uses public service announcements broadcast over local radio stations. When there is only one experimental condition, there is no need to use a subscript after the X.

The number of groups in the research design will depend upon the number of experimental conditions we want to observe. For example, we may want to study the difference between X (the intervention) present compared to X absent, or more of X compared to less of X. Each variation of the experimental condition requires a separate group. The number of groups then will be equal to the number of variations. Similar to the Os, the Xs can also be described in a key or a legend.

Note that each group involved in the research study is given its own line in research design notation. If there are three groups, there should be three corresponding lines of notation. Two events that occur simultaneously are represented by notation placed vertically one above the other. In the following example of group research design notation, for instance, two pretests were administered at approximately the same time, followed by the administration of an independent variable in one group and followed by two posttests occurring about the same time. The illustration below describes a study in which two different groups, for example, a treatment group and a wait list group, are given an anxiety scale at pretest (O_1) at approximately the same time. The first group is given an intervention (X), such as cognitive behavioral therapy, while the second group is still on the wait list. At the end of the intervention program, both groups are given the anxiety scale again (O_2).

O_1 X O_2

O_1 O_2

Random Assignment.   The third symbol, R, when placed in front of a row of group research design notation, denotes random assignment to groups. Random assignment can be accomplished in a many ways:

- Assign every other person who applies for services to one group or another.

- Flip a coin for each participant. Heads go in one group, and tails go in another.

- Assign a computer-generated random number to each participant. Put odd numbers in one group and even numbers in another group.

- Put all participants' names in a hat and draw them out one at a time. The first person is assigned to the first group, the second person to the second group, and so on.

When groups are randomly assigned, as illustrated in the research design below, the group with the experimental condition (or independent variable) is called the **experimental group,** and the group without the experimental condition is called the **control group.** For example, in the study of anxiety described earlier, if the members of the intervention group and the wait list group are randomly assigned, the notation below can describe the study.

R O_1 X O_2 (experimental group)

R O_1 O_2 (control group)

The purpose of random assignment is to create **pretreatment equivalency,** also referred to as **between-group equivalency.** The assumption is that groups that have been randomly assigned should be similar to each other in terms of the major variables that might impact the dependent variable. The rationale for using random assignment is that if the groups are equivalent before the introduction of the independent variable, any differences between the groups at posttest can be attributed to the independent variable. The assumption of pretreatment equivalency can be tested statistically by examining the equivalence of the groups on any variables believed to be important in terms of the dependent variable. These important variables typically are identified through a review of the literature. For example, when the observation involves individuals, the most common variables include age, sex, education, race/ethnicity, income, and family size.

When you are conducting group research, you need to distinguish between random assignment and random sampling. **Random sampling** is a means of selecting elements from a population so that each and every element has an equal chance of being selected. The intent of random sampling is to ensure that the subjects involved in the research represent the population from which they are drawn. Random assignment, in contrast, seeks to create between-group equivalence and is not concerned with the group's similarity to the population. For example, 50 people attend a program for parent education and are assigned to two conditions: one is a 12-week course and the other is a 6-week course. If the parents are randomly assigned to the 6- or 12-week course, that is random *assignment.* It does not tell us whether the parents, as a group, represent the population of parents in the community, the state, or the United States. Random sampling involves selecting the parents at random from the population before assigning them to a group. We discuss random sampling in the next chapter.

Assignment That Is Not Random (NR). The final symbol, NR, indicates that the process of assigning elements to groups was "not random." (An alternative format is to place a set of horizontal dashes between two or more lines of notation.) The NR symbol is optional. Generally speaking, if the notation does not include an R for random assignment, we can safely assume that the procedure was not random. Significantly, when the assignment procedure is not random, we cannot assume between-group equivalency. In such cases, the groups are said to be **nonequivalent.** In the absence of random assignment, the group that is *not* subject to the independent variable is called a **comparison group** rather than a control group, as shown below:

NR O_1 X O_2 (experimental group, assignment to groups is not random)

NR O_1 O_2 (comparison group)

Although we cannot assume pretreatment equivalency in the absence of a control group, we can examine the similarity between the comparison and experimental groups by using statistics. (We examine statistics in detail in Chapter 9.) A statistical analysis of the characteristics of two or more groups can gauge just how similar the groups are on observed variables that are believed to impact the dependent variable. For example, in the study of child neglect, the literature identifies family size as an important factor. In the absence of random assignment to groups, the social work researcher would want to know how equivalent the experimental and comparison groups were on family size before administering the independent variable, such as assignment to a homemaker mentor. The social worker would also want to know how similar the groups are regarding other important variables related to child neglect such as history of previous abuse, parent's stress level, parent's history of abuse, extent of social support, and substance abuse by a family member.

The study of nonequivalent groups and comparison groups is common in social work research. In many cases, either random assignment is not practical or there are too many objections to its use. For example, some agency administrators may prefer to assign clients based on which intervention or which social worker they believe will be most beneficial to the client rather than on a random basis. When random assignment is not a viable option, researchers frequently recruit participants from *preexisting groups*. Not only are preexisting groups plentiful, but they tend to be captive audiences. Classic examples are the students in a classroom and the consumers of a service. We discuss the use of preexisting groups in research in the next chapter.

*When someone inquires about the methodology used in a particular piece of research, he or she is usually interested in knowing about the research design, although the term **methodology** is also used in a broader sense to include sampling and measurement.*

Describing Group Research Design Notation

Researchers often need to communicate about group research designs in words as well as notation. To do so, they combine several common terms with notation. Different sources will sometimes use slightly different terminology to describe the same design. As long as the descriptions are clear, the terminology used is generally acceptable.

Cross-Sectional Designs.   The terminology used to describe the Os, or observations, depends in part on (a) whether an experimental condition is present and (b) the number of observations in the design. If there is only one observation, the group research design may be referred to as a **cross-sectional design.**

Pretests and Posttests.   If there are two observations and the first observation, O_1, occurs before the independent variable is administered, the first observation is called a **pretest.** Going further, if the second observation, O_2, follows the independent variable, it is called a **posttest.** Group research designs including pretests and posttests are sometimes referred to as **before-and-after research designs.** The interval between the pretest and posttest will usually depend upon the length of time it takes to administer the independent variable. For example, most programs designed to stop teenagers from engaging in sexual activity range from two to eight weeks in duration. In a research design to evaluate change in teenagers' intentions to abstain from sexual activity, the pretest would be administered just before the start of the curriculum, and the posttest would be administered at the conclusion of the curriculum.

Sometimes two pretests are administered before the independent variable is introduced. In these cases, the second pretest is referred to as a **delayed pretest.** We use delayed pretests when we want to assess the *normal* amount of change that occurs between two measurements before the introduction of an independent variable. The use of delayed pretests, although not common, is typically found in research when (a) there is no opportunity to observe the changes that occur in a control or comparison group, or (b) the population is maturing relatively quickly. For example, in a study of teenage abstinence from sexual behavior in Arizona, the researchers used a delayed pretest to assess changes in attitudes toward sexual abstinence that were occurring as part of the maturation process. Significantly, changes were found to be taking place in the absence of the independent variable—the abstinence-based curriculum. Advanced Skill Development 4.1 presents some useful guidelines concerning when and when not to use a pretest.

Follow-up Observations.   When two observations follow an intervention, the second one is referred to as a **follow-up observation.** These are required to determine whether observed differences between the pretest and the posttest are maintained over time. Follow-up observations help answer questions related

ADVANCED SKILL DEVELOP-MENT 4.1

To Use or Not to Use a Pretest

There are certain guidelines to help social work researchers decide when to use and when not to use a pretest (Fitz-Gibbon & Morris, 1987). First, a pretest is always recommended when the assignment to groups is nonrandom and between-group posttest results will be compared. The researcher can use the pretest to evaluate whether the scores of the assigned groups were comparable *before* the independent variable was introduced. Second, the use of a pretest is essential if researchers need to know how much change has occurred in the dependent variable over time, that is, from pretest to posttest.

Third, researchers can use a pretest to check the assumptions that have been made in planning an intervention program. For instance, is it true that parents identified as being at risk for child abuse and neglect have little knowledge of time-out techniques before their involvement in a program to promote parenting skills? A pretest can check this assumption.

Fourth, many programs have difficulty recruiting the target population for which they are designed. For example, voluntary screening programs for breast cancer that are designed specifically for low-income women from ethnic minorities often attract minority women from higher income and education levels (Abbott, Barber, Taylor, & Pendel, 1999). Pretests can be used to screen potential participants according to some preset eligibility criterion.

In other cases, researchers can avoid pretests in order to cut costs or save time. They should also avoid pretests for cases in which the act of taking the pretest would demoralize research participants. This might occur if the participants were to perceive the test as overly difficult or the subject matter as overly intrusive for a first meeting. Finally, researchers should not use pretests for cases in which taking the pretest would alter the way participants respond to the posttest, irrespective of the independent variable. For example, a pretest to measure knowledge of human sexuality may spark curiosity that leads to additional discussions or readings on sexuality before the posttest.

to the durability of outcomes. In the Arizona study on teenage abstinence, for example, a six-month, post-program follow-up observation assessed whether changes in attitudes toward sexual behavior were consistent with or stronger than posttest levels or whether they had regressed to pretest levels or below. Using group research design terminology, the abstinence example would be described as a one-group pretest-posttest research design with a delayed pretest and six-month follow-up. Using group research design notation, it would be represented as $O_1 O_2$ X $O_3 O_4$.

Many research studies do not include follow-up observations. In some of these cases, the researchers don't have the resources to pursue them. In other cases, they simply are not necessary. For example, the group research design O_1 X O_2 is commonly referred to as a pretest-posttest research design. In contrast, some designs employ three or more observations before and/or after the introduction of an independent variable. These designs are referred to as **time series** or **longitudinal** research designs.

The Number of Groups Involved.   Another part of the descriptive label given to group research designs relates to the number of groups that are involved. Group research designs employing only one group are commonly referred to as one-group research designs. For example, the design O_1 X O_2 is commonly known as a one-group, pretest-posttest research design. There is only one group, a pretest (O_1) is followed by the introduction of an independent variable (X), and then a posttest (O_2) is administered. With the addition of another group to the one-group, pretest-posttest research design, it becomes a two-group, pretest-posttest research design. Research designs with more than two groups are commonly referred to as **multigroup designs.**

Prospective and Retrospective Studies.   A final distinction in describing group research designs has to do with the timing of measurement. In a **prospective research study,** the researcher collects the pretest data and then observes the dependent variable as the independent variable is exerting its influence. In contrast, in a **retrospective research study,** the researcher does not observe the dependent variable until after the independent variable has exerted its influence. In other words, the prospective research study looks ahead in time, whereas the retrospective study looks back. The advantage of the prospective study is that the researcher can exert greater control over the research design, including sampling and measurement. The advantage of a retrospective study is that it probably costs less and requires less time. Whether research is prospective or retrospective is often a matter of feasibility.

At times the examination of a single phenomenon can involve both retrospective and prospective research. In the study of a home visitation program designed to prevent child abuse and neglect in Arizona, for example, researchers conducted a retrospective study to identify the factors that predicted substantiated child abuse and neglect in the participant population. The researchers examined the records of more than 8,000 families involved in the Healthy Families Arizona program since its inception in October 1991. They then used the results to ensure that the program was addressing the major risk factors identified in the study, such as premature birth and high levels of parental stress. The retrospective research was one step in helping the program prepare for a prospective, experimental study of child abuse and neglect prevention. The prospective study involved random assignment of at-risk parents to a treatment group and a control group and follow-up observations over the course of five years.

Retrospective research can also be a means of examining old data under a new lens. For example, researchers have used retrospective studies to provide more accurate counts of suicide, domestic violence, and shaken baby syndrome, which are often overlooked or improperly classified. Retrospective research in these areas is often conducted by reexamining medical records as well as coroners' and crime reports. In the next section we consider the more common research designs

Be careful when using the language of group research design. An income-support worker told me a story about how her office had differentiated clients assigned to the experimental group from those assigned to the control group. One day as the worker directed a client to her cubicle for an interview, the client asked, "Why are you trying to control me?" The word CONTROL was written in black marker across the front of the client's file.

within each of the three types of group research design, the research questions they are capable of answering, and their strengths and limitations.

Pre-experimental Research Designs

The simplest of all group research designs are those classified as pre-experimental. As we discussed earlier, a pre-experimental research design involves only one group or one round of observation, and participants are *not* assigned to groups through random assignment. Pre-experimental research designs tend to be less expensive and time consuming than experimental and quasi-experimental research designs because they do not involve multiple groups or multiple waves of measurement. We discuss two pre-experimental designs: the one-shot case study and the one-group, posttest-only.

One-Shot Case Study. The simplest of all pre-experimental group research designs is the **one-shot case study,** also known as the cross-sectional study. The one-shot case study is appropriate for answering exploratory and descriptive research questions related to what exists at a certain point in time. It can be used to answer questions about the level of knowledge or about functioning, attitude, behavior, or environmental circumstances at one point in time. It does not involve the introduction of an independent variable. An example of a research question that can be answered with a one-shot case study is What do incoming BSW students know about group research design? The one-shot case study can be used with research approaches that use only qualitative methods, only quantitative methods, or a combination of the two. When using group research design notation, the one-shot case study is illustrated simply as O.

One-Group, Posttest-Only. If the one-shot case study is implemented after the independent variable is administered, it becomes a **one-group, posttest-only research design.** This design can answer questions related to whether some minimum standard of achievement has been met. An example is the question What do graduating BSW students know about group research design? In this case, the BSW program is the independent variable.

The function of the one-group, posttest-only research design is to explore. It cannot produce knowledge about change because there is only one observation. Neither can it measure the impact of the independent variable because there is no means for comparison. This design only describes the dependent variable following the introduction of the independent variable. This design could not, for instance, answer the question of whether social work students increased their knowledge of research design while engaged in the BSW program. Nor could it determine whether students' knowledge of group research design at graduation was a result of participating in the program. The one-group posttest-only research design is illustrated as X O.

Quasi-Experimental Group Research Designs

Quasi-experimental group research designs are similar to pre-experimental designs except that they involve additional observation points or additional groups selected without random assignment. Quasi-experimental research designs are useful for answering research questions related to changes that occur over time. They are often employed when experimental research designs are not feasible. These designs are also employed in cases in which there are strong objections to implementing an experiment. In this section we discuss six quasi-experimental research designs.

One-Group, Pretest-Posttest. The simplest of all quasi-experimental designs, the **one-group, pretest-posttest research design,** measures the dependent variable both before and after the independent variable is introduced. Thus, it is useful for measuring change over the course of an intervention. For example, unlike the pre-experimental designs discussed earlier, the one-group, pretest-posttest design could answer the research question How much did BSW students' knowledge of group research design change over the course of their social work education program?

A major limitation to this design is that the observed change cannot be attributed to the independent variable because possible alternative explanations have not been ruled out. We discuss the most common of these alternative explanations later in this chapter in the section "Threats to Internal Validity." A second limitation of this particular design is that it cannot answer whether changes in the dependent variable are maintained over time. The one-group, pretest-posttest design is represented as O_1 X O_2.

Posttest-Only with Nonequivalent Groups. In the **posttest-only with non-equivalent groups** research design, the two groups are observed at posttest, with only one group receiving the independent variable. An example of a question this research design might answer is What are the differences in attitudes toward sexual abstinence among eighth graders who receive the "ABC" abstinence curriculum and eighth graders who do not receive any school-based instruction in abstinence?

Because the posttest-only design compares a group that has received the independent variable with one that has not, researchers sometimes interpret the findings as a measure of the impact of the independent variable. In fact, this design cannot answer questions on impact because it does not rule out competing explanations for the between-group differences. For example, in the abstinence study cited in the previous paragraph, let's assume that students in the abstinence program exhibited more positive attitudes toward sexual abstinence than students in the other group. Can we automatically attribute this difference to participation in the program? The answer is that we cannot, because other factors might have shaped the students' attitudes. It is possible, for instance, that the eighth graders in the group showing more positive attitudes (a) were younger, (b) were more likely to have previously attended a religious school, or (c) had a greater overall religious orientation than the eighth graders in the other group.

The posttest-only, nonequivalent group is illustrated as follows:

X O

O

Pretest-Posttest Comparison Group.   Unlike the posttest-only design, the **pretest-posttest comparison group research design** compares two groups at pretest as well as at posttest. Because the groups are not assigned randomly, we cannot assume that they are equivalent at pretest on important factors that may influence the dependent variable. However, although we cannot assume pretreatment equivalency, we can test it to some degree by using the pretest. As with the posttest-only design, even if the study finds a greater amount of change in the experimental group, the design does not allow for any statement on impact or causality.

Regardless of its limitations, the pretest-posttest comparison group design is useful for identifying changes from pretest to posttest and speculating about the impact of the independent variable. This design is illustrated as follows:

O_1 X O_2

O_1 O_2

Multigroup, Posttest-Only.   Researchers can use the **multigroup, posttest-only research design** to determine whether a certain standard has been achieved. In this design, several groups are used, and each group is exposed to different levels of the independent variable or to different independent variables. For instance, a researcher can use this design to compare the outcomes among groups of students subjected to three different abstinence-based curricula. This design also might suggest the best form of treatment for achieving a particular outcome. In turn, this process could lead to the development of hypotheses and further testing employing a more rigorous experimental research design.

The multigroup, posttest-only research design cannot tell us anything about within-group change because it does not include a pretest. The multigroup, posttest-only research design is illustrated as follows:

X_1 O_1

X_2 O_1

X_3 O_1

Simple Time Series.   A **simple time series design** can be either interrupted or noninterrupted. An *interrupted time series design* involves making at least three observations before the independent variable is administered followed by at least three observations after it is administered. There is, however, no maximum number of observations that may occur either before or after the intervention. The simple interrupted time series design is illustrated as O_1 O_2 O_3 X O_4 O_5 O_6. The *noninterrupted time series design* is similar except that no independent variable is introduced. It is used to assess the actual changes of a variable without outside intervention. It is based only on a series of measurements and is appropriate for descriptive research when the researcher's interest involves the trajectory of a problem or state. The noninterrupted time series design is illustrated as O_1 O_2 O_3 O_4 O_5 O_6.

Multiple Group Time Series.   Adding groups to a simple time series design with alternative interventions, or adding a comparison group, changes the simple time series design into a **multiple group time series design.** This design is used to lend greater support to the hypothesis that the independent variable is responsible for the changes that are occurring. For example, student attitudes about drug use may be measured in the three years before a Drug Awareness Resistance Education (DARE) program and three years following the program. A comparison group that does not have a DARE program is also measured. This design is illustrated as follows:

O_1 O_2 O_3 X O_4 O_5 O_6

O_1 O_2 O_3 O_4 O_5 O_6

Time series designs can be difficult to manage over a long time because participants frequently drop out before the study is completed. The tendency of participants to withdraw prematurely from a research study is known as **attrition.** Attrition occurs for myriad reasons, including illness, death, refusal to participate further, and the inability to contact participants who have relocated. When attrition rates become excessive, researchers are unable to fulfill the goal of the study, whether that is exploration, description, or explanation.

Although researchers agree that attrition can be a serious problem, they have not achieved a consensus on what constitutes too much attrition. Most researchers aim for a retention rate of 70 percent to 80 percent. However, in some studies an attrition rate of even 20 percent is unacceptable. An example is a research study that involves two or more groups in which the resulting between-group differences in outcome are small. In such cases, it is impossible to know which way the missing 20 percent would have tipped the scale. Conversely, if the research involves one group and there is a great deal of within-group variation, a 20 percent attrition rate would not be a problem.

Once you have mastered the concepts behind the notation O, X, R, and NR, you are ready to begin constructing your own group research designs.

Researchers often assume that the dropouts would have looked worse on whatever outcome is being considered. For example, a study of satisfaction with mental health services would assume that dropouts had lower satisfaction, which could explain their decision to drop out of services as well as the study. Maintaining low rates of attrition requires time and resources. We consider specific strategies to address attrition through sampling in Chapter 5 and through managing the research study in Chapter 7.

Experimental Research Designs

If the research design includes random assignment to two or more groups, it is a true experimental research design. Experiments are extremely powerful research tools for producing explanatory or causal knowledge, although they are not always welcomed by social workers and administrators (see Advanced Skill Development 4.2). The true experiment is marked by five common characteristics (Campbell & Stanley, 1963):

1. There is a temporal order in which the presumed cause (the independent variable) occurs before the presumed effect. If one variable is presumed to be the cause of a second variable, then logically it must be present before the second variable is observed.

2. The independent variable (X) is manipulated. For example, the researcher might examine X present versus X absent, smaller versus larger amounts of X, or variations of X.

3. The relationship between the independent variable and the dependent variable must be established. This is accomplished primarily through a combination of theory and prior pre-experimental and quasi-experimental research.

4. **Rival hypotheses,** defined as alternative explanations apart from the independent variable that might account for the outcome, can be ruled out. This is achieved primarily through the use of random assignment.

5. There is random assignment to at least two groups, including an experimental group and a control group.

The following sections review three experimental designs: (1) the classic experiment; (2) posttest-only, control group; and (3) the Solomon four-group design. We also discuss the technique known as *matching,* which can be used with both experimental and quasi-experimental designs to reduce sampling error.

True experiments have merit because they enable researchers to make valid conclusions about cause-and-effect relationships and they offer the highest internal validity of all research designs. Despite these benefits, however, when researchers suggest conducting an experiment, they often encounter resistance from social work practitioners and program administrators. Following are some common objections to conducting experiments and answers to these objections.

ADVANCED SKILL DEVELOP- MENT 4.2

Overcoming Objections to Experiments

- It is unethical to deny potentially beneficial services to otherwise eligible members of the population who will be included in the control group.

  - *Often the control group receives the services that are typically offered by the agency. They do not go without services. Or a wait-list control group is used because a waiting list is necessary due to the limited number of people who can be served at any one time.*

- People are not to be experimented upon, and random assignment violates our ethical norms.

  - *It is unethical to subject people to an intervention program when the belief in the effectiveness of the program is based more on faith than on fact. It is unethical to spend scarce dollars for social services on programs when there is no evidence that these programs actually work. Social work ethics mandates that we use the best tested methods. Experimentation is the best way to demonstrate the effectiveness of an intervention. Random assignment does not violate social work ethics. Experiments are also valuable because their results can help social workers and other proponents of change build needed support and cooperation for policy initiatives.*

- Assignment for treatment should be based on need and not randomization.

  - *Research can be done so that all who need services receive them. We often do not know which clients might benefit most from a particular new service. Research can help provide this information.*

- Steps taken to protect ethical standards such as informed consent may actually hinder the relevance of the findings because they may produce selection bias.

  - *This is true. Informed consent, however, is essential in protecting the rights of human subjects and takes priority over other concerns.*

- Experiments do not generalize to real-life situations. Because people are not "randomly assigned" in real life, the likelihood that there will be differences between those who volunteer for a random experiment and those who volunteer for the actual program may be great, especially if recruitment mechanisms differ.

  - *Experiments are one step in establishing the effectiveness of interventions and social programs. Additional evidence is needed to assess the transfer of the results to the "real world."*

continued

ADVANCED
SKILL
DEVELOP-
MENT 4.2

*Overcoming
Objections to
Experiments*
continued

- The quality and effectiveness of a program implemented in a tightly controlled experiment will be different when the program is implemented on a broad scale.

  - *Experiments should also be conducted on social programs that are broadly implemented as well as on tightly managed pilot programs so that the results will be applicable beyond the research context. An important consideration is replication of the experimental research findings—that is, demonstrating consistent results across comparable studies.*

- Experiments may overlook subtle but valuable program effects. For example, an experiment may measure only behavior change but not self-esteem.

  - *Use of theory and discussions with program staff should identify the relevant outcomes to be measured in experiments.*

- Experiments may impose on program operations. Program operators (e.g., social workers) may struggle with the loss of control, and as a result they may withhold cooperation by declining to assist with evaluation tasks, limiting access to participants, or sabotaging records.

  - *Program staff should be made aware of the benefits of the research, receive an orientation to the project, be given a chance to express their concerns, and be given the results of the study. Concerns about experimental design should be addressed early, and researchers should notify stakeholders about the practical and political aims of the project, how the mission of the program will be advanced, and how the experiment can add a rational dimension to policy making and funding decisions. In addition, experiments must be designed to cause minimal program disruption. In some cases, this stipulation may require that researchers add resources to the program to deal with aspects of the study such as participant recruitment and data collection. Assigning individuals other than program staff to recruit participants and collect data can help reduce the potential for researcher bias.*

The Classic Experiment.   In the **classic experiment,** also known as **pretest-posttest control group,** equivalent groups are formed through random assignment. The group called the experimental group is subject to the independent variable, whereas the control group is not. The changes that are expected to occur as a result of the independent variable are measured in both groups. Simply put, if the experimental group changes in the expected way and the control group does not change or changes in the opposite direction, then the independent variable was the likely cause of the difference. Using group research design notation, the classic experiment is represented as follows:

$$R \; O_1 \; X_1 \; O_2$$
$$R \; O_1 \quad \; O_2$$

Posttest-Only, Control Group.   As we saw in Advanced Skill Development 4.1, there are situations in which the use of a pretest is either not feasible or inappropriate. In these situations, an experimental research design that fills the requirement of an experiment without using a pretest is the **posttest-only, control group design.** Rather than employ a pretest, this design assumes that random assignment negated any significant initial differences between the experimental and control groups before subjecting the experimental group to the independent variable. In other words, the groups are assumed to be equivalent. In group research design notation, the posttest-only, control group design is represented as follows:

$$R \; X \; O_1$$

$$R \quad O_1$$

Solomon Four-Group.   The **Solomon four-group research design** combines the classic experiment and the posttest-only, control group design. This design is particularly useful when the act of taking the pretest might influence the posttest. Comparing the second group ($R \; O_1 O_2$) with the fourth group (RO_1) allows the researcher to estimate the amount of change, if any, that is attributable to taking the pretest—a phenomenon known as a **testing effect.** For example, in a study of attitudes about HIV/AIDS, the independent variable is an education program. Four groups are used, and members are assigned randomly to all four conditions. The first group (1) is given a pretest about their attitudes, the educational program, and posttest. The second group (2) is given the pretest and posttest, but not the educational program. The third group (3) is given the educational program and the posttest. The fourth group (4) is given only the posttest. If group (1) scores differ from group (3) scores, the pretest can be assumed to account for the difference since both got the educational program. If groups (1) and (3) scores are similar but higher than groups (2) and (4), the independent variable is assumed to have accounted for the difference.

(1) $R \; O_1 \; X_1 \; O_2$

(2) $R \; O_1 \quad O_2$

(3) $R \quad X_1 \; O_1$

(4) $R \; O_1$

Matched Samples.   One way to improve the comparability of the groups in experimental research is to combine randomization with matching. **Matching** is the process of finding elements with the same specified characteristics. For example, we could match on eye color, height, or weight.

In research, matching permits control on only a very small number of variables. For instance, suppose that in a study of preventing child abuse and neglect, we are interested in the variables of mother's age and racial background. We would assign at random one-half of the 18 randomly selected Native American women under age 25 to the control group and the other half to the treatment group. Similarly, we would assign at random one-half of the 26 randomly selected Native American women age 25 and over to the control group and one-half to the treatment group. In this way, matching serves to increase comparability.

Matching can also be used in quasi-experimental research. However, the use of matching does not change the design from quasi-experimental to experimental. Remember that an experimental design always requires random assignment.

LIMITATIONS OF GROUP RESEARCH DESIGNS

All group research designs have limitations that social work researchers should acknowledge explicitly. We have already discussed one major limitation; namely, that each specific group research design can answer some types of research questions but not others. For example, consumers of research, and even some researchers themselves, frequently want to generalize and to infer causation from even the simplest designs. Other limitations relate to the way that a research study is managed, such as taking preemptive steps to minimize attrition, and additional considerations in measurement and data collection that are discussed in Chapters 6 and 7. Fortunately, researchers can predict common problems such as attrition and poor quality control in the management of a research study. Consequently, they can take steps to prevent these problems or at least to diminish their impact. Case-in-Point 4.2 provides an example of what can happen when an experiment is conducted before a program is properly implemented.

Threats to Internal Validity

The amount of confidence we have that changes in the dependent variable are the result of the independent variable and not some other factor is referred to as **internal validity.** Factors that jeopardize that confidence are known as threats to internal validity. Perfect internal validity in a research study is rarely assumed to exist. The design features of a research study, however, can enhance the likelihood of an acceptable level of internal validity (Campbell & Stanley, 1963). Nine of the most common threats to internal validity are presented here:

1. **History effects** are a factor when the observed effect in a research study is influenced by an event that takes place between the pretest

Experiments tend to be lengthy and expensive to implement. For these reasons alone it is doubtful that researchers would undertake an experiment unless they felt that there was a reasonable chance of rejecting the null hypothesis, that is, the conclusion that there is no difference between the experimental and control groups at posttest. As the following study illustrates, strong research designs cannot compensate for weak or poorly implemented treatments (Duggan et al., 2004).

The Hawaii Healthy Start Program, a home visitation program designed to prevent child abuse and neglect, undertook an experimental research study of its services in the mid-1990s. Eligible families were randomly assigned to intervention and control groups and were interviewed annually for three years with an impressive follow-up rate of 88 percent. In the final analysis, the researchers found that the program had no significant impact on (1) any risk factor for child abuse, (2) child abuse and the use of nonviolent discipline, and (3) the use of community services by at-risk mothers to address specified risks for child abuse and neglect.

The researchers provided several reasons for the lack of positive findings. To begin with, they discovered that only 50 percent of all referred families received the recommended number of home visits according to schedule. The program also experienced a high attrition rate. Although it was designed for a three-year period, 10 percent of families had dropped out at three months, and 50 percent at one year. In addition, the program paid scant attention to the factors known to increase the risk for child abuse and neglect, particularly substance abuse, mental health, and domestic violence. The major reason for this shortcoming was that the home visitors lacked the training, skills, and supervision to address family risks for child abuse and neglect, to motivate families to change, and to link families with professional services. There was a lack of formal referral arrangements with professional services in the community to address salient risks and promote healthy family functioning.

The lesson learned from this evaluation is not that home visitation is ineffective but, rather, that no program should engage in experimental research until it has implemented an articulated model of change, or program theory, that is based on prior research and theory. Prior research should have investigated whether the program was using evidence-based practice and, if so, was being offered as conceived. In the case of home visitation, the program theory would identify the factors that the program must address in order to prevent child abuse and neglect. The training and hiring of home visitors should be guided by the knowledge and skills necessary to address the identified risk factors. The program theory helps clarify how the program differs from the status quo, that is, from what is regularly available in the community in the absence of the program. Program implementation should be monitored on an ongoing basis using pre-experimental and quasi-experimental research methods. The information obtained through research on the program should be used in a continuous quality improvement process. Program theory, attention to implementation, and attention to quality are essential if, as Duggan and her colleagues have demonstrated, there is to be a fair test of the intervention.

CASE-IN-POINT 4.2

When Good Experiments Go Bad

The Social Work Library

Visit the Social Work Library to access the Duggan articles.

and the posttest. When the event that influences the outcome occurs in one group and not the other, we call it a threat of **intrasession history.** The longer the study, the more likely it becomes that history might pose a threat to internal validity.

2. **Maturation** is a threat that occurs when an observed effect is due to the respondent's growing older, wiser, stronger, and more experienced between the pretest and posttest. Certain groups such as infants and children are more prone to maturation effects in the short term.

3. Testing effects, as mentioned earlier, involve the danger that observed effects are due not to the independent variable but to the fact that performance on a test is influenced by taking a pretest. Testing effects may be due to the number of times particular responses are measured and the chance that familiarity with the test enhances the participant's performance. In some cases, what we are measuring may be the ability of participants to remember the answers they perceive as correct.

4. **Instrumentation** refers to unintended changes in the way the dependent variable is measured over time. Instrumentation can arise from problems with the measuring instrument, the observer, and so on. For example, an observer may get bored or change his or her rating style during an experiment.

5. **Statistical regression** can occur whenever a group is chosen because they are extreme. In such cases, the tendency is for both very high scores and very low scores to move toward the population mean regardless of the treatment being offered. For example, very tall parents generally have children shorter than themselves, or the most anxious members of a group are likely to be somewhat less anxious at the next measurement.

6. **Selection bias** exists when the groups are not comparable before the study. In such cases, the change observed in the dependent variable could be due to pretreatment difference between the groups rather than to the independent variable.

7. **Experimental mortality** is the danger that an observed effect is due to the specific types of persons who dropped out of a particular group. For example, mortality can be a threat to the internal validity of a study that involves the GPA of high school students if high school dropouts are included at pretest but not included at posttest.

8. **Treatment contamination** can occur when the participants in one group learn about the treatment being offered to the members of

another group, or when program personnel provide some compensatory benefits to those who form the control group. In some cases, treatment contamination is serious enough to cancel an experiment, as illustrated in Case-in-Point 4.3. In other cases, treatment contamination occurs naturally, for example, when youth in the experimental group discuss on the playground what they learned in an HIV/AIDS education program with youth not in the program but in the control group.

CASE-IN-POINT 4.3

When a Research Cadillac Turns Out to Be a Lemon

Experimental design is often referred as the "gold standard" of research, or "the Cadillac of research designs." Experiments, however, are expensive, difficult to manage, and, at times, impossible to implement. Assessing beforehand the conditions under which an experiment is likely to succeed or fail can help to avoid wasting valuable resources, as this example illustrates.

In October 1995, the state of Arizona, with the assistance of a large national research firm, began randomly assigning individuals to an experimental group and a control group. The experimental group was subject to the state's welfare reform policies, known as the Empower Program, and the control group was subject to the preexisting social assistance program, Aid to Families with Dependent Children (AFDC). The intent of the experiment was to determine the impact of the state's welfare reform program on aid recipients. The impact would be measured by examining between-group differences in the receipt of public assistance and other outcomes related to employment and income. The study was implemented across four sites—three urban and one rural—to test for the replication of program effects. **Replication** is the process of duplicating the study. It can involve differences in time, location, and target population. Existing welfare cases were randomly assigned, as were new applicants for income assistance. Those cases that never became active and those that were denied benefits were dropped from the sample.

At the end of the first year, the total sample size was short of initial projections. This discrepancy was attributed to the state's improving economy. Not only were the numbers lower than expected, but attrition became a substantial problem, for two reasons. First, whenever participants transferred out of any of the four research sites to receive benefits at another site, they were automatically dropped from the study because only the welfare workers in the four research sites were trained to handle the groups differently. Second, whenever members of the original control group and the experimental group merged under one new case that received cash assistance, the members of both groups were lost due to "contamination." For instance, when a grandmother who was receiving income assistance applied for assistance for her grandchildren who were previously receiving assistance under another case, the cases were considered merged. Over the first 12 months, almost 20 percent of the research sample were lost because they either left the research sites or became part of the same case.

Staff turnover also influenced the study. Turnover was typically high in the welfare offices. As staff left, it became difficult to find replacement workers who were familiar with the old

continued

CASE-IN-POINT 4.3

When a Research Cadillac Turns Out to Be a Lemon
continued

welfare policies. Those workers who remained faced the task of keeping two sets of policies and procedures straight and still meeting strict workplace expectations on timeliness and accuracy. Participants and nonparticipants alike found it difficult to comprehend the study and often raised objections to the welfare workers about the different rules and benefits they themselves and their neighbors were subject to, further complicating the workers' jobs.

The final blow to the experiment came with the introduction of a new federal welfare program in 1996, Temporary Assistance for Needy Families (TANF). Once again, the rules and benefits for income assistance changed, and after one year, Arizona abandoned its welfare reform experiment. The procedural changes that accompanied welfare reform and the transience of the sample were not conducive to experimental research. In hindsight, the researchers could have used knowledge of the policy environment and the population to anticipate these difficulties before expending valuable resources on experimental research. They could have examined important research questions by using short-term pre-experimental and even quasi-experimental approaches.

9. **Resentful demoralization** is a reaction to being part of the control group. Sometimes membership in the control group is believed to be a negative state, causing resentment, anger, and demoralization that can inflate the difference among the two or more groups. For example, youth may see going to a ropes course as a privilege and those not selected to participate may be resentful, thus affecting their scores on a measure of commitment to the school.

Researchers generally assume that random assignment to treatment and control groups can negate the first six of the above threats. In contrast, the final three cannot be avoided by randomization. Rather, careful planning and preparation can often reduce their impact.

Threats to External Validity

A study with a high degree of internal validity allows us to make causal inferences regarding the sample and the setting that was studied. The question then becomes What about other settings and the larger population? These are matters of **external validity**—the degree that the research findings can be generalized to other cases not studied as well as to the population in general.

The basic issue behind external validity is whether an experiment is so simple, contrived, or in some other way different from the everyday world that what we learn from it does not apply to our everyday world. To maximize external validity, the study group must be representative of the larger target population so that the results can be generalized. We discuss strategies to achieve this objective in the next chapter on sampling. For now, we consider three major threats to external validity: reactivity, researcher bias, and multiple treatment interference.

Reactivity occurs when the situation being studied produces different results than would otherwise be found. Put simply, when people become aware that they are being observed or studied, they behave differently than they would under normal circumstances. Reactivity is also known as the **Hawthorne effect.** This term is derived from an experiment conducted in the 1920s to determine what factors would improve worker productivity in the Hawthorne factory of the Western Electric company in Cicero, Illinois. The study found that workers became more productive simply because they were aware that they were receiving more attention than they were accustomed to.

The second threat, **researcher bias,** occurs when researchers see what they want to see. In such cases, researchers interpret findings toward the positive for the experimental condition and toward the negative for the control and comparison groups. This is especially true when subjective judgments such as level of "empathy" or "creativity" are made. Researchers may be unaware of their tendency toward bias. In order to avoid researcher bias, it is best to use a **double-blind** study, that is, one in which neither the researcher nor the participant knows to which group a participant is assigned.

The final threat to external validity, **multiple treatment interference,** occurs when the effects of two or more treatments cannot be separated. This problem is common in social work because research takes place in real life rather than in a laboratory. Researchers have no control over what other resources people can access voluntarily or to whom they will speak. For example, in the research on the abstinence-only program in middle schools, it was difficult to find children who had not been subject to multiple forms of sex education in the schools before entering the program. Or someone in a group home may have advice from a religious counselor, grandparents, and custodial staff in addition to the regular program of activities.

CONCLUSION

The right research design is the research design that will do the best job of answering the research question while dealing with the contextual complexities of the environment. Instead of limiting themselves to a restricted number of preset group research designs, social work researchers should focus on design features such as the number of groups and observations, timing, and variations in the independent variable in order to construct the optimal design for the research context at hand. Identifying the potential for common problems like resistance to experimentation and participant attrition is key to the successful implementation of any research study. Experimental studies that examine research questions related to impact require additional attention so that the research results in a fair test of the independent variable and not a description of implementation problems. The next two chapters continue the discussion of the planning process that must occur before a research study can be successfully implemented.

MAIN POINTS

- When selecting a research design, you want to match the level of knowledge implied by the research question with the class of research design that is capable of producing that level of knowledge.

- All three classes of research designs—pre-experimental, quasi-experimental, and experimental—have value in the creation of knowledge for social work.

- Mastering the concepts represented by the four symbols of group research design notation puts the beginning social work researcher in a position to understand, communicate about, and select group research designs.

- Experiments are essential for testing causal processes.

- Research designs that do not include a pretest do not allow for an assessment of within-group change.

- Participant attrition threatens the success of any research study.

- Six of the nine threats to internal validity can be dealt with through random assignment.

- Before engaging in experimental research, you need to assess and deal with any contextual complexities that could derail the study. Particular attention should be focused on conditions that might lead to treatment contamination, resentful demoralization, and attrition.

EXERCISES: PRACTICING SOCIAL WORK

1. Read the "engage" section in the Black Feather case study on your CD-ROM. From the knowledge you gain through reading this introduction, develop one exploratory, one descriptive, and one explanatory research question.

2. For each research question you specified in the preceding question, identify an appropriate group research design that would enable you to answer each research question. Provide a rationale for your selections. For each research design you chose, outline the strengths and limitations.

EXERCISES: SOCIAL WORK LIBRARY

Select any explanatory research article referenced in the online library for Chapter 4. Articles linked to the explanatory question include Olds et al. (2004a, 2004b) and Pinderhughes et al. (2000).

After reading each article, respond to the following questions:

1. What was the research design? Write a descriptive title for the research design and, represent it using group research design notation.

2. What are the independent and dependent variables, if any, identified in the study?

3. What threats to internal validity, if any, are being controlled for in the study? How are they being controlled?

4. What threats to internal validity, if any, remained a serious concern? Explain.

5. What hypotheses are suggested in relation to the findings?

OTHER EXERCISES

1. When we deal with individuals in research studies, it is impossible to say that two groups are ever equal. When we randomly assign to groups, we say that the two groups are equivalent. What does equivalence mean in the context of random assignment to groups?

2. Explain the differences between a quasi-experimental and an experimental research design. What are the advantages and disadvantages of each?

CHAPTER 5

Sampling

Selecting a sample is often a balance between what you want to accomplish and the resources available.

S LIGHTLY MORE THAN ONE-HALF OF ADULTS IN THE UNITED STATES— 52 percent—report that they are opposed to allowing workers to invest part of their Social Security taxes in stocks or bonds, whereas about 44 percent are in favor. A large majority—88 percent—agree that major changes in Social Security are needed. Significantly, 53 percent favor higher taxes over reduced benefits, whereas 38 percent prefer to cut benefits (Saad, 2005). Do you ever wonder how researchers can speak for the nation with such confidence? Going further, how many of the more than 217 million adults in the United States do you think the research staff at the Gallup Organization contacted in order to make such sweeping claims? It might surprise you to know that the number was as few as 1,006.

So far, we have addressed the questions of how to select a research problem and how to formulate a research question and hypothesis (Chapter 3). Chapter 4 dealt with the topic of selecting a group research design to answer the research question and test the hypotheses. This chapter focuses on the question of where we get the **data,** the information that is collected—usually in the form of numbers or words—that will allow us to answer our research question or test our hypothesis. To accumulate our data, we need a **sampling plan** that outlines where the data will come from and justifies the choices we make along the way. Important choices in the formulation of a sampling plan include what to study and whether to collect data from the whole population, or whether to limit data collection to a sample. A **population** is the totality of persons, events, organizational units, and so on that the research problem is focused on. A **sample,** in contrast, is a subset of the population. As one example, if a researcher conducted a study of students at your school, the population would consist of the entire student body. Any subset of that population—for example, 100 students picked at random—would represent a sample.

In instances when sampling is the preferred approach, researchers must decide how to select the elements they wish to study. In sampling, the term **element** refers to each member or entity in the population. Another question that the sampling plan must address is How big should the sample be? Finally,

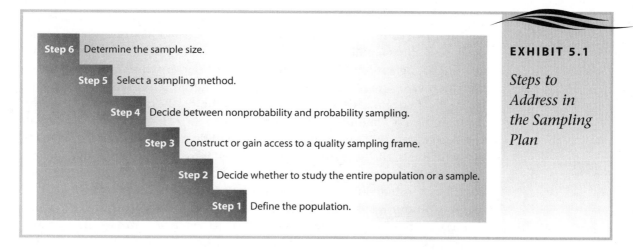

EXHIBIT 5.1

Steps to Address in the Sampling Plan

the plan must indicate whether the sampling method will permit inferences. By making an **inference,** the social work researcher is claiming that what holds for the sample is likely true for the population from which the sample was drawn. In the example just cited, the researcher would assume that the results of the study of 100 students could be generalized to the entire student population. Exhibit 5.1 outlines the steps that the researcher will address in the formulation of a sampling plan. This chapter prepares you as a beginning social work researcher to engage in sampling and to critique the most commonly used sampling methods. By the end of this chapter, you should be able to:

- Describe the difference between a sample and population.
- Explain the rationale for choosing to study either an entire population or a sample.
- Identify the two main approaches to sampling, and explain their key differences.
- List and discuss four types of probability sampling.
- List and discuss four types of nonprobability sampling.
- Discuss the concept of sampling error, and identify strategies to minimize it.

DEFINING THE POPULATION

The first step in developing a sampling plan is to develop clarity on the population that you wish to study. This task may sound straightforward and even simplistic. Why would a researcher question what he or she will be studying? In reality, deciding on the population elements can sometimes be tricky. Social work research sometimes focuses on individuals and at other times on aggregates of people such as families, couples, and entire communities. Let's assume that we are conducting a study in which the population elements are families. Although the category of "families" is very familiar, it nevertheless raises several basic questions. To begin with, within a given household, whom should we include in our definition of "family"? For example, do we define "family" simply as parents and dependent children? What about adult children and extended family members who live in the household? Going further, if we are studying adults, at what age do we begin to place older children who are living at home into this category? Does an individual become an adult at 18, 19, or 21 years of age?

To shift our focus somewhat, suppose our population consisted of elderly Chinese people. Would we restrict our study to American-born Chinese people, or would we also include elderly immigrants from China? What about immigrants from Taiwan and Hong Kong? A researcher must decide the boundaries of the population that is the focus of the study and define it so that others will be clear about exactly who is included and who is not.

Researchers can use dimensions such as place, time, demographic characteristics, behavior, membership, attitudes, and beliefs to help define the population. The goal in specifically defining the population is to help the researcher achieve (a) greater clarity about the focus of the research so that decisions are well thought out and (b) greater precision in reporting the research procedures and findings.

Step 1. Define the population.

There will be times in research when the population elements are not exactly the same as the **sampling units,** the entities from which the data are gathered. For instance, a social work researcher may be interested in preschool children, but the sampling units may be the parents of the preschool children because they are the ones who will respond to the researcher's request for information. The first step in developing a sampling plan, then, is to specifically define the population in terms of the elements and the sampling units.

Why Sample?

In the beginning of the chapter, we discussed a survey of the U.S. population that was based on a little more than 1,000 respondents. Why would a researcher whose ultimate interest is an entire population study only a sample of that population? The rationale for studying a sample generally involves saving time and money. Can you imagine how long it would have taken and how expensive it would have been if researchers at the Gallup Organization had tried to contact every adult in the United States to elicit her or his opinion on Social Security reform? The difficulties and costs involved in surveying the entire population probably explain why the U.S. Census is conducted only once every 10 years. A **census** collects data from every element in the population.

Conversely, in instances when the size of the population is relatively small, the researcher may want to study the entire population rather than a sample. This is the situation in many agencies and organizations that employ social workers. One guideline for deciding whom to study is to restrict sampling to populations with more than 100 elements. The decision to sample, however, is also based to a large extent on feasibility. Even when a population contains 100 elements, the researcher might have only enough resources to collect data on 50. Given this scenario, a small, carefully crafted research study based on a sample is better than no research study at all.

Step 2. Decide whether to study the entire population or a sample.

Developing a Sampling Frame

Once the researcher is clear about the population and has made the decision to sample, his or her next step is to obtain access to a **sampling frame**—a list of all the elements in a population from which the sample is selected. Together, the totality of population elements on the sampling frame is referred to as the **sampling universe.** The closer the sampling frame approximates the actual population, the less error that is introduced into the research study. The researcher's goal, then, is to gain access to a sampling frame that is comprehensive and free from error. For example, when the population is all schoolchildren in a district, the sampling frame may be a list of students obtained from the registrar's office in each school.

When a sampling frame does not include the entire population due to errors and omissions, we say that it is *biased*. For example, in the list of students, some may be missing because they are new to the district and the list is not yet updated. It might seem obvious, but it must be made clear that the lack of inclusiveness is due only or primarily to error. **Sampling bias** is defined as a problem with the selection of elements that produces systematic error in the research study. If all students with low test scores were left off the sampling frame, that would be a source of sampling bias. A sample that is drawn from a biased sampling frame cannot accurately represent the population.

At times, gaining access to a sampling frame is easy because it already exists, for example, a list of all juveniles in a detention facility. In other instances, you will have to develop the sampling frame from scratch, for example, a list of parents with adopted children in a specific school district. In either case, make certain to assess its quality very carefully. Is the sampling frame current? Is it inclusive of all the elements in the population? Is the information free of error? If possible, cross-check the sampling frame with other available sources. Sometimes you might have to add to or improve on an existing sampling frame. Do not worry if the elements on the sampling frame do not appear to be in any particular order—they do not need to be.

Social work researchers must be careful to include all of the elements on the sampling frame in the sampling process. If they exclude any part of the sampling frame, the elements no longer have an equal or a known chance of being selected. In such cases, the sample will not represent the population. For example, let's say that a researcher has a sampling frame of 150 individuals. Of these individuals, 100 provide contact information, and 50 do not. If the researcher selects only from the 100 who provide contact information, the sample will likely be biased. In other words, there will be a systematic difference between the sample and the population. The reason for this difference is that those individuals with contact information are probably different in some important ways (personality or motivation) from those individuals without contact information.

Sources of Error

How well we can generalize from a sample to the population depends on both sampling and nonsampling error. Error introduced by the sampling process can be of two types: sampling error and nonsampling error. We discuss strategies to reduce sampling error later in this chapter.

Step 3. Construct or gain access to a quality sampling frame.

Nonsampling error is not related to the actual sampling procedure and includes inadequate sampling frames, high levels of attrition or nonresponse, and measurement and data entry errors. We examine strategies to reduce nonsampling error, including assessing the quality of the sampling frame before sampling and implementing a plan to maximize retention, in Chapter 7. Finally, we address strategies to reduce measurement and data entry errors and attrition in the next two chapters.

SELECTING A SAMPLING APPROACH

The next step in developing the sampling plan is to decide which of the two main sampling approaches to use: probability sampling or nonprobablility sampling. **Probability sampling** is a procedure in which every element in the sampling universe has a known chance (probability) of being selected. Note that all probability sampling approaches involve random sampling. Recall from Chapter 4 that the process of random sampling is the best way to ensure that there is no systematic bias in the way elements are selected. In other words, it protects against bias. Similar to flipping a coin or rolling the dice, chance alone determines which elements will make it into the random sample and which will not. There is no purposive inclusion or exclusion of any element in random sampling. If the researcher randomly selects enough elements, the sample should be representative of the population. We will examine the question of how many elements are "enough" later in the chapter.

The major advantage of probability sampling is that it permits **generalization,** the process of applying the findings from the sample to the population from which the sample was drawn. As for the broader population beyond the sampling frame, the researcher can only hypothesize about the applicability of the sample findings. This is one reason why replication in research is so important, to test the limits of findings as they apply to additional settings and variations in the population.

Nonprobability sampling, in contrast, is a procedure in which all of the elements in the population have an unknown and usually different chance of being included in the sample. Thus, nonprobability sampling does not support the claim that the sample is representative and therefore does not permit generalization, only speculation. Given these shortcomings, you might wonder why a researcher would choose nonprobability sampling. The answer is that it is simpler to manage and less expensive than probability sampling. In addition, it is better suited to answer some types of research questions, as we discuss next.

The decision regarding what sampling approach to use will depend to a large extent on the goals of the research. Nonprobability sampling is most commonly used in exploratory research, in which the goals of the research are more concerned with discovery than with generalization. Recall from Chapter 3 that exploratory research tends to be qualitative because its purpose is to understand and give meaning rather than to quantify and generalize. For this reason, nonprobability sampling methods are often associated with qualitative research. In addition, nonprobability sampling methods are appropriate for situations in which it is either unfeasible or impossible to draw a probability sample. Such situations tend to develop when populations are difficult to access or when greater resources are required than are available. Nonprobability sampling is particularly appropriate if the study is a trial run for a larger study.

In contrast, research studies focused on descriptive and explanatory goals are better served by probability sampling because probability samples permit the researcher to generalize to the population. Also, because each element has a known probability of being selected, the researcher can estimate how well the findings for the sample will apply to the population. Because descriptive and explanatory studies are often quantitative in nature, probability sampling is most commonly associated with quantitative research. The research example presented in Case-in-Point 5.1 illustrates what happens when there is a mismatch between the sampling approach and the type of knowledge called for in the research question.

Probability Sampling Approaches

This section presents four common methods of probability sampling. They include three single-stage methods—simple random sampling, systematic random sampling, and stratified random sampling—and one multistage method, known as cluster sampling. The section describes each method, including its advantages and limitations and the types of situations in which it is used, and presents simple instructions for drawing probability samples.

One reason that the by-product of every good research study is two or three more research questions is because there are so many limitations on making generalizations.

Step 4. Decide between a probability and a nonprobability sampling approach.

Practicing Social Work

Try the exercises on the Practicing Social Work CD-ROM to practice the probability sampling methods. They can be found in the Resources folder under Reference Materials.

Shere Hite is known for her pioneering research on female sexuality in the 1970s. Her research has always commanded a lot of attention, and her study on the sexual practices and opinions of American women was no exception. Hite (1989) contributed substantially to watercooler and locker-room conversations by reporting that 84 percent of American women are not emotionally satisfied with their relationships and 70 percent of women married five years or longer are engaging in extramarital affairs. How did she come up with these rather astounding findings?

Hite conducted her research by distributing more than 100,000 questionnaires to women across the United States over a seven-year period. Many of her questionnaires were distributed through organizations, including churches, political and women's rights groups, and counseling centers. Other women received questionnaires by responding to Hite's calls for volunteer respondents. In the final analysis, approximately 4,500 completed questionnaires were returned, a response rate of 4.5 percent. Hite claimed that the 4,500 women included in her sample were representative of women in the United States based on demographic characteristics such as age and ethnicity.

Despite these assertions, several critics claim that Hite's research represents an extreme case of sampling bias, defined as the systematic tendency to overrepresent or underrepresent some segment of the population (Streitfield, 1988). In Hite's study, what segment of the female population do you think would have been most likely to respond to her 127-item essay questionnaire? Would some women be more likely than others to answer it? What characteristics might make the difference in responses? Unfortunately, because Hite selected a nonprobability sampling method, no one will ever be able to answer these questions accurately.

The point here is not that Hite's research has no value. In fact, her pioneering work on female sexuality has opened the dialogue on many topics that formerly were considered taboo, including cultural barriers to female masturbation and orgasm. The problem is that the sampling method that Hite chose did not allow her to adequately answer her descriptive research question on the sexual behaviors and opinions of American women. Because Hite's objective was to generalize from her study to the female population, she should have selected a probability sample. Had her sample been selected randomly, 4,500 responses would have been more than sufficient.

Simple Random Sampling.   In simple random sampling, the researcher selects elements from the entire sampling frame one at a time at random, so that each element has a known and equal chance of being selected. For example, if the sampling frame contains 50 elements, each element has a 1/50, or 2 percent, chance of being selected.

Simple random sampling can be performed manually using any random method. For instance, the researcher can write the sampling units on pieces of paper, put them in a container and shake them, and then pull them out at random until she or he reaches the desired sample size. The procedure used to

1. Define the population.
2. Secure a quality sampling frame.
3. Decide on the sample size.
4. Number consecutively all of the elements on the sampling frame.
5. Consult a table of random numbers like the one presented in Exhibit 5.3. Select a random or arbitrary starting point on the table, for example, by closing your eyes and placing your finger somewhere on the page. Decide in advance whether you will read down the columns or across the rows of the table.
6. Select the numbered elements from the sampling frame that correspond to the numbers chosen from the random numbers table. Ignore redundant or out-of-range numbers.
7. Sampling is completed when you have selected enough elements to meet the desired sample size.

EXHIBIT 5.2

Instructions for Drawing a Simple Random Sample

select the simple random sample will likely depend on the size of the sampling frame and the researcher's comfort with using computer software. If the sampling frame is relatively small, a manual process is manageable. If the sampling frame is large, manual methods can be tedious. For large samples, the researcher would want to use a computer program to number each element and generate a list of random numbers that matches the size of the desired sample. For example, if the desired sample size is 50 and the sampling frame contains 75 elements, the researcher would generate a list of 50 random numbers ranging from 1 to 75. The final step would be to match the list of 50 random numbers with the elements on the sampling frame.

A more common method of simple random sampling that involves the use of a random numbers table is described in Exhibit 5.2. A table of random numbers can be found at the back of this book and through an Internet search using the term "table of random numbers."

Simple random sampling works best with a population that is relatively **homogeneous,** that is, in which there is not a great deal of variation on variables of interest to the study. For example, a study of attitudes in a Mormon community in Colorado might safely use simple random sampling, whereas the same study would require a different sampling method in the more diverse areas of Los Angeles. If there is a great deal of variation on key variables in the population, as will be seen, a stratified random sampling method may produce a sample with less error—in other words, one that is more representative of the population.

Systematic Random Sampling. In systematic random sampling, the researcher computes a sampling interval based on the number needed for the sample. For

EXHIBIT 5.3

*Use of the
Random
Numbers
Table*

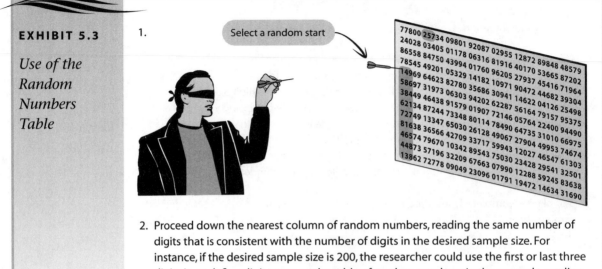

1.

Select a random start

77800 25734 09801 92087 02955 12872 89848 48579
24028 03405 01178 06316 81916 40170 53665 87202
86558 84750 43994 01760 96205 27937 45416 71964
78545 49201 05329 14182 10971 90472 44682 39304
14969 64623 82780 35686 30941 14622 04126 25498
58697 31973 06303 94202 62287 56164 79157 95375
38449 46438 91579 01907 72146 05764 22400 94490
62134 87244 73348 80114 78490 64735 31010 66975
72749 13347 65030 26128 49067 27904 49953 74674
81638 36566 42709 33717 59943 12027 46547 61303
46574 79670 10342 89543 75030 23428 29541 32501
44873 57196 32209 67663 07990 12288 59245 83638
13862 72778 09049 23096 01791 19472 14634 31690

2. Proceed down the nearest column of random numbers, reading the same number of digits that is consistent with the number of digits in the desired sample size. For instance, if the desired sample size is 200, the researcher could use the first or last three digits in each five-digit entry on the table of random numbers. In the example, reading the first three digits down the column from the random start, the first number is 149, the second is 586, the next is 384, and so on.

3. Match the random numbers from the table to the numbers assigned to the elements on the sampling frame. Select all of the elements for which there is a match until the desired sample size is achieved.

example, if a researcher has a list of 300 names and plans to sample 50, she or he would select every sixth name (300/50 = 6). The researcher then selects the first element using a random start within the sampling interval of 1 through 6. Finally, beginning with the random start, the researcher selects every sixth element until she or he reaches the end of the sampling frame. The process of systematic random sampling is described in Exhibit 5.4. As with simple random sampling, the elements in systematic random sampling have a known and equal chance of being selected.

A major advantage of systematic random sampling over simple random sampling is that the researcher does not have to number all of the elements on the sampling frame, a tedious task if the sampling universe is large. A second advantage is that the researcher does not need to match randomly chosen numbers with the numbers assigned to the sampling units. Finally, unlike simple random sampling, systematic random sampling can sometimes be used in the absence of a sampling frame. No sampling frame is necessary, for instance, if the elements are somehow organized in a way that permits the researcher to select elements at a regular interval. This process can be performed with either a manual filing system or a computer directory of electronic file names.

1. Define the population.
2. Secure a quality sampling frame. (In the absence of a sampling frame, access to a filing system that is representative of the population elements may work.)
3. Decide on the sample size.
4. Compute the sampling interval as follows:

$$\text{sampling interval} = N \text{ (population)}/n \text{ (desired sample size)}$$

If the computed sampling interval is not a whole number, alternate between using the first whole number immediately less than and greater than the computed interval. For example, if the sampling interval is 5.5, alternate between selecting elements at intervals of 5 and 6.
5. Select a random start within the first sampling interval. (In our example, the sampling interval is 5.5, so the random start would be a number ranging from 1 to 6.)
6. From the random start, select each element according to the sampling interval. When you reach the end of the sampling frame or the end of the filing system, you will have achieved the desired sample size.

EXHIBIT 5.4

How to Draw a Systematic Random Sample

When researchers employ systematic random sampling, certain quality control issues arise, even when they don't use a sampling frame. For example, it is not unusual for filing systems, both paper and electronic, to have missing files that generally go undetected until an audit is conducted. Thus, researchers must take care to ensure that the entire sampling universe is available for selection.

When using systematic random sampling, researchers must be alert to the possibility of order bias. **Order bias** occurs when the ordering in the sampling frame corresponds with the random start and the sampling interval in such a way as to underrepresent or overrepresent particular subgroups in the population. Consider, for example, a large child welfare agency and a sampling frame that is ordered by unit. Each unit is listed with the unit supervisor first, followed by five caseworkers. In this instance, drawing a systematic random sample could either overrepresent or underrepresent the caseworkers and the unit supervisors. If the researcher chose an interval of 6, for example, he or she would end up selecting only the supervisors.

Stratified Random Sampling. Researchers should adopt the method of stratified random sampling when they have reason to believe that (1) the outcome of interest varies among the different subgroups in the population, and (2) those subgroups run the risk of being overlooked or underrepresented in simple or systematic random sampling. For example, when researchers from the Gallup Organization examine public support for changes in Social Security, they know that the results will vary with the age of the respondent. For this reason, they make certain their samples include representatives from three subgroups: current retirees, young workers, and baby boomers who are approaching retirement. Using this method can reduce error by helping to ensure that the sample is more representative of the population than it might have been with simple or systematic random sampling.

To draw a stratified random sample, the researcher first divides the sampling frame into two or more strata to be sampled independently. The **strata** (*stratum*, singular) are categories of variables determined to be important on the basis of prior knowledge. For example, in a study of literacy in childhood, the parents' primary language is an important variable. The researcher in this case may decide to create three strata: children whose parents speak only English, children whose parents speak only one non-English language, and children with bilingual parents. In certain studies, the researcher may stratify the sample on more than one variable. For example, the study may further stratify the groups by language, such as Spanish and Korean if these are the primary languages of the participants. The more variables, however, the greater the number of strata, and the larger the sample size needed to ensure that each category or stratum is represented.

Stratified random samples can be of two types: proportionate and disproportionate. In **proportionate sampling,** the proportion of each stratum in the sample corresponds to its respective proportion in the population. Conversely, in **disproportionate sampling,** the size of the stratum is *not* the same as the proportion it constitutes in the population. Disproportionate sampling is used when the numbers of elements with certain characteristics are so few in the population that they need to be *oversampled* in order to be examined adequately as a subgroup and to be compared to other subgroups. **Oversampled** means the elements are sampled in greater proportion than their proportion in the population. For example, in a study of students' needs with a sample of 100, if only eight speak English as a second language, all eight might be included in order to better understand their needs. The process of stratified random sampling is described in Exhibit 5.5.

The task of creating the strata makes stratified random sampling considerably more complex than simple random or systematic random sampling. Thus, researchers who use stratified random sampling should limit the number of strata to only the most relevant categories. As with any research decision, researchers must be prepared to justify their choice of strata.

Disproportionate vs. Proportionate Sampling. When a researcher uses disproportionate stratified sampling, the probability of each element in each stratum being selected is no longer equal. Just the opposite, the elements in some strata have a greater chance of being selected than the elements in other strata because the strata vary in size. In such cases, if the researcher wants to make inferences from the sample back to the population, the sample data must be

1. Define the population.
2. Secure a quality sampling frame.
3. Stratify the sampling frame into relevant, mutually exclusive categories. Categories are *mutually exclusive* when each element belongs to one and only one category.
4. Decide on the sample size.
5. Choose between proportionate and disproportionate sampling.
6. Sample each stratum as previously described under simple random or systematic random sampling. Sampling is complete when you achieve the desired sample size.

EXHIBIT 5.5

How to Draw a Stratified Random Sample

weighted to account for the influence of the oversampled elements. **Weighting** involves adjusting the values of the data to reflect the differences in the number of population units that each case represents.

For example, if we chose to study homelessness and our population of interest was U.S. military veterans, we know that gender would be an important variable. The National Coalition for Homeless Veterans (2005) reports that 98 percent of veterans who are homeless are men and only 2 percent are women. If we want to study the incidence of lifetime homelessness among the veteran population in Washington, D.C., we would want to ensure that female veterans are represented in sufficient numbers in our sample. In other words, we would need to use stratified random sampling, disproportionate to size, to ensure an adequate sample of female veterans. Of course, the ability to stratify assumes that a quality sampling frame exists.

The pie charts in Exhibit 5.6 on p. 120 illustrate the difference between proportionate and disproportionate sampling. If we have a population of 40,617 veterans, as shown in Exhibit 5.6a, and we know that approximately 91% are men and 9% are women, we can calculate a proportionate sample. Given a target sample size of 220, if we were to use proportionate sampling, we would sample 200 men (91% of our total sample size) and 20 women (9% of our sample size). We calculate the proportion of men by multiplying the total sample size (220) by their percentage within the population (91%) represented as a decimal (91/100 = .91). In this instance: 220 × .91 = 200. For women, the sample proportion was calculated by the equation 220 × .09 = 20. When we look at Exhibit 5.6b, we must ask if our randomly chosen subgroup of 20 women would be representative of the entire population of 3,552 female veterans. Clearly we cannot make this assumption because our sample size is so small. Therefore, not only would we introduce significant error if we made inferences to the entire population based on a sample of 20 women, but we could not make any valid comparisons between male and female veterans.

One strategy to deal with this shortcoming is to use a disproportionate sampling technique, as shown in Exhibit 5.6c. In this case, 50% of our sample

EXHIBIT 5.6

Proportionate and Disproportionate Stratified Samples

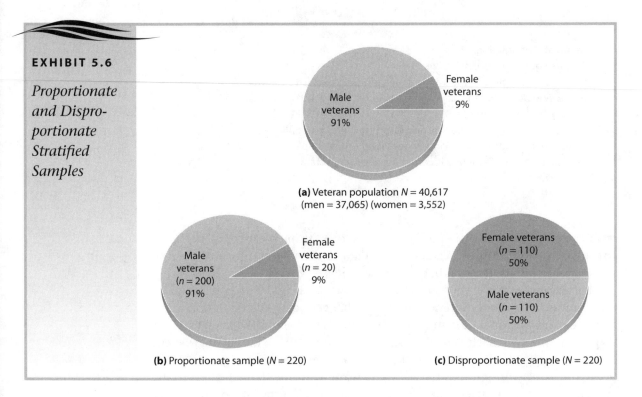

(a) Veteran population $N = 40,617$
(men = 37,065) (women = 3,552)

(b) Proportionate sample ($N = 220$)

(c) Disproportionate sample ($N = 220$)

would be female veterans, and 50% would be male veterans. Given our total sample size of 220, this would yield equal samples of 110 women and 110 men. If we randomly selected a sample consisting of more than 100 individuals in each subgroup, we could now examine male and female veterans separately and make between-group comparisons. If, however, we wanted to estimate the average income for the population of veterans from our disproportionate sample, we would need to weight the data for each case to take into account the overrepresentation of women—who typically have lower incomes than men—and the underrepresentation of men in the sample.

Cluster Sampling. Some populations cannot easily be represented on a sampling frame because they are so large or dispersed. One way to deal with this problem is through **cluster sampling,** the selection of elements from aggregates (groups) of elements. Let's use Exhibit 5.7 as an example. In this example, the sampling unit is students. However, the national student population is immense. How can we randomly sample such a population?

One approach is to first randomly sample clusters. In this case, the clusters are counties. If we were to end our sampling at this level, we would have performed a basic cluster sampling. However, because we want to sample individual students, we need to repeat the random sampling at increasingly targeted levels

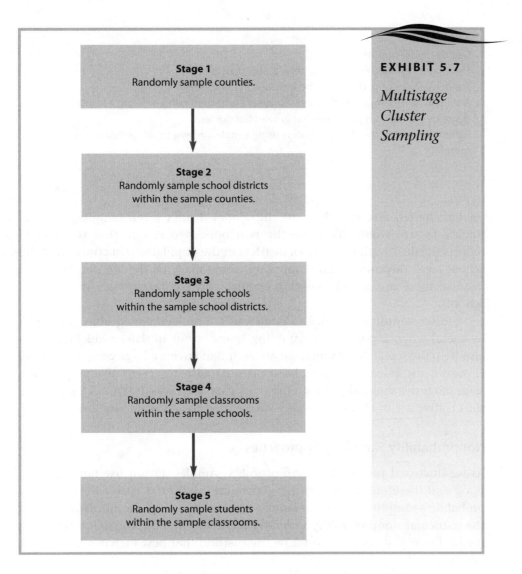

EXHIBIT 5.7

Multistage Cluster Sampling

Stage 1
Randomly sample counties.

Stage 2
Randomly sample school districts within the sample counties.

Stage 3
Randomly sample schools within the sample school districts.

Stage 4
Randomly sample classrooms within the sample schools.

Stage 5
Randomly sample students within the sample classrooms.

until we reach our sample population. That is, after we sample counties, we would then sample school districts, individual schools within districts, and classrooms within schools until we finally get to the students within the classrooms. This method of repeating random samples until we reach the sampling unit is referred to as **multistage cluster sampling.** Note that the more stages of random sampling, the greater the chances for sampling error, because error is introduced at each stage. The process of cluster sampling is described in Exhibit 5.8.

Cluster sampling can easily be combined with stratification. Within the level of school district, for instance, it may be important to stratify by size. Similarly, at the school level, it may be important to stratify by type: for example,

1. Decide on the population.
2. Develop a sampling frame of clusters; stratify if justified.
3. Randomly select the clusters to be included in the sample.
4. After you have completed the lowest level of cluster sampling, develop a sampling frame by enumerating each randomly selected cluster.
5. Randomly sample the chosen clusters using simple, systematic, or stratified random sampling.

public, charter, and parochial. At the school district level, sampling proportionate to size would likely be the best option to ensure that the sample reflects the distribution of school districts in the population. In contrast, at the school level, disproportionate sampling would likely be the method of choice because there are usually fewer parochial and charter schools than public schools.

Cluster sampling can make a large research project manageable, and it can be useful when a population sampling frame is not initially available. It can also help the researcher to manage research that covers a large geographic area. However, the researcher must be concerned with representativeness at each stage of cluster sampling and stratify if appropriate. Case-in-Point 5.2 illustrates the creative use of cluster sampling with a hard-to-access population.

Nonprobability Sampling Approaches

As we discussed previously, nonprobability samples do not use random sampling and therefore do not permit generalization. The decision to use a nonprobability sampling approach should be intentional, as should the choice of the particular nonprobability sampling method. The nonprobability sampling method that you choose should be the method that best matches the goal of your research.

This section describes four common types of nonprobability sampling methods: convenience, purposive, snowball, and quota. As with probability sampling, the sampling units in nonprobability sampling do not have to be human, with the one exception being snowball sampling.

Convenience Sampling. As its name suggests, **convenience sampling** selects the most available elements to constitute the sample. This may be based on geographic closeness, ease of access, or other opportunity such as members at a conference. The use of convenience sampling is common in social work research because it is relatively quick and inexpensive. The caution with convenience sampling is not to generalize to the broader population because there is no justification to claim that the sample is representative of the larger group.

CASE-IN-POINT 5.2

The Homeless Street Count

Populations that are relatively small in number, underserved, and stigmatized are particularly difficult for researchers to access. One population that fits this description is homeless individuals. Nevertheless, despite the difficulties involved, every year on one particular day communities all across the United States engage in an annual count of their homeless population.

Participation in the Homeless Street Count (the Count) is a condition of receiving federal funding under the Stuart B. McKinney Act Continuum of Care Awards. The McKinney Act provides the only major federal funding to address homelessness, and many communities rely on these funds to provide needed services. The federal government chooses the week of the Count, and participating locations select the date. On the specified day, workers and volunteers across the country count the homeless population one individual at a time. To guide the Count, the Department of Housing and Urban Development (HUD) has provided the following definition of homelessness: adults, children, and unaccompanied youth sleeping in places not meant for human habitation. Examples of settings that fit HUD's definition are streets, parks, alleys, dumpsters, abandoned buildings, campgrounds, vehicles, and stairwells. Note that this definition does not include individuals who move from home to home sleeping on couches and floors or in garages. The Count, therefore, might underestimate the number of people that we would define as homeless. The existence and clarity of the definition, however, make the Count possible.

Some jurisdictions participating in the Count use sampling in combination with straight counting. Researchers in the city of Phoenix, Arizona, for example, *stratify* geographic areas of the city into grids of low-density and high-density numbers of homeless individuals. The stratification is based on information obtained from previous Counts. All high-density areas are counted, whereas the cluster of low-density areas is randomly sampled. The low-density areas that are selected for inclusion in the sample are then counted.

Sampling the low-density areas saves time and resources, thereby making the task manageable. From the sample data, researchers compute the average number of homeless individuals in the low-density areas and then assign this number to the low-density areas that were not included in the sample. In other words, they make an inference to the population based on the information they obtain from the sample. How accurate are the results? The answer is that no one knows for certain. Nevertheless, these data are the best information available on the incidence of homelessness, and they are used to secure needed funding and to raise public awareness of homelessness in the United States.

Unfortunately, there is a tendency among some researchers to make this leap, as was illustrated in Case-in-Point 5.1.

Purposive Sampling. Researchers who use **purposive sampling** intentionally select the elements to be included in the sample. They may choose the elements they believe are good sources of information, possess varied perspectives or common experiences, or are extreme or deviant. Purposive sampling is sometimes referred to as *expert sampling* because the researchers choose individuals for their special knowledge and not necessarily for their formal training or education. The key to purposive or expert sampling is that selection is intentional and is consistent with the goal of the research. The researcher may be guided by her or his judgment or the advice of others.

Researchers frequently use purposive sampling when they collect information to assess community needs. In these cases, they select certain individuals because of their unique perspective on the community. Included in this group are schoolteachers, law enforcement personnel, health care providers, government officials, social service workers, business and apartment owners, elderly residents, youths, working parents, and homeless individuals. Case-in-Point 5.3 describes what can happen in a community needs assessment when researchers employ convenience rather than purposive sampling.

CASE-IN-POINT 5.3

Sampling for a Community Needs Assessment

Resources to meet social service needs are always scarce. For this reason, researchers perform an assessment of community needs to help set priorities and determine how to allocate scarce resources. Community needs assessments deal with such basic necessities as food, housing, income, health, and safety. In approaching the task of conducting a community needs assessment, researchers need to formulate a sampling plan that will guide them in determining where to access information for the assessment.

Understanding the different perspectives that can go into defining need is the first step before undertaking a community needs assessment. (See Chapter 11 for more information on needs assessment.) Basically, there are four different perspectives on need (Kettner, Moroney, & Martin, 2002). *Perceived need* refers to the ways in which the individuals in a community define their needs. *Normative need* is a judgment concerning what amenities the majority of people in a community should have, such as electricity, running water, and telephones. *Expressed need* examines the demand for services in relation to the inadequate supply. For instance, how many people sought shelter or food but did not receive it? Finally, *relative need* addresses the gap between the level of services existing in one community and those existing in similar communities or geographic areas. Ideally, a community needs assessment will include all four of these perspectives. In reality, the scope of a needs assessment will depend on the amount of time and resources available.

Recently a nonprofit organization partnered with a team of local researchers to conduct a community needs assessment for a small suburban city. To encourage broad participation, the researchers used press releases and flyers to invite local residents and service providers to a town-hall meeting. At the meeting, the researchers provided the attendees with summary information on the population, including employment, ethnicity, housing, education, and median income. The researchers then proceeded to gather people's perceptions on local need and their suggestions for change. The meeting attracted approximately 65 people, most of whom were service providers. As a result of the meeting, the researchers authored a final report and encouraged the community to continue to work on the major issues identified in the meeting. This method of understanding community needs has some serious difficulties. First, the perspective of service providers may differ from that of other residents. In addition, only people strongly interested in this issue are likely to attend a community meeting. They may not reflect the thoughts of the majority of the community.

CASE-IN-POINT 5.3

Sampling for a Community Needs Assessment
continued

 Web Links

Visit www.mhhe.com/ krysik1 for a link to tips on how to sample for a community needs assessment.

The category of perceived need suggests that the residents of a community, as well as people who serve the community by providing services to meet basic needs, should be asked about their perceptions of the community. The next logical question is How can we access those people? This question should be addressed in the development of a sampling plan for the community needs assessment. A sampling plan would describe and justify the sampling approach and the sampling methods. If the researchers had developed a sampling plan, they would have considered this question ahead of time. What approach or combination of approaches would you suggest?

Examining population data is a useful strategy for community needs assessment. Unfortunately, its use was limited to basic aggregate data in this case. Knowing that median income is $51,000 and that 48 percent of the population has attended at least some college does nothing to help understand or locate need in a city. A sampling plan would have directed the researchers to examine such data on a smaller scale. As one alternative, they could have sampled census tracts or city blocks as opposed to examining the city as a whole. A community needs assessment is an exercise in research, and all good research requires the formulation of a sampling plan that justifies the researcher's choices on the basis of what is required to answer the research question.

Snowball Sampling. This method of sampling relies on the human factor to provide information to further the sampling process. In **snowball sampling,** the researchers ask the initial participants to identify other potential participants until they have achieved the desired sample size, thus the term *snowball*. The number of participants builds as each person identifies multiple new potential recruits. Snowball sampling is useful for locating hard-to-access populations, and it can be used when no sampling frame is available. Going further, the researcher can deliberately ask participants to identify potential participants who have divergent ideas or perspectives. In this manner, the researcher can diversify the range of attitudes, behaviors, and other elements represented in the sample. Snowball sampling is used with populations such as sex workers, gay teenagers who are homeless, and members of gangs. It is based on the idea that people often know others in situations similar to their own.

Quota Sampling. The only nonprobability method that relies on prior knowledge of the population and a predetermined sample size, **quota sampling** involves substantially more work than convenience or snowball sampling.

Quota sampling parallels stratified random sampling in that it is concerned with the representation of certain population subgroups in the sample. Quota sampling most closely approximates proportionate sampling because it seeks to represent certain characteristics in proportion to their prevalence in the population. Quotas for each subgroup are set according to their estimated representation in the population. The major difference between quota sampling and

1. Identify key variables, and establish discrete categories.
2. Determine the representation of each category in the population based on prior knowledge.
3. Establish the desired sample size.
4. Calculate the quotas.
5. Sample using convenience or snowball sampling until you fill the quotas.

Step 5. Select a sampling method.

stratified sampling is that the selection procedure in quota sampling is not random. Using our example of veterans in the Washington, D.C., area, if the desired sample size is 50, then sampling quotas would be set so that 9 percent of the 50 elements are female veterans and 91 percent are male veterans. Quota sampling is often used at large events such as sporting events or concerts to conduct attitude surveys. Interviewers may be given a quota—for example, interview 25 men who appear to be over 60 years of age and 25 African Americans who appear to be between the ages of 18 and 25. Once the quotas are set, participants would be recruited through a nonrandom process (convenience or snowball sampling) until the desired sample size is achieved. The process of quota sampling is described in Exhibit 5.9.

WHAT IS THE CORRECT SAMPLE SIZE?

One of the major questions a researcher must address in planning a study is How big should my sample size be? There is no simple answer to this question. One key factor that affects this decision is whether the researcher has chosen to use a probability or a nonprobability sampling approach.

In nonprobability sampling, sample size is based on conceptual rather than statistical considerations. As a general rule in nonprobability sampling, the researcher selects elements until no new insights or observations are revealed. In snowball sampling, as we have seen, the researcher may intentionally sample for maximum variation. Convenience sampling often involves a small group of participants such as the students in a classroom. In such cases, the entire group should be included if resources permit. In purposive sampling, the sample size will be determined by the variation in experience, knowledge, and attitudes the researcher considers important to represent. For quota sampling, the desired sample size will be based at least in part on the number of categories that the researcher has predetermined to be important.

As with all research, sample size is a balance between what is desired and what is feasible. An increase in sample size in nonprobability sampling will not allow the researcher to claim that the findings are any more representative of the broader population than she or he could claim with a small sample. Why is this true? The answer is because nonprobability sampling does not involve random sampling; therefore, a nonrandom selection process is likely to introduce bias. Case-in-Point 5.1 provided a prominent illustration of the fallacy that increasing the size of a sample that is selected through nonprobablility sampling will generate more accurate results.

Probability samples are typically larger than those found in nonprobability sampling. In probability sampling, an increase in sample size actually *does* permit the researcher to claim greater representation to the population. For probability sampling approaches, sample size will be determined by a combination of these factors:

- desired precision
- degree of variability in the population on key variables
- plan for the analysis
- estimated nonresponse or attrition rate

Desired Precision

The question of how big a sample should be is determined to a large extent by the amount of sampling error the researcher is willing to accept. **Sampling error** is the degree of difference between the sample and the population from which it was drawn. In determining an acceptable degree of sampling error, the researcher must select a confidence level and confidence interval. The **confidence level** tells us how sure we can be that the results from our sample represent the population. The confidence level is selected by the researcher. By convention, most researchers in the social sciences use a confidence level of 95 percent as their standard. A confidence level of 95 percent means that if the same study were conducted 100 times with random samples drawn from the same population, it would represent the true population value 95 times. Of course, this definition implies that 5 times out of 100, the sample would *not* represent true population value. In other fields such as the medical sciences, in which decisions relate to life or death, and the physical sciences, in which decisions can be a matter of safety, a confidence level of 99 percent or higher might be chosen because the probability of being wrong is considered much too high.

The **confidence interval,** in contrast, is that *plus-or-minus margin of error* that we see mentioned in public opinion polls. The **margin of error** (usually expressed in percentage points) indicates how far the sample's results can stray from the true value in the entire population. The margin of error of a sample depends on the number of elements included in the sample. Margin of error, or the confidence interval, is calculated by the following formula: 1 divided by the square root of the number of elements in the sample. Thus, if the sample size is 50, we divide 1 by 7.1 (the square root of 50). This equation produces a margin of error of plus-or-minus (±) 14%. This means, for example, that if we conducted a survey to which 40% of those interviewed answered that they routinely used spanking as a means of disciplining their toddlers, we could be 95% confident that the true population figure would fall ± 14 of 40, somewhere between 26% and 54%. Conversely, there is a 5% chance that the true population figure would *not* fall between 26% and 54%; it could be higher or lower.

A range of plus-or-minus 14 percentage points is very large and does not tell us anything with an adequate degree of precision. A sample of 100 individuals, in contrast, would provide a narrower margin of error, plus-or-minus 10 percentage points. A sample of 200 would reduce the margin of error to plus-or-minus 7 percentage points. If our goal were a margin of error of plus-or-minus 3 percentage points, we would need a sample size of 1,000. The margin of error selected depends on how accurate the research needs to be. For example, since a close election may be decided by 1 percent of the vote, a very small margin of error is needed. On the other hand, if we need to know whether or not people are generally in favor of an after-school arts program, a larger margin of error (such as 10–15 percent) would suffice.

Although the size of the sample influences the margin of error, the size of the population does not. That is, it does not matter if we are interested in 200 million adults in the United States or in 10 million adults from Los Angeles County. In both cases, a randomly drawn sample of 1,000 is sufficient if we are willing to accept a margin of error of plus-or-minus three percentage points. This explains why the Gallup Poll relies on sample sizes of approximately 1,000 people to represent large populations. Researchers must keep in mind, however, that if they want to make statements about population subgroups, they need to consider the size of the subgroup in the sample when calculating the margin of error. The ability of a probability sample to represent the population from which it was drawn depends, however, on more than sample size. As discussed next, it also depends on other factors related to the population and the research design.

Managing Variation

Recall that when population elements are similar to a large extent on key variables, we say that they are homogeneous. In contrast, populations with greater within-group diversity are **heterogeneous.** Generally speaking, the more heterogeneous the population, the larger the sample size needed to accurately reflect the population. For a population with little variation on key variables, a relatively small sample usually is sufficient.

Fortunately, tables like the one in Exhibit 5.10 are available to help us determine a *base sample size*—the smallest sample size that will adequately

Confidence interval calculations are based on the assumption of probability sampling.

The law of diminishing returns states that at a certain point, more does not mean better. In sampling, once we pass a particular point, what is gained in accuracy is not usually justified by the cost.

Step 6. Determine the desired sample size.

POPULATION SIZE	VARIABILITY					EXHIBIT 5.10
	50%	40%	30%	20%	10%	
100	81	79	63	50	37	
125	96	93	72	56	40	
150	110	107	80	60	42	
175	122	119	87	64	44	
200	134	130	93	67	45	
225	144	140	98	70	46	
250	154	149	102	72	47	
275	163	158	106	74	48	
300	172	165	109	76	49	
325	180	173	113	77	50	
350	187	180	115	79	50	
375	194	186	118	80	51	
400	201	192	120	81	51	
600	240	228	134	87	53	
800	267	252	142	90	54	
1,000	286	269	147	92	55	
2,000	333	311	158	96	57	

EXHIBIT 5.10

Determining a Base Sample Size with a ± 5 Percent Margin of Error

This table assumes a 95 percent confidence level.
The base sample size should be increased to take attrition into consideration.

Source: J. Watson, 2001. How to determine a sample size: Tipsheet 60, University Park, PA: Penn State Cooperative Extension. Available at www.extension.psu.edu/evaluation/pdf/TS60.pdf.

represent the population—while taking into account the degree of variability in the population. If we do not know the variation in key variables, we should use the first column under the heading "Variability" because it assumes the greatest amount of variation, a 50/50 split. The column on the far right with the heading "10%" assumes that the distribution on the variable of interest is 90%/10%. Social work researchers would define such a population as homogeneous. In some instances, researchers must undertake a pilot study to understand the degree of variability before they make an informed judgment on sample size. One method of reducing variation in the population is to focus on a more homogeneous group of elements, that is, to define the population more narrowly; for example, they could sample only a specific income class rather than the full range of incomes.

Considering the Number of Variables

Another factor that influences sample size is the number of variables that researchers will consider in the analysis. When researchers break down the data

EXHIBIT 5.11

Income by Ethnicity

AGE IN YEARS	AFRICAN AMERICAN	HISPANIC	NATIVE AMERICAN	WHITE/ CAUCASIAN	ASIAN, PACIFIC ISLANDER
<19					
19–25					
26–32					
33+					

to analyze categories of multiple variables, what initially appeared to be a substantial sample size may no longer be large enough. Take the Healthy Families America program discussed in earlier chapters as an example. As shown in Exhibit 5.11, when researchers in that study examined parental stress across four categories of age and five categories of ethnicity, they ended up with 20 cells, each of which must contain data. As data are cross-classified, the sample size must increase to support the analysis. When the sample size is small, the number of elements in each cell can become quite sparse. A **sparse table** is one in which 30 percent of the cells have five or fewer elements. The use of sparse tables will invalidate many statistical tests. Statistical tests for small samples are discussed in Chapter 9.

In order for the sampling plan to take into account anticipated statistical analyses, the researcher must understand the variables that will be considered. The literature review the researcher conducts to help formulate the research problem and question is vital to identifying important variables for the analyses. As a strategy to determine whether the base sample size that was determined from a table such as the one in Exhibit 5.10 will support the planned analysis, the researcher can use the *rule of 10 elements per variable* included in the analysis. However, if the variables are nominal or ordinal, the researcher must also consider the number of categories in each variable. For example, if the analysis will include the variables age (young/old), race (African American, Hispanic, White, and Other), and gender (Male/Female), that requires a $2 \times 4 \times 2$ table that includes 16 cells. In this instance, the rule of 10 elements per variable would not be sufficient, and it would be better to use the rule for sparse tables; that is, no more than 30 percent of the cells should contain five or fewer elements. If the base sample size does not support the number of variables to be examined, or if several of the variables have multiple categories, the researcher will want to adjust the base sample size upward.

Accounting for Attrition

It would be highly unlikely not to observe at least some level of attrition in a research sample. If the research involves observation at one point in time, we are concerned with **nonrespondents,** those who did not respond for what-ever reason: refusal, language problems, illness, or lack of availability. If the study involves more than one round of measurement or observation, the re-searcher must be concerned with attrition, elements that are lost from one ob-servation to the next.

To avoid an additional round of sampling, we can estimate the expected level of attrition before the study begins and then compensate for it when we determine the initial sample size. To estimate attrition, we might look at the dropout rates in similar studies. In studies of home visitation programs to prevent child abuse and neglect, it is common to sample an extra 20 percent in addition to the desired sample size to account for attrition. If the desired sample size was 220 and the estimated attrition rate was 20 percent, we would calculate the number of additional sampling units needed by multiplying the total sample size by the percentage of expected attrition represented as a decimal: $220 \times .20 = 44$. Thus, the total sample size needed to account for attrition would be 264 (220 + 44). Chapter 7 provides strategies for managing attrition once the study is implemented.

CONCLUSION

The power of random sampling is evident in national opinion poll surveys that allow researchers to generalize findings to the nation based on the responses of 1,000 people. Social workers are often concerned with large numbers of people as well, for example, when studying attitudes about social policies, the adjust-ment of people with mental illness in the community, or the stability of place-ments for foster children. This chapter has presented the development of a sampling plan as a process requiring six steps, shown at the beginning of the chapter. Together these steps can be used as a guide in developing a sampling plan, as well as to evaluate the sampling procedures used in other studies. In contrast to what some researchers imply, the ability to generalize from a sam-ple to a population is not as dependent on sample size as it is on the sampling approach. Researchers should keep in mind the limitations of different sam-pling approaches and exercise caution not to generalize beyond what the sam-pling approach will support. Reduction of error is a goal in research, and prior knowledge of the research topic and the population can be used to tailor the sampling plan to minimize the potential for sampling error. Once a sample has been selected, the researcher is ready to measure variables in the sample and engage in data collection. The following two chapters present additional strate-gies for minimizing error associated with measurement (Chapter 6) and data collection (Chapter 7). Unless appropriate sampling is used, even the best measuring instruments and the most sophisticated data analyses will yield inaccurate results.

MAIN POINTS

- A sample is a subset of the population.

- Key to good sample selection is the development of a sampling plan that addresses how the population will be defined, the justification for sampling or including the entire population, the quality of the sampling frame, the sampling approach, the sampling method, and the sample size.

- Probability sampling is a procedure in which every element in the sampling universe has a known probability of selection. If enough elements are randomly selected, the sample should be representative of the population. The major advantage of probability sampling is that it permits generalization.

- Nonprobability sampling is a procedure in which all of the elements in the population have an unknown and usually different probability of being included in the sample. Thus, nonprobability sampling does not support the claim that the sample is representative of the population and therefore does not permit generalization.

- Sample size must be estimated in the design phase of the research. There are guidelines on how many subjects to sample based on population size. However, these guidelines can be improved upon through the consideration of desired precision, the number of variables considered in the analysis, the degree of variability within the population, and estimates of attrition or nonresponse.

- The amount of difference between the findings based on a random sample and the true value in the population, if it were known, is sampling error.

EXERCISES: PRACTICING SOCIAL WORK

Consult the sampling frame of tribal adults from the Black Feather case study on your CD-ROM. It can be found in the Resources folder under Tools; select Reference Materials and then Sampling Frame. Note that the list of names is ordered alphabetically.

1. Using the sampling frame provided and the table of random numbers, select a simple random sample of 20 adults. Indicate below:

   a. How you chose your random start

   b. The 20 random numbers you selected

   c. The 20 names that you selected

   d. Your assessment of how well the sample represents the population

2. Using the sampling frame provided on the CD-ROM, select a systematic random sample of 20 adults. Indicate below:

   a. The sampling interval you calculated

   b. How you selected a random start within the first interval

   c. The list of names you selected

   d. Your assessment of how well the sample represents the population

3. Using the sampling frame provided, select a stratified random sample of 20 adults. Indicate below:

   a. The categories you will choose to stratify the sample

   b. The percentage of the sample you will select from each stratum if you use proportionate sampling

   c. The number of elements you will sample from each stratum if you use disproportionate sampling

   d. Twenty names you selected using proportionate sampling

   e. Twenty names you selected using disproportionate sampling

   f. How your sample compares to the simple random and systematic random samples you selected for questions 1 and 2

4. Using the information from the Black Feather case study on your CD-ROM, create a hypothetical sampling plan for a community needs assessment. Would you use probability sampling methods, nonprobability, or a combination of the two? Justify your decisions. What cultural considerations would enter into your sampling plan?

EXERCISES: SOCIAL WORK LIBRARY

Read the articles by Saltzburg (2004) and Olds et al. (2004a) and answer the following questions for each:

1. How did the author(s) define the population?

2. What was the purpose of the research?

3. What sampling approach was used?

4. How was the sample selected for this research?

5. Were the sampling approach and the sampling method appropriate for the purpose of the research? Explain.

6. Did the author(s) discuss considerations of sample size? If yes, what were they? If no, what considerations on sample size do you think the author(s) should have addressed?

OTHER EXERCISES

1. Compare and contrast the advantages and limitations of probability and nonprobability sampling methods.

2. List five different techniques that you could use to draw a random sample.

CHAPTER 6

Measurement

Grownups like numbers. When you tell them about a new friend, they never ask questions about what really matters. They never ask: "What does his voice sound like? What games does he like best? Does he collect butterflies?" They ask: "How old is he? How many brothers does he have? How much does he weigh? How much money does his father make?" Only then do they think they know him
—Antoine de Saint-Exupéry, *The Little Prince*, 1943/2000, p. 10

IMAGES OF MEASUREMENT IN EVERYDAY LIFE ARE COMMONLY associated with the tools of our time. For instance, we use tape measures, clocks, and thermometers to measure concepts such as length, time, and temperature. How well we measure these concepts depends to a large extent on the tools we use. An atomic wall clock provides a much more accurate measure of time than eyeballing the position of the sun. Similarly, new advances in nanotechnology—technology at the level of the atom—are changing the ways in which doctors diagnose and treat cancer (National Cancer Institute, 2004). Doctors can now detect cancer at its earliest stages, pinpoint its exact location within the body, and direct anticancer drugs to the affected cells. These examples involving time and medicine illustrate the fact that measurement involves choice. To a large extent, the choices we make in measurement depend on the available technology, the skill level of the people who administer the measure, access to resources such as time and money, and the need for precision.

Measurement is also a fundamental concept in research. Certainly there is no one right way to measure each of the many concepts that are the subject of social work research. Take, for example, the concept of poverty. We often hear statements referring to the percentages of certain subgroups within the population who are living in poverty. Poverty statistics are bandied about as if there were an absolute division between people who are poor and people who are not poor. According to the official poverty measure in the United States, known as the *poverty threshold*, a four-person household with two dependent children earning $19,000 in 2004 was considered poor, while a household of the same size and structure earning $19,200 was *not* poor (U.S. Census Bureau, 2005).

What this example illustrates is that all measures, even well-established and accepted measures, have benefits and limitations.

Measurement becomes problematic when concepts are defined and then communicated as if they were independent of the measures used. The example concerning poverty serves to remind us that measurement is the representation of a concept, not the actual condition itself. Measurement is reductionist in the sense that it filters the information that will be considered. For example, the poverty threshold is based solely on income and family type and does not consider other things, such as health care costs. Measurement is also a social construction in the sense that it requires a decision about what to include and what to exclude.

Measurement can be defined as the process of assigning numbers or other symbols to characteristics or attributes of a concept according to specified rules. Given this definition, social workers must be diligent in critiquing the fit between concepts and their measures. The choices we make regarding measurement have important implications. Measurement is a vital component of our communication both within and outside the social work profession. It also forms the basis of our conclusions in social work research. Finally, we use measures such as the poverty threshold to target individuals for research and to determine whether they are eligible for important programs and benefits.

Measurement is so important in social work research that it is the focus of two chapters in this book. This chapter is concerned with the *concept* of measurement and the questions we must ask in order to make critical choices in selecting and evaluating measures. Chapter 7 then focuses on the *process* of measurement, which begins after we have selected the appropriate measures and are preparing to implement the study. By the end of this chapter, you should be able to:

- Describe the concept of measurement.

- List the pros and cons of different measurement options.

- Explain the four levels of measurement.

- Discuss the issues of measurement reliability and validity and their relationship to each other.

- Know where to search for existing measurement instruments.

- Know how to construct your own questions for use as measures in social work research.

FROM CONCEPT TO MEASUREMENT

In social work research, we are interested in measuring concepts that we call variables. In the context of measurement, a variable is simply something with no fixed numerical value; that is, its value can change or vary. For instance, if

One foot is short. One inch is long. —*Qu Yuan, Chinese poet and patriot (340 BC–278 BC)*

we were interested in the way parents discipline their preschool children, parental discipline would be the variable. Various options or categories within the concept of parental discipline include spanking, yelling, pushing, explaining, and time-out. The options within a variable, in this instance the different forms of discipline, are referred to as **attributes.** Variable attributes such as spanking, yelling, pushing, explaining, and time-out would be the focus of measurement. Thus we are concerned with measuring the attributes of variables.

When we communicate about concepts in everyday life, we often define them in a way that conveys a mental picture. As discussed in Chapter 3, this type of definition, similar to what we would find in a dictionary, is referred to as a *nominal definition*. The concept of disability, for instance, is defined by Webster's dictionary as "lack of competent power, strength, or physical or mental ability" (1989, p. 408). In order to consider a concept for inclusion in a research study, we have to go beyond a nominal definition to define it in a way that enables us to measure it. We call this type of definition an *operational definition*. The process of creating an operational definition involves defining a concept in detail so that it means the same thing to one person as it does to another.

In social work research, we can often adopt or build on operational definitions that have already been developed. Take the concept of childhood disability, for example. The U.S. Social Security Administration has defined childhood disability as "a physical or mental condition(s) that very seriously limits his or her activities *and* the condition(s) must have lasted, or be expected to last, at least 1 year or result in death" (U.S. Social Security Administration, 2005, p. 1). We could add to this operational definition by defining in greater detail the concepts of "child" and "mental condition." For example, we could define a child as an individual less than 18 years of age. We could adopt the definition for mental condition from the Americans with Disabilities Act: "any mental or psychological disorder such as mental retardation, organic brain syndrome, emotional or mental illness and specific learning disabilities" (Americans with Disabilities Act, 2004, p. 2). The greater the detail in the operational definition, the less room for ambiguity. Case-in-Point 6.1 illustrates the importance of considering cultural variability when operationalizing variables.

THE CONTEXT OF MEASUREMENT

Talking about measurement without referring to the research context in which measurement occurs is impossible. Measurement will vary depending on whether the researcher chooses a quantitative or qualitative approach to

**CASE-IN-
POINT 6.1**

*Operational-
izing Elder
Abuse*

The concept of elder abuse presents an example of the difficulties involved in moving from a nominal to an operational definition. A nominal definition of elder abuse could be "an occurrence in which an adult child or caretaker injures a senior, not by accident but in anger or with deliberate intent." To operationalize elder abuse, we would need to take the nominal definition further by deciding which indicators to use. This is not as simple as it seems.

There are some specific circumstances that would obviously seem to indicate elder abuse, for instance, the personal use by another individual of an elderly person's financial resources. A second indicator might be repeated and unexplained bruises on the elder's body. Both of these indicators are problematic, however, in that they correspond with typical changes in older adulthood. Regarding financial resources, some elderly adults mismanage their money as their short-term memory declines with age. As a result, adult children and caretakers often assume responsibility for the elder's financial responsibilities. Clearly, their actions are a form of assistance, not abuse. Similarly with the second indicator, elderly individuals tend to bruise more easily than younger people. To compound this problem, they may not be able to accurately explain the origin of their bruises due to memory loss, deteriorating mental status, and communication problems. Thus, for some elderly individuals, bruising indicates problems with balance rather than abuse.

Culture also complicates the operationalization of elder abuse. For example, some cultures define the placement of elderly individuals in skilled nursing facilities as a form of abuse, whereas other cultures interpret it as a sign of caring. The problem of operationalizing elder abuse—and many other concepts of interest to social work researchers—is that it involves subjective judgments and culture-bound definitions.

*No one operational
definition is right for all
research contexts.*

Source: Content for this Case-in-Point was contributed by Steve Wilson, Assistant Professor, School of Social Work, California State University at Long Beach and funded by the John A. Hartford Geriatric Enrichment in Social Work Education project.

answering the research question. The researcher's decision regarding the appropriate approach is based in part on the types of information that the researcher needs in order to answer the research question and also on the researcher's value system concerning the best way to investigate social issues.

Regardless of the particular approach the researcher chooses, however, at the most basic level there are only three ways to measure concepts: (1) ask questions, (2) make observations, and (3) consult existing records. The first two options involve the collection of **primary data,** or new data compiled by the researcher. The third option involves the use of **secondary data,** defined as data that were previously collected for a purpose other than the research at hand. The next section describes in greater detail the research contexts social workers are likely to encounter. It begins by contrasting measurement in qualitative and quantitative research.

Measurement in Qualitative and Quantitative Research

The type of measurement used in social work research is related to the research approach being employed in the study. As discussed in Chapter 1, quantitative and qualitative research are different perspectives, with different assumptions and different methods. Quantitative and qualitative research also approach measurement differently. The major difference is reflected in the quote from *The Little Prince* at the beginning of this chapter. Whereas quantitative research focuses on a limited number of predefined variables that generate primarily numeric data, qualitative research is holistic in its approach, and the data tend to be rich narrative descriptions. The main sources of data for qualitative research are unstructured observation and in-depth interviews. In contrast, researchers using a quantitative approach rely on structured observation, experiments, and survey research.

The interview in qualitative research is different from the interview in quantitative research. Qualitative research makes use of unstructured interviews, although the interview may be guided by a list of topics and subtopics or broad questions. In addition, the questions used in qualitative research do not ask participants to select from a number of predefined responses, as is often the case in quantitative research. Typical questions in qualitative research revolve around how people experience being part of a cultural group or subculture, how they describe or comprehend an experience or an event, and the discovery of regularities and patterns in people's experiences.

Quantitative and qualitative approaches to measurement both have advantages and limitations. As a result, some researchers combine aspects of qualitative measurement in quantitative research, and vice versa. For example, a study of home visitation to prevent child abuse and neglect may incorporate aspects of both quantitative and qualitative measurement. Because it is difficult to find a quantitative measure that captures the nature and quality of the parent-child relationship, the researcher may choose to use qualitative methods such as observations of parent-child interaction and in-depth interviews with the parents. However, the researcher may also collect quantitative data on the research participants from existing records to provide demographic and historical background. An early feminist researcher, for instance, observed female sweatshop workers and their male employers, conducted in-depth interviews, and incorporated statistical data from existing records in her book *Prisoners of Poverty: Women Wage-Workers, Their Trades, and Their Lives* (Campbell, 1883/1970).

In conducting a study, the researcher selects the approach to measurement that will provide the kind of data that will answer the research question. The next section describes three common contexts of measurement used in social work research: survey research, observational research, and research using existing records.

Survey Research

Survey research, which relies on questioning, is a popular method of gathering data in social work research. A **survey** is a systematic way of collecting data from a number of respondents. The survey can be used to determine what respondents know, believe, or feel or how they say they behave. Some surveys ask respondents to describe what they have done or how they felt in the past, whereas others ask respondents to speculate about their future intentions. Every research study that uses a survey as a data-collection method can be included under the umbrella of survey research. In contrast, efforts to sell something or to educate or persuade under the guise of a survey are *not* true forms of survey research, although they may be falsely identified as surveys. What differentiates selling and educating from survey research is that the sole purpose of survey research is to collect data.

 Web Links

Consult www.mhhe.com/ krysik1 for a list of resources on computer-assisted and Web surveys.

The measurement tool used to collect data in survey research, the survey instrument, is identified differently depending on the means of survey administration. A survey that is mailed to potential respondents or that is given in person is called a **self-administered questionnaire.** When interviewers ask survey questions in face-to-face or telephone interviews with respondents, the measurement tool is called an **interview schedule.** Another way of administering an interview schedule is through the use of **computer-assisted telephone interviewing (CATI),** in which the computer asks the questions and records the responses. Web surveys have also become popular in recent years. Chapter 7 discusses Web surveys and presents guidelines on how to choose among the different forms of survey research.

Structured and Semi-Structured Surveys.   The degree of standardization in a survey instrument is reflected by the degree of structure in the questions. Survey research can be characterized on a continuum between structured and semi-structured. In a **structured survey,** the interviewer asks the questions as they are written with the aim of standardizing the administration process as much as possible. The questions included in a structured survey are primarily **closed-ended questions**—they require the respondent to choose from a limited number of predefined responses. Closed-ended questions are useful because they produce uniform responses. Even probing questions such as "Can you please explain what you mean by that?" are scripted in a structured survey.

In a **semi-structured survey,** the interviewer is free to clarify the questions and follow up on the participant's responses. Unlike structured surveys, semi-structured surveys make use of **open-ended questions,** which ask respondents to respond in their own words rather than to select from a number of predefined responses. Open-ended questions are useful when the researcher cannot anticipate all of the answer categories and does not want to limit the responses. Seldom would a researcher administer a semi-structured survey by any

CLOSED-ENDED QUESTION

1. What have you been doing in the past four weeks to find employment?
   a. Checked with public employment agency
   b. Checked with private employment agency
   c. Checked with employer directly
   d. Checked with friends or relatives
   e. Placed or answered ad
   f. Read want ads

PARTIALLY CLOSED-ENDED QUESTION

2. What have you been doing in the past four weeks to find employment?
   a. Checked with public employment agency
   b. Checked with private employment agency
   c. Checked with employer directly
   d. Checked with friends or relatives
   e. Placed or answered ad
   f. Read want ads
   g. Something else, please specify_____

OPEN-ENDED QUESTION

1. What have you been doing in the past four weeks to find employment?

EXHIBIT 6.1

Closed, Partially Closed, and Open-Ended Survey Questions

means other than an interview because of the length of time and writing required in answering the open-ended answers. Exhibit 6.1 presents examples of closed, partially closed, and open-ended questions.

Limitations of Survey Research.   A major drawback of survey research is that individuals are not always honest about what they have done, nor do they always follow through with what they say they intend to do. For example, in a national Gallup Poll survey conducted a little over a week after the December 26, 2004, earthquake and tsunami in the Indian Ocean, 45 percent of respondents indicated that they had contributed money to the relief effort (Moore, 2005a). Four days later in a similar national survey, only 33 percent indicated that they had contributed money when responding to the same question that had been asked only days earlier. How could monetary donations decrease from 45 percent to 33 percent within a matter of days? The 12-point difference between the results of the two surveys was too great to explain by sampling error.

The Gallup Organization offered the following explanation for the difference: at the time of the first national survey, there was such media frenzy over the tsunami that people felt pressured to say that they had done something to help the victims. Researchers refer to the pressure to respond in a certain way regardless of whether the response is true as **social desirability.** Polls on voting behavior, for instance, customarily show the same skewed pattern, with more people reporting that they vote than actually do.

Another problem associated with survey research is recall. Simply stated, people's memories are not always accurate or reliable. This problem is especially acute for questions that either ask for a great deal of specificity or span a broad time period. How many adults, for instance, could accurately report how many newspapers they have read in the past six months? In contrast, most adults probably could accurately recall how many newspapers they have read in the past week.

Web Links

Consult www.mhhe.com/ krysik1 for a list of resources on survey research.

Observational Research

There are two main forms of observational research: pure and participant. In **pure observation,** the observer remains apart from the group, event, or person being observed. For this reason, pure observation is especially appropriate for use with nonverbal populations like infants. It is also useful for studying behavior across contexts, for example, in the classroom and in the schoolyard.

Pure observation tends to be highly structured in the sense that the researcher begins with a limited number of defined behaviors to be observed within a specified time and location. The researcher can observe behaviors in terms of three characteristics: (1) their frequency, defined as how often they occur; (2) their duration, meaning how long they last; or (3) their magnitude, or intensity. As an example, let's use crying as the target behavior. We could measure this behavior by the number of times the individual cried during a defined period, the duration in minutes of each crying spell, or the intensity of the crying. The next chapter examines various methods for recording observational data.

In **participant observation,** the observer becomes actively involved in the research setting. The degree of participation varies with the context of the research. A researcher may live in a housing project for people with mental illness to gain insight into their daily routines. Alternatively, a person may "hang out" on the street corner talking with unemployed men to better understand their lives. Participant observation makes use of interviews. However, in participant observation, the researcher uses interviews to clarify and interpret data rather than simply record the information. Moreover, the interview will vary across participants depending on the topics the participants wish to discuss. Nevertheless, the primary purpose of the interview in both survey and observational research is to collect data.

The advantage of observational research over survey research as a means of data collection is summarized in the saying "actions speak louder than words."

Observation eliminates the need to rely on participants' self-reports of their behavior and intentions. Observational research also avoids the problems of social desirability and recall that can afflict survey research.

At the same time, however, observational research has certain limitations or shortcomings of its own. One significant problem is that what the researcher observes in a specified segment of time is not always an accurate representation of what is typical. In fact, as we saw in Chapter 4, studies have shown that participants often adjust their behavior simply because they know that they are being observed. This problem of reactivity can interfere with accurate measurement. To illustrate by example, a popular measure used in research on parenting programs requires the observer to record within a one-hour home visit the number of times a parent makes eye contact and verbalizes to his or her infant. The problem is that when parents are aware that their parenting behavior is being observed, they may be more attentive than usual to their child.

A second problem associated with observation is **observer inference.** This problem relates to the meaning that the observer attributes to what he or she observes. The way an observer explains or understands a behavior, feeling, or attitude may be different from the way that the person being observed experiences it or would report it.

 Web Links

Consult www.mhhe.com/ krysik1 for a list of resources on observational research.

Existing Records

Paper and electronic documents, databases, and other nondocument artifacts of human behavior are included in **existing records.** Research using nondocument sources of existing records such as the analysis of trash are rare in social work. Existing documents, or secondary data, are valuable sources of information for social work researchers. We could, for instance, use existing records to answer our question about the prevalence of donations to the tsunami relief efforts in the immediate aftermath of the 2004 earthquake. One way of conducting this task would be to examine charitable donations reported on 2004 tax returns. A law introduced in January 2005 allowed taxpayers to claim cash contributions made specifically for the relief of tsunami victims up until the end of January 2005 (Internal Revenue Service, 2005).

Using existing records as a data source for social work research has many advantages. For example, using secondary data can help the researcher avoid the time and expenses involved in collecting primary data. Similarly, it can reduce the data-collection burden on respondents. Finally, some secondary sources such as the U.S. Census Bureau provide access to large samples of the population.

Existing sources of data also have limitations. Perhaps the most serious limitation is that the researcher has to work with whatever data are available, even if they do not include important variables for the study. A further problem is that the data might not be standardized. Consider, for example, a researcher conducting cross-national policy research that involves census data. One

 Web Links

Consult www.mhhe.com/ krysik1 for a list of resources on research with existing records.

problem he or she will encounter is that some countries, such as the United States, collect information on marital status, whereas other countries, such as France, do not. In addition, the number and types of categories used to record marital status vary from country to country. This lack of standardization can cause the researcher to exclude entire countries as well as certain key variables from the analysis. Despite these limitations, existing records are a significant source of data for social work research, and they should not be overlooked.

MEASUREMENT TOOLS

Researchers have developed a variety of measurement tools to help provide the data needed to answer research questions. In some cases—for example, when conducting interviews or observations—the researcher is the tool. In other cases, the researcher uses more standardized instruments and questionnaires. Standardized instruments differ from questionnaires in that they tend to focus on either one concept or a number of related and narrowly defined concepts. For example, the Center for Epidemiologic Studies Depressed Mood Scale (CES-D) measures a single condition, namely, depression. In contrast, the Mental Health Inventory is multidimensional and includes separate subscales on depression, anxiety, positive affect, and feelings of belonging. Although the Mental Health Inventory is broader in scope than the CES-D, the conditions it measures are all closely related and carefully defined. Questionnaires, in contrast, are usually designed to collect data on a number of areas.

The next section focuses on the use of standardized instruments and questionnaires as measuring tools. Researchers can be confident of their findings only if they believe the measuring tools they use accurately measure the variables of concern. Therefore, this section also focuses on the precision of measuring tools and the problems associated with error in measurement.

Standardized Instruments

Web Links

See www.mhhe.com/krysik1 for a list of online sources of standardized instruments and questionnaires.

For many concepts we are interested in measuring, a measurement instrument has already been developed. We call these existing measures **standardized instruments.** Standardized instruments are published and are readily available for use in social work research. They can be either self-administered or administered via an interview. These types of standardized instruments are referred to as *self-report*, because the participant provides the answers. In contrast, other standardized instruments are completed by the researcher while she or he is observing the participant.

Norms and Cutting Scores.   Standardized instruments are also more likely than questionnaires to have developed **norms,** meaning that they often contain

ADVANTAGES

- Standardized instruments are readily available and easy to access.
- The development work has already been done.
- They have established reliability and validity estimates.
- Norms may be available for comparison.
- Most are easy to complete and score.
- In many instances, they are available free of charge.
- They may be available in different languages.
- They specify age range and reading level.
- Time required for administration has been determined.

LIMITATIONS

- The norms may not apply to the target population.
- The language may be difficult.
- The tone might not fit with the philosophy of the program, for example, deficit based versus strength based.
- The target population may not understand the translation.
- The scoring procedure may be overly complex.
- The instrument may not be affordable.
- Special qualifications or training might be required for use.
- The instrument may be too long or time consuming to administer.

EXHIBIT 6.2

Advantages and Limitations of Standardized Instruments

information about how different groups score on the instrument. The usefulness of the norms depends on how accurately the normed population represents the target population. For example, norms are often developed based on college or university populations. These norms might not apply to noncollege populations of a different age or social class. Similarly, norms developed only on men may not apply to women. Researchers also must consider when the norms were established, as they may be outdated.

Some standardized instruments also have **cutting scores,** which measure the difference between two levels of a condition or performance. For example, a cutting score on a depression scale may indicate the level at which clinical depression is likely to occur. Researchers can develop cutting scores by calculating the difference in scores between a normative group and a group that is experiencing the problem. The development of norms and cutting scores is a major advantage of standardized instruments. Overall, as you can see in Exhibit 6.2, standardized instruments have many advantages relative to their limitations. When these instruments are available and are suitable to the research purpose, researchers should use them rather than develop new measures.

How Researchers Use Standardized Instruments.   Standardized instruments measure a particular concept by combining several items. In this context, the term **item** refers to a single indicator of a variable. Items can take numerous forms, such as the answer to a question or an observation of some behavior or characteristic. Standardized instruments use multiple items to avoid the biases inherent in a single item. In Case-in-Point 6.1, for example, we saw that the measurement of elder abuse takes into account multiple items such as bruising, financial responsibility, and cultural expressions of caring, because using only one of these items may not accurately measure the concept.

Social work students interested in developing standardized instruments are advised to pursue coursework in measurement theory, psychometrics, and statistics.

As with other forms of quantitative measurement, standardized instruments are reductionist devices. That is, although a standardized instrument can include multiple items, the researcher tabulates those items to achieve a single score. The way that the researcher tabulates the total score depends on whether the standardized instrument is an index or a scale. An **index** is constructed either by adding the scores assigned to specific responses or by adding the scores and dividing by the total number of responses to calculate an average score. A **scale** differs from an index in that it takes advantage of any intensity structure that might exist among the individual items, for instance, by weighting the responses to the individual items differently. For example, an *index* of depression would have items such as "Feels blue," "Has suicidal thoughts," "Unable to sleep." Each item would be counted as yes or no and given equal weight. The total number of items would indicate the level of depression. In a *scale,* each item might be scored on a 1 to 5 scale, from "Never" to "Almost Always." In addition, some items might be weighted. "Suicidal Thoughts" might be weighted as being three times as important as "Feels Blue."

How Researchers Access Standardized Instruments and Questionnaires.   Questionnaires are often used only for one particular research project, whereas standardized instruments can be used across a number of projects. Fortunately for today's social work researcher, the Internet has made the process of locating standardized instruments much easier than in the past. Researchers can locate many standardized instruments simply by typing keywords into an Internet search engine. In addition, most university libraries have a measurement section, and reference librarians can help researchers locate standardized measures. There are also published questionnaires that can be adopted or adapted for use in survey research. Examples are The American Drug & Alcohol Survey and The American Tobacco Survey. In some instances, scoring and report preparation services are advertised with the sale of questionnaires and standardized instruments.

Despite the availability of standardized instruments, using such a measure can involve more than just locating it and photocopying or retyping it. Some standardized instruments are copyrighted, and users must pay a fee and secure permission. Others are available free of charge when they are used for research but not when they are used for practice or program evaluation.

In some instances, the developers of standardized instruments specify minimum qualifications for the persons who will be administering the instrument. For instance, the qualifications specified to administer the Eyberg Child Behavior Inventory (ECBI) are "a degree in Psychology, Counseling, or a closely related field from an accredited 4-year college or university, plus satisfactory completion of coursework in test interpretation, psychometrics and measurement theory, educational statistics, or a closely related area; or license or certification from an agency that requires appropriate training and experience in the ethical and competent use of psychological tests." In the case of the ECBI, as with many standardized instruments, the qualifications are posted along with the information on purchasing the instrument (Psychological Assessment Resources, Inc., 2005). For some measures, it is difficult to find information on qualifications, permission process, and cost. In these cases, the researcher must search the literature and possibly even contact the developer.

Many instrument developers or publishers will mail or fax sample instruments upon request to a researcher who is considering them for research or evaluation. In some cases, publishers post copies of the instrument on their Web sites. Other instruments must be purchased up front, with a money-back guarantee. The social work researcher must be very clear about the costs of purchasing standardized instruments and questionnaires as well as the applicable refund policies, should they prove to be inappropriate.

Like all measures, standardized instruments have some degree of error. The amount of error depends on how accurate the measure is and how well we apply it. The next section examines the concept of measurement error.

Measurement Error

As discussed at the beginning of the chapter, a measure is not necessarily the same as the attribute being measured. Thus, a bathroom scale may indicate that a person's weight is 140 pounds, but other, more accurate measures may report that the weight is 150 pounds. The difference between the actual attribute and the measurement of the attribute is **measurement error.**

In some research contexts, the amount of measurement error is critical. The consequences of measurement error can be quite obvious in the physical sciences. A classic example is the loss of a Mars orbiter in 1999 that was worth $125 million. The loss occurred because one research team unknowingly was using metric units while another was using the Imperial system.

EXHIBIT 6.3

*Random and
Systematic
Sources of
Error in
Measurement*

MEASUREMENT SITUATION	TYPE OF ERROR
A person has a cold the day she takes a test and does a little worse than she normally would.	Random error—people's health or mood varies randomly.
The reading level of the scale is at ninth grade. Those with a lower reading level cannot understand it and skip many questions.	Systematic error—scores reflect reading level and not the variable being measured.

Measurement error can have critical implications in social work just as it does in the physical sciences. At times, an entire program is canceled as a result of a measurement error that fails to represent actual change in the target problem. Such an error leads to the inaccurate conclusion that the program had little or no effect on the population. Alternatively, a measure may erroneously show a positive effect and thus lend support to an ineffective program. In any case, social workers must attempt to minimize measurement error and maximize their ability to accurately represent what they are attempting to measure.

Measurement error can take two forms: random and nonrandom. **Random errors** are those that are neither consistent nor patterned. For instance, a respondent may misread a question and answer in a way that is contrary to her or his actual intent. Similarly, an observer may lose concentration and fail to record an instance of the target behavior. Random error is the less worrisome kind of error because it has no specific direction. In the best-case scenario, a mistake in one direction will be counterbalanced by a mistake in the opposite direction. For example, an observer who misses one instance of the target behavior might subsequently record two incidents as opposed to the one that actually occurred. The net result of these two mistakes is no measurement error.

In contrast, **nonrandom error,** also called **systematic error,** has a definite pattern. It is therefore the more worrisome source of error for social work researchers. For example, if the majority of respondents misinterpret a question and thus answer in a particular way that does not reflect their experience, systematic error is being introduced. Unlike random errors, systematic errors do not balance out. Rather, they accumulate and bias the research findings. Exhibit 6.3 illustrates the difference between random and systematic sources of error.

To minimize error, we need to be very selective about which measures we adopt. For this reason, we evaluate measures on the basis of validity, reliability, utility, and past performance. The next section examines the evaluation of measures in more detail.

EVALUATING THE QUALITY OF MEASURES

A quality measure is one that consistently and precisely measures what it is supposed to measure. If we measure our weight, we want a scale that is accurate no matter who steps on it. We want it to tell us our weight, not our blood pressure. We want it to be sensitive to changes, for example, if we take off our shoes. We want to trust that it will give us the same reading over and over again, assuming that our weight does not change. Finally, we want to know that it still works that way with the passing of time.

Social workers must consider these same qualities of a good bathroom scale when they are using a standardized instrument for measurement in their research. When deciding whether to adopt a standardized measure for a particular research study, the social worker should consider four characteristics of the instrument: validity, reliability, utility, and past performance. The degree to which the measure actually represents the concept of interest is referred to as its **validity.** Thus, validity exists when the researcher is actually measuring what he or she intends to measure. In contrast, **reliability** is the ability to find consistent results each time the measure is administered. A bathroom scale that measures the same person at 140 pounds at 10:00 a.m. and 150 pounds at 10:02 a.m., under the same circumstances, clearly is not reliable.

Good measures have both validity and reliability. Validity and reliability are not, however, absolutes. A measure can be valid and reliable in one research context and not in another. For example, a depression scale may accurately assess depression for college students in Nebraska but not for Native Americans on a reservation in New Mexico. For this reason, the researcher must also evaluate whether the measure is useful for the particular study in which he or she intends to use it.

Measurement Validity

A thermometer measures temperature. It does not measure weight. Therefore, if we are using a thermometer to measure weight, we are using an instrument that is not valid. A lack of validity represents a source of systematic error in the research study. Validity, however, is not an all-or-nothing proposition; rather, it is a matter of degree. Researchers use four methods to assess an instrument's validity. Two of these methods—face validity and content validity—involve subjective judgments by the researcher. The other two methods—construct validity and criterion-related validity—use empirical assessments of validity.

Face Validity. The first method, known as **face validity,** assesses the extent to which the measure appears to be valid to the people to whom it is being administered. That is, does the instrument appear to measure the concept "at face value"? For example, we would expect a depression scale to contain items about sadness, suicidal thoughts, grief, crying spells, and lack of energy. If the scale included items that asked about our hair color, favorite flavor of ice cream, and feelings regarding cats, it would not make sense on the face of it. Consequently, we would not take this scale seriously as a measure of depression. These negative feelings could affect our willingness to fill out the scale or the ways in which we answer the questions. Some researchers argue that face validity is not a true form of validity because it is concerned only with whether the instrument *appears* to measure what it purports to measure, but it cannot determine whether it is *actually* measuring the concept.

Technicalities aside, face validity is an important consideration in evaluating how a particular culture will respond to a specific measure. For instance, the concept of elder abuse discussed earlier can differ substantially from one culture to another. Items that measure elder abuse in one culture may be interpreted differently in another. These types of cultural differences can affect the respondents' willingness to cooperate, their ability to understand the questions, and the completeness of their responses.

Content Validity. The second method, **content validity,** is concerned with both the choice of the items and the degree to which the measure has captured the entire domain of the concept. Content validity is concerned with *why* the researcher selected the items. The developers of the measuring instrument should provide information about the rationale for their selection of items. The content of the items is often based on theory, reports of practice experience, and experts' judgments. In addition, an instrument should address the full range of a concept. A test of parenting knowledge, for instance, that includes questions related to children's requirements for sleep, nutrition, and stimulation but does not address age-appropriate toileting expectations or social skills would not be considered content valid. Whereas face validity is assessed from the perspective of the respondent, content validity is usually assessed from the perspective of people considered experts in the field.

Construct Validity. The assessment of **construct validity** is based on the way a measure is related to other variables within a system of theoretical relationships. For example, you would expect an individual's level of self-esteem to be related to depression but not to IQ or hair color. Basically, construct validity implies that the developers of standardized instruments form hypotheses regarding how the score on the instrument should relate to other concepts.

Construct validity involves two components: convergent validity and discriminant validity. **Convergent validity** is the degree to which the measure correlates highly with variables theoretically related to it. **Correlation** is a statistical test that provides a measure of the strength of the relationship between two sets of numbers or scores. Researchers use correlation as a means to test convergent validity. Chapter 9 explains correlation in greater detail. For now, it is enough to know that the **correlation coefficient**—the measure of the strength of the correlation—ranges from 0 to 1. The number 1 represents perfect correlation, and 0 represents no relationship. The closer the correlation coefficient is to 1, the stronger the relationship, and the greater the evidence of convergent validity. Thus, to validate the Index of Self-Esteem, a researcher might hypothesize that a respondent's score on this measure will be strongly correlated with a psychiatrist's rating of the client's level of depression.

A closely related concept, **discriminant validity,** is the degree to which the measure does *not* correlate highly with variables that researchers hypothesize to be *unrelated* to it. For instance, the researcher may assume that self-esteem should be only weakly correlated with variables such as age, gender, geographic location, and ethnicity.

One way to assess convergent and discriminant validity is to administer a scale to a sizable group of people, say 100 or more, along with a background questionnaire on age, gender, income, ethnicity, and some other scale that measures a concept that is hypothesized to be correlated with the concept of interest. If the resulting pattern of correlations matches the hypothesized relationships, the instrument has evidence of construct validity. If the pattern deviates from the hypothesized relationships, this is evidence that the instrument may be measuring something other than the concept it was developed to measure. For example, if you were testing a scale to measure depression, you would expect it to correlate highly (the hypothesized relationship) with other standardized measures of depression as well as with a measure of life satisfaction. In addition, you would *not* expect it to correlate highly (hypothesized relationship) with age, gender, ethnic group, or political party preference.

Criterion-Related Validity.   Researchers also use **criterion-related validity,** which assesses a measuring instrument in relation to its ability to predict some external criterion. This method has two forms: predictive and concurrent. **Predictive validity** refers to the ability of the instrument to predict a future state on some external criterion. For example, if a preschool student's score on the Eyberg Child Behavior Inventory (ECBI) can predict academic success in first grade, the ECBI is said to have predictive validity. The external criterion in this example is the record of academic success. **Concurrent validity,** in contrast, refers to the ability of a test to predict an external criterion as it concurrently exists. For example, the concurrent validity of the ECBI could be demonstrated by its ability to predict children's scores on the Perceived Self-Control Scale, another valid measure of child behavior.

Going further, criterion validity also maintains that the measure should be able to discriminate between groups based on the key variables. For example, a measure of depression should be able to discriminate between people who are in treatment for depression and those who are not. This form of criterion validity is referred to as **known groups validity.**

EXHIBIT 6.4	If Reliable, may not be Valid	A bathroom scale gives consistent measures but does not measure accurately.
Relationship between Validity and Reliability	If Reliable, may be Valid	A bathroom scale gives consistent measures and also measures accurately.
	If not Reliable, never Valid	A bathroom scale gives inconsistent measures, so it cannot be accurate.
	If Valid, then always Reliable	If the scale accurately measures your weight, it must be consistent.

Measurement Reliability

As discussed earlier, reliability refers to how consistent the results are each time a measure is administered. In general, a good measuring instrument produces similar results under similar circumstances. In contrast to validity, reliability is concerned with the introduction of random error into a research study. That is, the only time the outcome on a measure should fluctuate is when some real change has occurred in the target concept. For instance, a respondent's score on the Index of Self-Esteem should improve only if his or her self-esteem has actually increased. If there has not been any opportunity for real improvement in the person's self-esteem, the change in the score can be attributed to random error. Exhibit 6.4 illustrates the relationship between validity and reliability.

There are several tests that researchers can use to assess an instrument's reliability. Five basic tests are as follows:

- interrater reliability
- test-retest reliability
- parallel forms reliability
- split-half reliability
- internal consistency

The test that the researcher selects will depend upon the type of measure being considered. We examine the five tests next.

Interrater Reliability. For observational measures or existing records, **interrater reliability** is an appropriate test of reliability. To determine interrater reliability, two observers independently record their observations of the same incident or extract data from an existing record such as a case file. The results of the two observers are then compared for consistency, and a percentage of agreement is calculated. For example, if 10 instances of a behavior are recorded and the two observers agree on 8 of them, the percentage of agreement would be calculated by $8/10 \times 100 = 80\%$. Alternatively, a correlation coefficient could be calculated to measure the relationship between the data produced by the two raters.

Researchers can use the results from a test of interrater reliability to strengthen operational definitions and to formulate guidelines or decision rules to improve reliability. The level of reliability determined to be acceptable will vary depending on the degree of precision desired in the research study. In most cases, an agreement of 80%, or a correlation of approximately .80, would be considered acceptable. Researchers can reassess interrater reliability periodically to ensure that an adequate level is being maintained. A related measure of reliability is **intrarater reliability,** which refers to the extent of agreement of ratings by the same observer at different points in time.

Test-Retest Reliability.   If the measure is a standardized instrument or a survey instrument, **test-retest reliability** can provide a useful assessment of reliability. Test-retest reliability provides information on how consistent a measure is when it is administered twice in a relatively short time frame. The appropriate length for that time frame will vary with both the instrument and the target population. Generally, the time frame needs to be long enough so that the respondent cannot recall specific answers yet short enough to ensure that no real changes occur in the variable being measured. If the scores between the two administrations are similar, the instrument is said to have good test-retest reliability. As with interrater reliability, researchers can calculate a correlation coefficient using the two sets of scores (O_1 and O_2) to represent the degree of consistency between the two administrations.

Parallel Forms Reliability.   For standardized instruments that measure a single construct, the researcher can assess reliability through **parallel forms reliability.** In this test, the researcher correlates the scores from two versions of the same instrument. For example, a measure of mental health, the Mental Health Index, has two forms of psychological distress measures. Version 1 is based on the full battery of questions. To reduce the burden on respondents, the test developers created a new, shorter instrument by selecting a subset of Version 1 items. To assess parallel forms reliability, the researcher would calculate a correlation coefficient to measure the strength of the relationship between the scores on the two versions. Scores of .80 or better are considered to show good parallel forms reliability.

Split-Half Reliability.   A test related to parallel forms reliability, **split-half reliability** is used for standardized instruments that measure a single concept using several items. The instrument assesses split-half reliability by correlating half the items with the other half. Because all of the items measure the same concept, the two halves should correlate highly. Consider, for example, a depression scale that contains 40 items. If all items measure aspects of depression, half of the items should correlate highly with the other half. As with parallel forms reliability, a correlation coefficient of .80 or higher would be expected.

Internal Consistency. Researchers use **internal consistency** as a test of reliability for standardized instruments that either measure a single concept or measure multiple concepts but calculate a score for each concept—also referred to as each subscale—separately. Internal consistency is concerned with the extent to which all of the items included in the index or scale for a single concept hold together, or how consistently the items are scored. In a reliable instrument, all of the items would be expected to correlate with one another because they measure the same concept. Those items that are not scored consistently serve to weaken the instrument. Internal consistency is assessed by the magnitude of a statistic known as Chronbach's coefficient alpha, which measures the average correlation among all of the items. The alpha coefficient, as it is often referred to, is interpreted like a correlation coefficient in that it ranges from 0 to 1, with a 1 being a perfect correlation. An alpha coefficient greater than .80 suggests that all of the items are measuring the same concept.

Measurement Utility

Researchers must select among the many standardized instruments with demonstrated validity and reliability. The first step in making a decision is to be clear about the purpose of the measurement. Is the purpose to measure the current status of a variable (for example, level of assertiveness) or to screen for services based on a cutting score (for example, degree of risk for suicide)? If the purpose is screening, the researcher might require instruments with higher levels of validity and reliability. Moreover, if the researcher intends to use the measure for both screening and determining eligibility, the measure must be able to differentiate as accurately as possible between people who most need the service and people who do not.

In addition, the researcher must consider how long it will take respondents to complete the instrument. Some instruments, such as the Minnesota Multiphasic Personality Inventory-2 (MMPI) (Graham, 2000), can take more than an hour to complete. Others, such as Hudson's WALMYR Assessment Scales (Hudson, 1982), take 5 to 10 minutes. Going further, is the purpose to evaluate practice with a single case, or is it to conduct research on a broader scale? If the former, the researcher should select a measure that is sensitive to small amounts of change in the target problem.

After the researcher identifies the purpose of the measurement, his or her next step is to assess how well the measure fits with the intention of the program. For example, if the program is not designed or funded to increase readiness for preschool, it would be inappropriate to implement a measure of preschool readiness, even if this information would be "interesting." Similarly, self-esteem should not be included in a study simply because a valid and reliable measure of this variable is available. As a general rule, the measures should not drive the program or pull it in a certain philosophical direction. Rather, the program objectives, or the intervention, should drive the selection of measures.

Another question to ask when evaluating utility is Who is the measure for? If the measure will be used with an elderly population, the length and number of questions may be a barrier to completion. Similarly, if the mental status of the target population is in question, a self-report measure may not be the best choice. In addition, the researcher needs to evaluate whether the language on the instrument is appropriate for the target population. For example, some standardized instruments specify a suggested reading level for comprehending the scale. Going further, the language used in some scales is biased toward a certain social class. For example, a test that measures problem-solving ability using subjects such as golf and sailing might be biased against low-income respondents.

Other instruments may have been developed a long time ago or in another country. In such cases, the vocabulary might not be familiar to contemporary respondents. For instance, the item "I feel *downtrodden*" may be difficult for young people to understand because the word *downtrodden* is not commonly used today. Finally, respondents may react to the titles of standardized instruments, especially titles that convey problems or deficits. For example, the Social Emotional Loneliness Scale sounds much more positive when it is referred to by its alternative title, the Goals Scale.

Measurement Performance

After the researcher has assessed the validity, reliability, and utility of the various instruments, the final step in the decision process is to examine the literature to determine how the measure has performed in the past. If researchers have used a standardized instrument, they likely have commented on its benefits and limitations in a published study. It is advisable to use instruments that have shown conclusive results in previous studies. These studies provide some evidence that the instrument is able to make distinctions when it is used to measure the variables of interest to the study. If the literature indicates that the instrument has never or seldom produced any conclusive results, the researcher should be very cautious about adopting it.

Note that when the results of a research study are inconclusive or negative, the recommendation is almost always to change the intervention or to attribute the lack of positive findings to some aspect of the research design.

**ADVANCED
SKILL
DEVELOP-
MENT 6.1**

*Demonstrat-
ing Change
through
Measurement*

Two important distinctions can be made regarding items used in measures to demonstrate change in a target problem. These distinctions also apply in instruments used to predict the risk of an event such as recidivism, or repeated criminal behavior. For example, a study may wish to investigate which factors are useful in preventing recidivism of juveniles currently in detention. In this case, some measures are more useful than others. Researchers use the terms *static* and *dynamic* to refer to items that relate to a changing state versus a non-changing state. **Static measures** are by their nature not amenable to change, whereas **dynamic measures** are amenable to change. For example, "previously arrested" is a static measure, whereas "unemployed within the last 30 days" is a dynamic measure.

In the case of items related to juvenile detention, a measure may be static or dynamic. If a question asks "Has the juvenile ever been detained?" the score on the item for juveniles who have been detained is never going to change. Clearly, once a juvenile has been detained, that fact can never change. This type of item is referred to as a *static indicator.* Static measures are limited in their ability to identify groups with vastly different probabilities of the outcome, in this instance, recidivism. *Dynamic indicators,* in contrast, are able to show change. If the question asks "Has the juvenile been detained in the past 6 months?" the response is allowed to vary with the juvenile's change in status. In a measure designed to predict recidivism, dynamic indicators are more useful than static ones.

A second important distinction in measurement is the difference between trait and state measures. Whereas *static* and *dynamic* refer to the ability to show change, *trait* and *state* refer to measures that are related to personal characteristics, such as temperament and anxiety level. A **trait measure** is concerned with a relatively enduring or stable characteristic, whereas a **state measure** assesses a transitory condition or a condition amenable to change. Indicators such as personality and temperament are considered relatively stable characteristics or traits. In contrast, conditions such as depression and anxiety are considered temporary. When the goal of social work research is to predict risk or to evaluate the effectiveness of an intervention or treatment program, the researcher generally should select dynamic and state measures that are able to reflect change over time.

However, the problem may arise from the lack of sensitivity or accuracy of the measures themselves.

There are many occasions in social work research when a standardized instrument appropriate for gathering data is not available. For example, a research area may be so new that no instrument has yet been developed. Additionally, researchers might need to combine one or more standardized instruments in a larger survey that includes additional questions. In these instances, researchers need to know how to create their own research instruments. The principles of question design and questionnaire construction are essential to this process. Researchers can also use these principles to critique individual items as well as the overall quality of standardized instruments. Before researchers can construct and critique questions, they must understand another fundamental concept: levels of measurement. We turn to this topic next.

PRINCIPLES OF MEASUREMENT DESIGN

There are many occasions that require social workers to construct questions to be administered in an interview or by a self-administered questionnaire. There are also many occasions in which social workers have to evaluate standardized instruments. When these occasions arise, social workers should keep in mind two basic principles of measurement:

- Maximize response rate.
- Minimize the amount of error.

The design as well as the types of questions should all be developed or critiqued with these principles in mind. In an effort to maximize response rate and minimize error, social workers must pay attention both to formulating individual questions and, in the case of self-administered questionnaires and standardized instruments, to designing the layout, or look, of the instrument.

In designing measuring instruments, of primary concern are how the data will be analyzed and which statistical tests, if any, will be used to test the research questions. We discuss the relationship between level of measurement and statistical testing in Chapters 8 and 9. The next sections provide a foundation for those chapters. We examine level of measurement, a concept that researchers must consider before they design specific questions, and then discuss how to design measuring instruments to maximize response rate and minimize error.

Levels of Measurement

Classifying variables according to their level of measurement is important to mastering measurement in social work research. Level of measurement is not only a consideration in minimizing measurement error but also has significant implications for data analysis. In Chapters 8 and 9, we will see that the statistical tests used to analyze data depend to a large extent on the level at which the variables are measured.

Four levels of measurement can be distinguished and are generally presented in the form of a hierarchy. On the bottom of the hierarchy is nominal measurement, followed by ordinal, interval, and ratio measurement. The higher we climb up the hierarchy, the more mathematical functions we can perform with the data.

Nominal measurement classifies observations into mutually exclusive categories. Categories are *mutually exclusive* when each observation belongs to one and only one category. Variables such as gender, ethnicity, religion, and political party affiliation are examples of variables measured at the nominal level. The variable Gender, for example, has two categories, *female* and *male,* which is the minimum number of categories required to measure a variable. These two categories are mutually exclusive because if you belong to one category you cannot possibly belong to the other. We could argue, however, that these categories are not **exhaustive,** another requirement of nominal measurement, meaning that there is an appropriate category for each response. Thus, depending on the nature of the study, the researcher may want to add the category *transgender* to make the categories exhaustive. When the researcher is not able to predetermine all of the categories, she or he has the option of using a category labeled *other* with a write-in line to specify the additional response.

In nominal measurement, the attributes are not numerical categories. The researcher, however, typically assigns a number or a code to each variable value or attribute solely for the purposes of tabulation and statistical testing. Using the variable Gender as an example, the researcher could code all females as 1 and all males as 2. Significantly, the assignment of numbers to the values of nominal variables is purely arbitrary. In other words, the numeric codes associated with female and male have no quantitative meaning; they are simply category labels. Because these numbers have no meaning, when researchers analyze the data from nominal variables, it makes no sense for them to perform mathematical operations such as addition, subtraction, multiplication, and division. Although the computer will perform any mathematical function it is programmed to run, the results will be meaningless.

Ordinal measurement is common in social work and is often used in standardized scales and questionnaires. Variables can be measured at the ordinal level when the attributes of the variable can be rank-ordered from highest to lowest or most to least. Take the question "How satisfied are you with the level of involvement your family had in case planning?" The response categories could be listed as an ordinal variable with numeric codes as follows:

1 = very dissatisfied

2 = dissatisfied

3 = neither satisfied nor dissatisfied

4 = satisfied

5 = very satisfied

As we can see from this example, the categories of ordinal variables have a fixed order. Like nominal variables, the categories must be exhaustive and mutually exclusive. In contrast to nominal variables, however, the numeric codes assigned to the categories of ordinal variables have a quantitative meaning. Keep in mind that these numbers indicate only that one category is greater than or less than another. They cannot measure how much *more* or *less* one category is than another. Thus, in the above example, it does not make sense to claim that a score of 2 represents twice as much satisfaction as a 1, and so forth. The numbers assigned to represent the ordinal categories do not have the numerical properties necessary for arithmetic operations. Another example is education: (1) less than high school degree, (2) high school graduate, (3) some college, (4) college graduate, and (5) postgraduate credit or degree. We cannot say how much more, in terms of education, one category is compared to another. All we can comment on is whether one category is greater than or less than another.

Interval measurement shares the same characteristics as ordinal measurement in that the categories have an inherent order and indicate whether each category is less or greater than the other categories. What separates interval from ordinal measures is that interval measures also have the feature of equal spacing between the categories. Interval scales, however, lack a true zero point. Therefore, the numbers can be added and subtracted but not multiplied or divided.

True interval measures are hard to find in social work. In social work research, indexes and scales that combine the responses to a number of individual items measured at the ordinal level are treated as interval-level measures. For instance, the WALMYR assessment scales that measure concepts such as self-esteem have scores that range from 0 to 100 (WALMYR Publishing Company). A score of 0, however, does not imply a total absence of self-esteem. We cannot conceive of a situation in which there is a true absence of self-esteem. IQ is another interval measure that is commonly used in social work research.

Highest on the measurement hierarchy is **ratio measurement.** On a ratio scale, each number represents a precise amount. Ratio scales also have a true or absolute zero where we can actually conceive of the absence of the attribute. Examples of ratio measures are age in years, years of military service, amount of debt, and number of out-of-home placements. Ratio-level data are suitable for all basic mathematical functions: addition, subtraction, multiplication, and division.

A general rule in measurement is always to measure variables at the highest level of measurement possible. This practice provides the most detailed information possible about the variable. As we will see in Chapter 9, following this rule allows the researcher to conduct more powerful statistical analysis on the data. Keep in mind, too, that researchers can convert ratio-level measures into ordinal categories where appropriate. However, if they collect only ordinal data, they will not have access to the full range of information because they cannot convert ordinal to ratio data. For example, if researchers know that 30 people are between the ages of 18 and 29 (ordinal), they do not know the exact age of each individual (ratio).

Some researchers have a tendency to place data such as age and income that could be measured at the ratio level into ordinal categories. In some cases, this practice is justified. For example, researchers might wish to avoid errors that often occur when they ask respondents to recall an exact number. In other cases, researchers attempt to soften an overly sensitive question that respondents may not answer. For example, many people are reluctant to state their exact income, but they will indicate the range into which it falls. In most cases, though, researchers should keep ratio-level data ratio rather than place it in ordinal categories.

Remember that most variables are never inherently associated with a specific level of measurement. Rather, the way in which we operationally define them determines their level of measurement.

Tips to Maximize Response Rate

First impressions are important to achieving a good response rate. Therefore, at first glance, respondents should perceive the questionnaire or self-administered instrument as professional and inviting. They also must be convinced that completing the questionnaire or interview will not be either time consuming or boring. You can enhance the likelihood of conveying a good first impression by adhering to the following 10 basic design principles.

The Look. Although an effective instrument maximizes the available space, try to avoid creating a cluttered look and using small type. If you are using a standardized instrument that is poorly formatted, you might want to spend time redesigning it. Although the instrument's weight can affect its mailing cost, respondents are less likely to fill out a cluttered instrument with small type. Whenever possible, choose good design over a small cost savings.

The Purpose. One way to boost the response rate is to explain clearly to respondents why you are conducting the research. You can counter respondents' feelings of being put upon by demonstrating that their participation will benefit them or the larger society. Exchange theory suggests that people weigh costs and benefits in making decisions about what to do. Be explicit in addressing "what's in it" for the respondent.

The Guarantee. Assure respondents that the results will be kept confidential and that no services will be withheld or denied even if they choose not to participate. In addition, reassure them that the questionnaire or instrument is not a test and there are no right or wrong answers. Be honest about how long it will take to complete the task and whether any follow-up contact will be required.

Sensitivity.   If you plan to ask potentially sensitive questions, keep them to a minimum, make certain they are relevant, and position them later in the instrument. Also, keep in mind that sensitivity should be evaluated from the respondent's perspective, not yours.

Knowledge.   Avoid asking questions that the target population is not likely to know anything about. This practice is not only demoralizing, but it will discourage participation. For example, do not ask questions about current events if you are not sure that respondents are familiar with them.

Biased Items.   Asking respondents to respond to biased items fits better with political campaigning or sales than with research. Consider, for example, the question "Do you believe that all forms of abortion, the killing of preborn babies, should be illegal?" This question is biased because it defines abortion in a way that clearly is intended to elicit a negative response. The question does not need to include any definition of abortion. A better question would be "Do you believe that all forms of abortion should be illegal?"

Open-Ended Questions.   The major disadvantage to open-ended questions is the burden they place on respondents. In a self-administered questionnaire, respondents may need a lot of time to write and structure their responses. As a result, the responses may be illegible or incomprehensible. In addition, open-ended questions may discourage individuals who feel that they do not write or express themselves well. For these reasons, open-ended questions are most suitable in interviews. However, they should be used judiciously in all quantitative research. As a general rule, you should position closed-ended questions first.

Response Formats.   Two question formats that can help respondents complete the questionnaire or survey quickly and accurately are contingency questions and matrix questions. Use contingency questions to save the respondent time when not all questions may be relevant to all respondents. Contingency questions make the completion of a question contingent upon the response to a prior question. Matrix questions are used to display response categories across a number of questions when these categories are the same. Matrices use space efficiently and can reduce response time. See Exhibit 6.5 for an example of a contingency question and a matrix question.

Question Order.   The order in which you present the questions can affect the success of your research efforts. One valuable rule is to begin with questions that are likely to be interesting and engage the respondent. In addition, try to

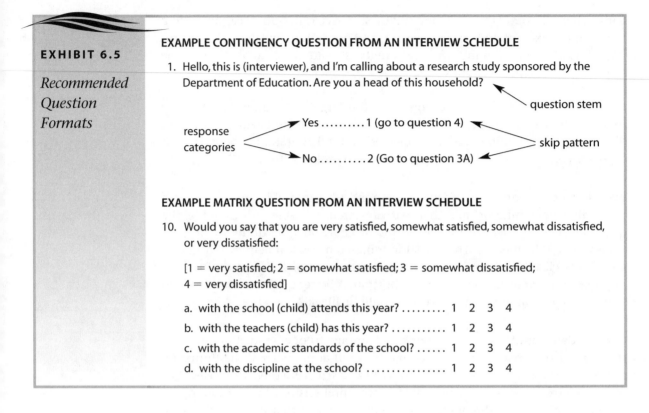

EXHIBIT 6.5

Recommended
Question
Formats

EXAMPLE CONTINGENCY QUESTION FROM AN INTERVIEW SCHEDULE

1. Hello, this is (interviewer), and I'm calling about a research study sponsored by the Department of Education. Are you a head of this household?

question stem

response categories

Yes .... 1 (go to question 4)

No .... 2 (Go to question 3A)

skip pattern

EXAMPLE MATRIX QUESTION FROM AN INTERVIEW SCHEDULE

10. Would you say that you are very satisfied, somewhat satisfied, somewhat dissatisfied, or very dissatisfied:

[1 = very satisfied; 2 = somewhat satisfied; 3 = somewhat dissatisfied; 4 = very dissatisfied]

a. with the school (child) attends this year? 1   2   3   4

b. with the teachers (child) has this year? 1   2   3   4

c. with the academic standards of the school? 1   2   3   4

d. with the discipline at the school? 1   2   3   4

group questions according to content area so that respondents don't have to constantly switch their train of thought. Within each content area, order questions according to their response format. For instance, group questions that are closed-ended together and questions that are open-ended together. To the extent possible, place closed-ended questions with the same response categories together. In self-administered questionnaires, begin with nonthreatening but interesting questions. In most cases, you should collect demographic information at the end to avoid making the survey appear like a routine information-collecting tool. The exception is interview schedules, where you may position demographic questions first to help you select the desired respondents and to establish rapport as quickly as possible.

Transitional Statements.   If a questionnaire is arranged into sections according to content area, you should introduce each section with a short statement that clearly explains its content and purpose. Transitional statements should sound natural and conversational. This transitional statement was part of a survey that sought to learn how nonprofit organizations develop, implement, and use the planning process:

The following items ask you some questions about factors related to your organization, its structure, and its daily functioning. The information you provide will allow us to describe the general character of the organizations represented in this study.

Tips for Minimizing Error

Not only must you get the target population to respond, but you must get them to respond accurately. There is an old saying from computer programming known as GIGO—"garbage in, garbage out." This saying implies that no amount of fancy analysis is going to fix a study that is based on incorrect data. Computers will analyze the data, and researchers will interpret the computer output and write reports. The quality of the research, however, depends on the accuracy of the data. Following are 11 tips that can help you minimize error in the data.

Audience.   Knowing the audience involves understanding respondents in a number of dimensions including language preferences and colloquialisms, age, culture, reading ability, mental status, and availability. Always try to avoid terms that respondents may not be familiar with, and consider if the language you use will be uniformly understood. A general rule is to write at the eighth-grade reading level, but this level may be too high for some populations.

In addition, the age and life circumstances of the respondent group might have implications for the length of the instrument. If mental status or respondent burden is an issue, you might have to use a different form of measurement such as observation. Alternatively, you could choose different respondents who you believe can answer the questions accurately. For instance, in the study of elderly individuals with dementia, it may be preferable to survey caretakers or adult children.

Clarity.   Check the instrument for spelling and grammatical errors that can change the intended meaning of the questions. Use simple language, and avoid abbreviations or slang, because someone is sure not to understand them. Always provide instructions for answering the questions.

Length.   Keeping questions as short as possible increases the likelihood that respondents will read, understand, and complete them. Aim for a maximum of about 20 words per question. At the same time, if you need to shorten questions, make sure not to leave out important information. For example, state explicitly whether the question is referring to past or current behavior.

Position.   Response categories should be positioned vertically underneath the question stem rather than side by side, as illustrated in Exhibit 6.6. Use a different labeling system for the question stem and the response categories.

EXHIBIT 6.6

*Good and
Bad Question
Presentation*

Example of recommended layout and labeling of question stem and response categories:

1. What grade are you currently in? (Please circle the letter corresponding to the correct response.)
   a. 6th grade
   b. 7th grade
   c. 8th grade

Example of poor layout and labeling of question stem and response categories:

1   What grade are you currently in?

  2   6th   2   7th   3   8th

1   What grade are you currently in?

6th _____   7th _____   8th _____

When you use the same labeling system for question stem and response categories, respondents sometimes mistakenly circle the label associated with the question stem. Present the number, symbol, or space for marking the answer to the left of the response categories rather than to the right. Indent the response categories to distinguish them from the question stem. Unless the questionnaire is in a booklet format, avoid using the back of the page, because it might go unnoticed. Make certain to keep every question together on one page.

Precision.   Precision clearly is essential to an effective instrument. As discussed earlier, some researchers sacrifice precision, for example, by moving from a ratio level of measurement to an ordinal level. As a general rule, you should take this step only if you believe that respondents will consider the question to be too sensitive and therefore will not answer it. In a trade-off between precision and response rate, go for response rate.

Detail.   Avoid questions that ask for too much specificity or recall. No question should require respondents to remember excessive detail or specifics from so far in the past that they are not likely to answer with any accuracy. Confine your questions within a reasonable time frame rather than asking global questions ranging over a long time. For instance, if you are interested in literacy activities in the home, asking respondents how many nights they have read to their children in the last month or more could prove difficult to answer. If you ask the same question within the time frame of the past week or less, they are more likely to respond accurately. If your interest is in the longer term, you could follow up with a second question asking whether their response is typical of the number of nights they read to their children on a regular basis.

Double Questions.   Avoid asking **double-barreled questions**—questions that ask respondents to give a single answer to a combination of questions. The following is an example of a double question: "Do you support abortion in the first, second, and third trimesters of pregnancy?" As a general rule, if the word *and* appears in the question, check to see if the item is a double question. The word *or* may also indicate a double-barreled question: "Do you support abortion, or are you a conservative?" If you want the answer to both parts of the question, use two separate questions.

Negative Wording.   Negatively worded items can be confusing and are easy to misread, thus contributing to error in the data. For example, the word *not* in the following question makes the item a negatively worded question: "Should the federal government *not* pay for children's school lunches?" It is easy to miss the word *not* in the question. The best remedy is simply to leave it out and ask "Should the federal government pay for children's school lunches?"

Instructions.   All questionnaires should begin by providing clear instructions for completing the instrument. If the instrument is an interview schedule, you must clarify which instructions should be read to the interviewee and which instructions are for the data collector. You can differentiate instructions by the style or color of type or by the way the instructions are offset.

Translation.   When you wish to translate a questionnaire either from or into a foreign language, if possible, secure the help of a native-language speaker whose background is similar to that of the majority of respondents. For instance, Spanish translations done in New York may differ from Spanish translations done in the Southwest, where the majority of Spanish speakers are from Mexico.

Social Desirability.   In the section on survey research, we discussed social desirability, that is, the tendency to answer sensitive questions based on what we believe we "ought to" do rather than what we actually do. One way to discourage socially desirable answers is to remind respondents that there is no right or wrong answer and that the value of the information depends on their open and honest responses. Social desirability can also occur when the survey attempts to educate respondents, as illustrated in Case-in-Point 6.2. The Case-in-Point also describes how placing questions within a series of related questions can influence respondents' answers.

Conduct Pretest of Measures

The measure that is right for one situation may not be right for another. How do you know if you are using the right measure? The answer is to conduct a

CASE-IN-POINT 6.2

How the Question Can Influence the Response

It is interesting to note how questions targeting the same basic information can produce different answers when they are asked in different ways. This was the case with three public opinion polls asking citizens about their attention to the Terri Schiavo case just before her death on March 31, 2005 (Moore, 2005b). In these polls, the percentage of the U.S. population who claimed they were following the story either *very closely* or *somewhat closely* ranged from 56 percent to 76 percent.

How can three polls taken at about the same time exhibit a difference of 20 percentage points? According to the Gallup Organization, the difference can be attributed to the amount of information the data collectors provided before asking the question. The purpose of polling is often to find out how many people are paying attention to an issue. To accomplish this goal, data collectors use language designed to jog the respondents' memories. The more information the data collectors provide, the more likely respondents are to say that they are paying attention to an issue.

One problem with this approach is that when data collectors provide respondents with information, the respondents are no longer representative of the general public. In addition, the information often influences the ways that respondents answer the question. In the Terri Schiavo case, the more that respondents were "reminded" about the case, the more likely they were to say that they followed it. The prompt may have conveyed the impression that the interviewer *expected* them to follow the case and that a *good and smart person* would be following it.

At times the very process of measurement affects the results.

Responses are also known to vary when questions are asked in a series. In some cases, the order in the series can increase the percentage of respondents who respond positively to the final item. For instance, the Gallup Poll findings on contributions for the relief of victims of the Asian tsunami in December 2004 could have varied because of the way the question about contributing money was asked (Moore, 2005a). In the first survey, the question was the third in a series of three questions that involved (1) praying for the victims, (2) donating supplies or material goods to the relief effort, and (3) contributing money for the relief effort. In contrast, in the second survey, the question was asked on its own. The results may have differed because when the respondents were asked if they prayed for the victims, they remembered that they had donated money during their religious services. In contrast, respondents who were asked only the money question may have forgotten these donations. Alternatively, the series of questions may have made respondents feel uncomfortable about admitting that they had done nothing. Therefore, they answered in a way they felt was more socially desirable.

pretest or pilot test. Chapter 4 discussed the use of pretests in experiments. These pretests assume that the measuring instrument is valid and reliable. Researchers use pretests to measure the level of the dependent variable prior to an intervention or independent variable. In contrast, an **instrument pretest** is a trial run of a measure with a group that is similar to the target population. It is used to assess the suitability of the measuring instrument. Pretests can be administered one-on-one or in a group. In a pretest, the researcher can evaluate how clear the instructions are, how well respondents understand the measure, and how difficult the measure is to complete. Pretests also can help researchers estimate problems with response rate and error. In addition, they can indicate how long it will take to administer the instrument. Pretests can be especially helpful in evaluating how accurately an instrument has been translated.

One technique for conducting pretests is to ask respondents to think out loud, and then you can tape or take notes on their comments, the expressions on their faces, and the speed with which they complete the questions. When you administer a pretest in a group, you can conduct a discussion in which the respondents can interact and respond to the comments of other individuals. In addition, you can analyze pretest data empirically. For instance, you can ask questions that attempt to elicit the same information in different ways and then compare the responses for consistency. This procedure can also help you to assess error in measurement. For example, you could administer three separate standardized instruments that measure depression. If the results of all three are not consistent, you can explore the reasons for the variability.

Some problems disclosed by the pretest can be fixed; others cannot. If the problem relates to an instrument or question developed specifically for the study, such as a poorly worded question, you can simply fix it. However, if the problem stems from a standardized instrument, you may or may not be able to fix it. Some developers of standardized instruments explicitly state as a condition of use that the instrument may not be altered in any way. If a standardized instrument does not perform as it should and there are restrictions on changing it, you might have to drop it completely from the study.

 Web Links

Visit www.mhhe.com/krysik1 for a list of resources for designing and administering surveys.

THE POLITICS OF MEASUREMENT

Despite the emphasis on the mechanics of measurement in this chapter, including the operationalization of variables, reliability and validity, and measurement error, the one thing that is certain is that measurement is not a pristine science. Measurement is greatly affected by the cultural and social contexts as well as the prevailing political climate in which it is constructed and applied, as illustrated in Case-in-Point 6.3. Keep in mind also that measurement has been used in the past to oppress population subgroups. Classic examples of this practice are found in studies of biological determinism that rank people of different races and genders on measures of intelligence. Many of these studies have concluded that women and minority groups are less intelligent than white males. Critics have denounced these works in part due to the studies' inadequate measurement techniques (Gould, 1981).

Data from the U.S. censuses of 1990 and 2000 offer a number of ways of identifying the relationships among individuals within the same household. In both censuses, respondents were asked to specify the relationship of all persons in the household to the householder (designated "head of household") based on five categories: (1) spouse, (2) child or other relative of the householder, (3) housemate/roommate, (4) roomer/boarder, and (5) unmarried partner.

Data on household relationships from the two censuses are not comparable, however, because of a change in the way the Census Bureau processed the data. In 1990, the census procedures did not allow for same-sex spouse combinations to occur. Thus, if a respondent indicated that a spouse was also of the same sex as the householder, the response was flagged as a "mistake," and the value corresponding to *spouse* was changed at random to any one of the other categories. Ten years later, if the respondent identified a same-sex spouse, the response was always changed to *unmarried partner*.

Why did the Census Bureau change the responses of individual respondents? The answer is because the federal government does not recognize same-sex marriages. The two censuses treated the relationship variable differently because at the time that Census 2000 was being prepared, there were several challenges in the courts to laws prohibiting same-sex marriage. The researchers at the Census Bureau realized that, because of the increased attention, more respondents would intentionally identify same-sex spouses on the census questionnaire. Therefore, they decided not to recode the spouse responses at random in the 2000 Census because people clearly had intended to indicate a same-sex preference. Therefore, they changed all "same-sex spouse" responses to *unmarried partner*. For this reason, the 2000 Census constitutes a more accurate count of same-sex couples than does the 1990 Census (U.S. Census Bureau, 2002).

CONCLUSION

The results of a study are only as good as the measures used to obtain the results. Measurement is a representation of the object or phenomenon of concern, and it is not to be confused with the actual object or phenomenon. Thus, choices in measurement must be based on which measures will provide the most accurate representation. Measuring instruments must be well designed with careful thought about the audience and the purpose for which they are intended. In addition, they must show evidence of validity and reliability. The choice of a research instrument is not an absolute; rather, it varies with the research context. No matter how valid and reliable a measure, it is only as good as the extent to which it has utility for the research context and the manner in which it is administered. Social workers must have a clear understanding of measurement both in conducting their own research and in critically assessing the research of others.

Once measuring instruments have been selected or designed, a researcher can begin to collect data. The next chapter on data collection focuses on the development and implementation of a data collection plan.

MAIN POINTS

- Measurement is the process of assigning numbers or other symbols to characteristics or attributes of a concept according to specified rules.

- Two important ways of obtaining data for social work research are asking and observing. Surveys are a popular form of asking and can involve self-administered questionnaires or interviews. A third source of data is existing records. All methods of data collection are subject to benefits and limitations, and the researcher's challenge is to pick the method that is feasible and will be the most accurate.

- Many standardized measures have been developed for use in social work research, and the Internet has made them increasingly accessible. Standardized instruments are often used in conjunction with surveys and sometimes as a means of structuring observation.

- Before choosing a measure or set of measures for a research study, we need to consider measurement validity and reliability. There is little point to conducting expensive data collection and analyses if the data are not valid and reliable.

- Validity is the extent to which the researcher is measuring what she or he intended to measure. There are four different types of validity to consider; two are empirical, and two require subjective judgments. All types of validity are important when assessing the accuracy of a measure.

- Reliability relates to the consistency of a measure in terms of whether all of the items are measuring the same thing in the same way each time. If a measure is reliable, it should produce the same results from one administration to another. There are a number of ways of assessing reliability, and the choice will depend on whether the measure is observation, questionnaire, standardized instrument, or existing record.

- Although it may seem like an easy task, question construction is complicated. The goal is to get the respondent to understand the question in the same way that the researcher intended it, and then to have the researcher understand the response in the same way that the respondent intended it.

- All measures are subject to error. Error may be introduced by chance, or it may be systematic. Social work researchers are most concerned with systematic error, as chance, or random, error can occur in either direction and has a way of balancing out.

- Pretesting measures is an essential step in preparing for measurement. The pretest should be conducted with a small group of respondents who are similar to the target population.

- Measurement involves political decisions as well as methodological decisions.

EXERCISES: PRACTICING SOCIAL WORK

1. Suppose you wanted to conduct a study of student success in the Black Feather community. Write down the steps you would take to measure school success.

2. Write four questions that you could use in your study of student success in the Black Feather community. In developing the questions, demonstrate your understanding of each level of measurement: nominal, ordinal, interval, and ratio.

EXERCISES: SOCIAL WORK LIBRARY

1. Compare and contrast the measurement techniques used in each of the following social work research studies: Drumm, Pittman, & Perry (2003); Beverly (2001); and Olds et al. (2004a).

OTHER EXERCISES

1. Construct questions to gather information on age, income, ethnicity/race, and sexual orientation. For the age and income variables, construct two separate questions to measure each variable at the ordinal and ratio levels. Write questions related to the variables as they would appear on a questionnaire, with question stem, response categories, and instructions for responding.

2. Conduct an Internet search to find how researchers are phrasing questions on ethnicity and sexual orientation. Evaluate different options using the two main principles of measurement: maximizing response rate and minimizing error.

3. Operationalize the term *substance abuse*. How would you take this concept and define it in a way that gives it common meaning and makes it measurable?

CHAPTER 7

Implementation: From Data Collection to Data Entry

D ATA COLLECTION MARKS THE BEGINNING OF THE IMPLEMEN-
tation phase of the research study. Prior to data collection, a lot of time
and thought has gone into identifying the research problem; specifying the research question; anticipating ethical considerations; choosing a research design
that will enable the researcher to answer the question; sampling; and deciding
how to measure the variables. This chapter focuses on implementation of the
research study, up to the point of analyzing the data. Implementation involves
choosing the most appropriate data collection method for the research; developing a data collection protocol; hiring, training, and supervising data collectors; collecting the data; constructing a database; and entering the data into the
database. This chapter pays special attention to two issues: (1) recruiting participants for the research study and (2) retaining participants in long-term
research studies. If researchers fail to anticipate and plan for problems with
participant recruitment and retention, these problems can derail the entire
research study.

   To help you develop your research skills, this chapter will use data from the
Black Feather Youth Survey, a survey of Native American youths that was administered as part of a community needs assessment. The data were collected in
North and South regions of the Black Feather community. Most of the data are
real, and a few variables have been added for illustration purposes. You will find
the data on the CD-ROM that accompanies this book, along with additional
information on the Black Feather project. You will find the survey and the data
files by clicking on Assess, then Community Needs Survey, and selecting the
appropriate file listed. Your CD-ROM has data from the Black Feather Youth
Survey in both Microsoft Excel and SPSS formats. Microsoft Excel is a spreadsheet program that is commonly available and relatively inexpensive. It is part
of the Microsoft package included with most computers. SPSS, short for the Statistical Package for the Social Sciences, is a popular program for analyzing social
science data. Many academic institutions have SPSS available for use by faculty
and students, but many social service agencies and organizations where social
workers are employed do not. Knowing how to enter and analyze data in both

formats is a valuable skill for social workers. We encourage you to work with the data in both Excel and SPSS to expand your skills.

Your academic institution or agency may have a different spreadsheet or statistical analysis software program (such as SNAP, SAS, MINITAB, or STATGRAPHS). Regardless of the program you use, the principles of data entry and analysis discussed in this and the next two chapters will still apply; only the details of using the software will vary. We have found that after we have mastered one spreadsheet or data analysis program, learning additional programs is relatively easy and can be accomplished with the help of a basic manual and sometimes a little help from a friend or technical support staff.

By the end of this chapter, you should be able to:

- Describe the strengths and limitations of different data collection methods based on the research context.

- Write a plan to recruit research participants.

- Write a retention plan to limit attrition in longitudinal research or evaluation.

- Write a data collection protocol that includes a training outline for data collection staff.

- Administer a measurement instrument.

- Create a database in SPSS and/or Microsoft Excel and enter data.

SELECTING A DATA COLLECTION METHOD

The previous chapter presented options in collecting primary data, including survey research, observation, and in-depth interviewing. Obviously, observation and in-depth interviewing need to be conducted in person. Within the broad category of survey research, however, there are a number of data collection options. As a result, a researcher who wishes to conduct a survey must decide which option will best fit the research. How does the researcher decide whether a survey should be self-administered or, alternatively, administered by a trained data collector? If the survey is self-administered, will it be sent by mail or completed in person either individually or in a group? Or will the survey be Web based or sent by e-mail? Alternatively, if the survey is to be administered by a trained data collector, will this individual conduct the survey in person or by telephone? In answering these questions, the researcher must remember the two objectives involved in all data collection tasks: minimize error and maximize response rate.

Previously there was a "known" hierarchy of survey response rates, with in-person administration producing the highest response rate, followed by telephone and then mail surveys (Dillman, 1978). However, extensive work in survey research methods has challenged this belief. In fact, with proper attention to detail, all three survey methods have been shown to yield satisfactory response rates (Dillman, 2000). The challenge then becomes matching the method of survey administration to the research context. This section reviews basic requirements and guidelines for selecting the most appropriate method of survey administration.

Mail Surveys

To conduct a mail survey, a researcher needs a complete mailing list with current and accurate address information. The researcher who selects this method assumes that the target population is reasonably literate and is motivated to complete and return the questionnaire. The major costs involved in a mail survey are printing and mailing. Thus, it is a less expensive method than in-person administration.

Given the amount of junk mail people receive today, one major concern associated with mail surveys is attracting enough attention so that the target group does not throw the survey away or put it aside and forget it. Another concern is that the survey will get lost in the mail.

In a mail survey, the researcher gives up control over which individual in the household or the organization will respond to the survey. Even though the researcher may provide a preference as to who completes the survey—for example, the adult female householder, the CEO, or the director of human resources—he or she cannot be certain that this request will be honored.

Measurement error can also be problematic in mail surveys, as the researcher has no control over respondents' skipping parts of the survey, writing illegibly, marking answers other than those intended, and answering in a socially desirable manner. Exhibit 7.1 summarizes the research conditions that need to be considered when deciding whether the research is best suited to mail surveys.

Telephone Surveys

In order for a researcher to use a telephone survey, the potential research participants must have access to telephones, and the researcher must have access to a list of current telephone numbers. If the survey is targeted to the general public and the researcher does not have access to telephone numbers, he or she can generate the numbers using some form of **random digit dialing** in which the researcher selects a geographic area and then uses computers to generate phone numbers randomly using the area code and/or first three digits of a telephone number. Telephone surveys do not require a certain level of literacy in the respondent population as do mail surveys, and they are better suited than mail surveys to less-motivated populations. Telephone surveys are also suitable for youth respondents, whereas mail surveys are not. Telephone surveys can be

EXHIBIT 7.1

Guidelines for When to Use a Mail Survey

Respondent characteristics	• Highly literate adult respondents with mailing addresses.
	• Motivated to respond thoroughly with attention to detail.
	• Suited to covering large geographic areas.
Survey questions and presentation	• Closed-ended questions that are simple and require no explanation, pretested on a similar population.
	• Attention to formatting and wording required.
	• Questionnaire short to moderate in length to minimize response burden and encourage motivation.
Resource requirements	• Accurate and complete mailing list.
	• Incentives provided in anticipation of response can improve response rates. Incentives are most commonly used when the survey is targeted to the general public or consumers of a service.
	• Cost of printing and mailing the questionnaire, follow-up requests, and return postage.
Skill requirements	• Design of the questionnaire.
	• Implementation of follow-up, including design of the follow-up, number of mailings, and response cards.
Examples of target groups	Alumni of a university, staff of organizations and agencies, professionals, consumers of a service.

used to administer open-ended questions as well as questions with complicated skip patterns. Closed-ended and partially open-ended questions should be kept simple in a telephone survey so that the respondent does not have to remember too many response options in order to provide an answer.

Unfortunately, the use of the telephone for administering surveys precludes the use of any visual aids that can help the participant to respond. If the participant has difficulty understanding a question, the data collector can repeat the question, offer clarification, and use prompts to encourage a response. Some researchers do not allow any prompts. Others do, although they prefer to standardize them for uniformity across administrations.

In a telephone survey, the researcher has greater control over which member of the household responds than in a mail survey. The researcher can also maintain greater control over the order in which the questions will be answered and the way in which the answers will be recorded. If the interviews are conducted in a room with several telephones, such as a call center, they can be

Respondent characteristics	<ul><li>Any level of literacy, youth and adult. Must be able to concentrate and maintain focus.</li><li>Must have access to a telephone and be able to hear well and communicate orally.</li><li>Initial motivation to respond need not be as high as in a mail survey.</li><li>The researcher cannot provide immediate incentives.</li><li>Suitable for large geographic areas.</li></ul>	**EXHIBIT 7.2** *Guidelines for When to Use a Telephone Survey*
Survey questions and presentation	<ul><li>Suitable for simple closed-ended (not too many categories to choose from), partially closed, and open-ended questions.</li><li>The researcher can use prompts and clarification.</li><li>Skip patterns can be used.</li><li>Less attention to formatting, design, and quality of paper.</li><li>Can be administered electronically without paper copies.</li><li>Length of the survey will depend on the characteristics of the population surveyed.</li><li>Surveys can be longer than those administered by mail.</li></ul>	
Resource requirements	<ul><li>Telephone costs if long-distance calling involved.</li><li>Possibly data collection staff, training for data collectors.</li><li>The researcher must have access to telephone numbers or be able to generate telephone numbers.</li><li>Possibly supervision and support for data collection staff.</li></ul>	
Skill requirements	<ul><li>Excellent verbal interviewing skills.</li><li>Ability to record answers accurately and quickly.</li></ul>	
Examples of target groups	Alumni of a university, staff of organizations and agencies, professionals, consumers of a service, youth, general public.	

monitored, and a supervisor can be present to provide oversight and answer questions as they arise. The major cost in a telephone survey is the cost of data collection. Telephone surveys are the most efficient data collection method in terms of producing data quickly, although that may change with the advent of Internet surveys. Exhibit 7.2 summarizes the research conditions appropriate for telephone surveys.

In-Person Surveys

In an in-person or face-to-face survey, the data collector meets with the participants, either in a group or individually. An in-person survey can be self-administered in the sense that the participant completes the questionnaire while the data collector is present. Alternatively, the survey can be administered as a structured interview in which the data collector reads the questions to the participant and then records the participant's answers. Whether the survey is self-administered or conducted as a structured interview will depend on the nature of the questions and the characteristics of the participant group. For instance, open-ended questions, skip patterns, and questions requiring prompts are best suited to a structured interview. A structured interview is also preferred over self-administration if the researcher (a) requires greater control and (b) is not confident of the participants' levels of literacy or motivation.

In-person survey administration is the preferred choice when the motivation to complete and return a mail survey may be low. Moreover, in-person administration provides the researcher with access to populations that do not have telephones, computers, and mailing addresses or postal boxes. In-person surveys are the preferred method when the respondents are either very young (pre-telephone age) or of advanced age. They are also recommended when respondents have certain disabilities related to hearing and mobility that would deter them from participating by telephone or in writing. Finally, in-person surveys are the most appropriate method for studies that deal with sensitive information such as grief and loss, violence, and illegal and deviant behavior. There is some question, however, as to the most effective method of survey administration for encouraging self-disclosure of sensitive, potentially embarrassing information and discouraging socially desirable responses.

The effectiveness of in-person surveys for collecting sensitive information is demonstrated in the motion picture Kinsey, *based on the true story of sex researcher Alfred Kinsey in the 1950s and 1960s. This film depicts the importance of using trained and skilled data collectors to elicit sensitive information.*

Of all the data collection methods associated with survey research, in-person surveys require the highest skill levels. Unlike the telephone survey, in which only what is said is important, in in-person data collection, the entire demeanor, appearance, and body language of the data collector are important. In-person administration can also be the most expensive method of data collection because it involves both travel and transportation costs. It is also the most time consuming of all data collection methods. Exhibit 7.3 summarizes the research conditions conducive to in-person survey administration.

Internet Surveys

The use of the Internet as a data collection tool is a relatively recent development. As computer literacy has increased and computer technology has evolved and become more affordable, the use of the Internet as a vehicle of survey administration has expanded dramatically. The flow of communication in an Internet survey is from computer to computer. By using the Internet, the

Respondent characteristics	• Appropriate when literacy and motivation are questionable. If incentives are important to motivate participation, they can be provided immediately.
	• Suitable for all age groups.
	• Accommodates disabilities such as hearing and concentration as well as some physical disabilities that would prevent writing or talking on the telephone.
	• Allows the greatest control over who answers the questions and control over administration of the survey, including question order and recording responses.
	• Most feasible with small sample sizes and when respondents are located in a relatively small geographic area.
Survey questions and presentation	• Appropriate for closed-ended, partially closed, and open-ended questions.
	• Appropriate for long surveys; response burden not as much of a concern as with the other methods.
	• The ability to use visual aids allows for the inclusion of complex questions.
	• Can include observational questions.
	• Appropriate for asking sensitive information.
	• Formatting and presentation not as important, unless the participant will be given a copy of the interview schedule.
Resource requirements	• Transportation.
	• Training, paying, and supervising data collection staff.
	• Incentives if applicable.
	• Formatting and printing of questionnaires.
Skill requirements	• Excellent interviewing skills and attending behavior; attention to speed and accuracy in recording data.
	• Appearance and attire are added considerations and must be appropriate for the target population.
	• Attention to safety while interviewing.
Examples of target groups	Incarcerated populations, homeless individuals, children and youths, elderly and disabled, and parents of preschool children.

EXHIBIT 7.3

Guidelines for When to Use an In-Person Survey

researcher can avoid the mailing and transportation costs associated with mail and in-person survey administration. Similarly, the researcher can avoid the labor costs associated with telephone and in-person interviews. Internet surveys have the potential to provide data quickly and cheaply. The major disadvantage—albeit one that is likely to lessen over time—is access. Many nonprofessionals still do not know how to use a computer, others do not have access to a computer outside of work, and not everyone with a computer has access to the Internet. All three of these aspects—knowledge, access, and Internet connectivity—are required of the participant in an Internet survey.

There are two types of Internet surveys: Web and e-mail. Web surveys have several advantages over e-mail surveys, one of which is presentation. Web surveys can employ color, graphics, audio, video, and other interactive features as well as automatic skip patterns, scoring, and response features. E-mail surveys, in contrast, are basically text messages that are either included in an e-mail message or attached to it as a separate word processing or spreadsheet document. Another advantage of Web surveys over e-mail is the simplified submittal process. The respondent need only left-click the mouse on the Submit Survey icon, and the survey is delivered. In contrast, e-mail surveys do not always make it back to the intended destination, either because they are returned to the wrong e-mail address or are not sent at all, or there is a problem in the delivery.

Web Links

For more information on Web surveys, visit Web Surveyor and SurveyMonkey, which can be accessed through www.mhhe.com/krysik1.

Although e-mail surveys do not require a great deal of skill or cost to design and distribute, Web surveys require researchers to be technologically savvy or to include discretionary funds in the research budget to hire a Web designer. Recently, the development of survey Web sites, such as Web Surveyor and SurveyMonkey, has greatly simplified the Web survey process. One issue the researcher will have to deal with in an Internet survey is getting through devices that are set up to block spam and being recognized as legitimate before being sent to the trash folder. Many legitimate communications are blocked because they are mistakenly identified as spam.

The Social Work Library

A valuable resource for designing and implementing Internet surveys is Dillman (2000).

Three key factors affect the respondent's ability to view Web surveys as intended by the researcher: (1) the respondent's computer operating system, (2) the speed and type of the respondent's Internet connection, and (3) the respondent's degree of computer literacy. Tracking survey response and conducting follow-up requests is much easier with e-mail than with Web surveys. Tracking has to be built into the design of Web surveys; otherwise, it is impossible to know who has responded and where to focus follow-up efforts. Exhibit 7.4 presents a summary of the research conditions suitable for Internet surveys.

Nonresponse in Survey Research

Regardless of the method of survey administration selected, all researchers need to concern themselves with nonresponse. Nonresponse, which we considered in Chapter 5, can be a particular problem when it follows a certain

Respondent characteristics	• Professionals in businesses, organizations, and government departments where computer use is expected and access is assured.	**EXHIBIT 7.4**
	• Inability to provide advance incentives to increase motivation.	*Guidelines for When to Use an Internet Survey*
Survey questions and presentation	• Closed-ended questions, attention to formatting and wording.	
	• Short to moderate in length to minimize response burden.	
Resource requirements	• Web survey design requires specialized knowledge and time spent in development, but once developed, both Web and e-mail surveys are low cost.	
Skill requirements	• Design of the survey.	
	• Implementation and follow-up.	
Examples of target groups	Staff of organizations, agencies, government departments, and universities, members of professional organizations.	

pattern that introduces bias into the study. This type of bias, called **nonresponse error,** occurs when the nonrespondents share certain characteristics that differentiate them from the respondents. For example, the respondent group may include a higher percentage of participants who have more free time to fill out the survey because they are retired, unemployed, or do not have children.

There is no consensus among researchers as to what constitutes a satisfactory response rate. This is because the relationship between response rate and nonresponse error varies. In some surveys, it may be possible to have only a 50 percent response rate and yet very little response error. In contrast, it is possible to have a very high response rate (for example, 80 percent) and substantial nonresponse error. A low response rate does not necessarily lead to nonresponse error, just as a high response rate cannot always eliminate or avoid nonresponse error. Rather, the size of the nonresponse error depends on how well the respondents reflect the total population of those surveyed and the variability within that population.

Opinion polls illustrate this phenomenon. For example, if the proportion of voters in the population who favor one candidate over another is very uneven, say 80 percent in favor of Candidate A compared to 20 percent in favor of Candidate B, then a response rate of 50 percent will not be problematic in terms of accurately predicting the winner. In this instance, a prediction can be made fairly accurately based on a moderate rate of response. In contrast, if the split in the population is fairly even—for example, 48 percent in favor of voting for Candidate A and 52 percent in favor of voting for Candidate B—then a high response rate will be critical to reducing nonresponse error and accurately predicting the outcome. The size of the nonresponse error is a function of both (1) the response rate and (2) the extent to which respondents differ from nonrespondents. Thus, in addition to reporting the response rate, researchers should compare respondents with nonrespondents on variables that might reasonably impact the dependent variable. In studying community members' attitudes about developing additional group homes for people with mental illness, for example, the researcher needs to know whether homeowners are equally represented among responders and nonresponders because homeowners often oppose group homes based on the fear that their property values will decrease. The procedure for calculating response rate is outlined in Advanced Skill Development 7.1.

Focus Group Interviews

Focus group interviews have become a popular method of data collection in recent years. We in the social sciences have adopted them from our colleagues in business and marketing. **Focus groups** typically involve a skilled moderator who interviews about 5 to 10 people in an environment that is conducive to sharing information. Focus groups are often easier to facilitate than other in-person methods of data collection such as structured and unstructured interviews because they are limited in time and in the number of questions that the interviewer can ask. Moreover, they do not require the same level of intense attending behavior—for example, expressions of attention and interest, verbal encouragers, and follow-up questions—as an in-depth interview or an in-person survey. They can also be enjoyable in that people typically take pleasure in sharing ideas in a nonthreatening and nonjudgmental environment. Researchers generally repeat focus groups with different groupings so they can identify trends and patterns in the responses.

Although the moderator has a great deal of flexibility in asking follow-up questions and providing clarification and prompts in the focus group, the actual interview questions are carefully predetermined. The majority of the questions are open ended. The questions are arranged in a logical sequence that contributes to the flow of discussion by beginning with the more general and proceeding to the specific. Due to the limited amount of time, the number of participants, and the open-ended nature of the questions, the number of predetermined questions is usually restricted to about 7 to 12. The number of questions will also depend on the time allotted for the group. The interview questions

ADVANCED
SKILL
DEVELOP-
MENT 7.1

*Calculating
Response
Rates*

A useful lesson in survey research is how to calculate response rates. It would seem logical to calculate a response rate by taking the total number of complete responses divided by the total number of possible respondents (the number of sampling units included on the sampling frame) and then multiplying by 100 to arrive at the overall response rate. For example, if you mailed 300 surveys and 240 were returned to you, your response rate is $240/300 \times 100 = 80\%$.

This method can, however, substantially inflate the rate of nonresponse. When calculating response rate, first subtract the number of nonresponse units from the total number of units in the sampling frame. **Nonresponse units** are those sampling units that could not possibly have responded because, for all practical purposes, they do not exist. For example, when the sampling units are households, nonresponse units would include vacant households and addresses without housing units, such as empty lots. In a telephone survey of households, nonresponse units would include out-of-service telephone numbers and business telephone numbers mistakenly included as residential.

Nonrespondents—those people who are legitimately counted in the calculation of nonresponse—include people who (a) refuse to participate; (b) terminate their participation partway into the survey (the definition of *complete* should be defined by the researcher); (c) cannot be contacted because they are not home when they are called or do not answer or send back the survey; (d) are unavailable due to death that occurred after the survey start date; and (e) are unavailable due to physical or mental inability, language problems, and miscellaneous other reasons. People unable to be verified as either nonrespondents or nonresponse units are also counted in the calculation of response rate. Reducing the total number of sampling units by subtracting the number of nonresponse units can significantly increase the response rate.

Here is the equation for calculating response rate:

$$\frac{\text{Number of complete responses}}{(\text{Number of sampling units} - \text{Number of nonresponse units})} \times 100$$

To illustrate the use of this equation, take the example of 300 surveys. The following are nonresponse units:

- 34 returned, not at this address and no forwarding address
- 5 deceased prior to survey date

Calculation of the response rate would then be $240/(300 - 39) = 240/261 \times 100 = 92\%$. A report of survey research should always include a statement of the response rate as well as a description of how it was calculated and the decision rules that were made.

can deal with feelings, attitudes, experiences, and knowledge. See Exhibit 7.5 for a sample of focus group questions that were used as part of a community needs assessment. The focus group was conducted with single adults who were homeless.

Like all social work interviews, the focus group interview should have a beginning, a middle, and an end, with transitions throughout. The beginning

EXHIBIT 7.5

Sample Focus Group Questions Used for a Community Needs Assessment

Introduction

Where is everyone from?

How long have you been in Greencourt?

1. What brought you to Greencourt?
2. What is life like for a person who is homeless in Greencourt? (Can you compare it to homeless life in other places?)
3. What are the major challenges you face on a day-to-day basis? What is keeping you homeless?
4. Where do you go to get help with the challenges you face?
5. Do you have any needs that are not being met? (Prioritize your three top needs.)
6. Do you think anyone should be doing something to address these needs? If yes, who (what organization or agency)?
7. What advice would you have for any agencies, organizations, or other groups trying to address the unmet needs of homeless individuals/families in Greencourt? What would a service have to look like in order for you to use it?

The Social Work Library

An excellent resource to guide the planning and implementation of focus groups and the analysis of focus group data is Krueger and Casey (2000).

serves to introduce the research study and the reason for requesting participation in the focus group. The middle is where the discussion around the focus group questions is facilitated. Transitional statements help participants shift from one line of questioning to another throughout the discussion. The end of the focus group provides a transition from the questioning to closure. For instance, the end would summarize the discussion and thank participants for their time. It would also inform participants of any opportunities for follow-up and how to access information from the research once it is complete.

Researchers select focus group participants who they believe can provide the type of information they are seeking. Thus, depending on the issue, researchers might focus on the participant's age, gender, position, occupation, interests, common experience, and so on. Overall, focus groups are a relatively cheap and quick method of collecting data, especially if the travel is limited. However, like any method of collecting data, if they are not well conceptualized and managed, they are a waste of time and resources. The most important consideration in deciding whether a focus group is the right data collection method for the research is the type of research question being considered. Whereas in-depth interviews, observations, and surveys can be used to answer exploratory, descriptive, and explanatory research questions, focus groups generally are limited to answering exploratory questions. Exhibit 7.6 summarizes the conditions for selecting the focus group interview as a method of data collection. In addition, the Web site for this book provides some useful tips on conducting focus groups.

Respondent characteristics	• Suitable for hard-to-reach populations, from school age onward.	**EXHIBIT 7.6** *Guidelines for When to Use a Focus Group*
	• Difficult if participant mobility is a problem and with disabilities that limit successful group participation.	
	• Possible to encourage participation through incentives.	
Survey questions and presentation	• Limited number of open-ended, carefully sequenced questions; few closed-ended questions to provide information on demographics and context.	
	• Not suitable for sensitive information considered too personal to share in a group context.	
	• Length will depend on the target group, but the interview generally lasts from one to two hours.	
	• Best suited to exploratory research questions.	
Resource requirements	• Comfortable space.	
	• Recording method (field notes, audio recording, flip charts, observation) may require transcript preparation.	
	• Incentives (monetary or otherwise).	
	• Other resources needed to secure participation such as transportation, child care, and food.	
Skill requirements	• Skilled facilitator with interviewing and group skills.	
	• Organizational skills to invite participants and arrange space.	
	• Attention to appearance and attending behavior.	
Examples of target groups	Resident subgroups of a community, consumers of a service, employees, members of a professional group, volunteers.	

Selecting among the Options

In some instances, the choice of a data collection method may be self-evident. For instance, if the purpose of the research is to evaluate a school-based abstinence education program, it makes sense to administer the survey in an in-person, self-administered, group format both before and at the end of the curriculum. Mailing surveys to students' homes or trying to contact them by telephone would only increase the cost of the research and would contribute to non-response error.

In contrast, a lengthy survey involving several open-ended questions would probably be best administered in person in a structured individual interview

**CASE-IN-
POINT 7.1**

*The NASW
Sampling
Frame: How
Would You
Like It
Served?*

For a price, individuals can rent the NASW membership list to use as a sampling frame. The purchaser must agree to one-time use per rental. This means that the list cannot be used over and over again but is restricted to the one-time, agreed-upon use. The materials that the researcher will send to the membership—for example, a self-administered questionnaire—must be submitted to and approved by the NASW before the researcher receives the list. The researcher can select from the entire list of approximately 153,000 members or a portion of the list. The cost to the researcher is calculated per 1,000 names. If the researcher elects, she or he may purchase additional membership information, including gender, income, age, work setting, member type, practice, function, work focus, years of experience, and ethnicity. Each additional variable is available at a set cost per 1,000 names.

format, unless the target participants are spread across an expansive geographic area, in which case a telephone survey would work best. Finally, a large national survey of professionals is probably best carried out using a combination of methods, including the Internet and regular mail. Conducting the first round of the survey using the Internet would significantly reduce printing and mailing costs. The researcher could then follow up using regular mail and even telephone surveys.

The decision of what data collection method to use should always involve answering the following two questions in this order:

1. Which method would most minimize measurement error?

2. Which method would yield the best response rate?

The decision about which method to use will be based to a large degree on feasibility. For example, if the budget does not include funds for travel or for hiring data collection staff, in-person data collection may not be feasible. As another example, if the time frame is short, a telephone or Internet survey may be a better alternative than a mail survey. Alternatively, the research study may be (a) scaled back to include a smaller sample; (b) restricted in terms of geographic area; or (c) shortened to include fewer questions, fewer focus groups, or fewer follow-up points. In some instances, the researcher might target a different group of respondents in order to fit the research with the budget. For example, instead of surveying children by using in-person individual interviews, the researcher might decide to survey parents by mail or interview teachers in a focus group. In some instances, the researcher might have to modify the research question. Case-in-Point 7.1 discusses access to a large sampling frame of professional social workers.

RECRUITING RESEARCH PARTICIPANTS

As discussed in Chapter 2, in order for the research to be considered ethical, participation must be a voluntary and informed activity. This fact does not prohibit researchers from taking reasonable steps to convince people to participate. The challenge for the researcher is to motivate respondents to comply without being coercive. Failure to achieve broad participation can result in a major source of error due to nonresponse. Further, it can lead to delays in starting the research study, and, in some cases, it can cause an entire study or evaluation to be canceled. Researchers will be well served by developing a recruitment strategy before the research begins. The next section identifies six strategies that can be used in the development of such a plan.

Cialdini's Six Recruitment Strategies

One way to encourage broad participation is to use Robert Cialdini's (1993) theory of "how to influence participation in survey research." Cialdini, an experimental social psychologist, describes six major tactics that researchers can use to encourage people to participate in survey research. Each tactic is governed by a fundamental psychological principle that directs human behavior.

According to Cialdini, technological advances in modern society have led to changes in the ways that people make decisions. The fast pace of modern life and the abundance of available information lead people to adopt a shortcut approach to decision making. Instead of rationally weighing the pros and cons of each decision, people often make decisions quickly on the basis of a single piece of information called a *trigger,* which, as the word implies, is something that leads people to choose one response over another. Cialdini claims that people make all kinds of decisions on the basis of triggers: decisions to give, to buy, to believe, and even to participate in research. He predicts that the tendency toward shortcut decision making will only increase in the future, thereby escalating the importance of understanding and using triggers in recruiting participants. The following sections present a discussion of each principle on which the six decision-making triggers are based: (1) reciprocity, (2) commitment and consistency, (3) social proof, (4) liking, (5) authority, and (6) scarcity. The six principles and their implications for the recruitment of research participants are summarized in Exhibit 7.7.

Reciprocity. Cialdini asserts that one of the most widespread and basic norms of human culture is embodied in the principle of reciprocity. The *principle of reciprocity* implies that we should try to repay in some form what another person has provided to us. People who take and make no effort to give in return are generally viewed negatively. For this reason, people go to enormous lengths to

EXHIBIT 7.7

Summary of Theory-Based Implications for Improving Recruitment

PRINCIPLE	IMPLICATIONS
1. Reciprocity	Providing an incentive, even of token value, at first contact and before a request to participate can improve compliance.
2. Commitment and consistency	Inducing an initial commitment and a reflection of self with a desired characteristic can be an effective means of gaining compliance with a further request that will be viewed as consistent with the former commitment. Once this new identity is established, future behavior is likely to be consistent even in the absence of a reward.
3. Social proof	Individuals who view others performing a behavior, especially if the other is perceived as similar, are more likely to follow suit. This principle does not generalize to situations in which the content might be considered too personal or embarrassing to be addressed in a group context.
4. Liking	Compliance is more apt to be obtained if the participant likes the requestor. Factors that influence liking are physical attractiveness, perceived similarity to the requestor, familiarity, and association with the positive. Number of contacts can increase familiarity. Praise and compliments act as positive reinforcement and can also increase liking.
5. Authority	There is strong pressure to comply with the request or endorsement of an authority figure.
6. Scarcity	Advertising in terms of a limited number of spaces and using a deadline tactic for enrollment can facilitate the impression of scarcity and value and can positively influence the desire to participate.

avoid being viewed this way. Undoubtedly, you have witnessed this principle in operation. Examples are supermarkets that give free samples to consumers to encourage them to buy, real estate agents who leave magnets on the door in the hope of gaining clients, and organizations that send pennies and address labels in the mail to encourage compliance with a request to donate.

Why do we see these types of examples with ever-increasing frequency? The answer to that question is simply "Because it works." This principle is so effective that it even works when the gift has little to no value to the recipient. This is good news for the social work researcher, who can use this principle to encourage participation in research on even the slimmest of research budgets.

According to Cialdini, this trigger is so effective it can overwhelm the influence of the other five principles. The strength of the reciprocity principle is evident in a study of 4,781 women recruited for a three-year longitudinal study on genital herpes (Young & Dombrowski, 1990). The majority of women recruited in all five sites reportedly stated that their participation was "out of gratitude for previous services they had received at the clinic." In all five sites, patients who had previously received family planning services were more likely than new patients to agree to participate in the study.

Don Dillman, a leading authority on survey research, favors providing advance incentives to increase response rates. Dillman's research has shown that small incentives, monetary or nonmonetary, provided with a request to participate in a survey are even more effective than the promise of larger incentives that are contingent on participation. Incentives, for example, could include a one-dollar bill, gift certificates, and drawings for a cell phone, cash prize, or DVD player.

Commitment and Consistency. This principle refers to the desire in most people to think and act in a steady or similar manner across different situations (Cialdini, 1993). Inconsistency is generally considered an undesirable trait, hypocritical at least, and at worst a sign of mental confusion. In recent political discourse, the term *flip-flopper* has emerged as a derogatory label for someone accused of being inconsistent. To apply the principle of commitment and consistency to research, the researcher begins recruitment by encouraging potential participants to make a small commitment that is consistent with a behavior that she or he will later request of them. Consider, for example, a study focused on a campaign to recruit blood donors. The study found that making a small initial request for permission simply to add a person's name to a list of potential blood donors and then calling the person 7 to 10 days later to discuss making a donation was a more effective means of recruitment than a straightforward request to donate (Hayes, Dwyer, Greenwalt, & Coe, 1984).

Significantly, not all commitments are equally effective at inducing compliance. Commitments generally are most effective when they are (1) active, such as signing an agreement to be contacted or to receive more information; (2) made in the public eye; and (3) viewed as internally motivated (Cialdini, 1993). This last point requires further explanation. For an example we will use a campaign to encourage people to join a bone-marrow registry, a list of volunteers ready and willing to donate bone marrow if identified as a match with someone in need. A follow-up study revealed that 13 percent of donors who were sent a letter praising them for being donors along with a questionnaire on their extent of altruism, commitments, and social support subsequently joined the registry. In contrast, only 6 percent of one control group who received only a brochure on the registry and 6 percent of a second control group who received a brochure with a letter asking them to join the registry actually joined.

The letter sent to the experimental group was designed to influence and reinforce their self-perception as donors, and the questionnaire was sent to actively reinforce that perception (Sarason et al., 1993).

The implications of this principle for recruitment to participate in a research study are (1) to create or build on an identity that is consistent with the request that will later be made to participate in research, and (2) to attempt a smaller, easier-to-achieve commitment before asking for a larger commitment that is consistent with the actions of the first commitment. For instance, in recruiting for a study on preventing child abuse and neglect, instead of asking mothers to sign up in the hospital after the birth of a child, the recruiter could acknowledge to the new parents that generally all mothers and fathers desire to be the best parents they can be (establishing an identity consistent with participation in the study) and ask if the parents would agree to have someone contact them to talk about the study in a couple of days (asking for a small commitment before the larger request for participation).

Social Proof.   The principle of social proof implies that we determine what is correct by finding out what others think is correct. That is, we perceive a particular behavior as correct in a given situation to the extent that we observe other people performing the same behavior. This principle is particularly relevant in a context of uncertainty, when the decision is unclear or ambiguous. In addition, the more we consider the people we observe to be similar to ourselves, the more likely we are to imitate their behavior. According to Cialdini, powerful imitative effects have been found among children and adults and in such diverse activities as purchase decisions and contributions to charity.

For an illustration of the principle of social proof, recall the study on genital herpes. The original recruitment strategy was to ask women to participate in the study at the end of a group session on contraception. This practice was soon abandoned after the recruiters realized that when one woman refused to participate, the rest of the group followed suit. In this case, social proof worked against the goals of the strategy. As this example illustrates, social proof is not an appropriate tactic to use when the subject matter of the research may be perceived as too personal or embarrassing to discuss in a group context. When the recruiters realized this fact, they changed their strategy from group discussions to individualized recruitment interviews. As a result, a higher proportion of attendees agreed to enroll in the study.

Liking.   The principle of liking has implications for the characteristics of the people conducting the recruitment as well as for the manner in which the study is titled and framed. People prefer to comply with the requests of individuals they know and like. One feature that influences liking is physical attractiveness. A second factor is perceived similarity: people tend to like people whom they view as similar to themselves. One strategy to enhance liking (and thereby encourage participation) is to praise, compliment, and demonstrate interest and concern toward potential participants. Increased familiarity through repeated contact can also facilitate liking, especially when the contact takes place under positive circumstances. Finally, you can increase liking through the process of association, that is, by connecting yourself with something perceived as positive, such as a child's school or basketball camp.

An example of the successful application of this principle is found in a demonstration project that sought to recruit and retain African American, Latino, Native American, and Samoan parents for a program aimed at preventing substance abuse among children (Harachi, Catalano, & Hawkins, 1997). The project, Parenting for Drug-Free Children, was marketed to parents as a program to strengthen and support families rather than as a drug prevention program. The project successfully recruited diverse groups of parents in an urban setting. Over a two-year period, it offered 27 workshops in which 455 individuals participated. The participants were 20% African American, 46% Hispanic, 7% Caucasian, 17% Samoan, 6% Native American, and 4% other ethnicity.

The recruitment strategies employed in the project were multifaceted. One strategy involved direct contact based on existing relationships: for example, a minister's spouse calling members of the congregation or recruiting at birthday and Tupperware parties. An alternative approach relied on direct contact with persons who were unknown to the recruiter but were perceived as having something in common with the recruiter. For example, a parent would call other parents whose children attended the same school. Community and church leaders helped identify recruiters within the targeted ethnic groups. For example, Spanish-speaking individuals conducted recruitment targeting the Hispanic population. Developing links with key community liaisons to support the project was an effective recruitment strategy. Significantly, other research studies have provided support for the success of community contacts in recruiting ethnic minority participants (for example, Chavkin & Garza-Lubeck, 1990; Herrerias, 1988).

Authority.   Society exerts strong pressure to comply with the requests of people in positions of authority. This tendency to obey authority figures originates in socialization practices that teach obedience as the correct mode of conduct. This principle is continuously reinforced because authority figures generally have the ability to reward and to punish. Psychologist Stanley Milgram (1963) demonstrated the strength of the authority principle in his study of obedience at Yale University. Milgram found that normal and psychologically healthy individuals were often willing to administer what they thought were dangerous levels of electric shocks to another person, based simply on the order to do so by an experimental scientist.

Not only do individuals tend to comply with the requests of people in authority, but they also tend to react to mere symbols of authority in an automatic way. For example, titles such as Dr. or Reverend; clothing, including police uniforms, badges, and pastoral robes; and automobiles, including fire trucks, police cars, and ambulances, tend to command respect and attract immediate attention. Think about how you react when you are driving and you notice a police car in the rearview mirror. Does your foot automatically lift off the gas pedal while your eyes shift nervously to the speedometer? What other authority figures or symbols do you tend to react to in an automatic way?

The strength of the authority principle for participant recruitment is illustrated in a study of a community mobilization strategy that involved church congregations in family recruitment for alcohol and drug prevention programs (Johnson, Noe, Collins, Strader, & Bucholtz, 2000). The programs ran between 20 and 25 weeks and consisted of two-and-a-half-hour sessions that focused on parents and their high-risk youths. The program developed church advocate teams (CATs) made up of 5 to 10 church staff and community members. The CATs then recruited families of high-risk children and developed links with other social programs. Church leaders also endorsed the program. Informational meetings were held, and advertisements were placed in church bulletins, newsletters, and the local media. The program also relied on telephone calls and in-person contact by members of the CATs to recruit families with high-risk youths. Five of the six sites were able to recruit the target number of at least 24 families using these methods.

Scarcity.   According to the scarcity principle, people assign more value to an opportunity when it is considered rare, in short supply, or available for a limited time. The scarcity principle works because people typically place greater value on things that are difficult to attain. There are plenty of everyday examples of this principle. Perhaps the most obvious cases occur as the holiday season approaches. During the 1983 Christmas season, for instance, ordinary Cabbage Patch dolls worth about $25 were in such high demand that they were being sold on the black market for as much as $2,000. In fact, people actually flew all across the world to *adopt* them.

In the case of participant recruitment, a request may be more effective if it is perceived as consisting of exclusive information. For this reason, directing requests to a specific name is more effective than using a general reference like "Dear Friend" or "Current Resident" or no reference at all. A related strategy is to inform potential participants that they are among a select number of individuals who have been offered the opportunity to participate and that their decision is time limited. For example, in an experimental study to examine the effectiveness of a child abuse and neglect prevention program, potential participants were told that they were among 200 local families being contacted and that they would be contacted within three days for their decision to participate.

Define the participant	Participants can be defined in terms of gender, age, ethnicity, sexual orientation, group, income, life experience, and so on.	**EXHIBIT 7.8** *Systems Framework for Tailoring Recruitment Strategies*
Goal clarity	The purpose of the research should be evaluated in terms of its relevance for the target participant. Take into account that the appeal of certain goals may vary among participants in the same target group.	
Use of contract	The contract or agreement to participate should be evaluated in terms of the target group.	
Meeting place	Is the meeting place for recruitment and later participation considered safe, accessible, and comfortable for the target group? Is it associated with a positive experience?	
Use of time	The time commitment and scheduling should be evaluated in terms of the target group.	
Relationship	The desired relationship between the research staff and the participant should be considered as well as the style of communication.	
Outside resources	The provision of outside resources may be necessary to remove barriers to participation. Child care, transportation, food, and referral to other resources may be required.	

Tailoring Recruitment to the Target Participant

The previous section discussed the application of six general principles that can influence the research recruitment process. This section develops that discussion by presenting a framework that researchers can use to tailor the recruitment strategy to the target participant. Two key objectives of any recruitment strategy are to anticipate and remove any obstacles to participation and to increase people's motivation to participate. The parallel to these objectives in social work practice is "beginning where the client is."

Social workers are generally familiar with thinking in terms of a **systems framework** (Bronfenbrenner, 1977). When designing an effective recruitment strategy, it is helpful to view the target participant as operating within a system. This system includes the microlevel of individual and family, which is grounded in the mesosystem comprising the participant's neighborhood, employer, church, schools, and recreation facilities. Beyond the mesosystem are the macro system and the exo systems, which include the local economy, the social service and educational systems, the mass media, and the government. Exhibit 7.8 presents a systems framework for tailoring participant recruitment strategies.

Define the Participant.   The first step in this framework is to define the target participant. In performing this task, researchers can consider a multitude of variables, including gender, age, ethnicity, income, preferred language, literacy, and experience. The more carefully the researcher defines the participant, the more precisely he or she can tailor the recruitment strategy. One real-life illustration of this principle involves two campaigns to recruit low-income and minority women for breast cancer screening (Abbott, Barber, Taylor, & Pendel, 1999). The first effort involved a traditional media campaign that distributed a generalized public announcement through newspapers, radio, local poster boards, church bulletins, hospital newsletters, and physician referrals. Significantly, the recruitment did not incorporate any culturally specific strategy, nor did it target low-income women or specific racial groups. Consequently, most of the participants recruited through this effort did not come from low-income or minority groups.

In contrast, the second recruitment effort involved a multistrategy approach specifically tailored to the target participant. The approach included health education sessions conducted at key locations within the community, such as housing complexes and local churches. Public service announcements referred to culturally specific events. In addition, recruiters actively sought the assistance of an African American newspaper columnist as well as community leaders such as church pastors. They also organized a telephone campaign. Another aspect of the strategy was to design pamphlets with graphics that incorporated the colors of the native African cultures and resembled Kente cloth. This tailored approach was effective in recruiting ethnic minority and low-income women.

Goal Clarity.   After the researchers have defined the target participant, the remaining steps in the framework are tailored to fit with the life circumstances of the target participant. The second step, for instance, involves the goals of the research. These goals should be clear and should be evaluated in terms of their relevance for the target participant. The key is to ask potential recruits to participate in something they want to do, as opposed to persuading them to do something they don't want to do.

Use of Contract.   The contract or agreement to participate should be tailored to the target participants. Is the language clear and understandable to the participants? Does it share important information that will motivate the participants and inform them of the expected role they will have in the research as well as the potential impact on their lives?

Meeting Place.   To improve success rates, recruitment efforts and activities should be located in a place that is easily accessible and considered safe by the participants. In the research study on genital herpes discussed earlier, adequate space was a critical factor in promoting positive interactions between the recruitment staff and the potential participants (Young & Dombrowski, 1990). Recruiters needed this space to conduct private interviews and to answer participants' questions. When women were provided with time and privacy to dispel their concerns, they often agreed to participate.

Use of Time.   A major consideration in any recruitment effort is that the research must be responsive to the complexities of the participants' lives. For this reason, recruiters should evaluate time frames to determine when they should ask people to participate. They should consider the season, day of the week, time of day, and overall time required for recruitment. For instance, if the research targets farmers, the strategy might be to contact them in the evening, during fall or winter, once harvesting is complete. If the research study involves parents of preschool children, early morning and evening may not be the best times to attempt contact, as they coincide with eating, dressing, and bedtime routines. Also, contacts with the parents of young children should be kept relatively short. If the research setting is a school, the researcher must plan around testing cycles. In an agency that receives public funds, contract renewal is a bad time to approach the administration with data requests. Researchers should always evaluate time frames for recruitment and research participation in relation to the life circumstances of the target participants.

Relationship.   Another responsibility of the recruiter is to assess whether the approach is sensitive to differences in culture, age, and gender or whether it needs to be modified along those lines. A related issue is whether the characteristics of the recruiter will appeal to the target participants. For instance, if the target population is youths who congregate at the mall, it may not be best if the recruiter is female and near the age of the youths' mothers. These youths may respond best to someone younger and not associated with authority. The recruiter should also consider which relational style fits best with target participants. Would potential participants respond best to someone they perceive as passive or to someone more directive and extroverted, for example.

Outside Resources.   Finally, the recruiter should use available outside resources to reduce the barriers to participation as they are perceived by the participants. For example, if the participants are caring for children or elders, the offer of outside resources should take into account the participants' roles as caretakers. Similarly, some low-income participants may have basic needs such as food, transportation, and safety. In addition or as an alternative to providing basic goods and services, providing information on community resources can be an incentive to participate. A list of local resources could include information on where to ask for food boxes, free or low-cost city bus tickets, and recreational programs for children from low-income families.

Gatekeepers.   Efforts to recruit participants do not always begin at the level of the participant. Sometimes recruitment efforts must begin with organizations that will help the recruiters achieve access to the participants. For instance, new parents are invited to participate in the Healthy Families Arizona program in the hospital at the time of birth. Efforts to recruit program participants for research, however, must begin with the Department of Economic Security that funds the program. From there, they must proceed to the program administrators and ultimately to the hospital administrators who offer the program to the parents.

In qualitative research, the individuals or groups who are essential in providing access to the research participants are referred to as the **gatekeepers.** The process of accessing the target participants is called **gaining entry.** The basic considerations in recruitment at this level are much the same regardless of whether the research is qualitative or quantitative. Strategizing about recruitment at the gatekeeper level involves many of the same considerations that are involved at the participant level. Gatekeepers have to be convinced that the research will produce more benefit than harm, that the participants' rights will not be violated, and that the research will be sensitive to the participants' needs and preferences. The gatekeepers must also be assured that the researcher has adequate skills and resources to carry out the research as described.

In addition to these considerations, gaining entry is a process of building trust. As such, it can be a quick process, or it can take considerable effort over a period of time, depending on the research context. Whatever the specific circumstances, the researcher must nurture those relationships over the life of the research project. This approach will ensure that the relationship will not end once the gatekeepers give their approval to proceed. To succeed in the process of gaining entry, the researcher should understand who the gatekeepers are and should strategize as to the best way to approach them and what messages to communicate to them. The researcher must then anticipate and respond to any barriers to participation. The framework in Exhibit 7.8 can also be used for strategically planning recruitment at the gatekeeper level.

Planning for Retention

The success of many research studies with more than one round of measurement—for example, a pretest/posttest or longitudinal research design—depends on **retention,** that is, the ability to retain participation of the same individuals over time. The opposite of retention is attrition, which can be characterized by permanent or intermittent loss. Permanent loss results when a participant withdraws from a study, dies, or cannot be accessed due to long-term incarceration or relocation without notice. Intermittent loss includes temporary difficulty contacting a participant, participant refusal to participate on a particular occasion, inaccurate location information, and other factors that result in missed appointments. Both intermittent and permanent loss of research participants are problematic, but permanent loss is by far the worse.

We know from Chapter 4 that attrition in longitudinal research is to be expected. In fact, considerable attrition should be expected. This section presents techniques that can enhance participant retention, even with populations that are prone to attrition. By carefully crafting a retention plan before the initial contact with a participant, researchers can improve their chances of retaining participants. Strategies to enhance retention should begin at recruitment, when impressions are made, relationships are developed, and participants establish a positive image of the research study or evaluation. Clearly, not all strategies will work with all participants. Therefore, researchers should develop a multifaceted retention plan. Whatever the specific plan, persistence, ingenuity, and flexibility are essential to achieving good retention rates.

Developing Rapport. Retention involves many of the same principles and considerations as participant recruitment. One common principle in recruitment and retention is liking. If the research participant does not experience a positive rapport with the data collector, does not trust the data collector or the study, or does not find participation interesting or enjoyable, he or she is not likely to continue to participate, even if incentives are provided. Strategies for developing rapport with participants include the following:

- Matching the qualities of the data collection staff to the characteristics of the participant. Personal attributes that can reduce attrition include perceived similarity to the participant.

- Training, supporting, and supervising data collection staff in establishing rapport (for example, adopting a nonjudgmental attitude, showing interest, listening attentively, being punctual, and adhering to procedures such as maintaining confidentiality).

- Maintaining contact with the participant between data collection periods if contact is otherwise infrequent, for example, intervals of six months or greater. Strategies for staying in touch include phone calls, personal visits, birthday/holiday cards, and periodic mailings. Reminder

The Social Work Library

See www.mhhe.com/krysik1 to access an annotated bibliography on retention.

The Social Work Library

An example of how retention can be proactively influenced is the longitudinal evaluation of the Hawaii Healthy Start Program (Duggan et al., 2004). This three-year experimental study achieved an overall retention rate of 81 percent with parents who were screened as at risk for child abuse and neglect, a population prone to high attrition. Although the study was conducted on an island, geographic context is only one factor in retention, but not the most important. The article is available online at the Social Work Library.

cards should be mailed to participants a couple of weeks before the scheduled contact.

- Providing continuity by limiting turnover in data collection staff.

- Conducting data collection in person whenever possible.

- Emphasizing the confidentiality of the data and respect for participants.

- Stressing the importance of the participant's contributions.

- Emphasizing the benefits of participation.

- Being accommodating and flexible with regard to the time and place of data collection.

- Adding a personal touch to all project communications. For example, you can create a project logo for all correspondence so that participants will recognize the communication and open it instead of discarding it.

Developing a Tracking System.   Research suggests that failure to locate participants is the greatest cause of attrition. Not surprisingly, then, persistence in trying to find participants is a key factor in retention (Sullivan, Rumptz, Campbell, Eby, & Davidson, 1996). Recruiters need to develop tracking systems for recording and updating contact information, providing reminders to contact participants intermittently, and recording the outcome of each attempt to establish contact. Tracking systems can be manual or automated, sophisticated or simple. Moreover, researchers can now use contact management software programs to help manage tracking efforts. A participant tracking system might include the following data:

- Information on as many ways of contacting the participant as possible (all telephone numbers, mailing address, postal box, e-mail, employer contact).

- Contact information for at least two friends or relatives who are the most likely to have stable residences and know the participant's whereabouts.

- Schedule of when to contact participants between data collection periods by sending birthday or holiday cards along with scheduled phone calls. Automated contact reminders can be built into computerized tracking systems.

- The outcome of all attempts to make contact.

- Updates of information at every data collection point, including changes in employment, outside contacts, and future relocation plans.

- List of community agencies that may have contact with the participant (educational institutions, treatment programs, criminal justice systems).

- List of places the participant likes to frequent.

Employers or agencies that serve the participant will generally not provide the researcher with information on any participant's whereabouts. Nevertheless, these contacts are often willing to deliver a message to the participant to make contact with the researcher. In addition, the participant can fill out a release-of-information form that grants family members, friends, and others permission to give the researcher information about the participant's whereabouts. In addition to collecting contact information, the researcher should inquire as to the best times to contact the participant. She or he should also consider cultural factors with regard to how, where, and when to contact participants.

Another strategy to improve the retention rate of research participants is to give the participants the researcher's contact information. This information can include a business card, a magnet with contact information, a card with the date of the next scheduled contact, and a request to call if any contact information changes. If a respondent has moved, the project staff can send a letter with "Do not forward, address correction requested" written on the envelope to obtain the respondent's new address from the postal service. Resources for locating participants include directory assistance, phone books, Internet locator sites, and relatives, friends, and other contacts. Setting up a toll-free number or encouraging participants to call the project office collect is another useful technique for managing attrition.

Minimizing the Research Burden.   One source of participant attrition is the perceived burden of the research. Several strategies can be used to reduce response burden:

- Reduce the length of the interview or questionnaire.

- Make the task fun as opposed to boring.

- Ask only relevant questions.

- Keep sensitive items to a minimum and place them near the middle to the end of the instrument.

- Make the location of data collection convenient and accessible.

- Reduce the frequency of data collection.

- Be flexible in scheduling times and locations and rescheduling.

- Facilitate communication by providing participants with a toll-free telephone number, business cards, magnets with project contact information, and stamped change-of-address cards.

Providing Incentives.   One method of encouraging participation is to reward participants for their initial and continued participation. Providing incentives can convey the sentiment that participation is important and can help motivate participation in follow-up contacts. It is common to provide incentives to private individuals but not to organizational participants, elected officials, or employees of a social service agency. The participation of these groups in research is usually viewed as a function of their employment or an extension of their civic duty. The use and value of incentives will ultimately depend on the research budget. When planning for incentives, the researcher can use the following strategies:

- Make the incentive large enough to be meaningful but not so large that it is coercive.

- Increase the value of the incentive over time to reflect the increasing value and importance of participation.

- Provide a schedule of incentives to participants at recruitment and at each data collection period thereafter while reminding them of the timetable and the requirements of the research.

- Provide small incentives to participants who inform the researcher of changes in contact information.

- Consider the type of incentive and its appeal to the participant. Some researchers do not like to use cash incentives because of concerns about the safety of data collectors in the field. Checks are useful in the sense that they can be mailed and tracked if they are lost, but they are not as flexible as cash. Gift certificates restrict how participants can use the incentive and may require participants to make arrangements for transportation. Nonmonetary forms of incentives, such as food, diapers, and toiletries, can also be considered and should be tailored to the population.

- Identify alternative sources of funding if the research budget is too tight to afford incentives. For example, researchers can elicit donations from local businesses and organizations. These donated incentives can include movie tickets, restaurant coupons, and sports items.

- Substitute a drawing—in which only one or a few participants win a prize—if incentives cannot be provided to everyone. Drawings are not a good idea when the participants are young children or very needy individuals. In these instances, researchers should make an effort to provide all participants with an incentive.

● Remember that incentives alone are not enough to encourage participation.

PREPARING FOR DATA COLLECTION

The plan for collecting data must be developed before participant recruitment begins so that data collection can begin immediately. Long intervals between participant recruitment and data collection will lead to problems with retention. To prepare for data collection, the researcher must develop a **data collection protocol,** a set of written instructions and policies that outlines the specific rules governing contact with participants and guides data collection. Like recruitment and retention plans, data collection protocols are a proactive step to prevent problems before they occur. The researcher will view the protocol as a work in progress. He or she will complete the protocol to the maximum extent possible in advance of the study and subsequently update it as questions arise, decisions are made, and problems are resolved.

Developing a Data Collection Protocol

The information that goes into the data collection protocol will vary with the context and scope of the research. The following items may be considered for inclusion in a data collection protocol.

Schedule of Measures.   This is a list that documents what data collection instruments will be administered in which observation periods, assuming there is more than one.

Policy for Participant Contact.   This section of the protocol outlines the general guidelines for contacting participants. It includes such information as (a) how far in advance and by what methods participants are to be contacted, (b) the minimum and maximum number of attempts to contact participants, (c) the interval or schedule for contact attempts, and (d) the procedure to follow in the event of a missed appointment. It can also include the specifics of what the researcher needs to do before making contact: mailing out a prenotice letter, printing a map of directions, and gathering the forms and instruments that will be used.

Tracking Procedures.   The protocol must specify the data needed for tracking, when to use the tracking procedure, and the appropriate sequence of tracking (for instance, the researcher would attempt personal contacts before contacting an employer).

Equipment. An effective protocol specifies the equipment needed to conduct an interview or observation. An example would be a tape recorder with set of spare batteries and a number of blank tapes. The protocol also outlines the testing procedures that must be conducted before using the equipment. Finally, it can list the equipment the researcher considers necessary for contact and safety, for instance, a pager or cell phone.

Answers to Frequently Asked Questions (FAQs). This section of the protocol consists of a one-page summary of answers to frequently asked questions, such as who is sponsoring the study, what the perceived benefits of the study are, when the study results will be available and how they can be accessed, and whom to contact to answer further questions or address concerns regarding the study. The one-page FAQs may be prepared as a handout to be distributed to participants and gatekeepers who want more information on the research.

Incentive Policy. The incentive policy states when and in what form incentives will be provided. It also indicates how the data collector will access the incentives and which accounting procedure will be used for tracking the incentives. For instance, when cash incentives are provided in person, participants should be asked to initial a receipt. In such cases, the protocol should specify the procedures for recording and filing initialed receipts.

Safety Protocols. An important feature of the protocol is the description of potential safety concerns with advice on what to do in the event the data collector encounters a problem. For instance, if the research requires home visits, the data collector may encounter situations in which he or she becomes aware of domestic violence, child abuse, drug use, or other illegal behavior. If the data collector must go into the field to collect data, the protocol should specify the requirements for reporting his or her whereabouts at all times. The collector should also be provided with a working cell phone and encouraged to dial 911 if a safety concern arises. All data collection staff should be outfitted with official identification tags that they can show participants when making home visits or in-person contacts.

Standardization of Administration. The protocol should include rules about administering the data collection instrument. In structured interviews, for example, interviewers must always read the questions exactly as they are written in each interview. Interviewers also must appear neutral at all times and never offer to the participant verbally or through body language any indication of whether they feel that the answer given is "right" or "acceptable." In questions in which the level of measurement is nominal or ordinal, interviewers must read the entire scale before the participant provides an answer, at least for the first few items in a series of questions where the response categories are the same.

Supervision.   The protocol should contain a policy for randomly checking the accuracy of the data and performance of the data collector in the field. This policy may involve observing data collection activities and eliciting participants' impressions of these activities. It is much better for researchers to discover a problem with data collection and take steps to correct it than to have problems brought to their attention by a participant or gatekeeper after data collection has been ongoing for some time. The protocol should also outline the policy on how data collectors can access a researcher or supervisor when they are in the field.

Probing.   The protocol should include examples of how to probe "don't know" answers. It should also contain responses to help participants say all they have to say about an open-ended question.

Communication.   The protocol should outline the terminology both to use and to avoid in discussing the study. For example, the study may be referred to as a *project* rather than a *study*. This section of the protocol should also provide guidelines concerning any specific letterhead, paper, header, or footer that must be included on all project correspondence. If there is a project logo, the protocol might state that it will appear on all correspondence. Also included is the procedure for proofreading all correspondence before it leaves the office.

Work Habits.   The protocol should explicitly state the project expectations for participants regarding punctuality, politeness, and return communication.

Record Keeping.   The protocol should specify which records the data collectors must keep during data collection: mileage, hotel, food, and other travel receipts. It should also indicate the time frame within which the collectors must submit all of their receipts, to whom, and how.

Securing the Data.   The rules governing data storage—for example, do not leave data in the car, do not carry data on discs, do not take data home—should be included in the protocol. In addition, the protocol should develop rules for the transfer of data if they pass between people or offices. The disposal of data—both hard copy and electronic formats—must be outlined in advance of the study.

Recording the Data.   The protocol should also include rules regarding how the data are to be recorded, including the use of pen or pencil, when and how to record, and procedures for checking the recording for completeness and accuracy.

Planning for the Analysis.   Researchers conducting quantitative analysis will want to plan the analysis in advance of implementing the study. This procedure serves a couple of purposes. First, it can help researchers to collect only those data that they believe are relevant and have a chance of being used. Second, it helps them determine whether they have considered all of the variables needed for the analysis. In contrast, for researchers engaged in qualitative research, analysis is a process that is conducted concurrently with data collection. Transcripts of interviews and observations should leave room for comments, tentative interpretations, and emerging hypotheses. Notes are important in describing how researchers analyzed the data and arrived at the conclusions. The protocol should remind researchers of these necessary steps.

Ethical Conduct.   Most ethical rules seem like common sense. Even so, the protocol should explicitly state them to prevent unfortunate ethical breaches from occurring. Rules of ethical conduct may be specific, such as "You do not approach or request contact with any participant outside the research context or for any purpose other than data collection." Rules of ethical conduct can also address less concrete situations such as the differences between a data collection interview and a therapeutic interview. There is no one set of ethical guidelines that will be appropriate for all research contexts. For instance, in ethnographic research in which the researcher often participates in the everyday life activities of participants over an extended period, the rules of ethical conduct may differ from those governing in-person survey research.

The Audit Trail.   An **audit** is a procedure in which an independent third party reviews the evidence of data collection in qualitative research. For instance, in relation to in-depth interviews, the audit trail could include the interview guides, audiotapes or videotapes, transcripts, list of participants, and the researcher's notes regarding the data collection procedures. Although auditing occurs after the study is completed, it must be planned in advance. Moreover, even if the audit does not occur, the researcher should keep the evidence available in the event that questions arise concerning the credibility of the study.

Journaling.   In qualitative research, the rules and decisions made as the research is conducted should also be recorded. This process is called **journaling,** and it becomes a crucial piece of the data in a qualitative study. The qualitative journal can include notes about research scheduling and logistics as well as reflections on self, research participants, and the data that are being collected. Journaling is also a helpful tool for quantitative research studies.

Decision rules must be made, recorded, and shared.

Decision Rules.   Once data collection begins, questions and problems will arise for which decisions must be made. Keep track of all decision rules (rules regarding how decisions are made) in writing, and make certain that the information is shared with all project staff through the data collection protocol. These steps will help ensure the integrity of the research project. The challenge of clear communication increases with the number of research staff and the division of labor, making the role of the protocol even more important.

Hiring and Training Data Collectors

Unless the study is small, the research participants may never actually meet the social work researcher who has designed and carefully crafted the study or evaluation. The data collection staff represent the research project to the participant. This point illustrates the importance of hiring and training data collectors who will represent the study in a professional and positive manner.

Advertising for data collection staff can include considerations of education, language skills, and requirements such as a valid driver's license, the use of a car, and proof of insurance. When advertising for staff, distinguish between what you require and what you desire in potential candidates. For example, if the research involves asking the data collectors to go into people's homes in economically disadvantaged areas or to meet with certain population subgroups, you probably desire staff with experience with these types of settings or people. If the work requires the data collector to speak, read, and write fluently in Spanish, you should state this fact as a requirement.

Actual decisions related to hiring should take into account the concepts discussed under participant recruitment, including factors related to liking. The final decision on hiring will be contingent on the candidate's signing a statement of confidentiality and agreement with a code of ethical conduct. The ultimate decision will be based on a reference check and possibly a criminal records check and drug screen. These extra steps are warranted when data collectors will be going into participants' homes and meeting with children or other vulnerable populations.

The researcher may want to set aside several days or even a week for training data collection staff. The data collection protocol can be used in training staff. Depending upon the scope of the research project, the researcher may want to develop a separate manual for training data collectors. Here are suggestions for items to be addressed in the training manual:

- Orientation to the employing agency.

- Agency policies and procedures.

- Overview of the research study.

- Self-awareness, including voice, posture, facial expressions, body language, and attire.

- Principles of participant motivation and rapport building.

- Other interviewing basics similar to what would be covered in a social work interviewing course. Among the most basic interviewing skills are speaking in complete sentences, clarity, speed, avoiding utterances and nervous gestures, conveying interest, asking for clarification, and maintaining neutrality.

In addition, time management is a necessary skill for data collectors, who must be in control of the interview at all times. They must know how to redirect and avoid getting caught up in chitchat and joking. Pacing is important to give participants time to think and respond without distracting them from answering.

The training of data collectors should include plenty of opportunities to observe and practice. Practice should include introducing oneself and the study to participants, administering the interview, and closing the interview. The success or failure of data collection will depend on how the task is presented. Before data collection begins, the data collectors need to familiarize themselves with each data collection instrument by completing it and administering it to one or more individuals. They must know the wording of each data collection instrument and approximately how long it takes to complete. They must be able to assure the participant of the importance of the data collected and to describe how the data will be used. An apologetic attitude on the part of the data collector immediately conveys to the participant the sense that the data collection is unnecessary and unwarranted. The data collector must repeatedly stress the importance of answering accurately and honestly. The research will not benefit anyone if the information is error ridden. Finally, the data collector must be sensitive to literacy problems. One way to avoid embarrassment over literacy is to offer to read the instrument to anyone who so desires.

As a final training requirement, the data collection staff should be required to enter the practice data that they collect into the project database. The purpose of this exercise is to illustrate the need for accuracy and completeness in data recording. Unless the data collection staff have an opportunity to actually use the database, they may have little understanding of the relevance or importance of the data that they collect. We discuss databases in the next section.

DEVELOPING THE DATABASE

A **database** is a grid that specifies all of the variables in the study. Typically the variables in the database are positioned in the columns beginning on the left and progressing to the right. If there are 90 variables, there will be 90 columns in the database. The data for each sampling unit are entered in the rows. The totality of data for each sampling unit (person or otherwise) is called a **record.**

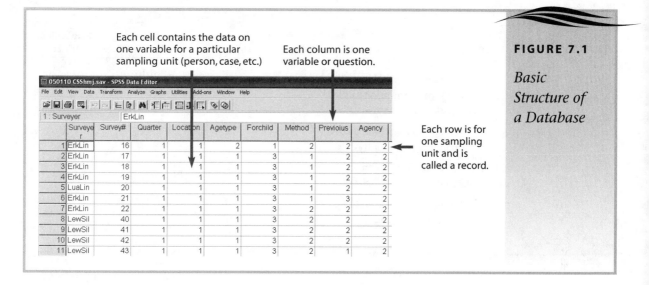

FIGURE 7.1

Basic Structure of a Database

Each cell contains the data on one variable for a particular sampling unit (person, case, etc.)

Each column is one variable or question.

Each row is for one sampling unit and is called a record.

Thus, if there are 50 participants in the study, there will be 50 records or rows of data in the database. The rows are numbered consecutively, with the numbers appearing on the left side of the grid, starting with 1. In the database, the data on each variable for each sampling unit are recorded in spaces called **cells.** The number of cells in a record matches the number of variables.

The structures of all databases are similar, regardless of the particular data analysis, spreadsheet, or data management program used. Figure 7.1 provides an example of a typical database with the parts labeled. It is good practice to develop the database before collecting any data. Constructing the database can help you identify and correct errors on the measures before you begin the study. Databases can be constructed manually, but this is seldom the case anymore, thanks to computers.

There are several steps to setting up a database. The first step is to determine the order in which the variables will be displayed. The order of the variables in the database should be consistent with the order of the variables on the data collection instruments. Following this rule will make data entry easier. Note that each question on the data collection instrument requires a column to record the response in the database. A question that involves either more than one part or more than one answer requires as many columns in the database as there are parts or possible answers to the question.

To illustrate the construction of a database, we will refer to the first four questions from the Black Feather Youth Survey. These questions are shown in Exhibit 7.9. A column in the database will represent each of the questions in Exhibit 7.9. The order of the variables in the database will correspond to the order of the items on the questionnaire. For instance, question 1 will be positioned before question 2, question 2 between questions 1 and 3, and so on. The

	YOUTH SURVEY QUESTIONNAIRE	STRONGLY DISAGREE	DISAGREE	NEITHER	AGREE	STRONGLY AGREE
EXHIBIT 7.9 *Black Feather Youth Survey Questionnaire*	1. When I get older, I plan to live in the same community as I currently live.	1	2	3	4	5
	2. When I get older, I plan to get a job in this community.	1	2	3	4	5
	3. When I get older, I plan to graduate from high school.	1	2	3	4	5
	4. When I get older, I plan to go to the doctor for regular checkups.	1	2	3	4	5

first variable in the database, however, is always reserved for the unique case identifier, explained in the next section.

Deciding on a Unique Identifier

As just mentioned, the first variable to be specified in a database will be the **unique case identifier,** which identifies the sampling unit for each particular record. The researcher must decide which system to use to assign unique case identifiers. Significantly, both SPSS and Excel allow you to enter both string data and numeric data. As their names suggest, **string data** consist of letters or words, whereas **numeric data** are numbers. It is possible, then, to use participants' names when you enter data, but this might not be a good practice for reasons of confidentiality. The preferred method is to store participants' names separately from their other data, even if you encrypt the file. **Encryption** is the translation of data into a secret code. It is the most effective way to ensure that the data are secure. To read the encrypted file, a person must have access to a key or password that enables him or her to *decrypt* the file, that is, to restore it to plain text. Another good reason not to use names is because two or more individuals often have the same name.

An alternative to using names is to use the participant's Social Security number (SSN). However, using SSNs could violate participants' privacy and possibly lead to identity theft. As a rule, unless it is necessary to collect SSNs, do not do it. A third option is to assign each participant a number. This number may be recorded on the hard-copy questionnaire or measures, or it may be associated with the participant's name in a file stored separately from the database.

Using a unique case identifier can help researchers avoid several common errors. For example, well-intentioned social workers who want to evaluate their programs sometimes administer a pretest to participants before an intervention and a posttest following the intervention. They then enter the data into a database without assigning any unique case identifiers to the data that will enable them to match the pretests and posttests of the individual participants. Mistakenly, some social workers think that calculating the average pretest and posttest scores for *all* participants and examining the differences will provide insight into changes that occurred over the course of the intervention. Clearly this assumption is false. In most interventions, some participants inevitably improve, some show no change, and some might even deteriorate. Generally speaking, when you analyze aggregate or group data rather than the data for individual cases, these variations remain invisible, and the scores come out looking "pretty average."

Another advantage to using a unique case identifier is that the researcher can easily go back to the original data if there appears to be an error in data entry. Sometimes the data that should be in a record are either left out of the database by mistake or entered incorrectly. The unique identifier allows the researcher to access the original data. If the researcher does not use a unique identifier, he or she has no way of going back to the original data and verifying the information or of gathering additional information from the sampling unit to correct the error.

Developing the Data Codebook

A **data codebook** is a listing of each variable in the order in which it appears in the database. The variables should be listed in the same order as they appear on the data collection tool (the interview schedule, questionnaire, or observational recording form, for example). The more variables included in the study, the more work will be required to develop the codebook. Fortunately, data analysis programs such as SPSS can develop the codebook directly in the program as the database is being created. In contrast, spreadsheet programs such as Microsoft Excel require the researcher to develop a separate codebook using either a different sheet in Excel or a word processing program such as Microsoft Word.

As its name implies, a codebook requires the researcher to develop a system of numeric codes that will be used to represent qualitative answers as numbers in the database. Codes are necessary for the response categories of variables measured at the nominal and ordinal levels. Take, for example, the four questions listed in Exhibit 7.9. These questions are measured at the ordinal level. The possible responses to each question are really labels that represent degrees of agreement with a statement. In this case, developing the numeric codes for these labels is easy because the participant is asked to respond to the questions using a continuum of numbers from 1 through 5. Thus, the code for the label "strongly disagree" would logically be the same as the response, that is, the number 1. Similarly, the code for "disagree" would be 2, and so on. Variables measured at the interval and ratio levels have numeric responses that have a quantitative meaning. In these instances, a code does not need to be specified, although some researchers use the word *actual* to clarify that they are entering the actual values.

Another, rather simple option for developing a codebook is to use a blank measurement instrument (such as the questionnaire or interview schedule) and write or type in the codes for the different responses to variables at the ordinal and nominal levels. Responses to partially closed questions that leave a space for "other" with a request to specify the response can be treated either numerically as an additional response category or as a string variable. Data analysis programs like SPSS and Excel are not suited to managing long string responses. Unless the response is treated numerically and assigned a mutually exclusive code, the answers to partially closed questions are best compiled in a word processing program.

In addition to developing codes for response categories, the creation of a database requires the researcher to assign a name to each variable so that it can be identified. Many data analysis programs like SPSS have certain conventions for naming variables. For instance, in SPSS, **variable names** cannot be more than eight characters long and may not start with a number or include any spaces. Next to the abbreviated variable name, the researcher will want to specify a **variable label,** a short description of the variable. Without variable labels, a researcher who uses a variable naming convention such as Q1, Q2, Q3 might not know what the variable names mean. In this regard, SPSS is more user-friendly than Excel, because it prints out the variable labels associated with the variables included in the analysis. In contrast, Excel requires users to refer back and forth between the analysis and the data codebook. For this reason, Excel users may want to avoid using variable names like Q1 and Q2 in favor of short, descriptive variable names such as "plnlive" for Q1, which refers to plans to live in the community, and "plnjob" for Q2, which refers to plans to get a job in the community.

Variable labels may also have certain restrictions in terms of the number of characters that can be specified. For example, the restriction in recent versions of SPSS for variable labels is 120 characters. Thus, a variable label for a variable named ID could be "Identification number." A variable label for question 1 in Exhibit 7.9 could be "plans to live in the community as an adult." Variable labels should be short and descriptive.

Specifying Missing Data

When using SPSS or other data analysis programs, the researcher will want to specify a code for each variable to represent **missing data**—those responses that are not provided, are illegible, or are out of range and an obvious error.

NAME		POSITION
ID	ID number	1
	Measurement Level: Scale	
	Column Width: 8 Alignment: Right	
Q1	Live in the same community when you get older.	2
	Measurement Level: Ordinal	
	Column Width: 8 Alignment: Right	
	Missing Values: 9	

Value	Label
1	Strongly disagree
2	Disagree
3	Neither agree or disagree
4	Agree
5	Strongly disagree

EXHIBIT 7.10

Sample SPSS Codebook for the Black Feather Youth Survey

Although specifying a value for missing data in the database is not required, it is strongly advised. The advantage of entering codes for missing data is that the researcher will know whether the otherwise blank space is a data entry error as opposed to a true missing value.

Often the code specified for missing data will be the same across many variables. Remember, though, that the codes used for missing data cannot be the same as any valid numeric response for that variable. For instance, on an ordinal scale ranging from 1 through 5, the code for missing data could not include any numerals from 1 through 5. It could, however, be any other numeric value of one or more digits, for example, a 9 or a 99.

If numeric codes are used in the database for missing data, they must be specified in the program as the value for missing data. If they are not specified as the value for missing data, the computer will simply treat them as numeric values. This happens by error from time to time, often with major consequences for the analysis. For example, in predicting risk of recidivism for juvenile offenders, a zero might be entered into the database to represent missing data. If the value of zero is being treated as a numerical value as opposed to missing data, however, it will lower the score for risk of recidivism by juveniles with missing data. SPSS has the flexibility to treat numeric values as missing data, whereas Excel does not. In Excel, missing data can be entered with a non-numeric symbol such as the pound sign (#), or the cell can be left blank.

Exhibit 7.10 displays the codebook for the first question that was developed in SPSS for the Black Feather Youth Survey. Notice that in an SPSS codebook, the variable name is positioned at the far left (ID) and the variable label is located

Computers do just what they are told to do. They do not have brains, and they are not capable of intelligent thought. Therefore, when we construct databases, we must be careful to define what variable values mean and to specify the values that we will use for missing data.

For step-by-step instructions on developing a codebook either in SPSS or manually, visit the Codebook tutorial on www.mhhe.com/krysik1.

to the right of the variable name (ID number). Note also that the codebook does not begin with question 1 but rather with the unique student identifier variable labeled ID. The second variable in the codebook corresponds with question 1 on the survey and is labeled Q1. This is the variable that refers to the participant's plans to live in the same community as she or he gets older. The response categories of the variable are listed as variable values under the heading "Value," and the corresponding value labels are listed to the right of each value. The variable is measured at the ordinal level in that the numerical values are ranked in order but do not have any quantitative meaning and are not suitable to be manipulated mathematically. Note that the ordinal variable values need to be listed in order from highest to smallest or most to least; they cannot be listed at random. The numbers under the heading "Position" close to the far right margin in the codebook are the columns in which the data for that variable are located.

Entering the Data

Once the researcher has collected all or at least some of the data, she or he will begin entering the data into the database. Quantitative data are typically entered directly from the questionnaire, interview schedule, or observational recording device. The researcher or data entry assistant proceeds through each data collection tool systematically from start to finish, keying in the responses for each variable. It may be useful to set the number pad on the computer keyboard in the lock position and use it for data entry. Data entry, however, is a matter of personal preference, and the objectives in order of priority are accuracy and speed.

Regardless of the process the researcher uses to enter the data, there are bound to be a few **data entry errors:** a wrong value entered here or there, a skipped question, and transposed digits. Depending upon the size of the database and the number of eligible sampling units, the researcher may need to check all or a portion of the data collection instruments against the database to look for data entry errors. Any errors that he or she detects should be corrected. If the researcher is checking only a sample of the questionnaires and finds very few errors, he or she may be reasonably confident that the entered data are accurate. Conversely, if the researcher discovers a number of errors, he or she should continue checking.

Certain data entry programs—some of which are available free of charge— enable researchers to set limits on the values that they can enter into a specific field. For example, if the valid responses to a variable such as Q1 on the Black Feather Youth Survey range from 1 to 5, with 9 specified as the value for missing data, the program will alert the researcher if she or he has entered any number outside that range in that particular field. The next chapter discusses checking the data for errors on a variable-by-variable basis. The completion of data entry and checking for errors represents a major achievement in the research process. The data are now recorded in a format that will enable the researcher to begin analyzing them.

The discussion of preparing data for analysis thus far has dealt only with quantitative data. The next section deals with preparing qualitative data for analysis.

 Tutorials

www.mhhe.com/krysik1 provides four tutorials for creating a database and entering data in SPSS and Excel. The tutorials include entering data into an existing data file and creating a database from start to finish.

PREPARING QUALITATIVE DATA

As we saw in Chapter 1, there are many types of qualitative research, and a discussion of each type is far beyond the scope of this book. Therefore, in this chapter and throughout this book, we focus on some of the commonalities in qualitative research. Perhaps the most basic feature common to qualitative data is that they tend to be in the form of words. The words can appear in various formats, including written documents such as letters, spoken and recorded words from interviews, and observational notes written by the researcher.

Qualitative data, like quantitative data, have to be processed before they can be analyzed. If the data are from an interview or handwritten notes, it is useful to transcribe or transfer them into a word processing program. Transcription takes time, so the researcher should plan for a ratio of approximately 1:3: one hour of recording will require about three hours of transcription. Transcription is a budget item that the social work researcher should not overlook. Transcription can also involve equipment costs, including tape recorders, transcription machines, and headsets. Written communication is easy to prepare, as it can be copied and pasted from one computer program to another.

If the researcher who collected the data is not doing the transcription, he or she must spend time reviewing and editing the transcript for errors. For example, in a recent qualitative study, a participant referred to Arizona's Medicaid program, the Arizona Health Care Cost Containment System, more commonly known as AHCCCS and pronounced "access." The person transcribing the interview wrote, "I didn't know if I was approached because I had access." The transcription was not consistent with what the participant intended, which was, "I didn't know if I was approached because I had AHCCCS." Checking for errors as the data is being prepared for analysis is equally important in quantitative and qualitative research.

The transcript of an in-depth interview or participant observation may include what was said, what was observed, and the researcher's thoughts and reflections. These three different types of information must be kept distinct from one another. The researcher can use labeling for this purpose. Additionally, if there was more than one person being observed, it may be necessary to know who said or did what. Assigning each person a brief identifier can make this task manageable. The researcher can use a simple system like A, B, C or something more descriptive such as Mum, Dad, and Grandma. In most cases, confidentiality concerns are the same in qualitative research as in quantitative research.

A key issue that arises when researchers prepare to enter their data is whether to use qualitative analysis software. Many computer-assisted qualitative data analysis software (CAQDAS) programs are available, and all have strengths and weaknesses and can perform different functions. Some of them can be used with graphics, audio, and video sources in addition to text. Two main questions researchers will need to answer are (1) should I use one, and (2) what program would best suit my needs?

Web Links

www.mhhe.com/krysik1 provides references to reviews of computer-assisted qualitative data analysis software as well as links to free teaching demos.

Keep in mind that the CAQDAS programs *aid* analysis, but they cannot *perform* analysis. The researcher must provide the guidance, while the computer makes the process less manual. (We address the analysis of qualitative data in Chapter 8.) In addition, these programs cost money and require time to learn. The researcher must decide whether the investment in time and money, as well as the potential benefits, are justified given the scope of the research and whether the researcher will have additional use for the software in the future. If the researcher is interested in using a CAQDAS program, she or he can consult published reviews in the form of books, articles, and online commentaries for help in choosing the program that will best meet her or his needs and budget.

WORKING WITHIN A BUDGET

Although the budget is certainly not the final consideration in preparing for data collection, we present it as the final topic in this chapter in order to provide an overview of the many different items that must be considered in a research or evaluation study. Exhibit 7.11 presents potential line items in a research budget. As you can infer from the number of items, research can be a costly and time-consuming endeavor. Research is not to be undertaken and then abandoned midway through because of a failure to budget adequately.

Which items the researcher includes in the budget will ultimately depend on the requirements of the funding source or sponsoring agency and the type of research design to be implemented. For multiyear projects, the budget may be developed by calendar or fiscal year as well as for the entire project. You can use the line items listed in Exhibit 7.11 as a guide for preparing a budget.

EXHIBIT 7.11

*Items for
Consideration
in a Research
Budget*

Labor
- Time for the researcher
- Data collectors
- Data entry
- Office support

Preliminary Research on the Problem Area
- Literature review
- Analysis of secondary data
- Primary data collection activities

Developing the Sample
- Accessing a sampling frame
- Recruitment

Measurement
- Purchasing measures, manuals, and scoring sheets
- Developing measures: constructing questions, pretesting, translating, formatting, printing
- Translation: measures, cover letters, informed consent documents, project correspondence
- Preparation of mailed packets and follow-up packets
- Internet surveys: Web design

Data Collection
- Hiring data collection staff (advertising, criminal record check, lab for drug screen)
- Training data collection staff (developing written materials, in person, and observation)
- Supervision and intra- and interrater reliability testing
- In-person (mileage, cell phones, rental cars, insurance)
- Mail survey (paper, envelopes, postage, preparation of address labels)
- Telephone survey (long-distance charges, toll-free telephone line)
- Tracking system (computerized or manual)
- Interim contact (cards, postcards, postage)

Incentives
- Number and value of incentives
- Incentives to report change of contact information

continued

EXHIBIT 7.11

Items for Consideration in a Research Budget
continued

Data Preparation
- Transcription
- Setting up the filing system for storing data as hard copy and electronically
- Database development
- Data entry (optical scanning)
- Verifying data

Equipment and Supplies
- Data recording equipment (audio/video recorders, blank tapes, laptops)
- Pens, markers, paper, stapler
- Focus groups: poster paper
- Day timers, palm pilots
- Pagers, cell phones

Data Analysis
- Database development
- Data entry
- Data analysis
- Report writing
- Consultant fees

Research Dissemination
- Report editing
- Report formatting
- Printing (extra for color inserts)
- Creating PDF files and posting on the Web
- Conference registration
- Equipment rental (overhead projector)
- Conference travel

Overhead
- Hardware (computers, scanners, copier, fax, overhead projector)
- Furniture (desks, telephones, filing cabinets)
- Space rental (office space, interview space)
- Software (word processing, tracking, data analysis, spreadsheet, presentation)
- University overhead (If research is conducted by a university faculty or institute on university time, the university often charges a percentage of the grant, often between 35 percent and 60 percent overhead.)

CONCLUSION

Preparing for data collection is a busy time for the social work researcher. A lot of planning and development has to go into managing the task of implementation. Managing a research project for success includes such steps as being strategic in planning for participant recruitment and retention. Development work requires writing a data collection protocol, a manual for training data collectors, and constructing a database and codebook. Even though data will not be entered in the database until after it is collected, developing the database before data collection begins can help pinpoint potential problems in the research or evaluation study. Depending on the scope of the research or evaluation, the data collection staff may be the "face" of the research to the participant. This makes hiring, training, and supervising data collectors of key importance to the success of the study. All steps in planning and implementing the research study are carried out with two main objectives in mind: minimizing error and maximizing response rate. This chapter concludes discussion of the implementation phase of the research process. With data in hand and entered in the database, the social work researcher is set to begin the process of data analysis. The analysis of qualitative and quantitative data is the subject of Chapters 8 and 9.

MAIN POINTS

- The researcher's choice of data collection method will depend on several factors, including characteristics of the research participants; size of the geographic area; requirements of the measures used (observation, in-depth interview; open-ended, closed-ended, or partially closed questions); subject matter; and the research budget.

- Failure to recruit and retain target participants in long-term research and evaluation studies can lead to the failure of any research project and at times even cancellation of entire programs. Researchers should be proactive and strategic in designing recruitment and retention plans to maximize success. Incentives can be used to encourage participation and retention but should only be one part of a multifaceted plan.

- There are many ways to calculate a response rate. The researcher must be explicit in reporting the method she or he has used and, when possible, examine the differences between respondents and nonrespondents. To avoid reporting inflated calculations of nonresponse, the researcher should subtract the number of nonsampling units from the original number of sampling units.

- Before participant recruitment begins, the researcher should develop a data collection protocol that will outline such items as the schedule of measures, the requirements for contacting participants, tracking procedures, the provision of incentives, recording requirements, data storage, and ethical considerations. The data collection protocol is a work in progress and will be updated as questions arise and decision rules are made with regard to data collection.

- For the novice researcher, collecting data will be unfamiliar and somewhat uncomfortable at first. Training and practice opportunities must be provided for data collectors so that they can assure participants of the importance of the data collected and describe its eventual use.

- Spreadsheet and data analysis computer software programs are available for analyzing and displaying quantitative data. Software programs are also available for analyzing qualitative data. Knowing how to use these programs is a valuable skill for social workers.

- Developing the database before data collection begins can help identify errors in the measures that can be corrected before implementation. With quantitative data, the researcher should always develop a unique identifier for each record in the database.

- Qualitative data that consist of the spoken word should always be recorded verbatim, in the first person as it is spoken, rather than in the third person as to what was observed. The preparation of in-depth interview data for qualitative analysis requires a labeling system that differentiates the researcher's observations, the identification of who said what if more than one person is involved, and the researcher's impressions and reflections.

EXERCISES: PRACTICING SOCIAL WORK

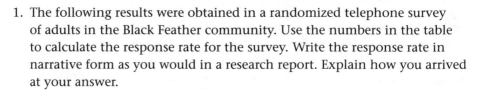

1. The following results were obtained in a randomized telephone survey of adults in the Black Feather community. Use the numbers in the table to calculate the response rate for the survey. Write the response rate in narrative form as you would in a research report. Explain how you arrived at your answer.

OUTCOME	NUMBER
Disconnected/nonworking number	47
Household refusal	173
No answer, not home	35
Unable to answer due to disability or language problem	37
Respondent did not complete the interview	52
Completed interviews	656
Total	1,000

EXERCISES: SOCIAL WORK LIBRARY

1. Compare and contrast the data collection strategies described in the articles by Saltzburg (2004) and Nichols-Casebolt and McGrath-Morris (2002).

OTHER EXERCISES

1. Create a database in SPSS that includes four questions from the Black Feather Youth Survey found on the CD-ROM that accompanies this book. The four questions to include are 1, 2, 32, and 33. To help with this task, use the SPSS tutorial found on the Web site for this book. The survey is located under Assess, Community Needs Assessment, Youth Needs Survey. Perform the following tasks for each of the four questions:

a. Develop a variable name.

b. Develop a variable label.

c. Define the variable values as appropriate given the level of measurement.

d. Specify a value for missing data.

When you are finished creating the codebook, print it. Then enter the data from the following table in your database. (Remember that the first variable in your database should be a unique student identifier.) When you have created your database, name it and save it to a disk.

NAME	QUESTION 1	QUESTION 2	QUESTION 32	QUESTION 33
Robert	1	1	15	1
Alex	2	2	17	2
Elizabeth	5	5	14	1
Juliana	4	4	17	
Isabel	4	4		2
Corrine	5	5	15	1
Nathaniel	2	2	16	2
Tyler	3	3	16	1
Terra	5	4	15	2
Alonso	1	2	17	1

2. Create a database in Excel for the same four questions and data presented in question 1. To help with this task, use the Excel tutorial also found on the Web site for this book.

a. Create the database.

    b. Enter the data.

    c. Name the database and save it to a disk.

    d. Create a codebook using a word processing program of your choice.

3. How do SPSS and Excel differ in the steps required to create a database?

4. How do the two programs compare for database creation: what do you prefer about either of the programs; what don't you like about either program?

CHAPTER 8

Describing the Data

Science is facts; just as houses are made of stones, so is science made of facts; but a pile of stones is not a house and a collection of facts is not necessarily science.

—HENRI POINCARÉ, FRENCH MATHEMATICIAN
AND PHYSICIST (1854–1912)

EXHIBIT 8.1 SHOWS RAW DATA AS THEY APPEAR IN AN EXCEL database. Exhibit 8.2 contains qualitative data as they appear in a text file. What do the data in either of these forms have to offer? The answer to that question in two words is not much. Raw data do not speak to us. In order to fulfill the purpose of research, we have to turn the raw data into information. Information is the ordering, summarizing, and analyzing of the data to enable us to formulate meaningful conclusions. Information, not data, will help guide social work practice. **Data analysis,** the focus of this chapter, is the process by which researchers turn data into information that can be used to determine the nature or cause of something in order to improve social work practice.

To analyze data effectively, the researcher must act like a detective and ask the right questions. Two important questions the researcher will try to answer through data analysis are (1) What is typical or common in the data? (2) What is the extent of difference or variation reflected in the data? For example, in a quantitative data set we may find that all of the respondents are teenagers. This is something they all have in common, and this is probably something useful to know. We may also find variation in the data, noting that the teenagers come from diverse economic backgrounds, with gross annual household incomes ranging from as low as $2,300 to as high as $56,000. These are examples of the useful information we can extract from quantitative data.

We also look for what data have in common in the analysis of qualitative data. We might look for themes or patterns in e-mail messages sent home from military troops deployed in Afghanistan, as in Exhibit 8.2. We might find, for example, that almost all of the service women and men repeatedly mention the sense of constant and immense danger. We also look for ways that qualitative data show variation. For example, the data may show that whereas

EXHIBIT 8.1

Raw Data in an Excel Database

ID	Q1	Q2	Q3	Q4	Q5
1	4	3	5	4	4
2	2	2	5	4	3
3	3	1	3	4	4
4	1	1	5	5	5
5		4	5	4	4
6	3	3	4	5	5
7	5	4	2	4	5
8	1	1	1	5	4
9	2	2	5	4	5
10	1	1	1	5	5
11	4	5	5	2	3
12	2	4	5	3	3
13	3	4	5	3	3
14	2	2	4	4	4
15	3	1	5	3	4

EXHIBIT 8.2

Qualitative Data in a Text File

Date – Thursday July 29, 2004 6:32 pm

Title: Kris from the Ghan

Hey everyone, I don't have a lot of time so I must be brief. It's pretty nuts here till about the 15th of Aug then I can phone maybe once a week or so but I'll write as many e-mails as I can. So what can I say? I made it here in one piece. It was a very long trip and not the most comfortable. Camp Mirage was like walking into a Sauna room with a winter jacket on, it was 125 degrees there. I arrived to Afghanistan camp Julien on Wednesday. I've been sleeping good as I'm still jet lagged. It is hot here, you don't stop sweating. It gets to like 95 by 7 am and then up to the mid 120s by the afternoon. My bunk space isn't much but it's a place to hang my head. A 6 by 8 cell is what I have but I am close to Jeff and all my buddies. Driving downtown Kabul is no treat. I think Afghanistan produces dust for the entire world. It is nuts down there. Like driving on the wrong side of the road against oncoming traffic while someone is hitting you with a blow torch and there is a burning pile of s--- under your nose. It stinks here. I've seen already people bathing in ditches or more like sewers. They hang their meat on hooks down town and it is covered with dust, flies and who knows what else. On a good note the camp is pretty good. The food is alright and the activities are ok. I won't have a lot of down time as I work on a 5-day workweek and hopefully I get a morning or afternoon off on one of these days. I can't wait till we get more English people here. Even this computer is all in French and so is the keyboard so sorry if there are typos. I miss you guys back home everyday but it feels like I am really a part of something great here despite the

EXHIBIT 8.2

Qualitative Data in a Text File
continued

inhumane territory. Anyways I gotta go to breakfast. It is 5 am here. I am 10 and a half hours ahead of you.

Gods Speed and Best Wishes

Love Kris

P.S. - Not to scare you all but, my first night here we had 3 RPGs fly over the camp and land half a mile away. I have also witnessed people getting beaten by the local police here for being idiots on the road, most of them deserved it though. I'll get pics for you as soon as I figure this computer out and I have time.

Source: Corporal Kristopher Denninger, stationed in Camp Julien, Afghanistan, from July 2004 to February 2005, sent to his parents, Reverend Clair (C.P.) and Joan Denninger. Used with permission.

The Social Work Library

Additional e-mails sent by Corporal Denninger from Afghanistan can be found at www.mhhe.com/krysik1.

some soldiers regularly refer to their sense of emotional connectedness to their comrades, others do not.

These two questions, What is common in the data? and How do the data vary? help guide analysis of both qualitative and quantitative data. In the analysis of quantitative data, the researcher answers these questions by using descriptive statistics. By contrast, in the analysis of qualitative data, the researcher often answers these questions by identifying categories and coding text. We explain and illustrate these processes later in this chapter.

Chapter 7 concluded at the point in the research process in which the researcher entered quantitative data into a database and organized qualitative data in terms of transcripts and notes. Although data collection and preparation are major achievements, the true value of the research comes in the form of analysis and reporting. This chapter addresses the kinds of information that qualitative and quantitative data have to offer. It also explains how to condense and extract this information from the quantitative database and the qualitative text. In addition, it focuses on how to *tell the story,* that is, extract and describe the information that emerges from data analysis in a concise and meaningful way. The instructional framework for this chapter is *tell me, show me, and let me try,* because when it comes to performing data analysis, a process that involves explanation, illustration, and doing facilitates learning.

Some students experience considerable fear when they think about statistics. If you are clutching your chest and feeling short of breath because you have some anxiety about working with numbers, take a moment, breathe deeply, and prepare to enjoy your journey. Remember that today most data analysis is done by computer. Nevertheless, you need to understand the logic of data analysis. The computer will then *do the math* for you. The information in this chapter and Chapter 9 may seem a little like learning a foreign language at first, but once you read the explanations, scrutinize the examples, and then try it for yourself, it will become much clearer. This chapter uses quantitative data from the Black Feather Youth Survey introduced in Chapter 1 for the purposes of illustration and practice. Qualitative data for practice are in the form of authentic e-mail messages written by a young army recruit to his parents during his first deployment to a war zone. The practice exercises and step-by-step instructions on the book's Web site are presented for both SPSS and Excel. The advantage of using these programs in tandem is that you can easily import the data from one program to the other, thereby allowing you to capitalize on the unique features of each one.

Can you do this? Yes, you can; and like many others before you, the authors included, you may find yourself excited about being able to derive meaning and draw conclusions from data because you will use the information to improve social work services and social conditions. By the end of this chapter, you should be able to:

- Conduct a preliminary analysis of quantitative data.
- Discuss how to select descriptive statistics based on level of measurement and distribution.
- Critique a frequency table.

CASE-IN-POINT 8.1

Avoiding GIGO: Garbage In, Garbage Out

In an experimental study to determine the effectiveness of an integrated case management program for children with multiple agency involvement, a researcher reported that 12 months into the study all 11 girls in the control group were pregnant compared to none in the intervention group. While the researcher was presenting that finding to a group of stakeholders, the results suddenly struck her as odd. What were the chances that 100 percent of the girls in one group would be pregnant? When the researcher checked the original data, she found that the results were indeed false due to errors that had been made in coding. In reality, none of the girls in the control group was pregnant—a very different story than what she had presented.

The moral of this unfortunate story is that databases almost always have errors: errors in recording, coding, and data entry. Researchers must take time to verify the data before analysis, not only to avoid making erroneous, embarrassing, and even damaging conclusions, but also because they have an ethical responsibility to ensure that their research is accurate.

- Develop a histogram and a bar chart.
- Code qualitative data for analysis.
- Discuss ways of validating the analysis of qualitative data.

VERIFYING QUANTITATIVE DATA

Once you have entered the data in the database, it is important to check them for accuracy before proceeding to analysis. Case-in-Point 8.1 presents one example of what can happen when errors are not corrected before analysis. In addition to correcting errors, **data verification**—checking to see that the information has been entered and coded correctly—serves the useful purpose of making the researcher more familiar with the data. Data verification may sound tedious because it has to be done variable by variable. The use of computer software programs such as SPSS and Excel, however, has made the procedure much simpler than in the past. This chapter presents the process of data verification as a series of four logically ordered steps:

- Ordering the data
- Examining the data graphically
- Recoding data
- Computing scales by combining multiple variables

We will now examine these four steps in detail.

Ordering the Data

The previous chapter mentioned the value of scrolling through the database, searching column by column for out-of-range values. (Remember that variables are in the columns and cases are in the rows.) This process, although useful, is not likely to identify errors in coding such as the one described in the example in Case-in-Point 8.1. The first step in verifying the data, then, is to put it into some type of order. Ordering the data will help the researcher determine more easily what values are represented for each variable and whether these values make sense.

You can order data sets by having the computer arrange the data in an **array,** that is, in ascending or descending order column by column. You can then browse each column to spot possible errors. A much more efficient means of ordering data is to construct a **frequency distribution** for each variable, which provides a count of how many times each variable value is represented in the database. It answers the question With what frequency does each value of a variable occur? A frequency distribution can be constructed for variables at all levels of measurement: nominal, ordinal, interval, and ratio. By using a computer program such as SPSS or Excel, you can accomplish this task in very little time.

Frequency Distributions at the Nominal Level.   For a variable measured at the nominal level, such as ethnicity, the frequency distribution shows how many different ethnic categories are represented in the data set and the frequency with which each category is represented. Exhibit 8.3 shows a frequency distribution generated in SPSS for the variable Gender from the Black Feather Youth Survey. When we examine the first two columns of the frequency distribution, we see that the variable value of male has a count, or frequency, of 90, and the variable value of female has a count of 98. That is, of the 190 respondents, 90 (47.4 percent) were coded as male and 98 (51.6 percent) were coded as female.

EXHIBIT 8.3

Frequency Distribution for a Variable Measured at the Nominal Level

GENDER

		FREQUENCY	PERCENT	VALID PERCENT	CUMULATIVE PERCENT
Valid	Male	90	47.4	47.4	47.4
	Female	98	51.6	51.6	98.9
	3	1	.5	.5	99.5
	4	1	.5	.5	100.0
	Total	190	100.0	100.0	

We also see variable values 3 and 4, each with a count of 1. Returning to our database or codebook, we check the valid codes for Gender and note only three codes: 1 = male, 2 = female, and 9 = missing data. This means that variable values 3 and 4 are not valid codes. In order to determine what the correct values are, we need to find the two errors in the database. (If the invalid responses have a frequency of more than 1, we need to find each occurrence of the error.) Once we locate the errors, we look for the identification number associated with each record (usually found in the first cell in the row), and we use it to look up the original hard-copy data collection instrument. We may find that the values were data entry errors; if so, we can fix them by typing the correct values in the database and saving the file. Alternatively, we may find that the questionnaires did not have valid responses. If we cannot determine the correct values, we would change the incorrect values to 9s to indicate missing data. Do not forget to save the corrected file, and always use the correct version.

Frequency Distributions at the Ordinal Level.   In the case of a variable measured at the ordinal level, the frequency distribution shows the range of values represented on an ordered continuum of responses. Exhibit 8.4 displays a frequency distribution created in SPSS for the Black Feather Youth Survey variable q9. This variable represents responses to the statement "I feel safe in my community." Notice that the frequency distribution table is titled with the variable label rather than with the variable name q9. This is a useful feature in SPSS. Examining Exhibit 8.4, we observe that the responses of the 190 youths spanned the entire range of responses from Strongly Disagree to Strongly Agree. In contrast to Exhibit 8.3, there are no apparent out-of-range values in this frequency distribution.

When you are reporting the percentage of respondents in one category—for example, 9.5 percent of the 190 youths strongly disagreed with the statement that they feel safe in their community—use the percentages in the fourth column labeled "Valid Percent." The third column, "Percent," happens to be identical to

Tutorials

See www.mhhe.com/krysik1 for detailed instructions on how to create a frequency distribution in SPSS and Excel.

		FREQUENCY	PERCENT	VALID PERCENT	CUMULATIVE PERCENT
			I FEEL SAFE		
Valid	Strongly Disagree	18	9.5	9.5	9.5
	Disagree	25	13.2	13.2	22.6
	Neither	51	26.8	26.8	49.5
	Agree	62	32.6	32.6	82.1
	Strongly Agree	34	17.9	17.9	100.0
	Total	190	100.0	100.0	

EXHIBIT 8.4

Frequency Distribution for a Variable Measured at the Ordinal Level

the "Valid Percent" column in Exhibits 8.3 and 8.4 because there are no missing data. The percentages in the third column, however, are calculated from the total number of cases, whereas the valid percentages are calculated from the total number of valid responses; they do not include cases with missing data in the calculation. Valid percentage represents the percentage of all cases for those we know. For an example of a frequency distribution with missing data see Exhibit 8.6 on p. 229.

Given that the data are ordered in a frequency distribution, the final column, "Cumulative Percent," calculates the total percentage up to that particular point. For example, the cumulative frequency distribution indicates that 22.6 percent of respondents answered either Strongly Disagree or Disagree. Thus, we could legitimately offer the following conclusion: "Of the 190 youths surveyed, 22.6 percent disagreed with the statement *I feel safe in my community.*" This type of information is useful when we are considering variables measured at the ordinal or ratio levels.

When examining frequency distributions for each variable, we should always ask, Does the information from the data make sense given what I know about the population or sample? This is often the only way to identify coding errors such as those described earlier in the erroneous reporting of the pregnant control group.

Frequency Distributions at the Interval and Ratio Levels.   Whereas frequency distributions are useful for verifying nominal- and ordinal-level data, they have limited utility when used with interval- and ratio-level data. This is especially true in large studies that have many records and many values represented for each variable. To illustrate this point, consider a hypothetical frequency distribution for the variable Ethnicity (nominal-level data). The frequency distribution will have the same number of categories represented regardless of whether the study includes 200 or 1 million individuals. The same observation holds true for a variable measured at the ordinal level, such as the statement "I feel safe in my community," that has a set number of predefined responses.

Now consider a frequency distribution for the variable Gross Annual Income, which is measured at the ratio level. The frequency distribution for 200 individuals would have a maximum of 200 different values. Although this number is not concise, it is manageable. The frequency distribution for 3,000 individuals, in contrast, could literally have as many as 3,000 different values listed. This number certainly would be unmanageable. Conversely, if we were to examine the age of the freshman class at a large university, there might be little variation even though there are thousands of students. Clearly, then, we must decide variable by variable, based on the number of records in the database and the expected variability in the data, whether a frequency distribution is appropriate for interval-level and ratio-level data.

Examining the Data Graphically

 Tutorials

See www.mhhe.com/krysik1 for detailed instructions on how to create a scatterplot for one variable using Excel.

As the old saying goes, "A picture is worth a thousand words." In the case of interval and ratio data, we might say, "A picture is worth a thousand data points." Each value entered in the database is a **data point.** When frequency distributions are inappropriate for verifying interval and ratio data as described previously, a graphic representation may be a useful alternative. Programs such as SPSS and Excel can produce plots to illustrate the types of information that a frequency distribution offers. There are different kinds of plots, but we will present the scatterplot because it is so frequently used with interval and ratio data. A **scatterplot** is a graphic representation of the values of one or two variables. In this chapter, we deal with only one variable at a time; in the next chapter, we deal with two variables.

We can draw an analogy between scatterplots and stargazing. Each data point on the plot is analogous to a star in the night sky. In examining scatterplots, we look for patterns in the data similar to those we search for in constellations. We can glean a great deal of information from examining a scatterplot, most of which we will discuss in Chapter 9. For the purpose of verifying data, however, we are interested primarily in detecting the presence of **outliers**—data points that are off by themselves, isolated from the other data points. If you think that this definition sounds rather arbitrary, you are right. Later in this chapter in Advanced Skill Development 8.2, we will present a mathematical method for judging whether an outlier should be excluded from the analysis. Take a minute to examine Exhibit 8.5. Which data points would you consider outliers?

Sometimes a data point that appears to be an outlier is actually an error. For this reason, we should verify the values of all outliers. For example, an outlier

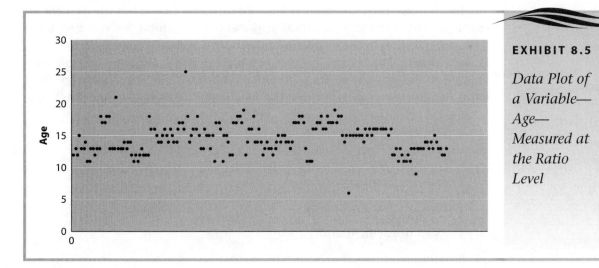

EXHIBIT 8.5

Data Plot of a Variable— Age— Measured at the Ratio Level

that shows age to be 143 is most likely an error. We use the same process of verifying suspect values as we do for out-of-range values. We (a) locate the value in our database, (b) find the associated record identification number, and then (c) go back to our original records to determine whether the data were entered correctly. In some cases, we may even return to the source of the data, as the error may have been introduced in data collection rather than data entry. If we verify that the extreme data points are not errors, we still want to make note of them. As you will see later in this chapter, true outliers will require us to be selective about how we report our analysis.

Whether we are examining data in the form of frequency distributions or graphically, we should adhere to the same process. Specifically, we should step back from the plot and ask, Based on what I know about the research, population, and sample, does this story make sense? Sometimes when we are immersed in the process of verifying data, it is difficult to "see the forest for the trees." It is vitally important, then, to take the time to reflect on the meaning suggested by the data. If the meaning doesn't make sense, there is probably a reason. At that point, we need to search a little deeper for possible sources of error.

Recoding Data

In the process of ordering the data and presenting them graphically, we may notice that some categories of certain variables do not have many cases in them. One explanation is that the categories were not well conceptualized. Another possibility is that in retrospect some categories either were not mutually exclusive or had little relevance to respondents. In such circumstances, we may decide to **collapse** some of the categories, that is, to combine two or more categories into a smaller number of categories. Collapsing categories has the effect of increasing the number of cases represented in a given category.

To illustrate the process of collapsing categories, consider the variable of ethnicity. The frequency distribution presented in Exhibit 8.6 was generated from one question in the evaluation of a Youth Life Skills program in the Black Feather project. The youths in the program were asked, What do you consider yourself to be? They were then provided with six responses to describe their ethnicity. The value labels listed in the codebook for this variable are as follows:

1. White, Non-Hispanic

2. African American

3. American Indian

4. Hispanic, Latino, Spanish

5. Asian or Pacific Islander

6. Other

WHAT DO YOU CONSIDER YOURSELF TO BE?

		FREQUENCY	PERCENT	VALID PERCENT	CUMULATIVE PERCENT
Valid	White, Non-Hispanic	269	50.8	54.0	54.0
	African American	99	18.7	19.9	73.9
	American Indian	52	9.8	10.4	84.3
	Hispanic, Latino, Spanish	21	4.0	4.2	88.6
	Asian or Pacific Islander	6	1.1	1.2	89.8
	Other	51	9.6	10.2	100.0
	Total	498	94.0	100.0	
Missing	System	32	6.0		
Total		530	100.0		

EXHIBIT 8.6

Frequency Distribution of Ethnicity

As we can see in Exhibit 8.6, a total of 51 youths, approximately 10 percent of the 530 respondents, selected the Other category to represent their ethnicity. These respondents subsequently were asked to specify what they meant. Examples of their responses include Indian; 25% Indian; Black and White; and four variations of Irish, including Irish, Irish American, Irish descent, and Irish full blood. Based on the respondents' descriptions of their own ethnicity, the researcher's next step is to create some decision rules about changing some of the responses coded as Other. One decision rule might be to code as 1 all responses that specify any variation of Irish. Similarly, the researcher might add a seventh category to represent Mixed Ethnicity. One purpose of creating new categories is to reduce the ambiguity within the categories. Changing a respondent's answers is acceptable, as long as the decision rule (what was done) and the justification for doing so (why it was done) are made clear when reporting the results.

The researcher considering the frequency distribution in Exhibit 8.6 might note two potential ethical dilemmas regarding the low frequency in the category Asian or Pacific Islander ($n = 6$). If the researcher's plan is to present data by ethnic category, she or he would want to collapse this category into Other. There are two reasons for this: (1) to protect the confidentiality of the six Asian youths represented in the sample, because in a small geographic area some people reading a summary of the research could reasonably guess the identity of the individuals from such a small subgroup; and (2) to discourage readers from drawing conclusions from the data based on such a small subgroup. This process of changing one value to another—for example, changing all 5s representing Asian or Pacific Islander to 6s representing Other, is referred to as **recoding.** Although recoding could be a tedious process and is subject to error when it is done manually, it is easily accomplished using available routines in computer programs such as SPSS and Excel.

Tutorials

See www.mhhe.com/krysik1 for detailed instructions on how to recode data in SPSS and Excel.

Statistical programs usually offer users the choice to create a new variable with the recoded results or to overwrite the existing variable. Recoding the variable into a new variable with a new name is always better than writing over the old variable. Otherwise, we will be unable to refer back to the original data. Finally, it is important to keep notes on decision rules made with regard to recoding in a file or a journal.

Computing Scales by Combining Multiple Variables

In Chapter 6, we discussed scales as one option in measurement. For many concepts—depression, for example—measurement using a single item would be unreliable. For this reason, researchers prefer to use a combination of items that, when combined, are represented by a single score. Sometimes researchers use a standardized scale; at other times, they create a scale from questions they develop.

The 31 items listed in Exhibit 8.7 represent questions included on the Black Feather Youth Survey. Notice that the response categories for each question are

EXHIBIT 8.7

The Black Feather Youth Survey Questionnaire

YOUTH SURVEY QUESTIONNAIRE	STRONGLY DISAGREE	DISAGREE	NEITHER	AGREE	STRONGLY AGREE
1. When I get older, I plan to live in the same community as I currently live.	1	2	3	4	5
2. When I get older, I plan to get a job in this community.	1	2	3	4	5
3. When I get older, I plan to graduate from high school.	1	2	3	4	5
4. When I get older, I plan to go to the doctor for regular checkups.	1	2	3	4	5
5. When I get older, I plan to go to the dentist for regular checkups.	1	2	3	4	5
6. When I get older, I plan to seek counseling if I have a personal or family problem.	1	2	3	4	5
7. When I get older, I plan to seek counseling if I have a drug or alcohol problem.	1	2	3	4	5
8. When I get older, I plan to go to the doctor if I feel sick.	1	2	3	4	5
9. I feel safe in my community.	1	2	3	4	5
10. If I have a health problem, I feel that I have someone I can talk to about it.	1	2	3	4	5

YOUTH SURVEY QUESTIONNAIRE	STRONGLY DISAGREE	DISAGREE	NEITHER	AGREE	STRONGLY AGREE
11. I don't feel respected by the adults in my community.	1	2	3	4	5
12. I feel connected to my community.	1	2	3	4	5
13. I trust the teachers at my school.	1	2	3	4	5
14. I feel connected to my family.	1	2	3	4	5
15. The police do a good job of preventing crime in this community.	1	2	3	4	5
16. I feel that I cannot talk to the police if there is a problem.	1	2	3	4	5
17. Parents are not involved with their kids in this community.	1	2	3	4	5
18. There is too much crime in this community.	1	2	3	4	5
19. When I grow up, I feel that I can get a good education in this community.	1	2	3	4	5
20. There is nothing to do for fun in this community.	1	2	3	4	5
21. There are too many drug dealers in this community.	1	2	3	4	5
22. Gangs are a problem in this community.	1	2	3	4	5
23. Family violence is a problem in this community.	1	2	3	4	5
24. Teen pregnancy is a problem in this community.	1	2	3	4	5
25. There is a lack of health care services in this community.	1	2	3	4	5
26. A lot of parents are using illegal drugs in this community.	1	2	3	4	5
27. I worry about being a victim of crime in this community.	1	2	3	4	5
28. A lot of teens are using illegal drugs in this community.	1	2	3	4	5
29. There is a lack of counseling services in this community.	1	2	3	4	5
30. There is a lack of good schools in this community.	1	2	3	4	5
31. There are not enough police officers in this community.	1	2	3	4	5

EXHIBIT 8.7

The Black Feather Youth Survey Questionnaire
continued

identical. Therefore, they could easily be combined into a scale. If we examine the list of items carefully, we might conclude that it would make theoretical sense to construct a number of one-dimensional scales, or scales that measure only one concept. For instance, 10 items on the questionnaire relate to perceptions of crime in the community (items 15, 16, 18, 21, 22, 23, 26, 27, 28, and 31). These 10 items could be added to produce a single "perception of crime" subscale score. Other scales could be developed for future health plans, future community plans, sense of connection, satisfaction with community services, and so on.

Assessing Internal Consistency.   Chapter 6 introduced the concepts of measurement validity and reliability. The section on reliability included a discussion of Chronbach's alpha, a statistic used to assess the internal consistency of the items included in a scale. Chronbach's alpha, commonly referred to as the "alpha coefficient," ranges from 0 to 1.0. Before calculating total scale scores to use in the analysis, the researcher should evaluate the scale's internal consistency using Chronbach's alpha. Scales in which the items are not scored consistently will have a relatively low alpha coefficient. Conversely, scales in which the items are scored consistently will have a relatively high alpha coefficient. A general guideline is that a scale used for research must have an alpha coefficient of .60 or greater (Hudson, 1991). In the case of a poorly performing scale, the researcher may want to reconfigure the scale by using different combinations of items and then recompute alpha.

The first step in computing an alpha coefficient is recoding. However, recoding is necessary only if some of the items are worded positively and some negatively. For example, questions 11 and 13 in Exhibit 8.7 are part of a subscale that measures "relationship with adults." High scores should indicate positive feelings about adults. If items are inversely worded—that is, low scores indicate high levels of positive feelings—the researcher would need to recode the scores for that item so that high scores are positive and low scores are negative. As you can see, question 11 states "I don't feel respected by the adults in my community," and question 13 states "I trust the teachers at my school." In order to combine these two variables into a single scale, the researcher would have to recode responses on question 11 to be consistent with the direction of the responses on question 13. Thus, if she or he wished to recode the items in a positive direction, the values of question 11 would be recoded as follows:

1 (strongly disagree) would become 5

2 (disagree) would become 4

3 (neither) = 3 (neither) (no recoding necessary)

4 (agree) would become 2

5 (strongly agree) would become 1

Once the researcher has completed recoding the data, she or he should save the data file under a new file name—for example, BFYSrecode—in order to differentiate it from the original data file. Once the researcher has saved the recoded file, there is no need to repeat the process, unless additional recoding is required.

Tutorials

See www.mhhe.com/krysik1 for detailed instructions on how to compute Chronbach's alpha in SPSS and Excel.

Calculating a Total Scale Score.   Regardless of the source of the scale, standardized or personally developed, each item is represented in the database as a separate variable. Therefore, we need to compute a total scale score by combining the values of the individual variables that make up the scale. There are many ways to calculate a total scale score. If the scale is standardized, the scale's author undoubtedly will provide instructions for scoring.

One way to calculate the total scale score is simply to add the responses to the different items in the scale. However, simply adding the values can produce misleading results if data are missing for some of the items. For instance, one individual with a score of 30 may have failed to respond to 4 of the 10 items on the scale. Another individual with a score of 30 may have answered every item. It is unlikely that these two individuals are actually equivalent on the construct being measured by the scale, even though their scores add up to the same value. For situations such as this one, the researcher might want to create a decision rule concerning the minimum number of responses that must be present for a total scale score to be calculated or considered in any analysis. If the scale is a published scale, the author may already have recommended such a rule. An example of such a rule is that at least 80 percent of the total number of items on the scale must be completed, or the total scale score will be calculated as missing.

Another way to deal with missing values is to use the **mean,** or average value, for that item as a substitute for the missing score. (We discuss the calculation of the mean later in this chapter.) For example, if the mean score for question 11 were 2.35, then anyone missing data for question 11 would be assigned that value in place of the missing data value. If the researcher inserts the mean for the missing data, the group mean for question 11 will not change, and there will be no missing values. Again, the researcher must explain this decision rule, in writing, in the research report.

Another problem with simply adding the value of the individual items is that the distribution of possible values on the scale may not permit easy comparison to other scale scores. Scale scores that can vary from 18 to 73 are more difficult to visualize than scores from 0 to 100. The additive method is especially problematic if a number of subscales are computed that have varying numbers of items per scale, resulting in unique scores for each scale. It is much easier to interpret and present data when all of the total scale scores have a standard and memorable range such as 0 to 100.

Fortunately, social work researchers have already figured out how to accommodate missing data and create total scale scores with a common metric of 0 to 100. One formula to accomplish this task is as follows:

1. Count the number of completed items in the scale (a).

2. Add the item responses (b).

3. Compute the highest possible score on the response scale for each item and subtract 1 (c).

4. Calculate the total scale score: (b − a) × (100)/a × c

To calculate the total scale score, begin by summing the item responses (b), subtracting from that sum the number of completed items (a), and then multiplying by 100. The resulting number is the numerator, the top number in the equation. The denominator, the bottom number in the equation, is calculated by multiplying the number of completed items (a) by the highest possible value on the response scale minus 1 (c). The final step is to divide the numerator by the denominator (Hudson, 1991). The example in Exhibit 8.8 uses data from the Black Feather Youth Survey to illustrate this equation.

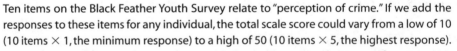

EXHIBIT 8.8

Computing Scales That Range from 0 to 100

 Tutorials

See www.mhhe.com/ krysik1 for detailed instructions on how to compute total scale scores in SPSS and Excel.

Ten items on the Black Feather Youth Survey relate to "perception of crime." If we add the responses to these items for any individual, the total scale score could vary from a low of 10 (10 items × 1, the minimum response) to a high of 50 (10 items × 5, the highest response).

To convert the total scale score from a simple total to a score that ranges from 0 to 100, we would calculate the score as follows. The item numbers are listed in the left column, and the responses to each item from one person are listed in the middle column. Any inverse or negative items have already been recoded. The computation is shown step-by-step on the right. The equation can be computed simultaneously for each case using a computer program such as SPSS or Excel.

ITEM	SCORE	COMPUTATION
15	3	1. There are 8 completed items.
16	4	2. The sum of the responses = 28
18	4	(without items 23 and 27).
21	5	3. The highest possible item response
22	3	is 5, and (5 − 1) = 4.
23	9 (missing)	4. Compute the equation:
26	2	(28 − 8) × 100/(8 × 4)
27	9 (missing)	= 20 × 100/32
28	4	= 2,000/32
31	3	Total scale score: 62.5

Once we have completed the four steps in data verification, we are ready to begin the analysis of the data set. The next section examines how to use descriptive statistics to explain the data.

DESCRIBING QUANTITATIVE DATA

The goal in describing quantitative data is to present as complete a picture of the data as possible in a concise and informative manner. To accomplish this, we use descriptive statistics. **Descriptive statistics** are measures used to summarize the many numbers included in the database into fewer numbers that are descriptive of the entire set of data. Descriptive statistics provide information for the aggregate data, rather than for each individual case or record included in the data. This is why descriptive statistics are commonly referred to as *data-reduction devices*.

The role of descriptive statistics is to communicate about the data, one variable at a time, without attempting to generalize. **Univariate analysis** refers to the examination of data one variable at a time. As we will see, the choice of univariate statistic is based on the level at which the variable is measured. Descriptive statistics are often categorized into two types: measures of central tendency and measures of variability. When these two types are used together, they are powerful statistical tools for describing the data.

Central Tendency

Central tendency refers to analysis that summarizes or represents all of the data related to a variable. It shows the degree to which the data are similar. There are three measures of central tendency, and they are probably very familiar to you, even though you may not recognize them by name. They are the mode, the median, and, the mean. Each of these measures can convey important and distinctive information about the **distribution,** defined as the values for a particular variable.

 Tutorials

See www.mhhe.com/krysik1 for detailed instructions on how to compute the three measures of central tendency in SPSS and Excel.

Mode.   The **mode** specifies the value that occurs most frequently in the entire distribution. We are asking about the mode when we ask questions of the data such as Do boys or girls constitute the majority of the sample? and What was the most frequently visited domestic violence shelter in the city? At times, more than one value in a distribution occurs with relative frequency. For example, three shelters may have topped the list of "the most frequently visited" in 2005. If so, we have more than one mode to describe what is typical.

When two values occur with the greatest relative frequency, the distribution of the data is said to be **bimodal.** When more than two values occur with

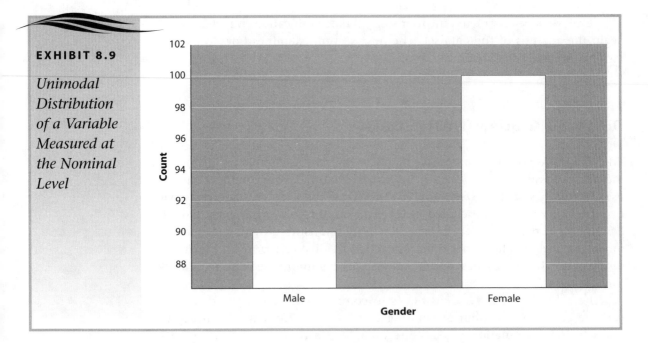

EXHIBIT 8.9

Unimodal Distribution of a Variable Measured at the Nominal Level

greatest relative frequency, the distribution is **multimodal.** A distribution with only one mode is **unimodal.**

We can use the mode to help describe the data at all four levels of measurement: nominal, ordinal, interval, and ratio. Exhibit 8.9 depicts a unimodal distribution for the variable Gender. In this example, the count on the y axis (the vertical axis, "Count") indicates that there are 90 males and 100 females in the distribution. Therefore, the mode is female. To represent the mode of nominal data graphically, we use a bar chart. The bar chart presented in Exhibit 8.9 was created in SPSS.

Exhibit 8.10 illustrates a multimodal distribution for the variable Gross Household Income. The data for this variable are continuous and are measured at the ratio level. A **histogram** is the graphic tool of choice to represent the distribution of continuous data. The histogram, a graph of a frequency distribution in which vertical bars of different heights are proportionate to corresponding frequencies, is shown in Exhibit 8.10. It was created using SPSS and shows several distinct peaks in the data, or several modes.

Practicing Social Work

See the CD-ROM that accompanies this book for detailed instructions on how to create bar charts and histograms in SPSS and Excel.

Median. Several variables of concern to social workers, including wages, rent, and housing prices, are typically reported as median values. For example, the U.S. Census Bureau reported that the lowest median home values were in the states of West Virginia ($78,200), North Dakota ($78,600), Mississippi ($78,700), and Arkansas ($79,902) (Buckner, 2005, p. 1). The **median** represents the 50 percent mark, or the value that divides a distribution in half so that

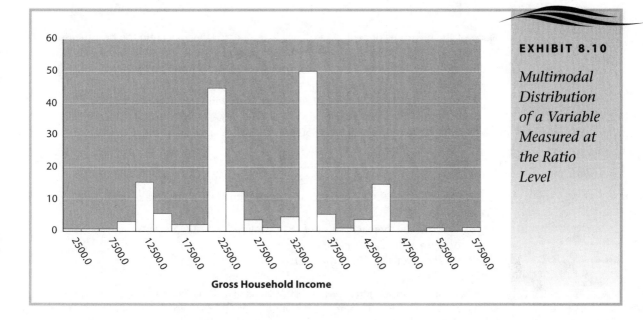

50 percent of the data points fall below this value and 50 percent above it. The median is meaningful only for data at the interval or ratio levels.

A preliminary step in determining the median for any distribution is to order the data. If the distribution has an odd number of values, the median is the number at the center of the distribution. If the distribution has an even number of values, we compute the median by calculating the average of the two most central values (adding them and dividing by 2). For example, consider the following distribution of values for the variable Years of Age:

10, 10, 11, 13, 14, 15, 15, 15, 16, 17, 18

The median in this example is 15 because it is the 6th of 11 values in the ordered distribution. Note that in this example, the median and the mode are the same. In many other cases, this will not be true.

Mean.   The mean, or the average as it is typically referred to, is probably the most commonly used and broadly familiar measure of central tendency. We use it to answer questions such as What is the average cost of child care in South Tucson? and What is the average life expectancy of African American males in the United States? Like the median, the mean is intended for use with interval- or ratio-level data. Sometimes it is also acceptable to calculate a mean for ordinal-level data; other times it is not. For example, reporting the average response to the item "I feel safe in my community" with a 1 representing Strongly Disagree and a 5 representing Strongly Agree would make sense. Reporting a mean of 2.5, however, for a variable that rank-orders income categories such as 1 (0 to $10,000),

See www.mhhe.com/
krysik1 for the answers
to questions 1–6 in
Advanced Skill
Development 8.1.

ADVANCED SKILL DEVELOPMENT 8.1

Selecting the Best Measure of Central Tendency

The Social Work Library

None of the measures of central tendency is the best; rather, selecting the best measure depends on how the data are distributed. For example, assume that we asked a sample of 10 individuals their age in years. Their responses were as follows: 25, 26, 27, 28, 30, 31, 32, 32, 33, 86.

The sum of the 10 numbers is 350. Answer the following seven questions:

1. What is the mode of the distribution?
2. What is the median of the distribution?
3. What is the mean of the distribution?
4. Which of the 10 values, if any, would you consider an outlier?
5. How does the outlier influence the calculation of each measure of central tendency?
6. Which of the three measures of central tendency best represents the typical age of those in the distribution?
7. What did you learn from this exercise?

When we are considering whether the median in particular is a good measure of central tendency, we must also examine the distribution of numbers. For example, if the distribution is heavily weighted at both ends, the 50 percent value may have little meaning. Take a minute to examine the following test scores, and then answer the following questions.

1, 1, 1, 1, 1, 3, 100, 100, 100, 100, 100

1. What is the best measure of central tendency? Why?
2. Is the median helpful in describing the data? Why?
3. Is the mean useful in describing the data? Why?
4. Is the mode useful for describing the data? Why?

2 ($10,001 to $20,000), 3 ($20,001 to $30,000), and so on, would not make sense. Means computed for nominal data are always meaningless, even though SPSS and Excel will easily produce them. If data are coded with a 1 for male and a 2 for female, for example, the average value for Gender might be 1.6, a meaningless value.

To calculate the mean, we sum all of the values in a distribution and then divide that sum by the total number of values. A special feature of the mean is that it is the only measure of central tendency that uses every value in the distribution in its calculation. This property of the mean makes it sensitive to extreme values, as illustrated in Advanced Skill Development 8.1.

Just because the computer computes, doesn't mean you should use it.

Variability

If we were limited to measures of central tendency to describe data, our descriptions would be incomplete and sometimes misleading. However, if we combine measures of central tendency with **measures of variability,** also referred to as *measures of dispersion*, we can provide a much more thorough description of the data. The words *variability* and *dispersion* imply the opposite of the word *central*. Measures of variability enable us to describe how the data differ or vary from what is common.

There are four commonly used measures of variability: minimum, maximum, range, and standard deviation. Like the median and the mean, measures of variability are intended for use with interval- and ratio-level data, although sometimes they are appropriately used with ordinal data as well.

Minimum, Maximum, and Range.   The **minimum value** is the lowest value represented in a distribution. Conversely, the **maximum value** is the highest value in the distribution. The **range** is the spread between the minimum and the maximum value. We calculate the range by subtracting the minimum value from the maximum value and adding 1. To illustrate these concepts, let's use the distribution of ages from Advanced Skill Development 8.1:

25, 26, 27, 28, 30, 31, 32, 32, 33, 86

The minimum age in the distribution is 25 years.

The maximum age in the distribution is 86 years.

The range in age is ([86 − 25] + 1) = 62 years.

A distribution with values that are similar in magnitude would be described as slightly variable or containing limited variation. A distribution in which all of the values are the same displays no variation. We would characterize this distribution of ages as variable. As will be seen in the next section, variability is measured with the standard deviation.

A common application of these three measures of variability is in describing the distribution of scores on a standardized scale. If a researcher were describing the results of a pretest of a depression scale, for example, the researcher might report, "The minimum score on the pretest was 14 and the maximum score was 68, a range of 55 points between the lowest and the highest scores."

Standard Deviation.   The final measure of variability, known as the **standard deviation,** is not widely used in everyday life, but it has a great deal of utility in statistical analysis. The standard deviation is a statistical measure of the amount by which a set of values differs from the mean. As with the mean, the calculation of standard deviation requires us to include every value in a distribution.

Calculating the standard deviation involves the following steps: (1) subtracting each value in a distribution from the mean of that distribution,

To calculate SD for a sample, the denominator is N – 1.

 Tutorials

See www.mhhe.com/krysik1 for an example of calculating the standard deviation in SPSS and Excel.

(2) computing the square of each of these numbers, and (3) adding the squares. The resulting number is called the *sum of squared deviations from the mean*, and it is the numerator in the following equation. The next step is to divide this sum by the total number of data points in the distribution (*N*). The standard deviation (*SD*) is the square root of this number. The formula for standard deviation is written as follows:

$$SD = \sqrt{\frac{\Sigma(\overline{X} - x)^2}{N}}$$

Σ is the mathematical symbol for summation.

$\overline{X}$ is the mathematical symbol for the mean.

x represents each value in the distribution.

You will probably never manually calculate a standard deviation because you will use the computer to do it for you. Standard deviation has three important uses:

- It enables us to compare the variability in different distributions.

- It is used in the calculation of many statistics, including the correlation coefficient, discussed in Chapter 6.

- It helps us interpret the scores within a normal distribution.

This section discusses the first function; the third is addressed in a later section titled "The Normal Distribution." The use of the standard deviation in calculating statistical tests can be found in many statistical textbooks and is beyond the scope of this book.

Regarding the first point, standard deviation reflects the variation in the scores so that we can compare different distributions. The size of the standard deviation is directly related to the variability in the data. That is, the greater the value of the standard deviation, the greater the variation in the distribution. The smaller the value of the standard deviation, the less the variability in the distribution, and the more clustered the data are about the mean. To illustrate these points, consider the following two distributions of age, which are identical except for the 10th values.

Distribution A: 25, 26, 27, 28, 30, 31, 32, 32, 33, 86

Distribution B: 25, 26, 27, 28, 30, 31, 32, 32, 33, 34

The mean of Distribution A is 35 years, not much different from the mean of Distribution B, which is 29.8 years. However, the standard deviation of

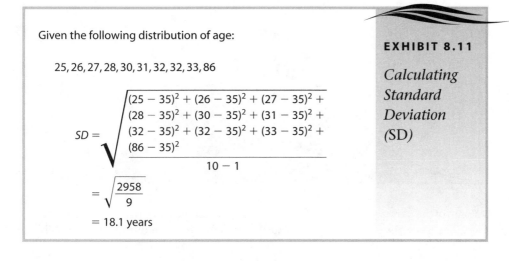

Given the following distribution of age:

25, 26, 27, 28, 30, 31, 32, 32, 33, 86

$$SD = \sqrt{\frac{\begin{array}{l}(25-35)^2 + (26-35)^2 + (27-35)^2 + \\ (28-35)^2 + (30-35)^2 + (31-35)^2 + \\ (32-35)^2 + (32-35)^2 + (33-35)^2 + \\ (86-35)^2\end{array}}{10-1}}$$

$$= \sqrt{\frac{2958}{9}}$$

$$= 18.1 \text{ years}$$

EXHIBIT 8.11

Calculating Standard Deviation (SD)

Distribution A is 18.1 years, compared to the standard deviation of 3.12 years for Distribution B. (See Exhibit 8.11 for an example of calculating the standard deviation.) By comparing the sizes of the standard deviations, we can conclude that the values are much closer to the mean in Distribution B, and we might assume that there is much more variability in Distribution A. What we do not know from these summary statistics about Distribution A is that an outlier is responsible for distorting the mean and the standard deviation. In fact, the values are actually quite clustered around the mean in Distribution A, with the single exception of the final value: 86. Clearly, then, combining information on the mean and the standard deviation with the minimum and maximum values provides us with a clearer picture of the two distributions, even if we do not review the raw data. We can use the *SD*, together with the mean, minimum, maximum, and *N*, to describe a small-to-large number of data points.

The Shapes of Distributions

Displaying continuous data graphically, as in the histogram in Exhibit 8.10, allows us to see at a glance how the data are distributed over the entire range of values. The shape of the distribution gives us an idea about what kind of distribution the data conform to. The data associated with many variables that are of interest to social workers are consistent with a type of distribution known as the normal distribution, the topic to which we now turn.

The shape of the normal distribution resembles a bell, which is why we often hear the term bell curve associated with its use.

The Normal Distribution. The **normal distribution** is a theoretical distribution of data that has several distinctive features. First, it is symmetric, meaning that one half is a mirror image of the other half. Second, because it is symmetric, it is also unimodal. Therefore, in a normal distribution, the data are distributed symmetrically about a single peak or mode. Third, 50 percent of the data

EXHIBIT 8.12

*Area under
the Curve
of the Normal
Distribution*

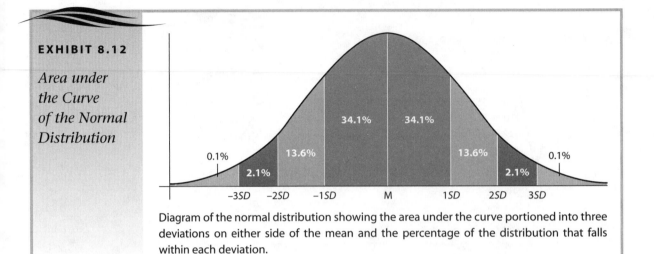

Diagram of the normal distribution showing the area under the curve portioned into three deviations on either side of the mean and the percentage of the distribution that falls within each deviation.

points fall on either side of the peak, indicating that the value of the median is the same as the value of the mode. Finally, the mean value of the distribution is precisely halfway between the ordered data points, indicating that it is also equal to the values of the mode and the median. Therefore, in a normal distribution: mean = mode = median.

Many things in life appear to have the characteristics of a normal distribution, perhaps accounting for its name. A normal distribution can be seen in a pile of raked leaves, the distribution of height and weight in the population, the age at which youths reach puberty, and most human talents and abilities. Other things do not have a normal distribution. Grades in graduate school are usually not normally distributed. They cluster at the high end. Wealth in the United States is also not normally distributed; households are clustered at the low end of the wealth continuum.

Because a normal distribution has several distinguishing characteristics, we can assess whether data are normally distributed without having to graph them. Put simply, if the mean, median, and mode are approximately equal, the data fit the profile of the normal distribution. Of course, the mean, median, and mode are precisely the same only when we have a very large number of data points; for small samples, they will differ slightly. When the data are consistent with the shape of the normal distribution, as shown in Exhibit 8.12, we can apply the mathematical properties of the normal distribution to the data using our knowledge of the mean and the *SD*. The mathematical properties of the normal distribution are as follows:

- The total area underneath the curve of the normal distribution, or any distribution for that matter, is always equal to 1, or 100%.

- The fact that the normal distribution is symmetric means that 50% of the distribution is found on either side of the mean.

- The distance of 1 *SD* to the left of the mean is the same as 1 *SD* to the right of the mean, and so on.

- If we partition the area under the curve, we know that 34.13% of the distribution of scores will fall within 1 *SD* from the mean. This means that 68.26% of the distribution will fall within plus-or-minus 1 *SD* from the mean (±1 *SD*). Another 13.59% of the distribution will fall between 1 and 2 *SD*s from the mean. This means that approximately 95% of the scores in the distribution will fall within ±2 *SD*s on either side of the mean. Another 2.14% of the distribution will fall between 2 and 3 *SD*s. Thus, a total of 99.72% of the area under the curve is accounted for within ±3 *SD*s from the mean. It is useful to know that falling outside of two standard deviations is a fairly rare event that happens only 5% of the time.

- Note that the curve does not touch the horizontal axis, or x axis, at ±3 *SD*s from the mean. Even though 99.72% of the distribution will be accounted for within 3 *SD*s on either side of the mean, the remaining .0014% of the scores will fall outside the lowermost and uppermost deviations.

This brings us to the third important use of standard deviation. If the distribution of the data conforms to the theoretical normal distribution, then the standard deviation permits us to interpret the scores within the distribution with great precision. If interval or ratio data are normally distributed, we usually report the standard deviation together with the mean so that the reader can get a better picture of how the data are distributed about the mean. Presenting the mean and the standard deviation together also indicates where a given score falls relative to other scores in the distribution.

Exhibit 8.13 presents a histogram showing the distribution of scores on a posttest of Life Skills. The data are from the Black Feather Youth Survey, and they represent the scores of 187 youths (*N* = 187). By considering the way the histogram conforms to the shape of the curve and comparing the mean, median, and mode, we could reasonably conclude that the distribution approximates the normal distribution. The mean and the median are equal at 64, and the mode is slightly lower at 58. The scores on the posttest ranged from a low of 17 to a high of 98.

Knowing that the distribution approximates normal, the mean equals 64.11, and the *SD* equals 14.91, we can draw certain conclusions about how the values are distributed around the mean. For example, because the mean posttest score was 64, we know that approximately 50 percent of the scores were below

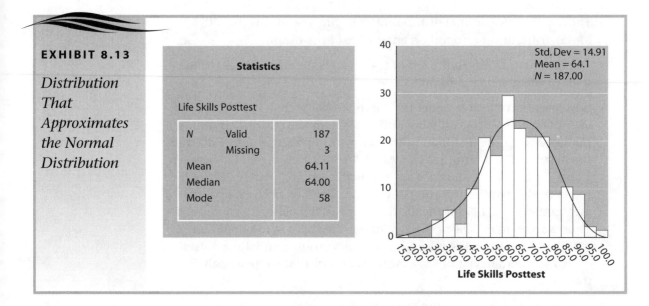

EXHIBIT 8.13

Distribution That Approximates the Normal Distribution

Statistics

Life Skills Posttest

N	Valid	187
	Missing	3
Mean		64.11
Median		64.00
Mode		58

Std. Dev = 14.91
Mean = 64.1
N = 187.00

Life Skills Posttest

that number and 50 percent were above it. We also know that approximately 68 percent of the scores in the distribution fell within one standard deviation from the mean—specifically, between the scores of 49.20 (64.11 − 14.91) and 79.02 (64.11 + 14.91).

Knowing that a distribution is normal can also help us determine whether a certain value is likely or unlikely to occur. Similarly, we can use the properties of the normal distribution to judge objectively whether an outlier should be excluded from the descriptive analysis, as illustrated in Advanced Skill Development 8.2.

Skewed Distributions. If a distribution does not appear symmetric when we plot it—that is, one half of the distribution is not a mirror image of the other half—we describe the distribution as a **skewed** or **non-normal distribution.** The term *skewed* simply means that it deviates from the normal distribution. If the scores trail out around the high end or the right side of the curve, we say that the distribution is **positively skewed.** Visually, the mode of a positively skewed distribution is to the left of the mean, and the curve extends to the right as if it had a longer tail on that side. Conversely, if the long tail is to the left of the mean and the mode is to the right of the mean, the distribution is **negatively skewed.** Exhibit 8.14 presents examples of positively and negatively skewed distributions. We can judge the direction in which the data are skewed by examining a histogram or by determining where the mean and mode fall on the distribution. Determining the type of distribution is necessary because, as we will see in Chapter 9, the types of statistical tests that can be used to analyze the data depend on the distribution of the data.

As we saw earlier in this chapter, the presence of outliers can severely distort the mean and standard deviation of a distribution. The social work researcher is likely to encounter at least one or two true outliers in her or his career, so the question becomes how to handle them. The application of Chauvenet's criterion is one technique for objectively assessing whether an outlier is so unlikely to occur in a sample that it should be excluded (Taylor, 1997).

Chauvenet's criterion uses the properties of the normal distribution to evaluate the likelihood that a data point of a certain magnitude is an unlikely occurrence. The probability that a data point will fall beyond 2 *SD*s on either side of the mean is roughly 5%, or .05. To apply Chauvenet's criterion, we multiply the total number of data points (*N*) by .05. If the result is less than .5, we can exclude the outlier. For example, consider the following distribution for age: 25, 26, 27, 28, 30, 31, 86. The value of 86 is an obvious outlier. There are seven data points in this distribution (*N* = 7), so the probability that the outlier (86) should be so far from the mean is calculated by .05 × 7 = .35. Applying Chauvenet's criterion, .35 is less than .5, so the outlier of 86 should be excluded from the analysis. The revised distribution (25, 26, 27, 28, 30, 31) has a mean of 27.83 and an *SD* of 2.32. These summary statistics are much more representative of the central tendency and variability in the data than the summary statistics calculated with the inclusion of the outlier ($\overline{X}$ = 35, *SD* = 18.13).

ADVANCED SKILL DEVELOPMENT 8.2

Deciding Whether to Exclude an Outlier

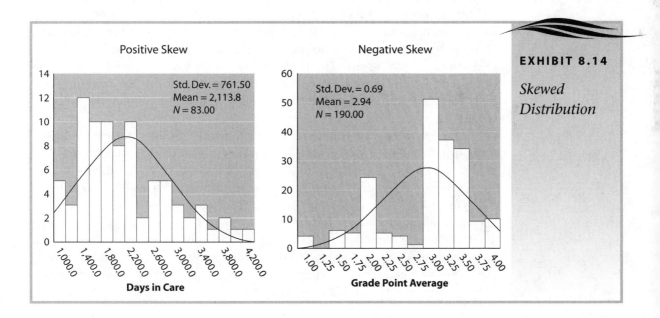

EXHIBIT 8.14

Skewed Distribution

Reporting Descriptive Analyses

Once you have analyzed the data in terms of central tendency and variability, you will want to report it to individuals and groups who have an interest in the results. One goal in this chapter is to provide you with some general tips and alert you to some common errors in reporting descriptive analysis. Reporting

EXHIBIT 8.15

*Sample
Frequency
Table*

CHARACTERISTICS OF YOUTHS IN RESIDENTIAL AND DETENTION PROGRAMS

VARIABLE	DETENTION (*N* = 116)		RESIDENTIAL (*N* = 145)	
	NUMBER	PERCENTAGE	NUMBER	PERCENTAGE
Race				
White	71	61%	92	63%
Nonwhite	45	39%	53	37%
Gender				
Male	90	78%	102	70%
Female	26	22%	43	30%

Source: Roe-Sepowitz, 2005. Adapted with permission from the author.

the results represents the culmination of your work in executing the research process. To do your research justice and to ensure that it has the desired impact on social work practice, you must report the results clearly and accurately. Chapter 12 outlines the various options for presenting research results, including conference and poster presentations, reports, and writing for publication. In addition, there are many books and style guides that describe how to communicate research results. The information we provide here serves two functions. First, it will help you present and describe data effectively. Second, it will help you read and critique the presentation of descriptive analyses by other researchers.

There are three ways to present descriptive analyses: in narrative or written form; displayed in a table; and graphically in bar charts, histograms, line graphs, and so on. A combination of these methods is often the most effective approach, and it serves as a guided visual tour through the results. It is unlikely that you will report every single finding from your study. Instead, you must choose carefully among the results that best fulfill the objectives of the research and that lead the intended audience to the conclusion revealed by the analysis. For this reason, you will want to begin the writing process by first designing the tables and graphics and then developing the written or spoken narrative around the presentation of the analysis.

Designing Effective Tables. A frequency table, like the one shown in Exhibit 8.15, is one of the simplest ways to organize and display data. The following guidelines will assist you in designing effective tables:

- Nominal and ordinal variables naturally order themselves into groups that lend themselves to frequency tables.

- To present interval and ratio data in a frequency table, you can divide the data into 6 to 15 equally spaced and mutually exclusive intervals.

- Some core information is standard and expected in the presentation of a table. To begin with, the variables go into the rows and the frequencies or other statistics in the columns. If you report percentages in the table, you must also report Ns, usually in the heading. Use horizontal lines to break up the sections of the table. An alternative is to present the table as a grid.

- Tables should be labeled as tables and numbered consecutively (Table 1, Table 2, and so on). In addition, they should be titled in a way that clearly describes the tables' contents.

- Each row and column in a table must have a heading.

- Use statistical symbols and abbreviations in tables to conserve space: % for percent, $\overline{X}$ for Mean, Mdn. for Median, Mo. for Mode, SD for standard deviation, and Min. and Max. for minimum and maximum. Use an uppercase, italicized N for the entire sample or population and a lowercase, italicized n to report the size of subgroups such as male and female.

- Always report valid percentages rather than absolute percentages in the tables. Remember that valid percentages are calculated without the inclusion of missing data in the Ns.

- Use notes at the end of the table for explanation, such as presenting operational definitions and decision rules and to document sources.

Developing Graphics. Most word processing programs can help you create graphics that you can integrate into the text with ease. You can also import graphics from Excel and SPSS. When you incorporate graphics into the text, you should refer to them as figures, number them consecutively, and describe each in a caption.

Interval and ratio data should be displayed in histograms and line graphs. Line graphs, such as the one shown in Exhibit 8.16, are recommended for displaying trend data, or data over time. This graph illustrates how attitudes toward police change over time. It represents a longitudinal study in which scores on an attitude scale were measured every five years from age 10 to age 30. Higher scores represent more favorable attitudes. What patterns do you notice?

In contrast, nominal and ordinal data are best displayed in pie charts, like the one shown in Exhibit 8.17, or bar charts. Always report valid percentages in the charts. A table can handle many variables at a time, whereas a chart is restricted to a single variable. Published articles often present categorical data in tables rather than charts due to space restrictions. In contrast, research reports and presentations generally are not restricted by space limitations.

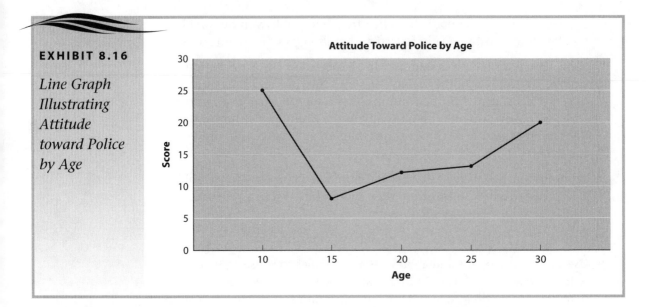

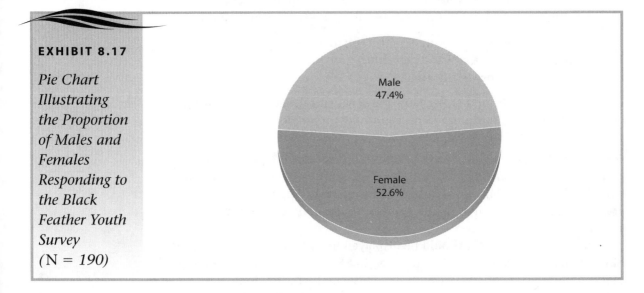

Finally, if the research report will be printed in black and white, avoid using graphics that require the reader to distinguish between too many shades of gray. The graphics should be large enough that all type is easy to read. A common size for a typical graphic is about half a page.

Writing the Narrative.   Most of the descriptive analysis will be presented in the results section of the research report or presentation. The results section should include only the presentation of the results. It is not the appropriate section to introduce theories or discuss the implications of the research. When you are writing the narrative, consider the following points:

- If the objective of the research is to compare two or more groups, instead of presenting aggregate information for the group as a whole, provide only the descriptive information for each group.

- The narrative should always address the data contained in the tables and figures, but it should avoid discussing every detail. It is best to pick out the two or three most salient points in each table or figure and discuss each one for emphasis.

- The tables and graphics should be placed near the location in the narrative where they are first mentioned. Otherwise, the reader has to flip back and forth between the text and the visuals.

- Interval and ratio data should be described with means, standard deviations, and *N*s. If the distribution of the data does not conform to the normal distribution, the median, minimum, and maximum values should be reported as alternatives.

- When reporting percentages, always report the corresponding *N*s.

- Use percentages only to compare groups that are similar in size. Otherwise, they can be misleading.

- Avoid reporting percentages for small groups. For instance, if 50 percent of the sample is less than 10 cases, reporting percentages can be misleading. Report actual numbers for small samples.

ANALYZING QUALITATIVE DATA

Analysis and reporting of qualitative data are very different from those of quantitative data. After you have collected all the data you want from the selected sample, or are unable to find any more unique insights, you continue the process of qualitative data analysis to reach the end point of reporting your findings. In qualitative data analysis, your task is to take a large amount of raw data, usually in the form of text, and condense it into something that is manageable without sacrificing meaning. There is no one right way to analyze qualitative data. The lack of a clear procedure for analyzing qualitative data does not imply, however, that this process is haphazard, unsystematic, or purely subjective. In fact, good qualitative analysis does follow a systematic process, and this process should be made clear when you report the study.

A major distinction between qualitative and quantitative research approaches involves the sequencing of data analysis in the research process. In

The Social Work Library

Read the articles by Westerfelt (2004) and Saltzburg (2004) online in the Social Work Library.

quantitative research, data analysis and reporting are the end stage of the research process. In qualitative research, data analysis is an iterative process, in which data are collected, analysis occurs concurrently, and more data are purposively collected. For example, Alex Westerfelt (2004) conducted a study of how faithfully a group of men infected with HIV adhered to their treatment schedules. Westerfelt describes the iterative process of data collection and analysis:

> I attempted to offset any bias on my part (that is, hearing only what was most important to me) by including another note taker and conducting three focus groups, modifying the interview guide after each group for inclusion of the new areas of inquiry that emerged. (p. 233)

Qualitative analysis also differs from quantitative analysis in its treatment of outliers. Whereas outliers are problematic—and sometimes excluded—when you analyze quantitative data, when you conduct qualitative research, you often look for outliers to make the research inclusive and holistic as opposed to reductionist. Chapter 2 discussed several different schools of qualitative research, for example, ethnography and grounded theory. Just as there are different schools of qualitative research, there are also many different approaches to the analysis of qualitative data. Our goal in this chapter is to present an overview of some of the major steps that are common in qualitative data analysis. The process we present includes four steps: (1) organizing the data into concepts, (2) developing the story, (3) validating conclusions, and (4) reporting the findings. To illustrate the process, we present examples from two published studies. The first is Alex Westerfelt's (2004) study of men who are HIV-positive, mentioned previously. The second is a study by Susan Saltzburg (2004) of the responses of parents when they first learn that their adolescent child is gay or lesbian. You can access each of these articles in the online Social Work Library.

Organizing the Data into Concepts

By the time the researcher has organized the data for analysis by transcribing interviews and compiling observations and field notes, his or her first task is to read through the entire collection of data. This is an important part of the analysis, and it can lead to different perspectives from those the researcher adopted when he or she considered the data piece by piece. As the researcher progresses through the data, he or she will note that some data have nothing to do with the research question and other data are not particularly relevant. This is the beginning of process known as **data reduction.**

During data collection and preliminary analysis, the researcher has made theoretical notes that include his or her thoughts about what the data meant, potential themes and concepts that seemed to emerge from the data, and additional questions. Now that the researcher has had a chance to consider the full text, including these notes, he or she can begin to identify concepts in the data, fitting them into categories. These concepts may or may not be consistent with those developed earlier. Nevertheless, the initial thoughts provide a good starting place. This process is described as follows by Westerfelt.

> I undertook a general thematic analysis, repeatedly reviewing both sets of notes [his and those of a graduate student assistant] to categorize recurring topics. These topics were further modified, adding others and grouping related categories together. (p. 233)

Once the researcher has selected the relevant categories, he or she begins coding the data. **Coding** is a method of categorizing qualitative data to make it manageable for analysis. In coding, the researcher marks portions of the text, notes included, with labels to indicate data that fit with the identified categories. Note that not all methods of qualitative data analysis involve coding, but many do. The researcher will mark the text with different levels of codes. For instance, in qualitative observations of the parent-toddler relationship, first-level codes might include *attachment, discipline, play,* and *education*. Subcodes within the category of attachment might include observations of *physical affection* such as *kissing, hugging,* and *touch*. The researcher records the codes and their meanings on a master list that organizes them by the different levels. The following example illustrates three levels of coding for the category of parent-child attachment that could be used to mark text.

ATTACHMENT	AT
AT: Physical affection	AT-PA
AT-PA-Kissing	AT-PA-K
AT-PA-Hugging	AT-PA-H

Coding is an iterative process. The researcher works through the text and refines the coding system, adding new categories and codes as required. The researcher must be aware of the different perspectives in the data and include them in the coding. Specifically, the **etic** perspective is that of the researcher, whereas the **emic** perspective offers the insight of the participant. It is important that the emic perspective be considered in the analysis, along with that of the researcher.

When the researcher has completed coding, she or he can reduce the data by extracting coded segments and organizing them by code. The researcher typically accomplishes this task through indexing the codes as to their location in the data so that the appropriate text can physically be brought together, compared, and summarized. Using a qualitative analysis software program, such as those discussed in Chapter 7, makes the extraction of text an easier task. The researcher can also use the copy and paste functions of a word processing program. Finally, the researcher can extract segments manually by literally cutting the text apart and organizing it by code.

Qualitative research is generally an inductive process, meaning that the researcher identifies categories and codes while collecting and analyzing data. Coding allows the researcher to move from raw data to the generation of concepts and theories. This approach is different from a deductive process that begins with a theory or framework and examines the data for the major concepts that are consistent with that theory or framework.

Developing the Story

The researcher engaged in the process of coding the data must constantly question how the emerging patterns or themes in the data relate to the initial research question. She or he will look for deviations from the themes in the data, areas of disagreement, and contrast. When the researcher finds contrasting data, she or he will search to identify the factors that can help explain the deviations.

The Social Work Library

Miles and Huberman (1994) illustrate many different forms of data displays in their book on qualitative data analysis.

A helpful tool in moving from data coding to the development of conclusions is to organize the categories, themes, and patterns into **data displays.** These can take many forms, but their basic purpose is to help the researcher describe and explain visually how the concepts in the data are linked. The data display further reduces the amount of text, making the task of drawing conclusions more manageable. A data display can take the form of a role-ordered matrix with defined rows and columns, like the one in Exhibit 8.18. Alternatively, it may map the relationships among concepts, the chronology of a process, or the steps involved in decision making. It may also present a typology. Data displays are limited only by the creativity of the researcher.

As with analyzing qualitative data in general, designing a data display is an iterative process. The researcher moves back and forth between the display and the data, revising and testing to see if the display fits for all of the data. When the researcher finds contrasting data, he or she must revise the display. As in quantitative analysis, the researcher must note the decision rules governing the design of the display for later reference and reporting.

As the reviewer refines the data displays, he or she inevitably observes patterns and themes, exceptions, and consistencies. Based on these observations, the researcher begins to draw conclusions, which he or she must explain in writing. Conclusions do more than summarize the data. Rather, they can involve rich descriptions with interpretations, theories, and questions and hypotheses for further research. At the same time, however, the researcher must be careful to avoid generalizing beyond the data. He or she should always check any conclusions against the original full-text data. If the conclusions do not fit with a subsequent reading of the data, they will need to be revised. Once the

ROLE		ANTICIPATED IMPACT OF CHANGE	PERCEIVED ROLE IN CHANGE	PERCEIVED PREPAREDNESS FOR CHANGE	PERCEPTIONS OF EXTERNAL SUPPORT FOR CHANGE	+ OR − PERCEPTION OF CHANGE
Administrator	Olivia					
	David					
	Kiley					
Case manager	Cowden					
	Terry					
	Alonso					
	Karina					
Foster care licensing personnel	AVC					
	Shalom					
	Pasqua					
	Delaney					
Foster parent	Mum J.					
	Dad C.					
	Mum I.					
	Mum T.					

EXHIBIT 8.18

Role-Ordered Data Display to Illustrate Perception of the Implementation of a New Foster Care Training Curriculum

conclusions fit with the data, yet another layer of validation will occur. Susan Saltzburg effectively describes this process:

> The steps for analysis include transcribing texts, discerning themes, reflecting on variations of meaning, translating to social work language, moving back and forth between the individual protocols (that is, interviews) to ensure that a structure emerging in one was not overlooked in another, and finally synthesizing the themes into the phenomenological summary. (p. 112)

Validating the Conclusions

The process of validating conclusions involves judging whether the conclusions that have emerged from the analysis are credible, defensible, and able to withstand alternative explanations. Researchers use numerous methods to validate the conclusions of qualitative data analysis. Here we discuss five of these methods: (1) triangulation, (2) respondent validation, (3) an explicit account of the data collection and analysis methods, (4) reflexivity, and (5) attention to negative cases.

The first method, **triangulation,** is the process of making comparisons among the results from different methods of data collection or different sources. For example, the researcher could compare the results obtained from observations to those obtained from interviews. Similarly, she or he could compare the results from a group of homeless individuals to the accounts of staff members at the homeless shelters. The second method, **respondent validation,** or **member checking,** as it is often referred to, involves reviewing the results of the data analysis with the participants of the research. The participants' reactions are then included in the report of the findings. This strategy is common in the qualitative approach known as participatory action research, discussed in Chapter 11.

Moving on to the third method of validation, because other researchers may wish to validate the claims of the study, the report should explicitly provide a clear description of how the data were collected and analyzed. For example, if the researcher coded the data, he or she must explain how the early coding was refined. Were some of the transcripts coded by an independent researcher and compared for reliability? How did the researcher create the data displays? How did the researcher structure additional data collection efforts based on the findings from the preliminary analysis? These are only some of the questions the results section of the research report should answer.

The fourth method, **reflexivity,** refers to the researcher's own reflections on how she or he might have directly impacted the research process, including the conclusions. Here, the researcher must take into account such factors as her or his age, gender, ethnicity, economic background, and profession as well as any relevant personal experiences. Reflexivity should be ongoing throughout the qualitative research process and should be addressed in the research report. Finally, the report of the findings should provide evidence that the researcher explored data that seemed to contradict her or his conclusions, sought cases that differed from the norm, and considered rival explanations for the findings.

Reporting the Findings

Whereas the style of writing required for reporting quantitative analysis is highly technical, qualitative analysis can be presented in a more literary style. In fact, the researcher often uses the first person ("I"). Nevertheless, qualitative research sometimes reports statistical information as well, especially to describe the sample. For example, Westerfelt reports, "Six respondents were living alone, and 15 were living with others (primarily partners)" (p. 234). The descriptions of the methods of analysis and the results are not as distinct in the qualitative research report as they are in the quantitative research report. In the qualitative report, the researcher will want to clearly explain her or his esoteric approach to the analysis. She or he also will likely present the data display or a revised version of it.

One of the most distinguishing features of the qualitative research report is that the author intersperses quotes both to illustrate and, to support the conclusions and to reflect the voices of the participants. In the Saltzburg example, the author discovered five common themes in her analysis. She used the themes as headings in writing her manuscript, and she provided quotes to illustrate each one. Although she includes verbatim quotes, Saltzburg is careful to protect the identity of the participants by labeling each with a title and a letter such as "Mother M" or "Mother J." An effective use of presenting quotes is found in the following excerpt from Saltzburg (2004), which she presented underneath the heading "Emotional Detachment."

> I can't stop the thoughts I have about homosexuality. This is what I've learned and what I believe. And now these apply to my child. It's awful to have these thoughts about one of your children. And I think that is what the depression and drinking was about. I felt so torn by all the awful thoughts I had about the child I loved. And I shut down from her and felt so empty. (Mother M) (p. 113)

In drawing a conclusion, the researcher should note for what proportion of the sample the conclusion applied. For example, Saltzburg reports, "Whereas all of the parents spoke about feeling stunned by the finality of their adolescent's disclosure, five alluded to a level of semiconscious awareness that they believed existed as far back as childhood" (p. 112). At the same time, however, the researcher must be careful not to turn the qualitative report into a quantitative study by reporting the frequency of occurrence for each coded segment of participant data.

The way in which the report is written will depend to a great extent on the qualitative method. Case studies (discussed in Chapter 10), for example, are intended to provide a holistic view of a subgroup, organization, or other single entity. Ethnography describes the culture of a group. Grounded theory aims at explaining a phenomenon. Whatever the qualitative method, the most important evaluative question for judging the qualitative report will be Did the findings fulfill the purpose of the research?

CONCLUSION

This chapter demonstrated the uniqueness of quantitative and qualitative data and the differences in the methods used to analyze these data. The use of personal computers has made the analysis and presentation of quantitative data much easier than in the past. The social work researcher, however, must tell the computer what to do. This requires knowledge of the different statistics and graphical formats that are right for each level of data and for the way that the data are distributed. There is much more diversity in the approaches used to analyze qualitative data; nevertheless, the analysis process is highly systematic and defined. This chapter examined the use of descriptive statistics to evaluate data and to summarize and describe it one variable at a time. The next chapter looks at using statistical tests to examine the relationship between two variables at a time.

MAIN POINTS

- Data are not useful in raw form. To have utility for social work practice, data have to be analyzed and turned into information. This requires social workers with sound research skills. Data analysis software, quantitative or qualitative, cannot turn data into information.

- An outlier is a value that is out of range relative to most of the data. In quantitative data analysis, we look for outliers by examining scatterplots or by developing frequency distributions for interval and ratio data. All outliers should be verified as to whether they are true extreme values or errors.

- In quantitative research, data analysis is a defined end stage of the research, whereas in qualitative research, the data analysis phase is an iterative process, in which data are collected, simultaneously analyzed, and more data are collected.

- Descriptive statistics are useful in providing an overview of the research to the reader. There are two types of descriptive statistics: central tendency and variability. Used in conjunction, they represent powerful tools for describing data.

- The value of the entire research process will be judged by the quality of the analysis as reported in the final report or presentation. If the report is not well conceptualized, accurate, or effectively written, the research will not have the desired impact: to improve social work practice.

EXERCISES: PRACTICING SOCIAL WORK

1. Verify the data in the SPSS Black Feather Youth Survey file on your CD-ROM. Do you detect any plausible errors? Outliers? The data file is located under Assess, Community Needs Survey, Youth Needs Survey.

2. Plot the age variable using Excel. Calculate measures of central tendency and dispersion using SPSS. Now remove case 14 and rerun the measures of central tendency. What measures of central tendency and dispersion are sensitive to extreme values? What measures of central tendency and dispersion are relatively unchanged by the deletion of case 14?

3. Find four variables in the Black Feather Youth Survey file, one representing each level of measurement. For each of the four variables, select the appropriate measures of central tendency and dispersion to describe the data in narrative and graphic form.

EXERCISES: SOCIAL WORK LIBRARY

1. Compare and contrast the approach to data analysis used by Saltzburg (2004) and Westerfelt (2004).

OTHER EXERCISES

1. Plot the distribution of gender in your classroom. What type of diagram did you use to represent this variable? Justify your choice.

2. Now plot the distribution of the age of students in your classroom. What type of diagram did you use to represent this variable? Justify your choice.

CHAPTER 9

Bivariate Statistics and Statistical Inference

Statistics can be used appropriately, or they can be misused. The challenge is to decide whether a particular application is one or the other.

MAKING INFERENCES COMES SO NATURALLY THAT MOST OF THE time we are not even consciously aware that we are engaged in the process. We make inferences when we mentally calculate the odds of a certain outcome based on prior knowledge and experience. For instance, what are the chances that this will be a good movie, based on my friends' recommendations? What are my chances of crossing a busy street without getting hit by a car? When the consequences are serious, we accept very low risk, as in crossing a busy street. Other times, we may have a higher risk tolerance, as in choosing to see a potentially bad movie.

Similarly, in social work practice we make decisions based on inferences about the odds of a particular outcome. Sometimes the consequences of making an error are serious. For example, what are the chances that a child will be safe if left in a home with a parent who has previously been abusive? At other times, the consequences of making the wrong decision are less serious. For example, what are the chances that shortening a parent education program from 16 to 12 sessions will reduce the program's effectiveness? This process of mentally calculating the odds is known as **logical inference. Statistical inference** is similar in that it involves making a calculated decision based on the results of an observation. Instead of making a judgment based on how we feel or think about the odds, as we do in logical inference, statistical inference relies on a mathematical calculation of the odds.

Statistical inference is based on **probability**—the odds or chances that something will happen based on the ratio of the number of favorable outcomes to the total number of possible outcomes. For example, if someone tossed a coin and correctly predicted that it would land heads up, we might not be too impressed, because we know there is a 50/50 chance of that person being right. Getting 50 percent heads and 50 percent tails is the typical, or expected, variation in tossing coins. If the person correctly predicted the outcome of a coin toss 70 times in a row, however, we might be either very impressed or very suspicious that the coin was not a regularly minted coin. In making inferences about the outcomes of research, we use the science of probability to assess the likelihood that our finding is the result of chance or typical variation in our object of study.

We all have an intuitive sense of probability. For example, if the average height of men is 5 feet 9 inches and the average height of women is 5 feet 5 inches, which of the following groups do you believe is all male and which is all female?

- Group 1: 5'8", 5'6", 5'4", 5'2", 5'4", 5'5", 5'6", 5'1"

- Group 2: 5'9", 6'1", 5'8", 5'7", 5'8", 5'9", 6'2", 5'6"

- Group 3: 5'6", 5'8", 6'0", 5'2", 5'7", 5'5", 5'7", 5'6"

You probably guessed that Group 1 is female, Group 2 is male, and Group 3 is hard to tell. You based your decision on your intuitive knowledge of probability. In statistical inference, we use math to estimate whether a sample reflects a population or whether the observed differences between the sample and the population are the result of chance—the chance that a particular observation is not representative of the population.

The previous chapter discussed ways to describe quantitative data one variable at a time using frequency tables, measures of central tendency, and measures of variability. In this chapter, we discuss **bivariate analysis,** statistical methods that enable us to go beyond the consideration of one variable to consider two variables at one time. Much of social work research is concerned with how two or more variables are related. This chapter also addresses **statistical significance testing:** determining the likelihood that the findings from sample data are *real*. In order to make judgments about the certainty of our findings, we must know not only the extent to which differences occur but also the extent to which they occur more frequently than we would expect by chance variation.

By the end of this chapter, you should be able to:

- Explain hypothesis testing by statistical inference, including the concepts *p*-level, rejection level, and statistical significance.

- Explain what is meant by Type I and Type II errors in hypothesis testing.

- Explain when to use parametric and nonparametric statistics.

- Explain the use of specific statistical tests for hypothesis testing, including Pearson's *r*, chi-square, various t-tests, and one-way analysis of variance (ANOVA), including how to interpret and report them.

- Explain the difference between a statistically significant result and a meaningful result.

- Given a quantitative research study using the statistical tests described in this chapter, explain what conclusions can and cannot be drawn from the data.

STATISTICAL SIGNIFICANCE TESTING

For most human attributes, there is variation; that is, there is a range of possibilities. People vary in height, in level of self-esteem, in political attitudes, in parenting skills, and so on. We assume that there is variation in any population. Thus, when we study a sample, it should also exhibit variation. We hope that the variation in the sample reflects the variation in the population from which the sample was drawn, especially if the sample selection was random and of sufficient size. As discussed in Chapter 5, selecting a sample that does not accurately reflect the true level of variation in the population is referred to as *sampling error*. In a hypothetical population of 500 students, for example, 70 percent support same-sex marriage and 30 percent do not. It is possible, but unlikely, to draw a random sample of 100 from the 500 students who are all against same-sex marriage. Based on this nonrepresentative sample, we would wrongly conclude that all students in the population are against same-sex marriage. We use inferential statistics to assess the likelihood that we have drawn a sample that does not accurately reflect the population.

We also use inferential statistics to test hypotheses. As we saw in Chapter 3, a hypothesis is a stated belief about the relationship among or between variables. The null hypothesis (H_o) is a statement that there is no relationship between the variables or no difference between the means of two groups. The alternative hypothesis or research hypothesis (H_1) is a statement that there is a relationship between variables or a difference between the means. Exhibit 9.1 provides examples of the different types of bivariate (meaning two variables) hypotheses.

In quantitative research, we use statistical tests to test hypotheses and make inferences. We begin by assuming that the null hypothesis is true; that is, we assume that no relationship between or among the variables exists unless the evidence indicates otherwise. If we observe a relationship between variables, we use statistical tests to determine the probability that sampling error is responsible for the observed relationship. For example, assume that we have drawn a sample of 300 people at random from a community. We then collect data pertaining to the income and mental health of the people in the sample. After examining the data, we find that a relationship exists between income and mental health. Specifically, people with lower incomes have poorer mental health, and people with higher incomes have better mental health. We are

TYPE	EXAMPLE
Null hypothesis (H_o)—No relationship	There is no relationship between income and mental health.
Two-tailed (nondirectional) hypothesis (H_1)—There is a relationship	There is a relationship between income and mental health.
One-tailed hypothesis (H_1)—Directional relationship	The greater the income, the greater the mental health.

EXHIBIT 9.1

Types of Bivariate Hypotheses

faced with two possibilities: (1) there is a "real" relationship between income and mental health; or (2) the sample does not reflect the population, in other words, we have a case of sample error.

One way to judge whether the finding is real or a product of sample error is through **replication,** doing the study again drawing multiple random samples from the population. If we get the same results in replication using several samples, we then gain confidence that the results actually reflect the population. Replication is an important means of advancing knowledge, and it requires time and resources.

Statistical significance testing—the process whereby we determine the probability that our findings are the result of sample error—also advances knowledge. As discussed in Chapter 5, this determination is influenced by the size of the sample and the degree of variability within the sample. Concerning sample size, it is intuitive that if you have a population of 1,000 people and you randomly sample 990, the sample will very closely reflect the population. If you sample 800 people, the sample will probably still closely reflect the population. But if you sample 50 people, the sample will be far less likely to accurately reflect the characteristics or views of the other 950.

Moving to variability, the lower the variability in the population, the smaller the sample that is necessary to be representative of the population. Conversely, the greater the variability, the larger the sample needs to be. Significantly, we can never be entirely certain that a finding is *not* the result of sample error. After all, strange samples do happen. The odds of winning the lottery are 40 million to 1, but someone still wins.

Statistical significance testing relies on probability to tell us the likelihood that the findings from the sample are the result of sampling error. For example, the probability of drawing an ace from a full deck of cards is 4 out of 52, or $4/52 = .07$, about 7 chances in 100. The probability that a relationship between variables or a mean difference found in a sample is a result of sample error is represented by the **p-value.** The p-value ranges from 1 (almost certain that the results are from sample error) to 0 (almost certain that the results are not based on sample error). Note that we are never completely certain that the results are

EXHIBIT 9.2	DECISION	TRUE ASSOCIATION	OBSERVED ASSOCIATION DUE TO SAMPLE ERROR
Type I and *Type II Errors*	Reject H_o and accept H_1	No error	Type I error
	Accept H_o and reject H_1	Type II error	No error

The only certainty in research is that the results will always have some uncertainty.

the product of sample error. Therefore, it is not correct to use the term *prove* in relation to hypothesis testing. Instead, we refute, reject, or support the null hypothesis. The statistical significance test is always a test of the null hypothesis; it is never a test of the research hypothesis.

The level we set the *p*-value as a criterion to reject the null hypothesis, the **rejection level,** depends on how willing we are to make a mistake in rejecting the null hypothesis. The decision of where to set the rejection level is arbitrary and is based on logic. In a drug study when someone's life is at stake, we may be willing to tolerate only a 1 in 10 million chance of being wrong. Most social science research, by contrast, uses a less stringent rejection level, generally .05. That is, there is only a 5 percent chance that the relationship found in the sample is due to sample error. When the *p*-value is at or below the rejection level, we refer to the result as "statistically significant." A statistically significant finding means that, based on probability, the result is not likely to be due to sample error.

Errors of Statistical Inference

There are two kinds of errors associated with statistical inference, as shown in Exhibit 9.2. **Type I error** occurs when we reject the null hypothesis, thereby inferring that a relationship that is observed in the sample actually exists in the population when, in fact, it does not. Going back to a previous example, we concluded that a relationship exists between income and mental health because the *p*-value is less than .05. It is possible, however, that there is no such relationship in the population.

Conversely, a **Type II error** occurs when we support the null hypothesis and conclude that there is no real relationship between the variables in the population when, in fact, there is such a relationship. For example, we test the relationship between income and mental health and conclude from a *p*-value of .16 (or any level greater than .05) that no relationship exists. It is still possible that income and mental health are related in the population but that the sample did not show the relationship because it was not representative. The higher the rejection level, the greater the likelihood of making a Type I error. Conversely, the lower the rejection level, the greater the likelihood of making a Type II error.

Impact of Sample Size

When considering the results of statistical significance testing, we need to take sample size into account. The larger the sample size, the more likely that we will find statistical significance, that is, the p-value will fall below .05. The reason for this rule is that large sample sizes are more likely to reflect the population, whereas smaller sample sizes have a greater likelihood of being skewed. As a result, whereas we might reject the null hypothesis at the .05 probability level with a sample of 250 ($N = 250$), we might not do so with a sample size of only 25 ($N = 25$). This conclusion holds true even when the observed relationship between the variables or the difference between the means in both samples is the same. As you might imagine, this makes interpreting the results of any one study more difficult. However, if we replicate the results in other studies with different sample sizes, we can have greater confidence that the relationship between the variables actually exists in the population. When the results of small sample studies are not significant but all point in the same direction— that is, they show a similar relationship between the variables—we can also have more confidence in the findings.

Small sample sizes increase the likelihood of making a Type II error of failing to reject the null hypothesis when it is false. For this reason, the researcher with a small sample size may decide before the study begins to set a higher rejection level, for example, .10 instead of the conventional .05.

Statistical Significance Testing in Nonexperimental Research

From the preceding discussion, you might conclude that statistical significance testing is appropriate only when the data are from true experimental research that includes a random sample. What if the data are from a convenience sample, or what if they represent an entire population? Recall from Chapter 5 that research with nonrandom samples and narrowly defined populations (population subgroups) is the norm in social work research. In contrast, research designs that involve randomization are less common in social work because they are often objectionable on ethical grounds and they are more difficult to manage, especially in small geographic areas where contamination between samples is more likely. If the sample is not truly random, the significance test can overstate the accuracy of the results because it considers only random sampling error and cannot assess the biases that result from other, nonrandom sources of error. In the absence of random sampling, how do we interpret the p-value?

The appropriate use of statistical significance testing is a research issue that has been debated by social workers in the past. To get a sense of where the profession stands on this issue today, browse through any number of research articles in recently published social work journals. What you are likely to find is many instances of statistical significance testing in studies employing quasi-experimental and even pre-experimental research designs. The consensus in social work seems to be that statistical significance testing is a formal and objective way of evaluating whether the strength of an observed relationship or the difference between means was small enough that it was likely a chance occurrence or large enough to suggest the possibility of systematic variation.

Statistical inference with nonexperimental designs does have some usefulness as long as the conclusions and recommendations based on the study are appropriate. For instance, generalization of the findings and claims of causation are not defensible in nonexperimental research. If the results of a study are not statistically significant and the study met all of the other requirements of defensible research, the researcher is justified in claiming that it is not a promising area of inquiry that warrants further research. In contrast, if the findings are statistically significant, the researcher could reasonably claim that further research is warranted and should involve, at best, a more rigorous research design and, at a minimum, replication.

The Social Work Library

If you are interested in delving into the arguments both for and against statistical significance testing, see Cowger (1984) and Glisson (1985).

COMMON BIVARIATE STATISTICAL TESTS

To examine the relationship between two variables, we use bivariate statistics. In Chapter 8, we saw that the choice of univariate statistic was based on the level at which the variable was measured. Similarly, the choice of bivariate statistic also depends on level of measurement as well as a few additional considerations. There are two classes of statistical tests: parametric and nonparametric. We use **parametric statistics** when at least one of the two variables being analyzed is measured at the interval or ratio level and is normally distributed in the population. We saw in Chapter 8 that when data are normally distributed they have certain mathematical properties: (a) the mean, median, and mode are roughly equal; (b) when they are plotted, they *approximate* a bell curve; and (c) they are from a random sample. The use of parametric statistics is the most common form of analysis in quantitative social science research.

In contrast, we use **nonparametric statistics** for analyzing data that (a) are not normally distributed, (b) are measured at the nominal or ordinal level, (c) were not randomly selected, and (d) were selected from a very small sample. The remainder of this chapter presents the most common parametric statistical tests used in social science research: Pearson's Product Moment Correlation Coefficient, three types of t-test, and one-way analysis of variance. In addition, it discusses one very common nonparametric test, chi-square. The chapter then concludes with a discussion of common pitfalls to avoid in using and interpreting tests of statistical significance.

Demonstrating or describing how to manually compute the bivariate statistical tests is not an objective of this book. Rather, this chapter is aimed at developing a conceptual understanding of select statistical tests, including the use, misuse, and interpretation of each test. There are many more statistical tests available than the ones presented here. The computation of the statistics presented in this chapter and additional statistical tests are addressed in courses focused on statistics, and they can be found in a variety of books on statistical analysis for the social sciences (see, for example, Craft, 1985; Fielding & Gilbert, 2002; Kerlinger & Lee, 2000).

You can easily perform the statistical tests presented in this chapter with the aid of a computer program such as SPSS or Excel. One objective of this book is to help you develop the skills to compute these tests using this software. To this end, the book's Web site contains step-by-step instructions on how to calculate each statistic in both SPSS and Excel. To expand your repertoire of research skills, we encourage you to use both programs to complete the practice exercises using the Black Feather Youth Survey data found on your CD-ROM.

Linear Correlation

Linear correlation is the degree to which two variables measured at the interval or ratio level are related, or co-vary. Linear correlation is concerned with how the values of the two variables vary in unison. For example, what is the relationship between education and income? Generally speaking, the more years of education people have, the greater their income. In such cases, in which the two variable values move in the same direction, we call the relationship a **positive correlation.** Of course, sometimes, for a variety of reasons, people who are highly educated do not earn a good income. Overall, though, the relationship holds true. In contrast, some variables relate in an opposite way. In most cases, for example, the more years of education adults have, the lower their depression levels. When variables co-vary in this opposite way—low scores on one variable co-vary with high scores on the other—we refer to the relationship as a **negative,** or **inverse, correlation.** Finally, there are cases in which the two variables seem to have little if any relationship. Height and IQ, for instance, do not co-vary. We say that these variables are unrelated. It would not be true that "the greater the height, the higher (or lower) the IQ."

Chapter 8 discussed the use of scatterplots to verify data. Also known as a *scattergram*, a scatterplot is also a useful way to depict the relationship between two linear variables. On a graph, we can plot the relationship between two variables. The **x axis** (the horizontal axis) represents one variable, customarily the variable we are using to make the prediction (the independent variable). The **y axis** (the vertical axis) represents the variable being predicted (the dependent variable). For example, we can plot the relationship between self-esteem and marital satisfaction, both of which are measured on an interval-level scale. We may hypothesize the relationship between these two variables as H_0: there is no relationship between marital satisfaction and self-esteem, and H_1: the greater the marital satisfaction, the greater the self-esteem. To test our null hypothesis, we give a random sample of married individuals a self-esteem scale ranging from 0 to 30 points. We also give each individual a marital satisfaction scale that varies from 0 to 12 points.

Exhibit 9.3*a* shows a scatterplot of the scores of the 36 individuals. Each point on the scatterplot represents one individual's score on both scales. In this example, scores on the self-esteem scale are plotted on the y axis and scores on the marital satisfaction scale on the x axis. Examining Exhibit 9.3*a*, we see that the first point on the left side of the scatterplot represents an individual with a score of 2 on the marital satisfaction scale and 8 on the self-esteem scale.

In general, from examining the pattern of points on the scatterplot, we can see that there is a positive correlation between self-esteem and marital satisfaction: the higher one's marital satisfaction score, generally the higher his or her self-esteem score. In addition, a straight line can be drawn through the points so that half of the points are above the line and half are below it. This is called the **line of best fit.** In the case of a positive correlation such as that shown in Exhibit 9.3*a*, the slope of the line will rise from left to right. In the case of a negative correlation, the line of best fit will slope downward from left to right, as shown in Exhibit 9.3*b*. When there is little or no correlation between the variables, the slope of the line of best fit will be approximately horizontal and the points will not form any pattern. Exhibit 9.3*c* shows a scatterplot illustrating no relationship.

As discussed in Chapter 6, a correlation coefficient is a number that represents the strength and direction of the relationship between two interval or ratio variables. The most common statistical computation of correlation is the Pearson's Product Moment Correlation Coefficient, called **Pearson's *r*** for short. By convention, the correlation coefficient is expressed as a lowercase, italicized *r*. It ranges from 1 (a perfect positive correlation) to -1 (a perfect negative correlation), with 0 indicating no relationship. In a perfect correlation, which seldom occurs in real life, all of the points on the scatterplot would fall on the line of best fit. The magnitude of the correlation coefficient indicates the strength of the relationship. The sign of the correlation coefficient indicates the direction of the relationship, that is, whether it is positive or negative. Positive numbers indicate a positive correlation, and negative numbers indicate a negative correlation. In the correlation between two linear variables, the correlation coefficient summarizes in one number what we can observe in a scatterplot. The correlation coefficient illustrates the utility of statistics—the succinct summary of raw data.

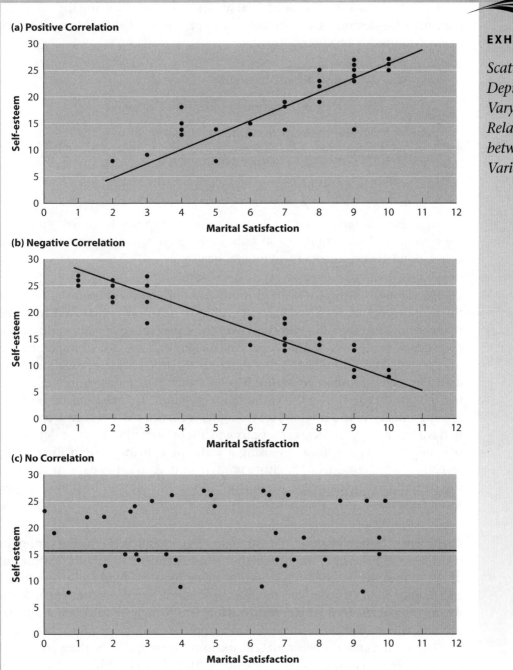

(a) Positive Correlation

(b) Negative Correlation

(c) No Correlation

EXHIBIT 9.3

Scattergrams Depicting Varying Relationships between Variables

How strong is a correlation? Social work researchers often use the following guidelines for describing the strength of a correlation coefficient in a research report (Guilford & Fruchter, 1973):

Less than .20: Slight, almost negligible.

.20–.40: Low correlation; relationship definite but weak.

.40–.70: Moderate correlation; substantial relationship.

.70–.90: High correlation; marked relationship.

.90–1.00: Very high correlation; very dependable relationship.

In a research report, the findings of a correlation would be written as follows: "In a random sample of 250 community members, there was a moderate correlation between income and mental health ($r = .47$)."

 Tutorials

See www.mhhe.com/krysik1 for detailed instructions on how to plot data and create a line of best fit.

Curvilinear Relationships.   Keep in mind that correlation is useful only when the relationship between two variables is linear. A **linear relationship** is one that continues in the same direction over the entire range of values and can be represented by a straight line. A person's height and age, for example, have a linear relationship from birth until about age 20. In contrast, correlation is not useful in a **curvilinear relationship,** in which two values do not continue in the same direction over the entire range of values. The relationship between income and age over a lifetime, for example, is curvilinear, because people tend to have less money in their early years and after they retire. You can determine whether the data are linear by using a scatterplot. If the pattern in the data reveals a consistent direction, either positive or negative, the data are linear. If the pattern curves markedly, the relationship is curvilinear. In that case, you should not use a correlation coefficient (see Exhibit 9.4).

Coefficient of Determination.   The strength of a correlation coefficient cannot be considered to have ratio-level properties. For instance, a correlation coefficient of .60 cannot accurately be described as being twice as strong as a correlation coefficient of .30. To compare the relative strength of correlation coefficients, we use the **coefficient of determination (r^2),** which we calculate simply by squaring the correlation coefficient. For example, if $r = .50$, $r^2 = (.50 \times .50) = .25$.

The coefficient of determination measures how much of the variance in one variable is explained by the variance in the other variable. For example, if a student's grade point average (GPA) and score on the Scholastic Aptitude Test (SAT) produce a correlation of .50 ($r = .50$), then SAT explains 25 percent of the variance in GPA. The remaining 75 percent of the variance is explained by other factors such as motivation, number of hours studying, academic preparation,

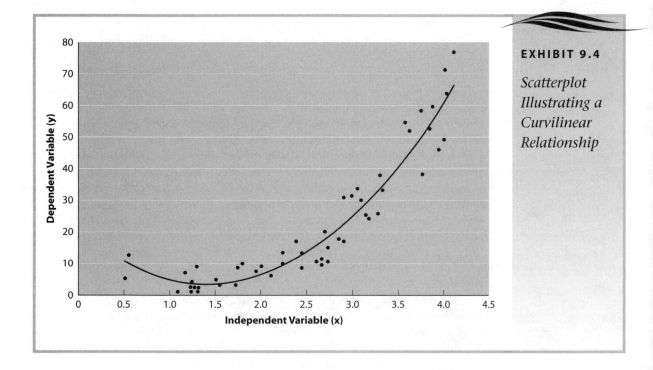

EXHIBIT 9.4

Scatterplot Illustrating a Curvilinear Relationship

previous course work, language skills, health, knowledge of the culture, and so on. Case-in-Point 9.1 demonstrates the use of Pearson's r and the coefficient of determination.

Hypothesis Testing with Pearson's r.   When you use a program such as SPSS or Excel to calculate a correlation coefficient, it also calculates a p-value. If you calculate a correlation coefficient manually, you can determine whether it is of sufficient size to reject the null hypothesis by consulting a table of critical values for r. You can find critical values tables at the back of this book. The minimum correlation value needed to reject the null hypothesis is located on the critical values table at the intersection of the sample size and the rejection level for a one- or two-tailed hypothesis. If the resulting correlation coefficient is equal to or larger than the value specified in the table, you can reject the null hypothesis.

The statement of null hypothesis for a test of correlation is represented by H_0: $r = 0$. The null hypothesis indicates that, in the population, there is no actual correlation between the two variables. If we set the rejection level at .05, from a small p-value ($p \leq 0.05$), we infer that there is no more than a 5 percent chance that the correlation between the two variables is really equal to zero in the population, and we describe the findings as "statistically significant." A p-value greater than .05 ($p > .05$) suggests that there is more than a 5 percent

Approximately 60 million adults in the United States are currently online. Going further, two-thirds of U.S. households with children use the Internet, with e-mail being the most frequently used Internet resource. As Internet use has increased, so has a phenomenon known as e-therapy. E-therapy includes therapeutic services conducted via asynchronous e-mail and real-time, chat-based communication. E-therapy Web sites are offered by a variety of professionals, including social workers, and they address a wide range of problems. E-therapy has a number of positive features, including easy access, stable support in a mobile society, and an alternative communication media. Concerns have also surfaced about e-therapy, including practitioners' abilities to meet ethical and legal standards for assessment, to develop positive therapeutic relationships without in-person contact, to provide availability, and to maintain privacy and confidentiality.

Given the growing use of the Internet by human service professionals, researcher Jerry Finn (2002) explored the attitudes of MSW students toward e-therapy. Finn developed two scales: one to assess beliefs about the effectiveness of e-therapy (EES) and one to assess beliefs about its ethics (EAS). Finn proposed that a relationship existed between these two sets of beliefs.

In a study of 378 MSW students at four universities, Finn discovered that, in general, students held negative beliefs about e-therapy, although very few had ever personally visited an e-therapy Web site or read a research article about e-therapy. Only 3.2 percent of the 378 MSW students surveyed agreed that e-therapy is as effective as in-person psychotherapy, and only 25.7 percent believed that a therapeutic relationship could be formed online. With regard to ethics, a minority of students believed that ethical standards could be met online.

In order to test the existence, strength, and direction of a relationship between students' scores on the two scales, EES and EAS, Finn used SPSS to calculate a Pearson's r. He found a substantial, positive relationship between the students' scores on the two scales ($r = .60$). Students who believed that the ethical requirements of practice could be met through e-therapy were generally more likely to have positive attitudes about the effectiveness of e-therapy. The coefficient of determination ($r^2 = .36$) indicates that 36 percent of the variance in beliefs about the effectiveness of e-therapy can be accounted for by beliefs about the ethics of e-therapy.

chance that the true correlation in the population is equal to zero. In this case, we claim that the correlation is *not* statistically significant.

In the research example in Case-in-Point 9.1, Finn conducted a test of statistical significance using Pearson's r to test the null hypothesis that there is no relationship between MSW students' attitudes toward the ethics of e-therapy and their attitudes regarding its effectiveness. In the published study, he reported that he found a statistically significant relationship between both sets of attitudes ($r = .60$, $p = .01$). Finn concluded that in order to change MSW students' generally negative beliefs about e-therapy, they would have to be assured that ethical standards could be met in online practice. Did Finn overstate the conclusions, generalize beyond the sample, or suggest further research?

n = 120		Age	Income	Depression
Age	r	1.00		
Income	r	.384	1.00	
Depression	r	.025	−.684	1.00

EXHIBIT 9.5

Example of a Correlation Matrix

To answer these questions, read the article, which is accessible via the Social Work Library.

Correlation Matrix.   A research report that identifies more than a few correlations often presents the findings in a **correlation matrix,** in which each variable is listed in the rows down the left side of the matrix and in the columns across the top of the matrix. The correlation between any two variables is found in the cell at the intersection of the row and the column. For example, in the matrix presented in Exhibit 9.5, the correlation (*r*) between age and income is .38, and the correlation between depression level and income is −.68. In a research report, you might read this finding reported as "There is a moderate inverse correlation between income and level of depression ($r(120) = −.68, p = .001$)." The number in parentheses after the *r* is the sample size.

Notice in Exhibit 9.5 that a correlation between a variable and itself is always 1.0, a perfect correlation. This is why the cells along the diagonal of a correlation matrix are always 1.0.

The Social Work Library

Visit the online library to access the article by Finn (2002).

Tutorials

To compute a Pearson's r in SPSS or Excel, use the step-by-step tutorials found at www.mhhe.com/krysik1.

Crosstabulation

Another common bivariate statistical test used in social science research is **crosstabulation.** We often want to determine whether there is an association between two variables measured at the nominal or ordinal level. For example, your community group is considering whether to build a new youth center, so it undertakes a survey to assess how the community members feel about this issue. In your survey of a random sample of 200 people, you find that 40 percent are in favor of the center and 60 percent are not. You would like to target an advertising campaign at the 60 percent who are not in favor in hopes of changing their position. It might be useful to know whether being male or female affects an individual's attitude toward the youth center. In other words, does someone's attitude *depend* on his or her gender? In this case, attitude is the dependent variable because it depends on the value of another variable, the independent variable, in this case, gender.

It is possible to describe the sample one variable at a time. For instance, you can use a frequency distribution like the one shown in Exhibit 9.6. Data in this

EXHIBIT 9.6	**ATTITUDE ABOUT THE YOUTH CENTER**		**GENDER**	
Univariate Analysis of Two Variables	In favor	105 (52.5%)	Female =	125 (62.5%)
	Not in favor	95 (47.5%)	Male =	75 (37.5%)

EXHIBIT 9.7

Crosstab, or Contingency Table, and Data

a

	FEMALE	**MALE**	**TOTAL**
In favor	Female and in favor (% of column)	Male and in favor (% of column)	Row total (% of total)
Not in favor	Female and not in favor (% of column)	Male and not in favor (% of column)	Row total (% of total)
Total	Column total (% of total)	Column total (% of total)	Grand total

Data for Crosstab

b

	FEMALE	**MALE**	**TOTAL**
In favor	80 (.64)	25 (.33)	105 (.525)
Not in favor	45 (.36)	50 (.67)	95 (.475)
Total	125 (.625)	75 (.375)	200

form, however, do not tell us whether men or women differ in their attitudes regarding the center. In order to find out whether attitudes differ by gender, we need to conduct bivariate analysis, that is, consider two variables at one time. We can conduct bivariate analysis for the community study by crosstabulation—tabulating one variable against the other in a table commonly referred to as a **crosstab,** or **contingency table.** Exhibit 9.7*a* explains the content of each cell, and Exhibit 9.7*b* shows the related data.

In the crosstab, the variable attitude is shown in the rows, and the variable gender is shown in the columns. The table could have just as easily been organized with attitude in the columns and gender in the rows. In order to see if women and men differ in their attitudes, we compare the percentages in the row labeled "In favor" for females (64%) and for males (33%). From examining the table, we determine that proportionately more women than men are in favor of the new youth center. It is important, however, to know the likelihood that this finding is a result of sample error. If we believe that this is a true finding, we might target our advertising campaign to men in order to increase their support.

Hypothesis Testing with Chi-Square.   **Chi-square** (X^2) is one commonly used statistic for testing the association between two variables measured at the nominal or ordinal level. It is pronounced "kī" (as in "pie") square. The variables included in a test of chi-square must each have two or more categories. Many nominal variables of interest to social work researchers are measured at the nominal level, including demographic variables such as gender, marital status, race, and type of disability. We also measure many dependent variables at the nominal or ordinal level, for example, recidivism (yes/no), level of improvement (none, some, a great deal), and placement (home, foster care, group home, other).

Although the chi-square test can be used with ordinal data, most statistical textbooks will claim that it is preferred practice to reserve chi-square for nominal data because the test does not make use of the rank-order information in ordinal data. Nonparametric alternatives to chi-square for use with ordinal-level data are the Mann-Whitney U, the Median test, the Kruskal-Wallis test, and the Kolmogorov-Smirnov test. These tests are not discussed in this chapter, but they can be found in most general statistics textbooks.

Chi-square is a nonparametric statistical test and thus does not assume that the data are normally distributed. It does, however, require a sufficient sample size so that all of the expected frequencies in the table are at least 5. The more categories in the data, the larger the sample size must be in order to meet this requirement. If it makes sense theoretically, the data for a table that is larger than 2 × 2 (2 rows × 2 columns) can be collapsed into a smaller number of rows and columns. The table cannot be any smaller than a 2 × 2. In a study that examines the relationship between satisfaction with an after-school program and grade level, for example, the frequencies shown in Exhibit 9.8 were produced.

Expected Frequencies and Observed Frequencies.   An assumption of the chi-square test is that no more than 20 percent of the cells will have an expected frequency of less than 5. **Expected frequencies** are those numbers that we expect to observe in each cell if there is no association between the variables. We calculate expected frequencies by multiplying the row total by the column total for any one cell and then dividing by the total N. For example, the expected frequency for the cell associated with high satisfaction and seventh grade would be calculated by (12 × 13)/24 = 6.5. Programs such as SPSS automatically calculate this information.

EXHIBIT 9.8

Crosstab of Grade Level and Satisfaction with an After-School Program

	7th GRADE	8th GRADE	9th GRADE	10th GRADE	TOTAL
HIGH Satisfaction	8	2	2	0	12
LOW Satisfaction	5	0	6	1	12
Total	13	2	8	1	24

EXHIBIT 9.9

Crosstab Illustrating Collapsed Categories

Student Satisfaction with the After-School Program

	JUNIOR STUDENTS	SENIOR STUDENTS	TOTAL
HIGH Satisfaction	10 (.67)	2 (.22)	12 (.50)
LOW Satisfaction	5 (.33)	7 (.77)	12 (.50)
Total	15 (.63)	9 (.37)	24

In Exhibit 9.8, because the number of 8th graders and 10th graders is small, we might collapse the data by combining 7th and 8th graders into a "Junior Students" category and 9th and 10th graders into a "Senior Students" category. Theoretically, this move makes sense because grades 7 and 8 are often considered middle school or junior high, whereas grades 9 and 10 are considered high school. In the absence of a theoretical justification, we must avoid collapsing the data simply to meet the assumptions of the chi-square test. Other statistical tests—for example, the Fisher exact test—are useful alternatives to the chi-square when the expected frequencies are small.

The table in Exhibit 9.9 combines 7th- and 8th-grade students and 9th- and 10th-grade students into two categories. Now each of the four cells in this 2×2 table has an expected frequency of at least 5, when the data are rounded to whole numbers. Comparing the percentages in the rows, we see that 67 percent of junior high students report high satisfaction with the after-school program, compared to 22 percent of high school students.

The *p*-value associated with the chi-square statistic indicates whether the observed frequencies differ from those we would expect if there were no association between the variables. In addition, it indicates the likelihood that the observed association is the result of sampling error. In effect, the chi-square statistic uses mathematics to do what we do on an intuitive basis. For example, if we tossed a coin 100 times, we would expect to get 50 heads, the expected frequency. If the result was only 48 heads, the **observed frequency,** we might not think that it was an unlikely result or much different from what we expected. However, if we observed only 3 heads, we might think that the observed frequency was much different from the expected frequency and was a very unlikely result.

Similarly, consider the example of a social work research project that tests the effectiveness of two different interventions to prevent further child abuse. Intervention A uses in-home coaching, and Intervention B uses group parent education classes. If the success rate—defined as no additional reports of child abuse for six months—for Intervention A is 69.2 percent, you would expect the success rate for Intervention B to be 69.2 percent (expected frequency) if the treatment was *not* associated with the outcome. If Intervention B has a success rate of only 20.8 percent, however, you might conclude that there is a meaningful difference between the two treatments because the observed frequency (20.8 percent) is much different from the expected frequency (69.2 percent).

As with other tests of statistical inference, we predetermine a rejection level and then test the null hypothesis at that level. In the case of this example:

- Null hypothesis (H_o): There is no association between the method of intervention and the occurrence of a subsequent report of child abuse at six months post intervention.

- Research hypothesis (H_1): There is an association between the method of intervention and the subsequent reporting of child abuse at six months post intervention.

- One-tailed hypothesis (H_1) (if you believe that one intervention is better): Intervention A will be associated with a lower rate of reported child abuse than Intervention B at six months post intervention.

Reading the Chi-Square Statistic. The formula for computing the chi-square statistic and the meaning of degrees of freedom (*df*) can be found in many statistics books and on the Internet. *Degrees of freedom* are calculated from the size of the sample. The value of *df* represents the number of values in the final calculation of a statistic that are free to vary. Researchers generally produce crosstabulation tables and calculate the chi-square statistic with the help of a statistical program such as SPSS or Excel. This section will focus on reading the results of a chi-square analysis and on the meaning of those results.

In the example of child abuse prevention, 50 parents were randomly assigned to either Intervention A or Intervention B. The data were analyzed using SPSS and produced the 2×2 crosstabulation table shown in Exhibit 9.10a. The numbers in the table are the observed frequencies and the associated percentages. The organization of the variables in the crosstab permits us to compare the success rate across the rows. From the table, we see the following results:

- Group A has a success rate of 69.2 percent ($n = 26$) compared with 20.8 percent ($n = 24$) for Group B.

- Looking at the far right column, both groups combined have a success rate of 46 percent.

The table in Exhibit 9.10b presents SPSS output for the chi-square test that allows us to determine whether the results are statistically significant at the preset rejection level of .05.

EXHIBIT 9.10

Testing the Success Rate of Two Interventions

Success × Group Crosstabulation

a

			Group		Total
			Group A	Group B	
Success	No	Count	8	19	27
		% within Group	30.8%	79.2%	54.0%
	Yes	Count	18	5	23
		% within Group	69.2%	20.8%	46.0%
Total		Count	26	24	50
		% within Group	100.0%	100.0%	100.0%

Chi-Square Tests

b

	Value	df	Asymp. Sig. (2-sided)	Exact Sig. (2-sided)	Exact Sig. (1-sided)
Pearson Chi-Square	11.768(a)	1	.001		
Likelihood Ratio	12.334	1	.000		
Fisher's Exact Test				.001	.001
Linear-by-Linear Association	11.533	1	.001		
N of Valid Cases	50				

a: 0 cells (.0%) have expected count less than 5. The minimum expected count is 11.04.

The calculation we are interested in is shown in the top row that reads "Pearson Chi-Square." The columns to the right show the output used to determine whether the chi-square test finds an association between the type of intervention and program success.

- **Value** (of chi-square): **11.768,** the value computed using a formula based on the difference between the observed and the expected values and the degrees of freedom. The larger the value of the chi-square statistic, the greater the association between the variables. See the critical values of χ^2 table at the back of this book to observe this relationship.

- **Degrees of freedom** (*df*): **1,** computed from the number of rows minus one (R − 1) multiplied by the number of columns minus one (C − 1). For a 2 × 2 table, the degrees of freedom value is always equal to (2 − 1)(2 − 1) = 1.

- **Asymp. Sig. 2-sided: .001,** the *p*-value for rejecting the null hypothesis in a two-tailed test.

In a research report, these results might be written as follows: "The association between the type of intervention and a subsequent report of child abuse at six months post treatment was statistically significant ($X^2(1) = 11.8, p = .001$)." Approximately two-thirds (68.2 percent) of the 26 parents in Intervention A had no further report of child abuse, compared with 20.8 percent of the 24 parents in Intervention B. Intervention A appears to be more successful than Intervention B in reducing further child abuse.

Case-in-Point 9.2 describes an example of the use of chi-square to test hypotheses.

Tutorials

To compute a chi-square statistic in SPSS or Excel, use the step-by-step tutorial found at www.mhhe.com/krysik1.

CASE-IN-POINT 9.2

Cyberstalking and GLBT Students

Cyberstalking is a new social problem related to the growth in Internet use. It is defined as receiving repeated, unwanted e-mail that threatens, insults, or harasses and would make a reasonable person fear for his or her safety. Because almost everyone on a college campus has an e-mail account, a university serves as a setting to explore the extent of cyberstalking that is taking place. In 2002, an exploratory study of 339 students at the Student Union Center at the University of New Hampshire found that approximately 10–15% of students reported receiving repeated e-mail that they felt either threatened, insulted, or harassed them (Finn, 2004).

Significantly, e-mail harassment was more prevalent among students who identified themselves as a sexual minority. Specifically, of the 16 students who identified themselves as gay, lesbian, bisexual, or transgender (GLBT), 5 (31%) reported receiving repeated e-mail from someone they did not know or barely knew that they perceived as a threat, an insult, or harassment. In contrast, 14.6% of heterosexual students reported receiving such

continued

CASE-IN-POINT 9.2

Cyberstalking and GLBT Students
continued

e-mail ($X^2(1) = 3.84, p < .05$). (Note: This should be read as "Chi-square with one degree of freedom equals 3.84. The probability that this result is due to sample error is less than 5%.") Similarly, 37.5% of GLBT students reported receiving such e-mail even after they told the e-mailers to halt all further communication, compared with 13.1% of heterosexual students ($X^2(1) = 7.37, p < .05$).

These findings are important because previous research had not addressed online harassment of GLBT students, and online harassment may reflect a broader hostile campus environment. Further research is needed to better understand the similarities and differences in the extent and nature of online harassment targeted at GLBT students and how that compares with the experiences of heterosexual students. In the meantime, colleges should make clear that harassment of any kind related to sexual identity is not acceptable and will not be tolerated. If these results are replicated in further research, colleges should institute prevention and education efforts that directly target online harassment related to GLBT students.

In considering this report, keep in mind the following points:

- This is an exploratory study of one university at one point in time.
- The number of GLBT students in the sample is small.
- The students who use the student union may not be a representative sample of students.
- The validity and reliability of the measure of the dependent variable is unknown.

What recommendations would you make based on the results of this research study?

t-TESTS: COMPARING THE DIFFERENCE BETWEEN TWO MEANS

As we have seen, crosstabulation enables us to assess the relationship between nominal and ordinal variables. However, social work researchers are often interested in differences both between and within groups that are measured at the interval and ratio levels. Regarding differences between groups, we may ask, Is one intervention more effective than another? Or, do men and women differ in their benefit from parenting classes? Within-group differences are conveyed by questions such as Do people behave differently at the end of an intervention program than they did at the beginning? A **t-test** is used to assess group differences that are expressed in either interval or ratio data. The t-test is a parametric statistic that assesses (a) whether group differences are greater than what we would expect based on chance and (b) whether sample error might account for the observed differences. Because the t-test is a parametric statistic, the assumptions of normality in the population and random sampling apply. If the data are not normally distributed, we could consider a nonparametric test or some sort of transformation of the data. These topics are covered in more advanced statistical textbooks.

There are three different kinds of t-tests: the independent samples t-test, the paired sample t-test, and the one sample t-test. Each has a particular use, as discussed next.

- The **independent samples t-test** compares the means of two independent groups. It assesses the likelihood that the means of two groups are equal or that they come from the same population. For example, an independent t-test would be used to test whether a treatment and a control group differed in their level of depression following an intervention program. In addition to the assumptions of normality and random selection, the groups must be independent; that is, each member can belong to only one of the categories of the nominal-level variable.

- In contrast, **paired samples t-tests** are concerned with changes in measures from the same individuals at two points in time. We would use a paired samples t-test to compare the pretest and posttest scores of the participants in a program designed to teach assertiveness skills to a group of shy teens. The test is based not on the overall group mean and variance but on the difference between the pretest and posttest scores for each individual.

- The **one sample t-test** estimates the likelihood that a single sample comes from a given population. In other words, is the sample typical of the population? We would use a one sample t-test to test whether a group of children in a specific neighborhood had health problems similar to those of other children their age in the population.

 Tutorials

To compute the independent samples t-test, paired samples t-test, and one sample t-test in SPSS or Excel, use the step-by-step tutorials found at www.mhhe.com/krysik1.

Independent Samples t-Test

The independent samples t-test compares the mean scores and the degree of variation on the dependent variable in two independent groups. The calculation of the t-test can be found in many statistics books and is beyond the scope of this chapter. The degrees of freedom (*df*) are also considered in the calculation. In the case of an independent samples t-test, they are equal to $N - 2$, and as such they are a function of the sample size. Statistical programs will produce the t-statistic, degrees of freedom, and the corresponding *p*-value. As with other tests of statistical inference, a rejection level is specified in advance of conducting the test, usually .05. The following example illustrates the use and interpretation of the independent samples t-test.

A study of satisfaction among consumers of mental health services in Pennsylvania used two different methods of survey administration: telephone and in person. The researcher wondered, "Do these two methods produce the same results?" In both methods, the interviewer read a list of 25 items to consumers and recorded their responses. The items covered areas such as satisfaction with appointment times, relationship with the therapist, and knowledge of grievance procedures. For example, one item was "My service provider spends enough time with me." The interviewer asked consumers to rate their level of agreement with each item from 1 (strongly disagree) to 5 (strongly agree). The researcher then summed the item scores to produce a total satisfaction score that could range from 25 to 125.

The null hypothesis was that there is no difference in reported satisfaction between those consumers who were interviewed by telephone and those who were interviewed in person. Conversely, the research hypothesis was that there *is* a difference in reported satisfaction between the two groups. Because the independent variable (method of interview) is measured at the nominal level with only two categories and the dependent variable (satisfaction) is interval, the researcher used an independent samples t-test to test the null hypothesis. The results are summarized in Exhibit 9.11. The first table shows a difference in the means of the groups (118.5 and 108.1). It appears that consumers surveyed in person averaged higher satisfaction scores than those surveyed by telephone.

EXHIBIT 9.11

Independent Samples t-Test

Consumer Satisfaction for Telephone vs. In-Person Interviewing

	Method of Interview	N	Mean	Std. Deviation
TOTAL SATISFACTION	In Person	14	118.5	3.0
	Phone	60	108.1	3.3

Independent Samples Test

		Levene's Test for Equality of Variances		t-Test for Equality of Means		
		F	Sig.	t	df	Sig. (2-tailed)
TOTAL SATISFACTION	Equal variances assumed	.030	.864	2.641	72	.010
	Equal variances not assumed			2.676	19.835	.015

The second table is part of the SPSS output. It indicates that there was a statistically significant mean difference in satisfaction based on the method of survey administration. The results would be reported as ($t(72)$ = 2.64, p =.01). Note the following:

- t = 2.64.

- (72) is the degrees of freedom, calculated as $N - 2$.

- p = .01 is the probability that the result is due to sample error or chance.

How should the social work researcher interpret these findings? The following are all viable explanations.

- There are real differences in consumer satisfaction based on the interview method. The agency should use only one interview method.

- There are real differences between interview methods. In-person interviews are likely to show higher satisfaction because of social desirability; that is, people are afraid to be critical in person. The agency should use only telephone interviews.

- There are real differences between interview methods. These differences might result from the ways in which the survey is administered. The agency should investigate whether the interviewers administer the questions the same in person as they do on the telephone.

- Even though the mean differences were statistically significant, the average amount of difference was small and relatively meaningless. Nothing need be done.

- The result could be a Type I error, that is, a result of sample error. The study should be replicated to see if the results are the same.

Which of these interpretations would you support, and why?

Paired Samples t-Test

A **paired samples t-test,** also known as the **dependent samples t-test,** is used to determine whether there is a statistically significant difference between the mean values of the same measurement on each person made under two different conditions. The test is based on the differences in scores for each person at two points in time. As with the independent samples t-test, statistical programs will produce the t-statistic and p-value and calculate the degrees of freedom. The null hypothesis is that the difference in the mean values is zero. The research hypothesis is that the difference in the means is not zero. The following example illustrates the use and interpretation of the paired samples t-test.

A preliminary study of foster youths aged 7 to 17 years found that they were less likely to learn computer skills than other youths of comparable age (Finn, Kerman, & leCornec, 2003). In response to this finding, Casey Family Services began a unique program in which they gave foster families a computer and Internet connection to improve the children's computer skills. The study involved a pretest in which the participants rated their own computer skills on a scale from 1—very few or no computer skills—to 5—very skilled. Approximately one year later the evaluators administered a posttest using the same measure. The results from the analysis of the paired means are presented in Exhibit 9.12 in SPSS format.

The null hypothesis is that there is no difference between the pretest and posttest scores for the youths. The research hypothesis is that there is a difference. The mean pretest score—2.6—is located on the top row of the SPSS output, and the mean for the posttest—on the second row—is 3.5 ($t(36) = 6.15$, $p = .001$). Note in the SPSS output that the p-value is written as .000. This is due to space limitations in the table. In a research report it would be safe to state the p-value as .001, meaning that the probability of the null hypothesis being true is less than 1 in 1,000. The findings indicate a statistically significant increase in the ratings of foster care youths regarding their computer skills between pretest and posttest.

EXHIBIT 9.12

Analysis of Paired Means

Paired Samples Statistics

		Mean	N	Std. Deviation	Std. Error Mean
Pair 1	rate computer skills	2.595	37	1.1170	.1836
	rate computer skills	3.4595	37	.90045	.14803

Paired Samples Test

	Paired Differences							
				95% Confidence Interval of the Difference				
	Mean	Std. Deviation	Std. Error Mean	Lower	Upper	t	df	Sig. (2-tailed)
Pair 1 rate computer skills rate computer skills	−.86486	.85512	.14058	−1.14998	−.57975	−6.152	36	.000

Note that we can drop the minus sign from the t-test statistic in reporting. We always check the statistical output to verify the direction of the mean difference. For instance, did the youths' ratings of their computer skills increase or decrease from pretest to posttest? There have been cases in which researchers reported a certain direction of change that was consistent with their expectations, when the data suggested a significant finding in the opposite direction.

How should we interpret these results? Consider the following possibilities.

- The youths improved their computer skills after one year in the program. This is one indicator of program success.

- The result is a Type I error, and no real difference exists. This is always possible. The *p*-value, however, suggests that this is highly unlikely.

- The youths have come to like the staff over a year in the program and gave higher ratings just to "be nice." Thus, the difference in the scores is a result of social desirability and not real program change.

- Some other factor accounts for the change in scores. For example, the schools may have begun a new computer training initiative just as the program was beginning. Without a control group, this cannot be ruled out.

How would you interpret the findings? Can you think of alternative explanations for the results? Locate the value of *t* (6.15) and degrees of freedom (36) on the table of critical values for *t* at the back of the book. What do you observe about the statistical significance of the finding?

One Sample t-Test

We use the **one sample t-test** to compare the mean of a variable measured at the interval or ratio level in a sample with the known or estimated mean in the population. This test helps us evaluate whether the sample is typical, or representative, of the population. The known mean of the population is called the **test value.** The null hypothesis is that there is no difference between the sample mean and the test value. The research hypothesis is that there is a difference.

For example, we know that the mean IQ in the United States is 100. We would like to determine whether the IQ in a sample of 10 youths is different from the population mean. A one sample t-test using SPSS produced the results shown in Exhibit 9.13.

The table indicates that the mean IQ for the 10 youths is 106, which is slightly higher than the national average. The t-test, however, indicates that the difference is not statistically significant at the .05 level ($t(9) = 1.85$, $p = .098$). Therefore, we cannot reject the null hypothesis. Instead, we must conclude that there is no difference between these youths as a group and other youths in the

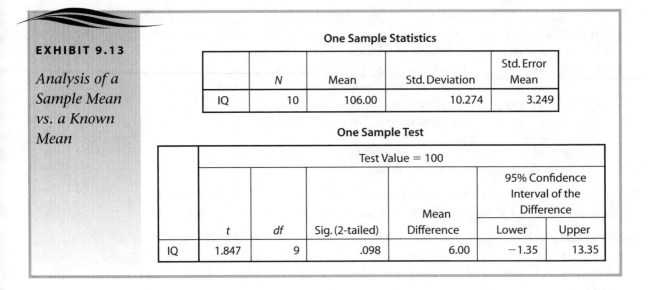

One Sample Statistics

	N	Mean	Std. Deviation	Std. Error Mean
IQ	10	106.00	10.274	3.249

One Sample Test

	Test Value = 100				95% Confidence Interval of the Difference	
	t	df	Sig. (2-tailed)	Mean Difference	Lower	Upper
IQ	1.847	9	.098	6.00	−1.35	13.35

population. Because the one sample t-test is based on the mean and standard deviation, *some* of the youths may have IQ scores significantly above or below the test value. As a group, however, they do not.

ANALYSIS OF VARIANCE

One-way analysis of variance (ANOVA) is a parametric statistical test that compares the means of more than two groups. We might wish to test three treatment conditions or analyze certain behaviors among four different socio-economic groups, for example. In this way, ANOVA is very similar to the independent samples t-test. In addition, it has the same requirements, except for the number of groups. In fact, an ANOVA calculated to assess the difference between two groups will provide results consistent with the t-test.

ANOVA produces an *F* statistic that serves the same purpose as the *t* value. The computation of *F* can be found in statistics books such as those referenced earlier and listed in the references at the end of this book. A statistical program such as SPSS will produce the *F* statistic, degrees of freedom, and the *p*-value needed for hypothesis testing. The null hypothesis is that the means of the dependent measure do not differ. The research hypothesis is that there is a statistically significant difference between at least two of the group means. The one-way ANOVA tests the mean differences between each of the groups as well as the difference between the mean of each group and the *grand mean* (or overall mean) of the combined groups.

The F statistic indicates only that there is a statistically significant difference among the groups. **Post-hoc analysis** compares the means of each of the groups two at a time in order to determine which groups differ. If the F statistic is associated with a p-value that is less than the rejection level, typically .05, then the means of at least two of the groups differ at a level that is statistically significant. If the p-value is greater than .05, none of the groups will be significantly different, and the post-hoc analysis is unnecessary. Many post-hoc tests are available, some of which are included in SPSS.

The following example illustrates the use of one-way ANOVA: A study examined the leadership style of three categories of agency personnel: administrators, supervisors, and direct service workers. Thus, Agency Personnel is the independent variable, and it is measured at the nominal level. High scores on the dependent variable, the Leadership Scale, indicate a preference for authoritarian leadership. Exhibit 9.14a shows the output produced using the ANOVA function in SPSS.

A full discussion of post-hoc analysis can be found in many statistics textbooks. For one example, see Casella and Berger (1990).

ANOVA

Leadership

		Sum of Squares	df	Mean Square	F	Sig.
a	Between Groups	1355.072	3	451.691	4.051	.008
	Within Groups	32779.559	294	111.495		
	Total	34134.631	297			

Multiple Comparisons

Dependent Variable: Leadership

LSD

	(I) Primary job responsibility	(J) Primary job responsibility	Mean Difference (I-J)	Std. Error	Sig.	95% Confidence Interval	
						Lower Bound	Upper Bound
b	Direct Service	Supervision	−4.938*	1.925	.011	−8.73	−1.15
		Administration	−5.159*	1.949	.009	−8.99	−1.32
		Other	−2.566	2.912	.379	−8.30	3.17
	Supervision	Direct Service	4.938*	1.925	.011	1.15	8.73
		Administration	−.221	2.543	.931	−5.23	4.78
		Other	2.371	3.339	.478	−4.20	8.94
	Administration	Direct Service	5.159*	1.949	.009	1.32	8.99
		Supervision	.221	2.543	.931	−4.78	5.23
		Other	2.592	3.353	.440	−4.01	9.19

EXHIBIT 9.14

Comparing the Means of More Than Two Groups

The result would be written as $F(3,294) = 4.01$, $p = .008$. The numbers in the parentheses are the degrees of freedom, calculated from the number of categories of the independent variable (3) and N minus the number of categories ($297 - 3$). Since the p-value of F is less than .05, the results suggest that there is a difference in leadership style among administrators, supervisors, and direct service workers.

Having accumulated these data, we need to employ post-hoc analysis to determine which of the groups actually differ. Exhibit 9.14*b* shows the post-hoc analysis using the Least Significant Difference (LSD) test, one of several post-hoc tests available in SPSS. Note that the mean difference between groups is presented in the second column. For example, the mean difference between direct service workers and supervisors is 4.98, which is slightly less than the mean difference of 5.16 between direct service workers and administrators. In contrast, the mean difference between supervisors and administrators is much smaller: .22. The asterisk (*) indicates those group differences that are statistically significant at the .05 level. The p-value is given in the column labeled "Sig."

What can we conclude from this study?

- Social workers in different positions have different preferences for leadership style. The statistically significant differences are between direct service workers and administrators and between direct service workers and supervisors, but not between administrators and supervisors.

- Given the p-value of .008, it is unlikely that the result is from sample error.

- Although the differences are statistically significant, they may not be meaningful. All groups may have a preference for non-authoritarian leadership, but the preference of direct service workers is a little stronger. To know whether the results are meaningful, we would need to know that the norms for leadership scores and outcomes in the real world conform to a particular level of leadership score.

- The results indicate that more research is needed.

 Tutorials

To compute a one-way ANOVA in SPSS use the step-by-step tutorials found at www.mhhe.com/krysik1.

Exhibit 9.15 summarizes the six statistical tests reviewed in this chapter. Along with each test is an example of the type of question that the test is suitable to address and the level of measurement of the variables that each test requires. Advanced Skill Development 9.1 provides guidelines for reporting findings.

STATISTICAL TEST	RESEARCH QUESTION	LEVEL OF MEASUREMENT
Pearson's correlation (r)	Is there a relationship between two variables?	Two variables, each measured at the interval or ratio level.
	Is there a relationship between income and longevity?	
Chi-square (χ^2)	Do observed values differ from those expected if there is no association between the variables?	Independent variable: nominal or ordinal. Dependent variable: nominal or ordinal.
	Do men and women differ in their support of group homes in their community?	Typically at least one of the variables is nominal. Not a preferred test for ordinal data.
Independent samples t-test (t)	Do the two groups come from the same population? Do their means differ?	Independent variable: measured at the nominal level with only two categories.
	Is Intervention A better than Intervention B in reducing the number of missed school days?	Dependent variable: interval or ratio.
Dependent samples t-test (t)	Does the average value of two measurements of the same dependent variable differ?	Independent variable: nominal. Dependent variable: interval or ratio.
	Do the pretest scores on self-esteem differ from the posttest scores?	
One sample t-test (t)	Does a single sample come from a specific population? Is a sample typical of the population?	The test value is measured at the interval or ratio level.
	Is the level of ADHD in the community similar to the level in the rest of the state?	
One-way analysis of variance (ANOVA) (F)	Are the means equal, or do the means of three or more groups differ?	Independent variable: nominal with more than two categories.
	Is there a difference between 7th, 8th, and 9th grade in the number of missed school days?	Dependent variable: interval or ratio.

EXHIBIT 9.15

Summary of Select Bivariate Statistical Tests

ADVANCED SKILL DEVELOP-MENT 9.1

Suggestions on Reporting the Findings

 Tutorials

More complex statistics, such as multiple regression analysis, are available for examining the relationship among a larger number of variables. Many of these statistical tests are the subject of advanced courses in statistics. For readers who would like to get started with multivariate statistical analysis, a brief tutorial on multiple regression is available at www.mhhe.com/krysik1.

The reporting of statistical results tends to follow certain conventions. It is customary to include the symbol for the statistical test, for example, r, t, F, or X^2, along with the actual value achieved (such as $r = .60$) and the degrees of freedom if applicable to the test. The degrees of freedom are placed in parentheses after the test symbol, for example, $t(24) = 5.11$, $p = .001$. The researcher should always report the exact p-value if available, thus the equal sign in the example. Note the statistical symbols that are italicized and the use of parentheses and punctuation. The value of the statistic is reported to two decimal places, and the entire p-value is presented.

The rejection level used to test the null hypothesis should also be reported. If the same rejection level is used for all analyses, it should be reported near the beginning of the results section, for example, "a rejection level of .05 was used for all analyses." Rejection levels are also correctly referred to as *alpha levels*. It is also important to know whether the reported p-value is associated with a one-tailed or two-tailed test of the hypothesis. In addition to the statistical significance of the findings, the researcher should comment on the importance of the findings, for example, by calculating and interpreting a coefficient of determination for r and presenting means and standard deviations for t and F. Chapter 12 covers additional information on reporting research, and you can consult style manuals such as the *Publication Manual of the American Psychological Association* (APA, 2001). Different style guides will use slightly different conventions. Choose a style and be consistent, and if writing for publication, check the required style of the journal you would like to publish your manuscript.

SIX COMMON PITFALLS TO AVOID IN SIGNIFICANCE TESTING

This chapter concludes by alerting you to six common pitfalls that frequently occur in statistical significance testing. You can use the information in this section whether you are engaged in producing research or critiquing research.

1. Equating statistical significance with importance.

2. Inferring the magnitude of the results from the size of the p-value.

3. Mistaking the rejection of the null hypothesis for confirmation of the research hypothesis.

4. Fishing for statistically significant relationships.

5. Inferring causation from statistical significance.

6. Failing to consider statistical power.

The first major pitfall that researchers must avoid is to equate statistical significance with importance. Statistical significance is *not* synonymous with importance. We may find, for example, that, compared to children living in group home arrangements, more foster children prefer chocolate ice cream over vanilla. Moreover, the difference is statistically significant at the $p < .05$ level. Nevertheless, that finding is not *important* in terms of helping us provide services. Ultimately, we must judge the importance of the results.

The second pitfall to avoid is inferring the magnitude of the results from the size of the p-value. A key point here is that when the sample size is large even small differences and weak relationships will be statistically significant. Sometimes even small differences may be important; other times they will not. We must be careful not to automatically interpret a small p-value as a strong relationship between variables or a large difference between independent or related groups. A weak correlation is still a weak correlation, whether the associated p-value is .1 or .0001. As mentioned earlier in the chapter, the size of the p-value is related to the size of the sample, regardless of the strength of the relationship. The magnitude of the result should be described through the coefficient of determination for r, the presentation of mean differences and standard deviations for t and F, and percentage differences for X^2.

In addition to these techniques, the researcher can calculate a statistic known as the effect size (*ES*). Calculating the effect size statistic allows the researcher to compare the magnitude of effects across studies. Statistical significance can be important, but it does not tell you the most important thing, that is, the size of the effect. Effect size can be calculated with the following formula:

(experimental group mean − control group mean)/control group standard deviation

For example, in a study to increase self-esteem, the mean for the experimental group is 50 and standard deviation is 2.2. The mean for the control group is 46 and standard deviation is 2. Using the formula for *ES*, $(50 − 46)/2 = 2$. An *ES* of 0 would indicate no effect (no difference between the groups). *ES* scores greater than 0 indicate greater change in the experimental group than in the control group. The *ES* can be used to compare studies using different methodologies. For example, a second study of self-esteem using a different intervention and different measure for self-esteem was found to have an effect size of .65. If both studies were methodologically sound, the *ES* indicates a stronger effect size for the first study (*ES* = 2) than for the second study (*ES* = .65). Although both studies were found to show significant improvement in the experimental group at the .05 level, social workers using evidence-based practice would give greater consideration to the first method rather than the second when selecting which self-esteem program to use in their practice since it has a stronger effect size. For further explanation of effect size, see an advanced statistic book such as Cohen (1977).

A third pitfall is to mistake the rejection of the null hypothesis for confirmation of the research hypothesis. Rejection of the null hypothesis simply means that it is unlikely that the observed findings are the result of sample error. The null hypothesis deals only with chance as a possible explanation for the findings. It does not rule out other sources of error in measurement or interpretation. Thus, it does not lead to blind confirmation of the research hypothesis. Support for the research hypothesis must also take into account the research design, the quality of the measurement and data collection, theoretical support, and the findings of related research.

The fourth pitfall is fishing for statistically significant relationships. Beware of the study that reports a large number of statistical tests. When the rejection level is set at .05, 1 in every 20 statistical tests (5 percent) is statistically significant by chance alone. In a study with many variables, if 100 statistical tests are computed, 5 of those are likely to produce false results, and there is no way of telling "real" differences from chance differences. To avoid this pitfall, plan statistical analyses in advance based on theoretical considerations and then run only the minimum number of tests necessary. For example, we use ANOVA to test the differences between more than two means so that we can avoid using multiple t-tests.

The fifth pitfall is inferring causation from statistical significance. Statistically significant results do not imply a cause-and-effect relationship. For example, if we find a positive correlation between self-esteem and marital satisfaction, we cannot conclude that one causes the other. We know only that the two variables tend to vary together. To support causation, we must use an experimental design in which threats to internal validity and extraneous variables are controlled.

The final pitfall is the failure to consider statistical power. **Statistical power** relates to the ability of a statistical test to detect a true relationship when one exists—in other words, to correctly reject the null hypothesis. Statistical power analysis involves calculating the probability of committing a Type II error based on the type of test, the sample size, and an estimate of the strength of the relationship. Thanks to pioneering work by Jacob Cohen (1977), social workers can make a judgment about the power of many statistical tests by consulting the appropriate statistical power table in his book.

Significantly, some statistical tests are considered more powerful than others because of the way they are calculated. For instance, some tests make use of each value in the data set for their calculation rather than relying on summary statistics. Another factor in the power of a test is level of measurement. Parametric statistics, for example, are more powerful than nonparametric statistics because they rely on variables measured at the interval or ratio level rather than categorical data. Because statistical power is related to the type of statistical test, there are multiple statistical power tables. If we were using Pearson's *r*, for example, we would consult a statistical power table for linear correlation.

Ideally, researchers should consider statistical power during the planning stages of a research study so that they can ensure they have an adequate sample size to correctly reject the null hypothesis if a true relationship exists. If researchers do not consider statistical power during the planning stages, they should conduct a statistical power analysis following any study that fails to reject the null hypothesis. Performing this analysis allows researchers to comment on the adequacy of the sample size, given the magnitude of the relationship. Many studies that report null findings fail to consider the impact of sample size on the significance of the results.

CONCLUSION

As consumers of social work research, we need to understand and critically assess the statistical information presented in research articles and other forms of research presentations. In addition, the credibility of your own research will depend not only on your ability to use scientific methods but also on the appropriate use of statistical procedures when conducting your research and describing your findings. Stating and testing hypotheses using the correct statistical tests for the types of questions you wish to examine and the types of data used to answer the questions are integral to the development of evidence-based practice.

Statistical tests when used correctly are wonderfully powerful. When applied in conjunction with appropriate research designs, they tell us the likelihood that a finding is "real" rather than based on chance. They allow us to test and support our theories and notions about what is important and what works in social work practice, effectively allowing us to advance our knowledge base. They allow us to present evidence that others can understand and attempt to replicate.

On the other hand, knowledge of statistical tests helps us understand the computer adage GIGO: garbage in, garbage out. This is especially important when others who do not share social work's goals may seek to use statistics to misrepresent the facts or draw unfounded conclusions related to data about social problems or program effectiveness. Knowledge of statistics empowers social workers to critique the evidence presented by others in a rational and professional manner.

Statistics do not exist in a vacuum. They are based on data from research projects and program evaluations related to social work practice, however imperfect. The next two chapters discuss the evaluation of social work practice. Chapter 10 focuses on single subject research, which involves assessing the outcomes of a single system such as a person, family, group, or community. Chapter 11 discusses the evaluation of social work programs, focusing on the effectiveness of programs based on the overall outcomes of the intervention efforts.

MAIN POINTS

- The choice of statistical test depends largely on the level at which the variables to be considered are measured. Other requirements of statistical tests can involve normality—how well the data in the population conform to the normal distribution, random sampling, and sample size.

- Bivariate statistics consider the relationship between two variables at a time. This is in contrast to univariate statistics that focus on one variable at a time and to multivariate statistics that are used to analyze more than two variables at a time.

- Parametric statistics are used to analyze data that meet certain assumptions, including normal distribution in the population from which the sample was drawn, random sampling, and measurement of at least one of the two variables being considered at the interval or ratio level. Common parametric statistical tests include Pearson's *r*, the t-test, and ANOVA.

- Nonparametric statistics represent an alternative to parametric statistics when the assumptions of parametric tests cannot be met, or when the sample size is very small. For instance, when both variables in a bivariate analysis are measured at the nominal or ordinal levels, we have no choice but to use nonparametric statistics. Chi-square is a popular example of a nonparametric test.

- Tests of statistical significance provide us with the likelihood that relationships between variables or differences between means are the result of sample error. They are a test of the null hypothesis, and not a test of the research hypothesis.

- Hypotheses are rejected or supported on the basis of statistical significance testing as well as through the replication of research studies. Both statistical significance testing and replication are important ways of advancing the knowledge base of social work.

- There are conventions in reporting tests of statistical significance that include always reporting the test, the test statistic, the degrees of freedom if applicable, and the exact *p*-value available in the statistical output when a computer program such as SPSS is used in the calculation.

- The informed social work researcher will be careful to avoid common errors in conducting and interpreting tests of statistical significance, for example: (1) equating statistical significance with importance; (2) conducting "fishing" expeditions to try and find statistically significant results; (3) inferring causation on the basis of statistically significant results; and (4) failing to consider statistical power. The power of a test to correctly accept or reject the null hypothesis is based on a number of factors, including the type of test used, sample size, and the level of measurement of the data. Researchers should make certain to examine statistical power when the null hypothesis is not rejected.

EXERCISES: PRACTICING SOCIAL WORK

1. You are interested in differences related to crime between the northern and southern regions of the Black Feather communities.

   a. Find all of the questions related to crime, gangs, or violence on the youth survey. The file is on the Web site for this book. Recode the answers to each question so that Agree and Strongly Agree are combined into one category and Disagree and Strongly Disagree are combined into another. Recode the "neither" category as missing data.

   b. Use chi-square to test for regional differences related to crime. What do you conclude?

   c. Add the scores for items related to crime to create a scale with a single total. For this question, you will want to use the data as entered (not recoded). Use an independent samples t-test to examine regional differences related to crime. What do you conclude?

   d. What percentage of the youths are female in each region? What percentage are male? Use chi-square to determine whether the proportion of females and males is the same in the two communities.

   e. Using the scale you created in (c), determine whether attitudes about crime are related to the youths' ages.

EXERCISES: SOCIAL WORK LIBRARY

1. Read the articles by Finn (2002, 2004). Discuss his choice of statistical tests in each article.

2. Critique Finn's presentation of the results of statistical testing.

OTHER EXERCISES

1. You give a random sample of 100 social work research students a pretest similar to their final exam and a posttest final exam. Their scores range from 30 to 100 on the pretest and from 30 to 100 on the posttest. You also

collect demographic data: age, sex, hair color, and eye color. Which statistic would you use to answer the following research questions? Explain your answer.

   a. Are there more men in one section?

   b. Does one section score higher on the test than the other?

   c. Is age associated with test scores?

   d. Is there a difference in score by hair color (blond, brunette, redhead)?

   e. Did students improve from the pretest to the posttest?

2. You want to test the relative effectiveness of couple counseling with and without a spouse included in the intervention. You notice that about half the couples at the agency are in individual counseling and half are seen as couples. You sample 20 clients, with 10 in each condition. The dependent variable is the individual's score on a marital satisfaction scale. You do both a pretest and a posttest.

   a. Write a null hypothesis for this study.

   b. Write the research hypothesis. Would you use a one-tailed or two-tailed hypothesis? Why?

   c. Would you use a parametric or nonparametric statistic? Why?

   d. Which statistic would you use to test group differences at posttest?

   e. How would you check to see if marital satisfaction is related to length of marriage?

3. If you had to make either a Type I error or a Type II error in the study described in question 2, which would it be? Why?

CHAPTER 10

Single Case Research

Sometimes the magic works, sometimes it doesn't.
—Thomas Berger, *Little Big Man*

SOMETIMES WE ARE INTERESTED IN ANSWERING RESEARCH questions that are probabilistic. That is, research tells us which result is most likely to occur for groups of elements such as individuals or families. For example, group-level designs (see Chapter 4) may allow us to evaluate whether one intervention is more effective than another. In many cases, however, social workers are interested in the results of a single case. This is especially true for workers involved in clinical practice. It is not enough to know that "most" people improve with a particular intervention. Rather, we need to know whether a specific situation is actually improving due to *this* intervention. To obtain this knowledge, we need to engage in single case research, the topic of this chapter.

There are two types of research that examine single cases: single subject research and case study research. People sometimes confuse these two different approaches. **Single subject research (SSR)** focuses on a quantitative approach to documenting changes over time in a limited number of specific variables such as behavior or attitudes. SSR is often used to document the process and outcomes of change efforts in clinical practice or organizations. In contrast, **case study research** is generally used to learn about a new phenomenon, to develop theories, to identify and understand important variables, and to provide specific examples of the phenomenon under study. The case study represents an in-depth, intensive, detailed qualitative study of an individual or particular unit as a group. It may include quantitative data, but it focuses on more holistic processes. SSR answers the question Did change occur? In contrast, case studies focus more on why and how the change occurred. Both approaches are based on scientific methods in that (1) they are planned, (2) they are clearly delineated, (3) they require the collection and interpretation of data, and (4) they are open to scrutiny and replication. In addition, both methods contribute to evidence-based practice.

By the end of this chapter, you should be able to:

- Describe the difference between single subject research and case study research.

- Describe the advantages and disadvantages of using SSR and case study research.

- Clearly define and operationalize variables to be used in an SSR design in measurable terms.

- List and describe the steps in carrying out SSR.

- Describe and state the purpose of various SSR designs.

- Use Excel to graph and analyze data collected in SSR.

- Describe the purpose of, and the methods used in, case study research.

SINGLE SUBJECT RESEARCH

Research can help social workers decide which interventions are most likely to produce positive changes for their clients. For example, in treating depression, is a combination of counseling and medication more effective than either medication or counseling alone? Research suggests that it is (Antonuccio & Danton, 1995). As another example, would a mentor program help improve a 10-year-old child's self-concept and grades in school? Research suggests that it would not (Barron-McKeagney, Woody, & D'Sousa, 2003).

Although basing interventions on research evidence is a useful starting place, this practice has its limitations, for example:

- There may not be conclusive (or any) research evidence on the issue to be addressed.

- The research evidence may show mixed or even contradictory results in several studies.

- The research may not be generalizable to your specific client population. Studies with urban foster children may not generalize to rural foster youth, for example.

- Even when studies find consistently effective outcomes, not *all* people in the studies show positive outcomes. Usually, at least some people show no change or may even get worse.

Social work values and our commitment to knowledge-based practice require us to evaluate the specific outcomes of our work with clients. Single subject research, also known in the literature as *single system design, single case experimental design, within subject comparison,* or *n of 1 research,* provides us with systematic methods for answering the question Does my intervention with this client system (individual, family, group, organization, or community) create change that is consistent with our agreed-upon intervention goals?

The Single Subject Research Model

Single subject research is based on a clinical research model that views services as a problem-solving experiment. Repeated data collection provides information about the process of change over time. These data are especially useful in clinical practice because they monitor the outcomes of our interventions throughout the period when we are providing services. In addition, they do not require us to perform sophisticated statistical analysis in order to evaluate success. SSR follows the logical steps of a scientific experiment.

- Through assessment, areas for change, known as *targets,* are identified, and goals are established. The hypothesis is that intervention will change the targets in the desired direction.

- Goals—the dependent variables in social work research—are operationalized. That is, they are defined in measurable terms. This process includes identifying the short-term goals that must be accomplished in order to reach the long-term goals.

- A specific type of single subject research design is selected.

- A **baseline phase** is established in which the dependent variable is measured repeatedly before the intervention is introduced.

- An intervention—the independent variable in social work research—is introduced.

- After the intervention has been introduced, the dependent variable is measured over time on a regular basis. This step is known as the **intervention phase.**

- The data are evaluated, usually using a graph, in terms of the desired goal(s).

Defining Variables.   In social work research, as in any scientific research, we must clearly define and measure all of the relevant variables. Specifically in SSR, we must define the dependent variable, whether goals or targets of services, in a way that enables us to measure it. This process may involve measuring the duration, frequency, or magnitude of the client's behavior.

As an example of this process, assume that you are working with a child who frequently throws temper tantrums. How would you measure this behavior in scientific terms? One option is to operationalize "tantrums" as "the number of minutes crying or screaming after being told 'No.'" This definition is based on duration. An alternative definition is "the number of outbursts per week." In this case, you are focusing on frequency. Finally, you can operationalize tantrums in terms of the intensity of the outburst. Here, you are focusing on the magnitude of the behavior. A more positive approach would be to define "compliance"—the number of times a child obeys a request the first time it is made—as a goal of the intervention. As with the number of outbursts, this definition is based on a measure of frequency.

Whenever possible, you should define your goals in terms of positive rather than negative behaviors. At the very least, your goals should include developing positive behaviors as substitutes for the negative behaviors that you wish to eliminate. When you are dealing with more complex behaviors, such as depression, you can break them down into measurable subgoals such as "number of negative self-statements," "time spent with friends and family," or "score on the Hudson Generalized Contentment Scale." Whenever possible, you should assess the dependent variable using valid and reliable measures. Examples of these measures are behavior counts, self-reports of feelings or experiences, existing records such as attendance records and teachers' homework-completion charts, and standardized scales. One strategy that can help you measure the dependent variable is **triangulation,** which involves using several different measures or sources to assess progress. For example, both compliance behavior and tantrums can be measured at home and at preschool, thus providing four indicators of a successful outcome.

Baseline Phase. A **baseline** is a series of measurements taken before an intervention is introduced. During the baseline phase, researchers establish the pattern of behavior before the intervention. Ideally, during this phase, researchers take measurements until a stable pattern emerges. A minimum of five measurements is useful to establish a baseline. In general, though, the more baseline measurements taken, the greater the certainty of the pattern.

As an example, a baseline may measure the number of times a child has a tantrum when told "no." The pattern of the baseline can fall into one of four categories: ascending, descending, stable, or unstable. If the pattern is *ascending,* the tantrums are becoming more frequent. Conversely, if it is *descending,* the behavior is decreasing without intervention. If the pattern is *stable,* the behavior is staying at about the same level. Finally, if the pattern is *unstable,* the behavior does not exhibit any fixed pattern; instead, it is sometimes ascending and sometimes descending in an inconsistent manner. In the baseline phase, if the

The Social Work Library

Visit www.mhhe.com/krysik1 for a list of online measurement resources.

pattern in the data suggests a trend of dramatic or continuous improvement, intervention may not be warranted. Success in the intervention period is defined as change relative to the baseline period.

Social work researchers frequently establish a baseline during the assessment phase after they have identified the areas for change. This process may involve developing instructions for monitoring behavior on a regular basis (for example, hourly or daily) or for completing assessment scales that have been validated for a series of measurements (such as the Clinical Measurement Package) (Hudson, 1982). The measurement can be performed by the social worker, the receiver of services, a third party such as a teacher or family member, or any combination of these individuals. The decision about who will conduct the measurement is important. It is essential to devise a measuring plan that will not be overly burdensome and that can be carried out reliably.

The most commonly used method, except with children, is self-report. Self-report, however, can be subject to bias and reactivity. For example, a youth reporting his or her own disruptive behavior in the classroom may minimize the extent to which this behavior takes place. One way to minimize bias is through unobtrusive observation—observing a person in ways that he or she will not notice. For example, a teacher or parent aide may keep track of the youth's behavior during the day. Here again, triangulation of data can help enhance the validity of the results.

In some cases, intervention must begin immediately, and there is no time to collect new baseline data. In these cases, we can use a **retrospective baseline,** one based on past experience. Examples of retrospective baselines are descriptions of behavior based on personal memory, on notes from a diary or journal, or on formal school records such as class attendance. Clearly, we must carefully consider the validity and reliability of retrospective baseline data.

Intervention Phase.   Data that are collected in the baseline phase continue to be collected in the intervention phase. The intervention, or independent variable, should be specified as clearly as possible. SSR is not associated with any particular theory of human behavior, and it can be used with any intervention approach. The intervention should clearly establish who will do what, when, and under what circumstances. Such specification is easier in some approaches than in others. For example, it may be easier to specify interventions that use behavior modification than those that use play therapy. To the greatest extent possible, specification should include the following elements: (1) the responsibilities of all parties, (2) the frequency of appointments, (3) expectations of behavior during intervention sessions as well as in the natural environment, and (4) rules concerning how data are to be collected. Exhibit 10.1 illustrates and summarizes the basic steps in SSR.

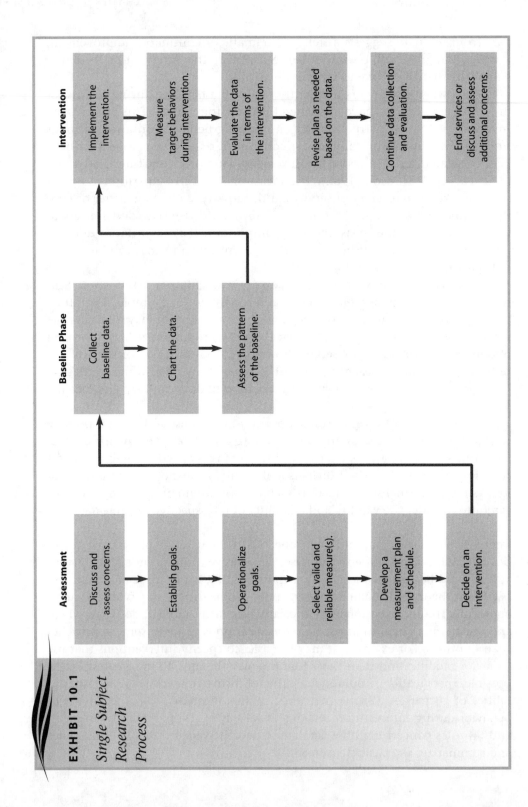

EXHIBIT 10.1

Single Subject Research Process

Assessment

Discuss and assess concerns.

Establish goals.

Operationalize goals.

Select valid and reliable measure(s).

Develop a measurement plan and schedule.

Decide on an intervention.

Baseline Phase

Collect baseline data.

Chart the data.

Assess the pattern of the baseline.

Intervention

Implement the intervention.

Measure target behaviors during intervention.

Evaluate the data in terms of the intervention.

Revise plan as needed based on the data.

Continue data collection and evaluation.

End services or discuss and assess additional concerns.

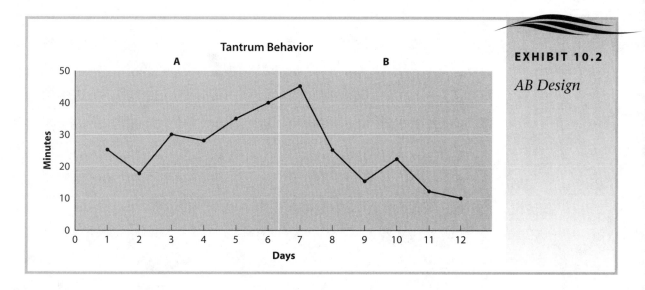

EXHIBIT 10.2

AB Design

Single Subject Research Designs

A variety of SSR designs have been used to evaluate practice in social work and other helping professions (Bloom, Fischer, & Orme, 2003; Franklin, Gorman, Beasley, & Allison, 1996; Kazidin, 1982). We discuss the following five designs: AB design, multiple baseline design, multiple component design, reversal design, and changing criterion design.

AB Design.   By convention, the letter *A* is used to designate the baseline phase, and *B* is used for the intervention phase. A vertical line separates the baseline phase from the intervention phase on a graph. An **AB design** simply measures the dependent variable during the baseline and intervention phases. Exhibit 10.2 shows a typical AB graph in which the dependent variable "tantrum behavior" is defined as the number of minutes the child spends pouting, begging, crying, or screaming after being told that it is bedtime. The line separating the baseline and intervention phases falls between Day 6 and Day 7. Note that the baseline is ascending, indicating that the behavior is getting worse. In contrast, the behavior appears to be improving, or descending, during the intervention period. These results suggest—but do not prove—that the intervention is succeeding.

Multiple Baseline Design.   A **multiple baseline design** is useful in illustrating the trend in the target variable in two or more related areas. It is assumed that the trend is the result of the intervention. For example, in the "tantrum" case, we could use a multiple baseline design to track compliance as well as tantrums. Exhibit 10.3 illustrates a multiple baseline design that tracks compliance both at home and in school. Note that the intervention, which uses a token behavioral

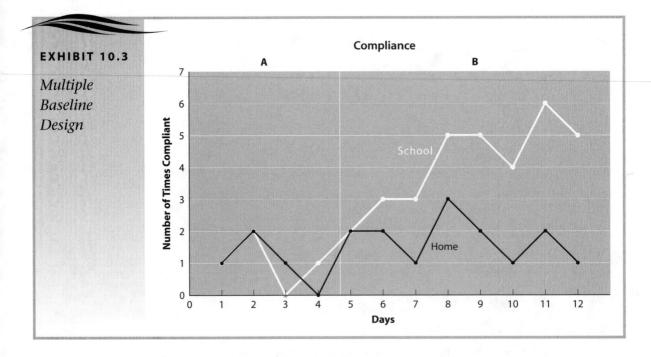

EXHIBIT 10.3

Multiple Baseline Design

system to reward compliance, appears to be successful at school but not at home. In this case, further assessment would be warranted to understand the reasons why behavior has not changed at home. Depending on the results of this assessment, we might need to develop a new intervention for the home.

Multiple Component Design. A **multiple component design,** sometimes known as an **ABC design,** involves the use of sequential interventions or changes in the amount or intensity of the same intervention. For example, in the case of an anxious six-year-old girl who was constantly biting her fingernails to the point of drawing blood, her parents recorded the number of times each week that they found her biting her nails. Meanwhile, the girl's social worker used play therapy for four weeks. Unfortunately, this intervention produced only limited results. The social worker and the parents then agreed to try a behavioral approach in which they made no comments when the nail biting occurred, but the girl was rewarded for each hour she went without biting her nails.

Exhibit 10.4 graphs the results of both interventions. Clearly, the girl's nail-biting behavior declined far more dramatically after the behavior therapy was introduced. It should be noted, however, that a multiple component design does not specify which components were effective. In other words, we can conclude from Exhibit 10.4 only that play therapy followed by a behavioral approach was effective. We *cannot* determine whether continuing the play therapy or using the behavioral approach alone would have been as effective.

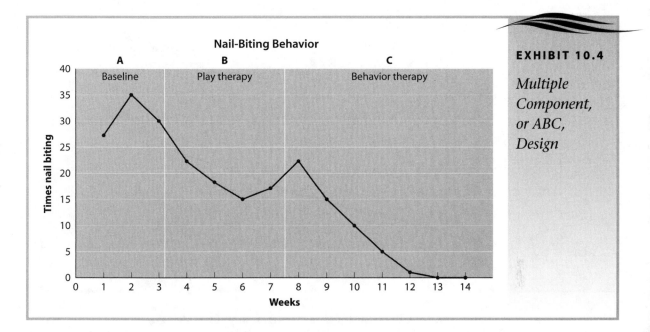

EXHIBIT 10.4

Multiple Component, or ABC, Design

The different phases of a multiple component design can be defined in a key or legend. An alternative strategy in this case would be to change the intensity rather than the mode of treatment. For example, the social worker could increase the play therapy to three times per week. In that case, the B phase in Exhibit 10.4 would be weekly play therapy, and the C phase would be play therapy three times per week.

Reversal Design.   Researchers use a **reversal design** to provide greater assurance that the intervention is responsible for the observed changes in behavior. In this method, as with the AB design, a baseline period is followed by the intervention. In a reversal design, however, the intervention phase is then followed by a third phase in which the intervention is withdrawn. Next comes a fourth phase in which the intervention is reintroduced.

This type of research is common in drug studies. Exhibit 10.5 illustrates a reversal design that is being used to test the usefulness of meditation for reducing the pain associated with migraine headaches. In the baseline phase, the subjective intensity of headache pain is charted on a 10-point scale for one week. After one week, the intervention—meditation—is introduced. After the meditation successfully reduces headache pain for two weeks, it is stopped in the third phase, and the effect of stopping the meditation on the headache pain is monitored. In the fourth period, the meditation is reintroduced.

Exhibit 10.5 illustrates a pattern in which the client reported a significant decrease in pain while using meditation and a major rebound after the meditation was stopped. These results strongly suggest that the meditation is a

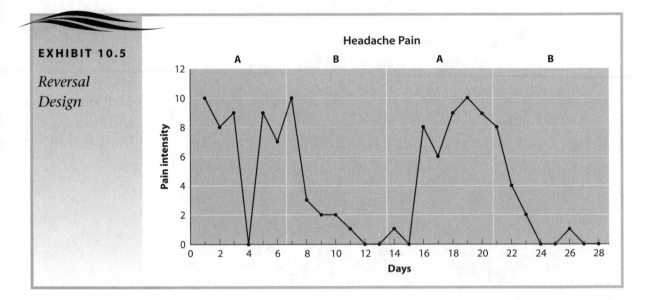

EXHIBIT 10.5

*Reversal
Design*

successful intervention for this client. In a reversal design, when the pattern of the behavior increases or decreases after the intervention is withdrawn, the intervention is the likely cause of the change. Note, though, that a reversal design does not test the possibility that the meditation had a placebo effect or that other chance circumstances were responsible for the pattern of improvement.

Reversal designs may not be appropriate for many social work interventions, for a couple of reasons. First, withdrawing an intervention that is helpful just to test for reversal effects would be unethical. In addition, many interventions would not have reversal effects because personality changes or new behaviors are expected to continue after the services are terminated. For example, a social worker would not expect parents who have learned better parenting skills through parent education classes to return to their former behavior after the classes have ended.

Changing Criterion Design. A **changing criterion design**, also referred to as a **changing intensity design**, is useful when the goal is to reduce (or increase) a specific behavior gradually. This approach is often used in monitoring interventions related to withdrawal from addictions to substances such as cigarettes or alcohol. Exhibit 10.6 shows the results of an intervention to reduce cigarette smoking. In this case, the client counts the cigarettes smoked each day and records the number on a paper attached to the cigarette pack. After the baseline phase (A), the client and social worker establish a goal of reducing the number of cigarettes smoked each day from an average of 16 to 13 (B1). When the client reaches the goal of 13, the goal is reduced in the next phase to 9 (B2). When the client reaches that goal, the goal is reduced to 4 cigarettes (B3), and so on until the client achieves the goal of not smoking at all (B5). Each phase

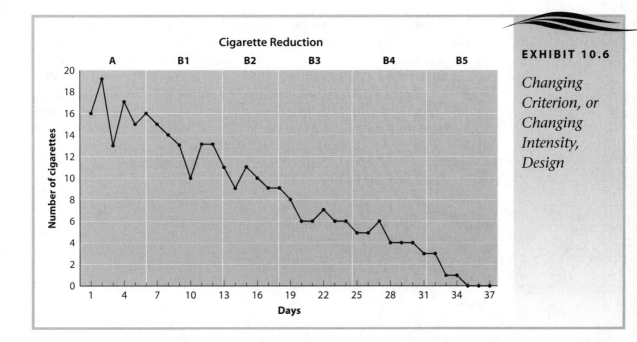

EXHIBIT 10.6

*Changing
Criterion, or
Changing
Intensity,
Design*

can last for a different period of time. Despite the length of the phase, however, the criterion remains in place until it is reached. Subscripts can be used to denote the change in the criterion at each phase of the study.

WHAT IS "SUCCESS" IN SINGLE SUBJECT RESEARCH?

People may define success in a number of different ways. Some people consider even the attempt to make positive changes a success. Others may view any change in the desired direction a success, and still others might consider only the complete resolution of a problematic situation a success. Social workers are generally interested in **therapeutic success:** the situation for which a person seeks services is resolved. Abuse and neglect of a child has stopped; an adolescent is no longer missing school; a nursing home resident is participating in social events; a married couple is engaged in problem solving rather than in destructive communications. Therapeutic success is achieved when clients have reached the goals of the services.

Researchers may define other types of success, including experimental and statistical success. **Experimental success** refers to the situation in which the intervention has produced a clear improvement—that is, measures in the intervention phase are better than the average of the baseline phase—but the goals have not been completely reached. In the case of the child who throws tantrums, the child may have improved from having tantrums every night to having a tantrum only once or twice a week. In contrast, **statistical success** refers to situations in which changes in the intervention period are greater than would be expected by chance variation. For example, if a student missed an average of 16 days of school per month with a standard deviation of 2 days during the baseline period but missed only 10 days during the intervention period, this difference would show statistical success because it was a change of more than two standard deviations. As we saw in Chapter 8, changing more than two standard deviations indicates a great deal of change from a student's typical or average behavior. Missing 10 days of school each month, however, cannot be considered therapeutic success.

Analyzing Single Subject Research

We can analyze SSR visually through a graph, statistically through the use of statistical software, or through a combination of these methods. In this section, we consider various methods of evaluating the success of social work interventions.

Graphing SSR Data.   A graph of SSR should have a title, and each axis should be labeled. The horizontal (x) axis indicates units of time (days, weeks, or months). The vertical (y) axis indicates increments of the dependent variable (number of minutes, number of days attendance, score on an anxiety scale, for example). Typically, researchers use a line graph to show changes over time. As noted earlier, *A* denotes the baseline phase, and *B* indicates the intervention phase. Additional letters, *C, D, E,* and so forth, denote additional interventions or changes in intensity of the intervention. Exhibits 10.2–10.6 are all examples of SSR graphs.

Visual Examination of the Data.   One method of determining the success of an intervention is to "eyeball" the data, that is, to look at the pattern of the intervention phase in relation to the baseline phase. In some cases, we can clearly see that goals have been reached and the intervention is successful (for example, in Exhibit 10.3, for compliance at school). In other cases, we can clearly see that the intervention has not been successful. We assume that an intervention has not been successful when (a) there appears to be no difference between the baseline phase and the intervention phase or (b) the intervention phase shows that the situation is getting worse rather than better (for example, in Exhibit 10.3, for compliance at home).

Split-Middle Method.   This visual approach assumes that the trend of the baseline will continue over time if the intervention is not successful. It is called the *split-middle method* because the baseline is split in the middle. We use the mean of each half of the baseline as a point through which we plot a *predictor line*.

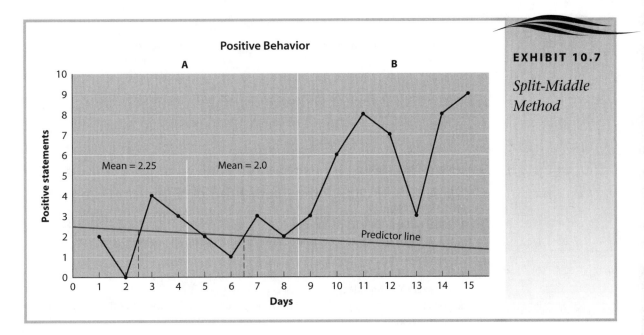

EXHIBIT 10.7

Split-Middle Method

(If the baseline scores show extreme variation, we can plot the median rather than the mean.) We then extend the line connecting the plotted means or medians into the intervention phase. If most of the points in the intervention phase are above or below this line (depending on the direction of the goal), we consider the intervention to be successful.

For example, consider a situation in which a goal of services is to increase a mother's use of praise and positive reinforcement in changing her child's behavior. We can see in Exhibit 10.7 that the mean of the first half of the baseline is 2.25 and the second half is 2.0. These points are plotted in the center of each half of the baseline, and a predictor line is drawn to indicate the trend of the data. Because the majority of points in the intervention phase are above the predictor line, the intervention is considered a success.

The Standard Deviation Method.   As its name suggests, the standard deviation method assumes that the baseline represents a person's typical behavior and that the behavior varies in a manner similar to the normal distribution. In that case, approximately 68 percent of behavior will fall within one standard deviation of the mean of the baseline phase, and 95 percent of behavior will fall within two standard deviations. Based on this assumption, a social worker may assume that if the mean of the intervention phase is outside of one standard deviation of the baseline mean, the intervention is considered successful because it represents a shift away from previous typical behavior. Alternatively, a social worker may use more stringent criteria and choose a change of two

EXHIBIT 10.8

Single Subject Design Tutorial— Graphing with Excel

You are tracking the number of minutes of fussing behavior on a nightly basis.

Baseline: 25, 38, 27, 30, 25, 30, 20

Intervention: 30, 35, 25, 20, 15, 10, 15, 10, 10, 15, 8, 10, 8, 5, 5, 10, 5, 8, 5, 0, 5, 3, 5, 1, 0, 5, 0, 3, 0, 0

Follow-up: 0, 0

GRAPHING WITH EXCEL

1. Enter all the data in the first row (in order, baseline first). The date will be in cells A1 through AM1.
2. Highlight the data (click and drag).
3. Click the chart wizard icon; select **Line** (be sure the **Rows** option is selected); click **Next**.
4. Click the **Titles** tab. Chart Title = Bedtime Behavior; Category X = Days; Category Y = Minutes.
5. Select the **Legend** tab. Click the **Show legend** box so that the legend is not visible. Select **Next**.
6. Select **View as an object in sheet 1**.
7. Click **Finish**.
8. Select **View/Toolbars/Drawing** if drawing tools are not already available.
9. Use the Line tool to draw a vertical line at the end of the baseline just after entry 7 on the x axis. Draw another vertical line at the end of Day 21 to separate the B phase from the C phase. Draw a vertical line at Day 35 to separate the C phase from the D (follow-up) phase.
10. Use the Textbox tool to add the letters A (for baseline), B (first intervention phase), C (second intervention phase), and D above each section. Also use the Textbox tool to label the baseline and standard deviation lines.

FINDING THE MEAN AND STANDARD DEVIATION OF THE BASELINE WITH EXCEL

1. Put the cursor in an empty cell, for example, A3.
2. Select the **Insert Function (fx)** button. Select **Average**.
3. In the Number 1 box, type **A1:G1** (this means A1 through G1) to select the average of the first seven days.
4. Move the cursor to another empty cell, for example, A4.
5. Select the **Insert Function (fx)** button. Highlight **STDEV**.
6. In the Number 1 box, type **A1:G1**.
7. In cell A5, subtract one standard deviation from the mean. In Excel, you can do this by typing **+A3-A4** or **=27.86-5.64** and pressing **Enter**.
8. Use the Line tool to draw the mean and the one standard deviation and two standard deviation ranges on the graph. (Note: Using different colors for these lines will add visual clarity.)

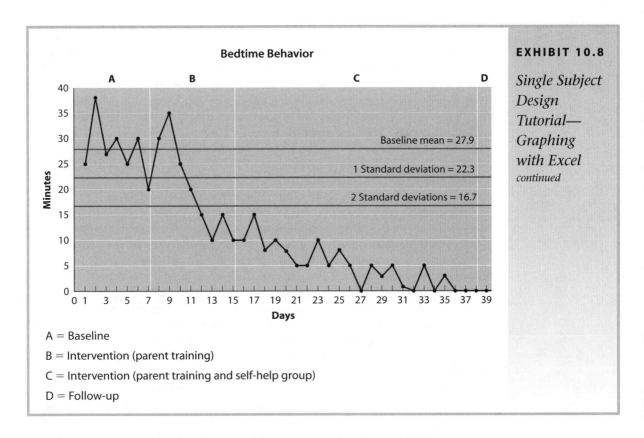

Bedtime Behavior

A = Baseline

B = Intervention (parent training)

C = Intervention (parent training and self-help group)

D = Follow-up

EXHIBIT 10.8

*Single Subject
Design
Tutorial—
Graphing
with Excel*
continued

standard deviations to represent success. When we use this method, plotting the standard deviation lines on the SSR graph can help us represent the results visually. We can easily calculate the mean and the standard deviation of the baseline phase and the mean of the intervention phase using a spreadsheet program such as Excel or statistical software such as SPSS. Exhibit 10.8 provides a tutorial and graph illustrating this method using the one standard deviation rule. Case-in-Point 10.1 describes the case undertaken by a family service agency.

When analyzing the graph in Exhibit 10.8, a social worker might make the following observations:

Other methods of analysis involve the use of trend analysis, t-tests of mean differences, chi-square analysis, and binomial probability. These methods are beyond the scope of this chapter and can be found in Bloom, Fischer, and Orme (2003) and Weinbach and Grinnell (2004).

- The baseline ranges between 20 and 38 with a mean of 27.9 (top line) and standard deviation of 5.6. The pattern is somewhat unstable with no clear direction. The middle line represents one standard deviation from the mean, and the bottom line represents two standard deviations.

- Visual inspection of the result shows a clear pattern of improvement and suggests that the goal has been reached.

Mr. and Ms. C. sought assistance from a family service agency because they were "worn out" trying to get their son to sleep at night. Mr. and Ms. C. were caring and involved parents who spent a great deal of time interacting with their six-year-old son, Jon. Ms. C. explained that things were fine during the day and evening, but they became chaotic and difficult at bedtime. When Jon was told that it was time to go to bed, he began to cry and whine. He said he was afraid of ghosts and wanted to sleep in his parents' bed with them. If his parents put him in his own bed, he cried and shouted about monsters and ghosts, and he clung to whichever parent attempted to put him to bed. Further, he usually left his bed and slept with his parents before the night was over. The parents were inconsistent, alternately threatening, coaching, and usually giving in to restore peace to the home and "meet their son's needs."

The parents agreed that the goal was to have their son go to bed after being told it was bedtime, spend 15 minutes of quiet time with his parents, and then sleep through the night in his own bed. The social worker asked the parents not to change their behavior during the next week. They were to keep a nightly journal noting the number of minutes Jon spent fussing before he went to sleep. The goals (dependent variables) are to decrease fussing and to have Jon sleep in his own bed. In the tutorial in Exhibit 10.8, the data indicating the amount of fussing for the first week (baseline) are presented. The parents noted that the week was typical of what they had been experiencing for the past year.

The intervention to which Mr. and Ms. C. agreed consisted of weekly parent education sessions focusing on the following strategies: (a) implementing a consistent bedtime routine, (b) setting limits, (c) ignoring all talk of ghosts and monsters, and (d) putting Jon back in his own bed when he left it. In addition, they were to praise Jon when he went to his own bed and reward him by reading him a story in the morning if he slept through the night in his own room. After two weeks, the parents and the social worker agreed that additional support and parent education would be useful. Mr. and Ms. C. then began to attend a weekly support group in which parents shared experiences and engaged in mutual problem solving.

Exhibit 10.8 also shows data for the next four weeks (intervention) using an ABC design. During the second week of the intervention, Jon's behavior began to show improvement, and it continued to improve throughout the intervention period. Mr. and Ms. C. ended services after five weeks, but they continued to attend the parent support group for the next three months. Follow-up telephone calls at one week and then one month after the end of services found that appropriate bedtime behavior continued.

- Behavior has improved considerably by the end of the first week of intervention, and measurements fall below two standard deviations from the baseline mean. These results would indicate experimental and statistical success, although the goal is not yet completely reached.

- By the end of the intervention phase, all measurements are below two standard deviations from the baseline mean, and the goal of bedtime without fussing appears to have been reached.

- Follow-up at one week and then one month confirms that the behavior change has been maintained.

Benefits of Using Single Subject Research to Inform Practice

The purpose of single subject research is to inform practice by monitoring the effectiveness of social work interventions. The use of SSR should enhance the quality of services and help build the social work knowledge base. It does so in several ways, which we discuss next.

Better Services. SSR promotes better services by documenting both the process and the outcomes of services on an individualized basis. Social workers who monitor progress will know whether an intervention that works for most people is effective with a specific client. In addition, social workers can change their approach when ongoing data collection indicates that it is not achieving the desired outcomes. Moreover, by monitoring many cases, social workers will learn the typical process of change for an intervention. This information will help them assess their progress during interventions and educate clients about the process of change.

Enhanced Relationships. SSR may promote a more collaborative relationship between social workers and their clients by opening up communication through a joint review of the data. In addition, SSR promotes discussions about the reasons that progress is or is not being achieved. Finally, communication with others (such as a parent, teacher, or counselor) during the process of collecting data promotes better understanding of the problem during the baseline phase. It further encourages everyone concerned to consider what factors other than the intervention may be impacting the problem.

Evidence of Progress. SSR provides concrete evidence to consumers about the progress of the interventions. For example, it provides important information about when to stop, change course, or refer elsewhere because the intervention is not working.

The Larger Context. Social workers can use SSR to evaluate services in a larger context. Given this individualized approach to evaluation, generalization to others with similar concerns is not possible from single cases. However, by using SSR with many cases, a social worker can accumulate information about the effectiveness of a particular type of intervention. This information can help answer questions about the usefulness of an intervention, the speed at which change can be expected to occur, and for whom and under what circumstances the intervention is successful. A social worker's cumulative SSR with a specific concern provides valuable feedback about practice. When such cases are collected and analyzed across all social workers in the agency, even greater generalization is possible. SSR can provide an inductive and empirical method for building evidence-based knowledge.

Promoting Critical Thinking. SSR uses an empirical, research-based orientation to services. For this reason, it may promote critical thinking about the efficacy of practice methods that have been based primarily on "practice wisdom" or authority. Thus, SSR both supports innovation and reinforces the use of interventions supported by research.

Efficiency. SSR is efficient in that it can be incorporated into practice with little additional time or expense. SSR avoids many of the costs and disruptions of group-level research projects. There is no need for research consultants, random assignment, or the extensive collection, input, and analysis of data. Data collection in SSR can generally take place as part of the assessment and intervention processes. Data analysis is relatively simple and straightforward.

Drawbacks of Using Single Subject Research to Inform Practice

In spite of the potential of SSR to inform practice, there has been some criticism and resistance to its use in social work. These arguments are based on both pragmatic and methodological concerns. Any form of evaluation may be threatening because it can highlight ineffective practices. In addition, even simple evaluation methods require a social worker's time and commitment. Next, we consider the major criticisms of SSR.

Impracticality. SSR is impractical. It takes away time that might otherwise be used for direct services. The use of SSR, however, fits within an evidence-based practice approach in which specifying goals, assessing systems, monitoring improvement, and documenting processes and outcomes are integral components of service delivery. The time needed for data collection is often minimal, and computer software makes graphing and analyzing results a fast and simple task. Nevertheless, social workers may resist the work involved in SSR.

Limited Scope. SSR is appropriate only for behavioral interventions that focus on simple behavior change. This is an erroneous belief. In practice, SSR is not tied to any particular theory or intervention approach. It can be used to monitor any kind of change, including changes in personality, attitude, relationships, and the environment.

Limited Validity. SSR has limited validity. SSR does not have the internal validity needed to establish cause-and-effect relationships or the external validity needed to generalize to broader populations. Although these criticisms cannot be refuted, they also apply to the majority of research done on social work practice that uses nonrandom samples, with small groups of participants, in limited settings. Nevertheless, SSR allows us to accumulate data that can lend empirical support to the use of specific practice methods.

Inadequate Time Series Measures. SSR lacks adequate time series measures for many concerns brought to social work practice. Many of the measures used to evaluate more complex variables such as self-esteem, marital satisfaction, family environment, and community integration have not yet been tested for reliability and validity as repeated measures. For example, a self-esteem scale may have been found to be a valid measure when it is given only once. However, the effect of the *testing* itself is unknown. In other words, taking the test on a weekly basis for several weeks may change a person's responses as she or he becomes either familiar or bored with the test. In addition, the test may not be sensitive to small changes that occur on a weekly basis. When using SSR, indicators based on behavior rather than a written scale may be more valid measures of change. Behavioral indicators are often available for concerns brought to social workers. In addition, some measures such as Hudson's Clinical Measurement Package (Hudson, 1982) have been validated for repeated administration. Much work remains to be done in this area.

Individual Focus. SSR focuses on individual change rather than system change. Although this criticism is valid concerning much of our practice with individuals, families, and groups, there is nothing inherent in SSR to prevent a focus on system change. Ultimately, it is people who seek services. For this reason, the results of services must be documented based on the well-being of those who seek them, whether the change effort is directed at people or at systems in the environment.

Little Research on Effectiveness. Finally, there is no evidence that social workers who use SSR are more effective than those who do not evaluate their practice. Little research has been done in this area.

CASE STUDY RESEARCH

Case study is the rich, detailed, and in-depth description and analysis of a single unit or small number of units. The unit may be at any system level: individual, family, group, organization, community, or even the larger social system. Case studies focus on discovering key system elements, such as history, motivation, and worldview, as well as on deriving patterns and processes that explain how the system functions. Case studies appear in the form of narratives of events and descriptions of personalities and situations. With individuals or families who seek social work services, a case study documents the background, history, environmental context, and reasons for seeking services. Case studies help social workers develop empathy by encouraging them to see the world from the perspective of the person or people being studied. A case study also documents the process of the intervention, using detailed notes and/or recordings to keep a record of services and to hypothesize the reasons why interventions are or are not effective. The goal is to understand the person in the environment in order to increase understanding of human behavior and to help develop effective interventions.

Published case studies of social work services are valuable research tools because they transmit knowledge about new methods while helping workers avoid ineffective interventions. Case studies employ primarily qualitative methods, which have a long tradition and an important role in the development of knowledge in the social sciences and medical research. The works of Sigmund Freud (1909) in psychiatry and Jean Piaget (1972) in child development provide classic illustrations of the use of case study research to develop and document new theories of practice and human behavior.

Social work researchers can use case studies for exploratory research when they know little about a phenomenon. For example, a researcher might use a case study to understand the experiences of *throw-away teens*—homeless teenagers who have been forced to leave home by parents or caregivers. The researcher's goal would be to obtain an in-depth understanding of the motivations, lifestyle, and consequences of being a throw-away teen and the culture in which this phenomenon exists. The researcher would study one teen (or a few teens) in this situation and attempt to understand his or her worldview, needs, motivations, and social niche. This effort might involve in-depth interviews with the person; the person's family, friends, and acquaintances; neighbors; school and medical personnel; and the police. In addition, the worker would carefully document relevant treatment strategies and issues, including engagement strategies, background, assessment, and successes and failures. From this cumulative data, the worker might develop and test a theory of throw-away teens.

Researchers also use case studies for explanatory research in which the goals are to establish cause-and-effect processes and to explain the reasons why things happen the way they do. Social workers can use this material to increase their understanding of, and empathy for, these teens as well as to inform intervention efforts and provide information that might be useful in prevention campaigns.

Researchers have also used case studies to understand larger systems such as organizations and communities. The qualitative methods that researchers use to study larger systems include participant observation, in-depth interviews, examination of personal documents (such as letters and records), and informal conversations to obtain the subjective experiences of individuals in the system and to understand their social construction of the world (Yin, 1994). Researchers might also collect quantitative data as part of an overall description.

Two case studies that focus on larger systems are presented here. Case-in-Point 10.2 provides insights into the social and cultural dynamics of an inner-city

Elijah Anderson, in his 1999 book *Code of the Street*, focused on understanding the impact of poverty and lack of opportunity on the everyday life of an urban inner-city neighborhood in Philadelphia. He explained street behavior and why it differs from mainstream culture. Anderson, a university professor living in Philadelphia, became a "regular" in the neighborhood, spending a great deal of time as a participant observer. Using a combination of purposive, snowball, and convenience sampling, he conducted intensive interviews with a wide range of community members, including "old heads" (elders), families, pregnant teens, students, drug dealers, and store owners. From his interviews and observations, he provided rich detail to support his explanations of the reasons for interpersonal violence, teen pregnancy, crime, drug use, and other social problems of the inner city.

Anderson divided families in the inner city into two broad categories. The first category, "decent" families, adheres to mainstream values. In contrast, "street-oriented" families do not identify with the broader society. Anderson focused on the daily pressures that shape the choices and goals of both types of families. Regardless of a family's values, everyone must learn the "code of the street." Anderson explains that the code is based on "respect," that is, being treated with the deference one expects based on his or her status in the community. This unwritten set of rules is based largely on an individual's ability to command respect through physical violence or the threat of violence. In addition, every individual must understand when and how to defer to others. The code is a powerful and pervasive form of etiquette that dictates the ways in which people learn to negotiate public spaces. The code of the street is functional. Its purpose is to establish status and reduce violence. Through narrative examples from interviews and descriptions of daily life, Anderson explains the code as a response to poverty, racial prejudice, alienation, and lack of opportunity. These forces create an economy based on illegal activities and a subculture at odds with mainstream culture. Both stable and street families must learn to negotiate this subculture. He concludes that the causes and solutions to social problems in the inner city are social and economic, not personal.

Code of the Street illustrates many strengths of a case study. It provides detailed accounts of people's motivation, behavior, activities, and responses to their environment in a way that makes them real for the reader. It examines and explains behavior that outsiders may not understand. It uses a flexible research design that could be altered by the needs of the study. The author's choice of who is interviewed about what topics emerges as he begins to understand the community. Finally, the study is based on actual experiences and firsthand accounts, and it is not time limited. In general, it provides a comprehensive, holistic view of community processes and events.

This study also illustrates the limitations of the case study method. How do we know that this neighborhood is like other inner-city neighborhoods? How much did the author himself, an African American middle-aged professor, influence the material that he gathered? The author provided money to one respondent as part of their relationship. Might this act have influenced what the respondent told him? How representative are the people Anderson selected for interviews? Did people respond to Anderson as a professor and a professional person, thus limiting and shaping what they said? Would another researcher of a different age, race, and gender reach similar conclusions?

Code of the Street provides an in-depth look at the culture and struggles of a community. How might this study be combined with quantitative methods to document the service needs of the community?

Through case study research, Janenne Allen and Richard Boettcher (2000) describe two attempts to pass a tax levy that would be used to fund the majority of mental health and alcohol and drug treatment services in Franklin County, Ohio. The first attempt to pass the tax, which was set to expire in the coming year, failed. The second attempt saw the tax pass by an overwhelming margin. The research question addressed by this case study could be characterized as "How can social workers promote a successful tax campaign to ensure the funding of mental health services?"

Allen was a participant in the second campaign. She describes herself as "an informal, behind-the-scenes liaison among the providers, the Board, and the political professionals." This role enabled her to outline in a comprehensive manner multiple perspectives on why the first attempt failed and to describe in detail the processes put into place for the second campaign. Allen and Boettcher's article offers two especially useful pieces of learning for social workers confronted with a similar problem. First, the authors explain both campaigns in reference to theories of community practice. For instance, they discuss theories on coalition building, conflict management, and influence in relation to the campaign. Thus, the reader knows not only what was done, but why. Second, the authors present detailed data on fund-raising and expenditures for the second, successful campaign. This material makes the political process more transparent. In addition, it allows social workers and other activists to replicate or adapt the authors' strategies to a different setting.

This study is an example of the power of combining qualitative and quantitative data. The qualitative data used in the case study include observations, the researchers' perceptions, and the findings of a focus group. In addition to the specific information about income and expenditures, the quantitative data presented in the case study include the findings from polls that were used to shape the message to the voting public. For instance, Allen and Boettcher write, "It was clear from the previous election and from polling that 40% of the voters were solidly against the levy, no matter what messages they heard during the campaign. Another 40% were solidly for the levy at the outset. The persuadable 20% tended to be Republican and politically Independent women. ... It was essential to victory that most of the campaign efforts and dollars be pitched to this 20%" (p. 33).

Case study research, as this example illustrates, is a form of qualitative research in that it is holistic. However, this fact does not preclude the use of quantitative data. Without the combination of qualitative and quantitative data, the researchers would not have been as successful in describing the efforts to pass the tax levy.

urban neighborhood. Case-in-Point 10.3 describes how social workers helped pass a tax levy to fund needed services in their community. As with individual case studies, researchers document their material through case notes and/or recordings. They then analyze these materials to develop or test theories, insights, patterns, themes, and processes.

As with any research method, a case study must conform to accepted standards of reliability and validity. Reliability is obtained through careful documentation that is available for verification. Validity depends on the researcher's ability to conduct unbiased observation and accumulate evidence that respondents are reporting honestly and accurately. Case studies have a number of advantages. They are often high in external validity; that is, they focus on life as it is happening, not as someone reports on a predetermined questionnaire or through a contrived experiment. In addition, case studies consider the full context of an event rather than looking at the event in isolation. Further, they provide the kind of rich detail that promotes the development of explanatory theories and may help others understand and have empathy for people in difficult circumstances. Finally, case studies promote a holistic view of people rather than focusing on social work practice as a few behaviors to be changed.

Despite all of these advantages, people who believe only in a positivistic philosophy of science—one based on a measurable objective reality—criticize case studies for several reasons. First, they argue that case studies can never be replicated because the depth and quality of information cannot be re-created. Imagine trying to re-create years of community interviews! More important, critics maintain that case studies have very limited value because their samples are so small that the results cannot be generalized. No evidence can be provided that the experiences of one person or object of study are similar to those of others.

In social work research, case studies and quantitative research often complement each other. Researchers use case studies to develop theories and share new methods while using quantitative methods to test hypotheses derived from these theories and to test generalization. Quantitative methods often show the extent of a problem in numerical terms, while qualitative methods show the true human impact in an emotionally powerful way. Researchers often use this combination of quantitative and qualitative data in writing grant proposals to fund human service needs. Case-in-Point 10.3 illustrates how two social work researchers used both methods to study a political development in Ohio that had consequences for social policy.

CONCLUSION

Social workers need to assure the people they work with, themselves, and the public that their services are effective. Case studies provide rich, detailed descriptions of the impact of social problems on people and the use of social work practice in creating change. Single subject research designs offer an efficient, cost-effective method for evaluating practice that is individualized and consistent with social work ethics and practice methods. SSR enhances practice in that it promotes specificity in assessment and accountability of results. SSR documents practice outcomes for individual social workers and can provide generalizable evidence of practice effectiveness when the SSR data from many cases are combined and analyzed. "Sometimes the magic works, sometimes it doesn't." Social workers need to know whether it "works" each time they use an intervention.

MAIN POINTS

- Social work values and ethics require that social workers use tested, effective methods to promote positive change. They also require that social workers document the outcomes of their services.

- Although social work research is a useful starting place for selecting an evidence-based intervention, we cannot know whether the intervention suggested by the research will be effective for a particular person, family, group, or community.

- Single subject research provides systematic methods with which to monitor the process and outcomes of change efforts on an individualized basis.

- Single subject research uses a clinical research model that follows the logical steps of good practice and research: formulating problems, setting and operationalizing goals; developing procedures for collecting data; collecting baseline data; specifying and introducing the intervention(s) with ongoing data collection; analyzing the data; and making decisions based on the data.

- A variety of single subject designs can be used depending on the goals and the degree to which the researcher needs to draw conclusions about the causal nature of the independent variable. These designs include AB, multiple component, multiple baseline, changing criterion, and reversal designs.

- Practitioners may define success differently than researchers do. A practitioner may define success as reaching agreed-upon goals. A researcher may view success as reaching a significant level of change, even if the goals are not completely reached.

- Single subject researchers often use spreadsheet and statistical programs to simplify the process of data recording, graphing, and data analysis.

- Single subject research has advantages and disadvantages. It is a practical, easy-to-use method of documenting the results of practice on an individualized basis. It promotes assessment and accountable, evidence-based decision making. At the same time, it has also been criticized for (a) taking time away from service delivery; (b) lacking appropriate measures for many problems; (c) lacking experimental control, which prevents researchers from reaching conclusions about cause-and-effect; and (d) focusing on personal rather than systemic change. Critics further contend that there is no convincing evidence that the use of SSR improves services.

- Case studies use qualitative research methods to examine social work practice and to provide in-depth examination of social concerns that explore new issues, describe social events from a holistic perspective, develops and tests theories, and provides examples to illustrate social concerns. Case studies are often high in validity but criticized for their lack of generalizability.

EXERCISES: PRACTICING SOCIAL WORK

1. From the Black Feather project, suggest one research question that could be answered using single subject research and one question that could be answered using the case study method. How would the information gained from these two methods differ?

EXERCISES: SOCIAL WORK LIBRARY

1. Read Singer (1996). Discuss the research process described in the article. Provide a critique of each of the steps as presented by the author.

OTHER EXERCISES

1. In single subject research, we need to be able to operationalize the dependent variable. How would you operationalize the following?

   a. She's a bad student.

   b. He's depressed.

   c. She's shy.

   d. He's always criticizing me.

2. Use a spreadsheet program to present the following single subject design.

   A new radio advertising campaign was initiated in order to recruit volunteers for the Senior Care Center. A retrospective baseline found the following number of people volunteering each month: 12, 15, 22, 14, 24, 15. The number of volunteers was tracked for the six months of the radio campaign. The total number of volunteers for the next six months was 28, 22, 18, 16, 18, 20.

   a. Graph the data.

   b. Enter the vertical lines to represent the baseline and intervention phases.

    c. Find the mean and standard deviation of the baseline.

    d. Enter one and two standard deviation lines on the graph.

    e. What do you conclude about the effectiveness of the intervention?

3. You wish to do research about people with multiple body piercings. Outline ideas for conducting a case study method for understanding this group. What are the strengths and limitations of the case study method you describe?

CHAPTER 11 ━━━

Evaluation of Social Work Services

If we help only one child, we consider ourselves a success!

SOCIAL WORKERS SOMETIMES USE THE OPENING QUOTE, OR A version of it, when they are asked to discuss their goals and to show evidence of their success. The sentiments expressed in the quote, though noble and heartwarming, are not the way the real world operates. More than ever before, we live in an age of evidence and accountability. Not only is social work's reputation as a profession dependent on providing scientific evidence that programs are successful and cost effective, but as social workers, our ability to live by our ethics and to secure funding for the programs we believe in is also at stake. So far in this book, we have discussed research tools and methods for answering questions of interest. Sometimes these questions are theoretical, and sometimes they are related to social work services. In addition, we have discussed the kinds of questions that can be answered by research, the methods and research designs we use to answer these questions, and the strengths and limitations of these methods and designs.

This chapter deals with the application of research methods to answer some practical questions about social work services: Do social work programs work? If they do work, are they cost effective? In order to answer these questions, we must clearly define what we mean by *program* and *work*. A **program** is a set of activities designed to reach specific objectives. A program can be used to produce change at any system level. Some programs involve clinical change in individuals and families, whereas others attempt to change organizations or communities. For example, a program can focus on a specific objective such as improving communication among individuals. Conversely, it can encompass an entire agency's activities, such as a program to reduce child abuse and neglect. Regardless of their scope, all social work programs are intended to improve the quality of life for people. If a program accomplishes this goal, we say it works.

Finding out whether the program works is a complex process. We can think of a program as based on a theory of practice. Theory states that if we perform a specified set of activities, certain changes will take place. If these changes do not take place, there are two possible explanations. First, the program does not have **treatment fidelity,** that is, the program is not being delivered as intended. To determine whether this is the case, we must collect evidence about the ways the program functions. Second, if we find that the program is operating as intended and yet the desired changes in people or systems are not occurring, we must conclude that our theory of practice was wrong. The program doesn't work.

Program evaluation refers to the use of research methods to answer questions related to planning, evaluating, and improving social work programs. Program evaluation is often divided into two major categories: formative evaluation and summative evaluation. This distinction is really one of purpose rather than method.

Formative evaluation is research conducted for the purpose of informing program improvement efforts. For instance, examining immunization levels of program participants compared to the overall immunization completion rate in the state may indicate that the program is doing well or, conversely, that the program should be doing better. Formative evaluation is directed at collecting information that can be used to target improvement efforts. **Summative evaluation,** in contrast, is for the purpose of judging the overall effectiveness of a program and lends itself to decision making about the future of the program. Based on information from the summative evaluation, important decisions will be made regarding whether or not the program should continue to be funded as is, should be terminated, or should even expanded.

Whereas the formative-summative classification is based on purpose, there is also an evaluation typology based on focus. In this chapter, we discuss nine different types of program evaluation, each with a distinct focus. These include needs assessment, evaluability assessment, implementation evaluation, quality assurance, program monitoring, consumer satisfaction, process, outcome, and cost evaluation. The different types of evaluation are related. Process evaluation provides information that the program is "doing things right" but not necessarily that it is "doing the right things." Even when a program is implemented as designed, process evaluation does not provide evidence that it is producing the intended changes in the people or communities. This is the focus of outcome evaluation. The combination of process and outcome evaluation is needed for evidence-based practice.

In addition to providing basic definitions related to program evaluation, and the functions and types of program evaluation, this chapter explains that program evaluation always occurs within a social and political context. The chapter concludes with a discussion of the politics of evaluation and strategies for maximizing the likelihood that program evaluation will be used to enhance social work services.

By the end of this chapter, you should be able to:

- Define what is meant by program evaluation, and list and explain the reasons why program evaluation is a necessary part of social work practice.

- Define four different perspectives on need and describe strategies for the assessment of community needs.

- Describe a variety of strategies for the evaluation of programs and explain the methods and purpose of each one.

- Recognize and write specific and measurable objectives that can be used in program evaluation.

- Describe the use of a logic model in conceptualizing program evaluation.

- Explain the use of cost analysis and benefit/cost analysis in program evaluation.

- Explain the difference between participatory evaluation and other evaluation strategies.

- Describe the political and organizational issues associated with program evaluation and what can be done to minimize them.

NEEDS ASSESSMENT

The development of a program must first include evidence that the program is needed. **Needs assessment** is the application of research methods to determine the nature of the problem, whether the problem warrants a service, and whether services currently exist to address the problem. In addition, where a need exists, needs assessment helps identify the most effective program to meet that need. Needs assessment can help social workers plan programs by identifying the extent of local problems or by documenting the existence of new concerns. It can also assist workers in establishing budgets by helping them choose between funding new services or increasing support for existing services. Unless researchers conduct systematic needs assessments, already limited resources can be wasted addressing lower-priority problems or even problems that do not exist. Keep in mind, too, that developing new programs and maintaining funding for existing programs are political processes. Funding depends on the outcome of conflicts among competing interests. Providing empirical evidence that a program is needed is essential to creating public awareness and convincing the community to establish and maintain social programs. Needs assessment focuses on questions such as these:

- What are the major social problems in a community?
- What is the extent of unmet need in a community?
- Are enough people in need to justify a program?
- Do people know about an existing program? If so, how do they perceive it?
- If you develop services, will people use them?
- Where should services be located?
- What barriers prevent people from accessing existing services?
- How do stakeholders view the need for new services or the usefulness of existing services?

Types of Information for Needs Assessment

In order to assess need, we must identify the different perspectives that are being investigated. One widely used classification system identifies four perspectives on need: felt need, expressed need, normative need, and comparative need (Gillam & Murray, 1996).

Felt Need.   The first perspective—**felt need**—refers to what people say they need. Felt need is generally assessed directly from the people involved through surveys, focus groups, and community forums. Always keep in mind that what people report can differ dramatically from how they actually behave. For example, a parent may concede that a parent education program is needed but may not attend the program.

One example of felt need is a study conducted shortly after September 11, 2001. The New York Department of Health and Mental Hygiene surveyed people living in the area of the World Trade Center. They found that 28 percent of the sample ($N = 414$) received supportive counseling of some type after the destruction. Approximately 33 percent of the individuals surveyed thought they would benefit from any or additional supportive counseling. When projected to the 12,300 people residing in these neighborhoods, this result indicated that there were about 4,000 individuals who felt they would benefit from counseling (Community Health Works, 2001). This does not mean, of course, that all 4,000 people would participate in counseling services if they were actually offered.

Expressed Need. As the name implies, **expressed needs** are those that are expressed in action. Consider the saying, for example, that people vote with their feet. Or consider a scenario in which 30 students come every week to an after-school program that is designed for 15 pupils. This is an expression of the need for an expanded program. Documentation from waiting lists or other agency records can also be a source of expressed needs. Expressed needs often underestimate the actual need. For example, if students know the after-school program is always crowded, many of them may not attend. Also affecting expressed need is the cultural acceptance of help-seeking behavior. In some cultures, admitting a problem or reaching out for help may be a sign of weakness or cause shame.

Normative Need. In contrast to felt need, which is defined by the people themselves, **normative need** is defined by experts. These definitions reflect what the experts believe people generally need based on a set of data or criteria. According to the 2005 federal poverty guidelines, for example, a family of four needs $19,350 per year on which to live (Federal Register, 2005). Accrediting organizations are another source of normative need. They may mandate, for example, that a staff ratio of 1 social worker for each 15 nursing home residents is needed. Thus, normative need may be guided by professional standards.

Comparative Need. Finally, **comparative need** is defined based on comparisons with similar populations. This approach is sometimes referred to as **rates under treatment.** For example, if most communities of approximately 50,000 residents have at least one group home for individuals with developmental disabilities, it may be reasonable to assume that *my* community of 50,000 needs a group home. Census data, information from other surveys, and rates of people under treatment in other communities can be used to show comparative need and may be an inexpensive way to conduct a needs assessment. However, we must be careful to justify that the compared groups are truly equivalent in important areas.

Research Methods in Needs Assessment

Given the different perspectives on needs and the difficulties involved in meeting the requirements of well-constructed research, such as appropriate sampling and instrument development, triangulation (use of several methods that point in the same direction) is useful in establishing the validity of the findings. Researchers use a variety of quantitative and qualitative methods to obtain information for needs assessment. These methods include surveys, focus groups, community forums, key informants, and the analysis of existing records.

Surveys. Mailed questionnaires, telephone surveys, or face-to-face interviews can provide generalizable information about felt needs. As we saw in Chapter 7, survey development involves considering methods for recruiting participants and designing the instrument. In addition, the sampling method must be appropriate, the instrument must be valid and reliable, and the response rate must be adequate to avoid response bias.

Focus Groups.   As discussed in Chapter 7, focus groups are meetings of about 5 to 10 people that generally last from one to three hours. In needs assessment, participants discuss their felt needs and/or expressed needs in some detail. Focus groups allow both the researchers and the participants to explore the relevant issues and to provide in-depth examples of experiences and opinions. Representation in the focus groups should be carefully considered and justified to avoid biasing the results. Focus groups may be repeated to look for similarities and differences in the results.

Community Forum.   Inviting community members to discuss community needs is an important step in establishing commitment to new services. A **community forum** is especially useful when a program is thought to be controversial, because the individuals who agree to participate are likely to be those who feel strongly about the issue. Consider a scenario in which a school board in an inner-city neighborhood proposes a program in which truant youths will be arrested by police and held until their parents pick them up. A community forum may disclose that although parents want their children to attend school every day, they view a policy of arresting their children as harassment of the minority community, and they strongly support other methods to improve school attendance.

Key Informants.   Some members of the community may have expertise about the needs and reactions of the community. Interviews with these **key informants** provide detailed, in-depth, qualitative information about the needs and reactions of the community. They also can help researchers discover the reasons that the community is not using existing services. Key informants may be professionals such as police, teachers, health specialists, and social workers who have direct experience with the populations to be addressed or the services to be developed. They may also be informal community leaders such as elders, religious leaders, business leaders, and activists. The rationale and justification for using particular key informants should be identified as part of the needs assessment.

Web Links

Visit www.mhhe.com/krysik1 for a list of online data sources where existing data can be accessed by zip code or census tract.

Analysis of Existing Records.   Census data, published reports, police and court records, agency case records, newspaper accounts, and even suggestion boxes can provide information to help assess the need for a program. For example, an analysis of the zip codes of current users of agency services may reveal areas of the community that are not being reached by the program. Similarly, census data combined with published reports of similar communities may provide information to justify the need for new services. For example, census data may indicate a significant increase in the population of senior citizens within the community, while published reports reveal that similar communities have food programs for this population. Together, these data suggest that such services are needed within this community. Case-in-Point 11.1 describes a combination of quantitative and qualitative research methods of obtaining information for a community needs assessment.

CASE-IN-POINT 11.1

Using Mixed Methods to Define Community Need, by Judy Krysik, PhD

At the present time, I am engaged in a community needs assessment of an old, inner-city area. The purpose of the needs assessment is to provide reliable information for planning future health and social services. As a social worker employed in this capacity, I am both a researcher and an artist. As a researcher, I must work with stakeholders to define the purpose of the needs assessment, to chart and follow a course, and to make ongoing judgments about the quality of existing sources of information I encounter along the way. I must be able to explain to community participants the implications of using data that are subject to error because of the way they were collected. I must analyze quantitative and qualitative data and present them in such a way that both the research methods I used and the limitations of those methods can be clearly understood by anyone who reviews my work. To be successful, I must draw on my knowledge of core areas of social work such as interviewing techniques, theories of human behavior, and strategies for seeking help in a culturally diverse context. As an artist, I am free to use my creative abilities to weave the quantitative and qualitative data into a story that reflects the reality of all of the residents of this small community. The story must fulfill the intended purpose of the needs assessment, and at the same time, it must engage the different audiences such as policy makers, agency administrators, and community members.

To fulfill the purposes of the needs assessment, I use both quantitative and qualitative research methods to gather information on the residents of the area, the problems they experience, their strengths, and the barriers they face in dealing with their problems. In research terms, the combination of quantitative and qualitative data-gathering techniques makes the needs assessment a mixed-methods study.

On the quantitative side, the needs assessment involves the analysis of secondary data. A major source of secondary data is the U.S. census. Census data include the number of people in the community; their gender, ethnicity, age, income, and marital status; the estimated value of their housing; and the number of grandparents responsible for raising grandchildren.

Another key source of secondary data is the State Department of Health. This agency provides information such as the number of women giving birth, their ages, the prevalence of babies born with low birth weights, and the amount and quality of prenatal care that the mothers received. Finally, data from the city police department reveal the number of violent and property crimes as well as miscellaneous crimes such as traffic crashes, gang involvement, and domestic violence. Significantly, all of these data are available via the Internet. By entering location information such as zip code, census tract number, or Internet-based crime mapping resources, I can retrieve the data within a matter of minutes

continued

and at no cost. In contrast, data on topics such as immunization, oral and physical health, the cost and availability of child care, child abuse and neglect, and juvenile crime are also automated, but they are not accessible to the general public. To access these data, a researcher must submit a formal request to a designated person in each agency.

Analyzing the quantitative data for the needs assessment is fascinating when it is taken to the lowest denominator—the census tract. A *census tract* is a small statistical subdivision of a county designated to have between 2,500 and 8,000 people and to be homogeneous with respect to population characteristics, economic status, and living conditions. The data reveal a microcosm of diversity within this geographically small community. Examining the community as a whole does not have the same impact, because all of the extremes are averaged together, making everything look "pretty average." In contrast, by focusing on census tracts, I discover that some clusters of the community are very affluent, predominantly white, and English speaking, whereas other areas are poor, are composed primarily of minority group members, have low levels of education, and are not fluent in English. In some areas, 100 percent of the schoolchildren are eligible for the Free and Reduced Price Lunch Program, and more than 70 percent are classified as English language learners. These secondary data are precise and could not be obtained from individual interviews of residents or by observation.

Qualitative data also play a role in the needs assessment. These data exist in the form of written case documents and individual and group interviews. In many ways, the qualitative data fill in the missing pieces of the picture.

In this particular community, there is a large group of homeless individuals, primarily single men. The residents believe that the homeless population is attracted to the area because of the services available there. However, according to a group of nine homeless individuals participating in a focus group, this is not the case. In fact, they pointed out that only one service is available to homeless people in the community—a dining hall that serves dinner four days per week and provides shower facilities. Further, these men knew that more services are available in the downtown area, including mail service, food, and shelter. Nevertheless, they prefer to remain in an area without services in order to escape the violence and craziness of downtown. They view themselves as different from the downtown homeless population in that they are less drug crazed and violent. In fact, they claim that even if the one service they have closes, they will not move.

In talking with homeless people, I soon learned that safety is a relative concept. For example, in the past four months, homeless individuals in this community have experienced three brutal attacks. One man reportedly had most of his teeth knocked out with a two-by-four while waiting at a bus stop. Another man had his skull smashed with rocks while he was sleeping in a dumpster. A third man was knifed in three places and had to be rushed by ambulance to the hospital emergency room. The interview data from the homeless population are rich with descriptions of their everyday lives and with their ideas of how to deal with the problems they confront.

The only other data available on the homeless population consisted of a count of how many homeless individuals were sighted on a particular day and where. The qualitative data add a perspective on homelessness that is not present in the quantitative data. Listening to the stories of traditionally hard-to-reach members of the community such as homeless people and undocumented families is essential to truly understanding their needs.

EVALUABILITY ASSESSMENT: DEFINING MISSION, GOAL, AND OBJECTIVES

Once the evaluator determines the need for the program, development begins with designing the overall program. In some instances, the determination of need may lead to the development of new programs and, in others, a critical examination of a program that already exists. In order for a program to be evaluated, its purpose, goal, and objectives must be defined clearly enough for social workers to measure the extent to which it has reached its objectives. This process involves understanding the program in terms of administrative structure, resources, activities, definition of objectives, assessment tools and methods, and the time frame for achieving its objectives. To determine whether an existing program can be evaluated, researchers conduct an **evaluability assessment,** an assessment of the clarity of the program's mission, goal, objectives, and measures.

Program Mission and Goal

Social work programs do not exist in isolation. Rather, they are generally provided within the context of an organization. Programs stem from the mission of the organization. The first step in evaluability assessment is to determine whether the proposed or current program fits within the organization's mission. Almost every organization has a **mission statement** that succinctly states its purpose and focus. See Exhibit 11.1 for two examples of mission statements.

THE INTER-FAITH COUNCIL FOR SOCIAL SERVICES MISSION STATEMENT

The Inter-Faith Council for Social Services meets basic needs and helps individuals and families achieve their goals. We provide shelter, food, direct services, advocacy and information to people in need. We accomplish this through strong partnerships with volunteers, staff and those we serve. We rely on the active involvement of caring individuals, congregations and other community organizations.

BURLINGTON COUNTY BOARD OF SOCIAL SERVICES MISSION STATEMENT

The Burlington County Board of Social Services is committed to excellence in providing services to individuals, to families, and to the community by:

Preserving and Restoring Families

Promoting Self-Sufficiency

Providing Information and Referrals

Protecting the Well-Being of Children, the Elderly, and the Disabled

EXHIBIT 11.1

Mission Statements

Programs are developed to accomplish the mission. The next step is to establish the goal that stems from the organization's mission. Recall from Chapter 3 that the goal is a general statement about what the program should accomplish. Whereas mission statements relate the overall purpose of the agency, goals relate to specific programs. Goals are ideals in that they may never be achieved. The following are examples of the goals of a child welfare protective services program:

- Create a safe environment for all children.

- Create a permanent living environment for all children.

Program Objectives

Goals are not directly measurable and need not be fully accomplished for the organization or program to be successful. After establishing goals, program evaluation focuses on stating specific, measurable **objectives.** Some objectives, known as **process objectives,** relate to activities that the agency must accomplish in order to achieve its goals. In contrast, **outcome objectives** relate to changes in people or larger systems produced by the program. Changes in program recipients are often referred to as **outcomes,** whereas a change in the larger community or social system is called an **impact.** To understand how these concepts apply to social work programs, consider the example of DARE, a program that provides drug and alcohol awareness education. The desired outcomes are to increase the knowledge and influence the attitudes of students in the program, whereas the intended impact is to decrease the number of arrests of juveniles in the community for drug-related problems. Outcome objectives focus on the accomplishments of the program.

Evaluators should clearly identify the objectives so that the evaluation can explicitly determine the extent to which they are accomplished. To do this, the objectives should specify the following information:

- What specific, measurable changes will occur?

- In whom/what targets will changes occur?

- By what method will changes be measured?

- What is the time frame in which changes will occur?

The following are examples of objectives that do *not* meet the preceding criteria:

- "The program will increase the number of adoptions by 10 percent." (Among whom? By when?)

- "Staff will develop an appreciation of cultural diversity by the end of the training." (*Appreciation* is vague. How is it measured?)

EXHIBIT 11.2

*Program
Design for a
Child Welfare
Agency*

- *Goal:* Children should have permanency in their living arrangements.
- *Process Objective:* All cases will have a permanency plan within three months of intake.
- *Measures:* The percentage of cases that have written permanency plans as judged by supervisor; the percentage of cases in which the plan has been implemented; the percentage of cases with no permanency plan.
- *Outcome Objective:* Ninety percent of children are living in a permanent arrangement within one year of intake.
- *Measures:* The percentage of children living with family or a relative; the percentage of children in foster care; the percentage of children in permanent residential care; the percentage of children in temporary care.

- "To decrease the number of consumers who do not keep their appointments at the agency by 15 percent." (By when?)

In contrast, the following are examples of clear and measurable objectives:

- "At least 80 percent of parents will attend at least six sessions of the parent education classes during the next year." (Process objective)

- "Staff will involve 20 high school seniors in developing two antismoking community awareness campaigns by the end of the year." (Process objective)

- "The program will increase the number of female-owned businesses by 5 percent a year for the next three years." (Outcome objective)

- "All state mental hospital patients will be in community housing placements by June 30, 2006." (Outcome objective)

Exhibit 11.2 gives an example of a clearly stated goal, objectives, and measures associated with a program for a child welfare agency.

Logic Model

When conducting an evaluability assessment of an existing program or designing a new program, it is useful to place goals, objectives, and measures in a more comprehensive format. For this reason, program evaluators frequently employ a **logic model** to chart the path from the social conditions that necessitate the program to the evaluation of program outcomes and impact.

Exhibit 11.3 shows the types of information included in a logic model. The model begins by specifying the social conditions that must be changed to improve the quality of life for the target population. Identifying these conditions

Not everything that can be counted counts, and not everything that counts can be counted. — Albert Einstein

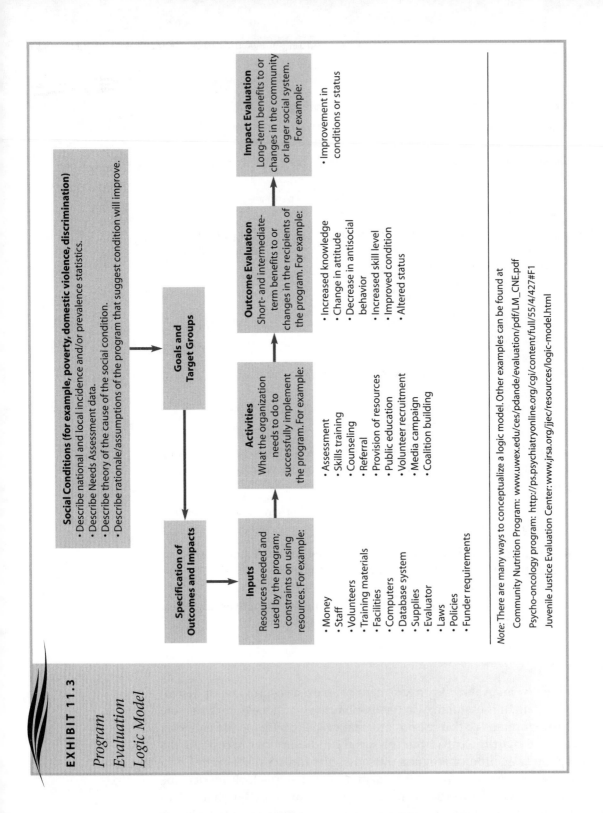

EXHIBIT 11.3

Program Evaluation Logic Model

Social Conditions (for example, poverty, domestic violence, discrimination)
· Describe national and local incidence and/or prevalence statistics.
· Describe Needs Assessment data.
· Describe theory of the cause of the social condition.
· Describe rationale/assumptions of the program that suggest condition will improve.

Goals and Target Groups

Specification of Outcomes and Impacts

Inputs
Resources needed and used by the program; constraints on using resources. For example:

· Money
· Staff
· Volunteers
· Training materials
· Facilities
· Computers
· Database system
· Supplies
· Evaluator
· Laws
· Policies
· Funder requirements

Activities
What the organization needs to do to successfully implement the program. For example:

· Assessment
· Skills training
· Counseling
· Referral
· Provision of resources
· Public education
· Volunteer recruitment
· Media campaign
· Coalition building

Outcome Evaluation
Short- and intermediate-term benefits to or changes in the recipients of the program. For example:

· Increased knowledge
· Change in attitude
· Decrease in antisocial behavior
· Increased skill level
· Improved condition
· Altered status

Impact Evaluation
Long-term benefits to or changes in the community or larger social system. For example:

· Improvement in conditions or status

Note: There are many ways to conceptualize a logic model. Other examples can be found at
Community Nutrition Program: www.uwex.edu/ces/pdande/evaluation/pdf/LM_CNE.pdf
Psycho-oncology program: http://ps.psychiatryonline.org/cgi/content/full/55/4/427#F1
Juvenile Justice Evaluation Center: www.jrsa.org/jjec/resources/logic-model.html

leads to the development of goals for change. The focus of change in a logic model is on the benefits for the target population, not on the provision of services. Therefore, it is the desired benefits—the desired outcome and impact—that drive program development. The need for resources follows from the outcomes and impact. These resources are then used to implement program activities.

Process evaluation involves selecting measures and research designs to provide information to assess the "Activities" section of the logic model. This process involves obtaining information about what, when, where, how often, by whom, and for whom services are delivered. Similarly, outcome evaluation uses measures and research designs to provide information regarding the accomplishment of the outcome and impact sections of the logic model. The changes generated by the services may occur in many areas, including knowledge, skills, attitudes, values, behavior, status, and condition. In addition, they may include system changes in policies and procedures.

IMPLEMENTATION EVALUATION

After the need for a program has been established and the program has been designed and funded, it is ready to be implemented. Starting a new program involves a great deal of work. Staff must be hired and trained, consumers of services must be recruited, record-keeping procedures must be put into place, intervention processes must be developed, and interventions must be delivered. Implementation evaluation focuses on the processes and activities that are established to implement the program. It helps workers develop the program by providing data in the early stages of development. These data may include who uses the program, the types of services the program is to provide, the length of services for particular issues, the extent to which staff implement the program components, and the reaction of staff and consumers to the services. Case-in-Point 11.2 illustrates how a family services organization used implementation evaluation to help establish a computer training program for foster children.

QUALITY ASSURANCE AND PROGRAM MONITORING

Once a program has been implemented as designed, evaluators must continue to collect data about the program to be sure that it continues to function as intended. In addition, the program might have to be adjusted in response to changes in the environment. Therefore, evaluators need to collect program data to know what changes are taking place and to supply information for evidence-based decision making. Two methods that ensure the program continues to

Access to, and comfort with, information technology can be viewed as a form of privilege. Those who have it are advantaged in that they possess skills that are necessary to succeed in today's information society. Specifically, they have access to resources, such as employment opportunities, college scholarships, internship opportunities, education and training, news, social commentary, social support, and entertainment, that create both financial opportunity and involvement with the larger community. One group who tends to lack access to technology and technology-related skills is foster children. This problem occurs for a number of reasons. First, foster children are more likely to be part of groups without access to technology, that is, low-income people, minority groups, and single-parent families. Second, they frequently must overcome barriers such as residential instability, educational discontinuity, and emotional and behavioral problems associated with family disruption. Third, caseworkers generally perceive developing children's technology skills as beyond the scope of their plans for developing independent living skills in foster youth. A study by Casey Family Services (CFS) found that foster children lagged behind the biological children of the foster parents in their development of technology skills (Kerman, 2000).

CFS then initiated a program, Building Skills–Building Futures (BSBF), that provided computers and Internet connection to 32 foster families in order to bridge the digital divide (Finn, Kerman, & leCornec, 2004). The program model was developed by a steering committee composed of agency administrators, information systems staff, the BSBF project director, foster care workers, foster parents, outside technology and education consultants, and a university-based evaluator. The model included the gift of a computer, printer, software, and Internet connection to participating families; access to community training for foster family members in how to use the computer and Internet; and the integration of technology into ongoing foster care services through the development of an Information Technology Plan (ITP) between foster family members and their social worker.

Three months into the program, the CFS evaluator conducted an implementation evaluation of BSBF. Among the questions in the evaluation were the following: Did family members receive their computer and Internet connection? Were they able to set up and use the computer? To what extent were they actually using the computer? Did family members participate in community-based technology training opportunities? Did families develop an ITP? How satisfied were family members with the program thus far? The evaluator gathered information from telephone interviews with foster parents as well as from separate focus groups with foster parents, foster youth, and foster care workers.

Early experiences implementing the BSBF program resulted in changes to the original program model with regard to timing, entry criteria, and curriculum.

- In one case, a new foster family who received the full complement of hardware and software left the program only three months later and refused to return the computer. As a result, the administration determined that developing ITPs with families will take place before hardware is installed in their homes. In addition, a family would receive hardware only after serving as a foster family for at least six months to ensure that they are committed to the goals of the BSBF program.
- Several participants identified two additional workshops that would have been helpful to enhance computer security: (1) introduction to virus protection software

CASE-IN-POINT 11.2

Building Skills— Building Futures
continued

and (2) Internet filtering software such as Net Nanny. In response, BSBF provided all participating families with Net Nanny software as well as training in monitoring Internet use by children.

- Fewer than 25 percent of family members had made an ITP with their social worker. A major reason for this low number was that social workers did not believe they could "mandate" that parents and biological children develop ITPs. In addition, workers felt that they did not have the time to focus on technology when they needed to address other, more important issues. As a result, the program model was changed so that only foster children would develop an ITP, thus reducing the workload on social workers.

- Social workers' own skill deficits, whether real or perceived, presented another obstacle to integrating the model within ongoing services. Some social workers expressed doubts about their ability to help families develop technology skills due to their own limited knowledge in this area. As a result, the project director, who had extensive experience in information technology, took the lead in developing ITPs with families. At the same time, she trained the accompanying social workers in the ITP process.

- Finally, interviews with parents revealed that very few had either participated in community training themselves or involved their children in additional training, even though CFS would pay for the training. They claimed that time restrictions, child care needs, and other priorities prevented them from attending training sessions. As a result, the program began to explore other models of training, such as recruiting "computer buddy" volunteers to visit the child in the home and offering training at the agency in conjunction with other family appointments.

Although families expressed a high degree of satisfaction with the BSBF program, implementation evaluation found that the original program model required additional policy development in several areas: (a) program eligibility, (b) the need for alternate training methods, (c) a change in ITP responsibilities, (d) additional training of social workers to help families develop their technology skills, and (e) modifying outcome goals to include only the foster children and not biological children. Understanding the need for change early in the program contributed to the satisfaction of participants in the program and helped overcome some of the initial resistance from social workers.

meet the needs for which it was designed are quality assurance and ongoing program monitoring.

Quality Assurance

One type of formative evaluation is **quality assurance,** sometimes known as the **model standards approach.** In quality assurance, an accrediting body, outside consultant, or agency-based committee defines the standards for a quality program—for example, the staff-to-client ratio, the types of records to be kept, and staff qualifications—as well as the procedures to be followed and

 Web Links

Visit www.mhhe.com/krysik1 for an online link to the accreditation process offered by Healthy Families America.

charted on a regular basis. The entity that sets the standards reviews the evaluation. This approach often involves a regularly scheduled site visit in which the evaluators review a variety of data sources such as interviews, observation of the program, and agency records. Quality assurance generally focuses on agency policies, processes, and procedures. However, it may also evaluate the impact of services on consumers.

Program Monitoring

Another type of formative evaluation is **program monitoring,** in which the evaluator routinely collects and reviews data over time. These data include the number of people seeking services, consumer demographic information, types of services requested, caseload ratios, dropout rates, and reasons for termination. Program monitoring provides, ongoing data for program planning and management. The evaluator may also track the outcome of services for consumers, usually through ratings of perceived improvement by social workers. The widespread use of computers and database systems allows organizations to track and analyze such information.

CONSUMER SATISFACTION

Quality assurance and program monitoring evaluate the functioning of the program from the organization's perspective. However, to evaluate a program comprehensively, we need to assess the views of the consumers of the services regarding the quality and effectiveness of the services. Research on consumer satisfaction seeks to provide the consumers' assessment of the convenience, appropriateness, and outcomes of the services they receive. Consumer satisfaction is a type of formative evaluation because it is collected to improve program functioning. It assumes that systems exist to produce specific outcomes and that, to achieve these outcomes, certain attitudes, processes, and services need to be in place.

Consider mental health services as an example. The desired outcomes of mental health services are to reduce symptom distress and help an individual (a) function on her or his own, (b) improve her or his performance and productivity at work or school, (c) develop a system of natural supports, and (d) gain access to health care services. To achieve these outcomes, a mental health system must offer a wide range of service choices that are voluntary, easily accessible, culturally appropriate, focused on recovery, and designed to promote consumer inclusion (MHSIP Task Force, 1996). Consumer satisfaction research may assess a consumer's *perceptions* of all of these aspects of services. Again, however, it cannot assess how well the services are actually achieving these outcomes.

Often the answer to a question depends on whom we ask. For example, healthcare providers may have a different perspective on the quality and outcomes of their services than the consumers of those services do. For this reason, the consumer satisfaction movement has become prominent in recent years, primarily in the areas of health and mental health. This movement is founded on the belief that the consumer "voice" is an important component in evaluating and improving a system. Consumer groups view themselves as partners in the health and mental health systems. They believe that they should be involved not only in evaluating services but also in developing the actual evaluation methods and tools. Social workers value the empowerment of people who are receiving services, and they can help facilitate research on consumer satisfaction.

Consumer Satisfaction: Obtaining the Information

Researchers can obtain consumer satisfaction information by a variety of methods, all of which have strengths and limitations. Some organizations are established specifically to assess consumer satisfaction. They generally conduct surveys based on a random sample of consumers who use the system. Other organizations survey consumers by mail or telephone at the time the consumers terminate services or as part of a quality-review process. Focus groups are useful when organizations want consumer input about specific issues. Exhibit 11.4 provides an example of consumer satisfaction questions developed by and for mental health consumers.

From a research perspective, information obtained from consumers is only as good as the methods and designs used to obtain it. Consumer satisfaction surveys should be based on the use of appropriate samples with high return rates, reliable and valid instruments, thoughtful choices about research design, and appropriate data analysis. Evaluators must employ a sampling method that ensures selection of a representative group. If evaluators give a survey only to consumers who complete services and not to consumers who drop out, consumer satisfaction rates will be inflated. Similarly, if they provide surveys that are written only in English and that require a ninth-grade reading level, people who do not speak English and people with lower reading levels will not be represented. Reassuring consumers that their responses will remain anonymous will also help reduce bias in the sample. Participants may worry that their answers will affect the quality of their services if their provider becomes aware of their responses.

Evaluators should also consider the consumer's ability to complete a survey. In mental health services, for example, low energy and lack of concentration can make answering a survey difficult. Thus, surveys should be kept short and simple. When necessary, interviewers should assist consumers, for example, by reading the questions to them or writing their responses for them. Finally, the survey results should be made available to consumers, along with an explanation of how the information will be used to improve services.

EXHIBIT 11.4

Sample Evaluation Questions

CONSUMER SATISFACTION EVALUATION QUESTIONS

1. I know whom to call to ask questions about my HealthChoices plan.
2. I was given the necessary information on how to access other services that I needed.
3. I have a choice in selecting or changing my service provider.
4. I know whom to call if I have a complaint or grievance about my services.
5. I am satisfied with the scheduling of my appointments.
6. Lack of reliable transportation has prevented me from keeping my appointments.
7. My service provider spends sufficient time with me.
8. Program staff respects the role of my ethnic, cultural, and religious background in my recovery/treatment.
9. I trust my service provider.
10. I feel that I am an equal partner on the treatment team.
11. I was informed of the advantages and disadvantages associated with my therapy or treatment.
12. My treatment promotes recovery.
13. I feel that my service provider and I work together as a team.
14. My service provider focuses on my strengths.

---

1 = Strongly disagree   2 = Disagree   3 = Neither agree or disagree   4 = Agree   5 = Strongly agree
NA = Not applicable

OUTCOME EVALUATION QUESTIONS

15. I can deal with daily problems.
16. I'm able to control my life.
17. I'm able to deal with crisis.
18. I like how I feel about myself.
19. I feel optimistic about the future.
20. I enjoy my leisure time.
21. I'm building a social support network.
22. I handle school or work.
23. I can deal with people and situations that used to be a problem.
24. The specific issues or problems that led me to seek services are . . .

---

1 = Much worse   2 = Worse   3 = About the same   4 = Better   5 = Much better   NA = Not applicable
Source: J. Finn, 2004, Consumer Satisfaction Consultation Report. Consumer Satisfaction Services, Harrisburg, PA.

Consumer Satisfaction: Understanding the Limitations

Although consumer satisfaction surveys are an important component of formative evaluation, they have certain limitations. We need to understand these limitations when we are interpreting the results. To begin with, as already discussed, satisfaction is not equivalent to actual changes or outcomes, although we often assume that that they are highly associated. Satisfaction may be related to expectations as much as to actual performance. Assume, for example, that a valid and reliable survey with a high return rate was given to a random sample of mental health consumers in two counties. The results indicated that consumer satisfaction in County A is much higher than in County B. How should we interpret these results? Here are three different but viable conclusions:

- Services are, in fact, better in County A, accounting for higher consumer satisfaction.

- Services are not better in County A, but the culture of County A is one in which people are more likely to say "nice" things.

- Services are not better in County A, but people's expectations of services are lower. Thus, people give high ratings even to mediocre services because the services met or exceeded their low expectations.

As these examples illustrate, you should always interpret satisfaction surveys with caution. Whenever possible, employ a triangulation approach using several measures when you evaluate the quality of services.

PROCESS EVALUATION

As we've seen, the implementation and processes of the program are the focus of process evaluation. It is an assessment of the activities performed by the organization and the quality with which the organization delivers these activities. For example, mental health services might collect information about the number of people served, the size of the workers' caseloads, the time between intake and ongoing services, the number of contacts before services are terminated, and the number of people who drop out of services before the goals of the program are reached. Process evaluation helps ensure that both the theoretical model upon which the program is built and the steps that are necessary to carry out the program are implemented as intended.

Because process and outcome evaluations are interrelated, researchers use both methods to test the program's theory of intervention. Unless researchers know whether the program is being delivered as intended, they cannot draw conclusions about the program's ability to achieve its goals. After researchers have completed process evaluation, they use outcome evaluation to seek evidence that the program has made positive changes in the target population.

OUTCOME EVALUATION

To accomplish outcome evaluation, researchers must first identify the types of changes that are being sought (a political decision), how these changes would be best measured (a research methods decision), and whether the changes are worth making (a political decision).

In the past, human service agencies could obtain funding and legitimacy for their programs by reporting process evaluation findings such as the number of clients served or the number of units of service delivered. More recently, funding decisions are being made on the basis of the outcome of the program for people and the impact of the program on the larger community. The Government Performance and Results Act of 1993, introduced in Chapter 1, specifically sought to hold federal agencies accountable for achieving results by setting program goals, measuring program performance against those goals, and reporting publicly on the program's results (Office of Management and Budget, 1993). The emphasis on outcomes has also been adopted by nonprofit organizations and private foundations in making their funding decisions. As a result, evaluation now must include both process and outcome evaluation.

Asking the Right Questions

The question "Does the program work?" is too simplistic. A more useful question has multiple components, based on a combination of process and outcome evaluation:

What services? (process)

Provided to whom? (process)

Produce what changes? (outcome)

For whom? (outcome)

Under what circumstances? (outcome)

For how long? (outcome)

Compared to what? (outcome)

At what cost? (cost)

Program evaluation can focus on one or any combination of these questions, depending on the needs of the organization, the resources available, and the feasibility of conducting the evaluation. We now take a more detailed look at each of these questions.

What Services?   Services may include therapy, support, education, training, pro-viding concrete resources, recreational experiences, changes in environment, or other activities used by social workers to create change. Regardless of the type of intervention, the services must be described, and program evaluators must assess whether the program is being carried out as planned.

Provided to Whom?   The targets of the program must be specified. In addition, it is useful to know to whom the program is actually being delivered. For exam-ple, a program aimed at adult education is restricted to people over 50 years of age. In this case, the demographic characteristics of the program recipients—including age, race, sex, income level, and education—as well as other charac-teristics that researchers believe to be relevant to the program outcome (such as severity of difficulty at intake) should be tracked. These data are essential to ensure that the target audience is being reached. Moreover, they enable researchers to generalize the results to the population actually being served.

Produce What Changes?   The objectives of the program must be stated in terms of outcomes in the target system and, when possible, the program's impact on the larger community. The extent to which evaluators can attribute changes to the influence of the program will depend on the sampling method used, the use of valid and reliable measures, and the use of research designs that control for problems with internal validity.

For Whom?   Just as demographic and other relevant characteristics can influ-ence who attends a program, they can also affect which people benefit from the program. It is useful to collect and analyze demographic and other information that suggests who has benefited in order to examine the reasons for differential success and to make appropriate generalization of the results. For example, pos-itive perceptions of a DARE antidrug program among 6th-grade and 9th-grade students in New Mexico were highly related to attitudes toward the police. In contrast, among 12th graders, perceptions were most closely associated with patterns of drug use. Thus, programs offered in the 5th or 6th grade should help build a more positive attitude toward police among students; with older stu-dents, the program should focus on people who are already using illegal sub-stances (LaFree, Birkbeck, & Wilson, 1995). See Case-in-Point 11.3 for a discus-sion of the effectiveness of the DARE program.

Under What Circumstances?   After identifying the individuals or groups who have benefited from the service, the next step in evaluation is to specify how the program is to be delivered. For example, is the program delivered by profession-als or by volunteers? If by professionals, what is their academic degree or theo-retical orientation? Is the program delivered in 6 weeks or in 10 weeks? Is it voluntary or court mandated? Although the range of circumstances seems

Perhaps you are familiar with the program Drug Abuse Resistance Education (DARE). DARE began in Los Angeles in 1983 and has since been adopted in school districts in all 50 states. The DARE program is generally a 17-week curriculum ranging from 45 minutes to 1 hour once a week. It is administered by uniformed police officers who attend classes in fourth through eighth grades to provide information about alcohol, tobacco, and other drugs and to teach strategies for students to resist the use of these drugs. The primary purpose of the program is to prevent substance abuse among youth.

A number of positive outcomes have been attributed to DARE. These outcomes, however, are related specifically to the attitudes and opinions of students, teachers, and parents rather than to their actual behaviors. For example, an evaluation of DARE in South Carolina with 341 fifth graders in 1989–90 found that after three months the program had improved participants' scores on attitudes toward the following issues: (a) avoiding substance use, (b) assertiveness, (c) positive peer association, (d) avoiding association with drug-using peers, and (e) avoiding alcohol use (Harmon, 1993).

In contrast, several studies, especially longitudinal studies of long-term impact, found that DARE had no effect on actual drug or alcohol *use* when equivalent comparison groups or control groups were used. For example, a five-year study of 2,071 students in Kentucky found no significant differences between intervention and comparison schools with respect to cigarette, alcohol, or marijuana use at post-program intervals of either 1 year or 5 years (Clayton, Cattarello, & Johnstone, 1996). Similarly, a 10-year follow-up study of 1,000 students in a midwestern area compared students who had attended DARE at age 10 with students who had not. The study found few differences between the two groups in terms of either actual drug use or attitudes toward drugs. Significantly, in the follow-up, in no case did the DARE group have a more successful outcome than the comparison group (Lynam et al., 1999).

These results raise a fundamental question: How and why did a program that has been shown to be ineffective or, at best, no more effective than standard education become so popular and widely used? One explanation is that teaching children to refrain from drug use is a widely accepted approach with which few individuals would argue (Lynam et al., 1999). These "feel-good" programs are ones that everyone can support; therefore, few people consider it necessary to critically evaluate their effectiveness. A second possible explanation is that programs such as DARE *appear* to work. In fact, most children who go through DARE do not abuse drugs or become delinquent. What many people fail to realize, however, is that the same conclusion applies to most children who don't attend a DARE program. A final explanation is the tendency of policy makers, practitioners, and the public in general to embrace short-term programs to solve complex social problems. Some experts believe that the public is looking for a *panacea*, a "cure" that is simple, available, effective, and inexpensive (Finckenauer, 1982). In the case of DARE, the public wants to believe that a little education at an early age with a person in authority will solve the nation's substance abuse problems. Therefore, they avoid examining the outcomes too carefully, lest they discover that their "solution" isn't really working.

Overall, the results of program evaluations focusing on the effectiveness of DARE are mixed and contradictory. Attitudes change in the short term, but behavior does not change in the long term. Thus, it is difficult to conclude whether DARE "works." Nevertheless, these evaluations highlight the importance of asking the broader question: What services, provided to whom, produce what changes, for whom, under what circumstance, for how long, compared to what, at what cost?

infinite, the analysis should focus on those variables that the evaluator considers to be important because of his or her theoretical orientation or past experience.

For How Long?   This question refers to the length of documented changes. Is the program measuring change only at the conclusion of the program? Is change maintained? If so, for how long? Are there follow-up data? This information is useful in determining both the success of the program and the appropriate generalization.

Compared to What?   This question focuses on the ability of the program evaluation design to establish a cause-and-effect relationship between the program and the outcomes. Some evaluations do not use comparison or control groups. They are interested only in changes at the end of the program. Therefore, they assume—and not always correctly—that changes are a result of program interventions. Other evaluations are interested in the relative effectiveness of the program compared to a different intervention or to no intervention at all. When programs use random assignment and control groups with reliable and valid measures, they are better able to establish both the effectiveness of the program and the link between the program and its outcomes.

At What Cost?   Human services rely on funding to deliver their programs. Service providers seek to deliver the best services in the most cost-efficient manner. Program evaluation can assist providers in this process by making the following types of analysis:

- Cost analysis: the costs of delivering the program.

- Cost-effectiveness analysis: the comparative costs of delivering different programs or different levels of the same program.

- Cost/benefit analysis: the cost in relation to quantifiable benefits.

COST EVALUATION

Funding for human service programs is limited, and organizations compete for these scarce funds. Therefore, service providers must be able to offer evidence that their services are cost effective in order to make optimal use of funds and to maintain support from funders and the public. A variety of questions are related to funding: Is this program the most efficient way of delivering the service? What are the benefits and costs of the services? Are the benefits worth the cost? Although financial considerations are not the only reason for making decisions about funding for programs, they are becoming increasingly important.

EXHIBIT 11.5

Cost-Effectiveness of Men's Domestic Violence Treatment Models

PROGRAM A	
Number of Participants:	60
Cost per participant:	$1,000
Total cost:	$60,000
Success rates:	40%
Number of successes:	60 x .40 = 24
Cost-effectiveness:	$60,000 / 24
	$2,500 per success

PROGRAM B	
Number of Participants:	50
Cost per participant:	$1,500
Total cost:	$75,000
Success rates:	70%
Number of successes:	50 x .70 = 35
Cost-effectiveness:	$75,000 / 35
	$2,142.85 per success

Cost-effectiveness analysis (CEA) estimates the net costs and effects of an intervention compared with some alternative. It assesses the costs of the program per successful outcome. CEA assesses program outcomes in natural, or nonmonetary, units. For instance, if the program is aimed at preventing premature births, one nonmonetary outcome would be the rate of premature births. The CEA might compare the costs of two alternative methods of producing the same outcome. This is a form of CEA called **cost minimization analysis.** It is concerned with such questions as Is individual or group counseling more cost effective? Is a 12-week program as cost effective as a 16-week program? To compute a cost-effectiveness ratio, you divide the total cost of the program by the success rate. Exhibit 11.5 compares the cost-effectiveness of two programs that use different models to provide treatment groups for men who engage in domestic violence. As you can see, although Program B treats fewer men at a greater cost, it has greater effectiveness, so its actual cost per successful outcome is lower.

In contrast to CEA, **cost/benefit analysis (CBA)** expresses all costs and benefits in monetary units. For instance, the health care cost to employers of a premature birth is $41,546 (March of Dimes, 2005). This total takes into account all costs over and above the normal birth expenditure of $2,830 for a healthy, full-term baby. These extra costs include $33,824 in hospital expenses, $4,561 in physician office visits, $395 in medication expenses, and $2,766 in lost employee productivity. To arrive at a cost/benefit analysis of a program to prevent premature births, the researcher would multiply the number of premature births prevented by the health care cost of $41,546 for the total dollars saved by the program. She or he would then subtract this total from the cost of operating the program to arrive at a final cost savings. All of the researcher's assumptions and sources must be clearly specified and available for scrutiny in the presentation of the cost/benefit analysis.

In 1992, the Michigan Children's Trust Fund (CTF) conducted an analysis of the cost of child abuse versus the cost of child abuse prevention (Caldwell, 1992). The Michigan CTF is a statewide, nonprofit organization dedicated solely to preventing child abuse and neglect. CTF estimated the annual cost of child abuse in Michigan at $823 million. Included in this total were the costs associated with low-birthweight babies, infant mortality, special education, protective services, foster care, juvenile and adult criminality, and psychological services. These costs included

- Average lifetime taxes that each child who died from abuse would have paid: $26,937. Thus, the deaths of an estimated 16 children per year from child abuse result in $430,992 in lost tax revenues over their lifetimes.

- The annual cost of hospital care for children injured in child abuse: $4.98 million.

- Expenses for special education services that 25 percent of all abused children will receive at $655 per child annually: $6.46 million.

The CTF estimated the overall costs of prevention programming to be $43 million annually. Thus, the overall cost/benefit ratio is 1 to 19 (43/823).

This cost/benefit analysis clearly suggests that the long-term benefits of prevention programming more than justify its costs. Social workers can use this type of information in advocacy efforts with legislators and funding organizations to provide evidence of the benefits of prevention programs.

In tallying costs, the researcher should consider both direct and indirect costs. **Direct costs** are the costs of goods and services provided to participants by the agency or organization. Examples are the payment of out-of-home placements for foster children, clothing allowances, and dental care. **Indirect costs** are expenses that are not directly related to one case, for example, air-conditioning and accounting services. Note that although these indirect costs apply to multiple cases, they would not exist in the absence of the program. In contrast, costs that would be incurred in the absence of the program—for example, the agency director's salary in an agency with multiple programs—should not be included in the analysis. Case-in-Point 11.4 describes an example of cost/benefit analysis.

In addition to direct and indirect costs, all programs involve **opportunity costs,** which are the costs of resources, capital, labor, and natural resources, measured in terms of the value of the outputs that could have been produced by using the same resources in a different way. For example, if a parent spends four hours per week attending counseling services with a child, the opportunity cost is the four hours of lost wages to the parent. Organizations should consider opportunity costs for consumers of services when they plan and implement programs. If these costs are too great, the targeted groups might not use the services. In addition, compensation for opportunity costs, such as an allowance for child care and transportation for low-income families, can be built into the program budget.

Another kind of opportunity cost is related to the relative value of the program. All programs have opportunity costs in that funds used for the program are unavailable for a different set of services. Evaluators, in conjunction with other stakeholders, should consider these kinds of opportunity costs as part of program planning. Moreover, stakeholders should review opportunity costs as information about the effectiveness of the program becomes known through program evaluation.

Cost analysis in social work tends to rely on the direct and indirect costs typically recorded by accounting systems because these costs are concrete and relatively easy to measure. In tallying actual costs, we can consider both the private and the public cost. For example, if the government subsidizes child health care, the portion of the health care costs that consumers pay is the private cost, and the portion funded by the government is the public cost.

THE POLITICAL CONTEXT OF PROGRAM EVALUATION

Program evaluation involves political as well as methodological decisions. Political decisions focus on the relative value of the goals to be accomplished and the allocation of resources to reach those goals. Politics are also concerned with who makes decisions about how the evaluation will be conducted and how the results of the evaluation will be used. Program evaluation is costly in terms of time and money, and it can lead to political difficulties if the results are not as the organization had wished. Nevertheless, most organizations routinely evaluate their programs and make the results known to various concerned parties. Clearly, these organizations perceive some value in this process. In this section, we will discuss how an organization can benefit from an effective program evaluation. We will then explore many concerns regarding the evaluation process that are common among social workers and administrators.

Participatory Evaluation

The question of whom to involve in planning and implementing a program is both philosophical and political. In many cases, professional program evaluators have carried out the evaluation methods described in this chapter without involving the people who are being evaluated, whether those people are agency staff, clients, or other community members. This lack of involvement has sometimes engendered resentment and resistance from the targets of the evaluation. These negative feelings may be due to the belief that the evaluation does not focus on the right outcomes, the evaluation is disruptive and wastes time, and the information from the evaluation will not be shared or will not be of use to the people being evaluated.

More recently, some evaluators have begun to include participants in the entire evaluation process. **Participatory evaluation,** sometimes known as **empowerment evaluation,** is the use of evaluation concepts, methods, and findings to promote program improvement and self-determination (Fetterman & Eiler, 2001). It is based on principles that view research as a means of empowering people and creating social change by creating a partnership between researchers and the people they are studying (Finn, 1994). Participatory evaluation is designed to help people help themselves and improve their programs using a form of self-evaluation and reflection. It differs from more traditional evaluation in that program participants, including administrators, service providers, and people receiving services, serve as a group to conduct their own evaluation. The participants are involved in, and make decisions about, all phases of the evaluation. An evaluator's function in this model is to provide a consultative, facilitative, or coaching role while members of the evaluation team determine for themselves the best way to evaluate the program.

Empowerment evaluation typically involves the group in a number of steps or phases. First, the group defines and refines the mission of the program. Thus, the final mission statement is produced by a democratic group process rather than imposed by the administration or the history of the organization. For this reason, it creates a shared vision and direction.

The next step, known as "taking stock," involves prioritizing and evaluating the organization's current activities and practices. In this phase, the group generates a list of key activities that are crucial to the functioning of the program. For example, in a parent education program, key activities might include recruiting parents at local schools, offering parent education classes, providing volunteer telephone support for parents, and maintaining a 24-hour crisis line. The group prioritizes the list of activities by identifying the ones that are most important to evaluate. The evaluator's role is to facilitate this process rather than to predetermine the focus of evaluation. Group members then rate how well the organization is functioning on each activity. These ratings are used to promote a dialogue about the functioning of program activities.

Finally, the group makes plans for future improvements in the program based on the previous phase of assessment. The group decides on goals and objectives and then selects strategies for achieving them. In addition, it identifies and collects evidence that the program is achieving these objectives. Participatory evaluation has been used in a variety of social work intervention settings, including tribal reservations, inner-city schools, battered women's shelters, adolescent pregnancy prevention programs, and substance abuse prevention programs (Fetterman, Kaftarian, & Wandersman, 1996).

Benefits of Program Evaluation

Why do organizations evaluate programs? The answer is that an effective evaluation can benefit the organization in at least five key areas: (1) it is consistent with professional ethics; (2) it can influence social policy and practice; (3) it is an essential component of the funding process; (4) it can improve decision making; and (5) it helps promote efficient services.

Professional Ethics.   The NASW *Code of Ethics* (5.02) has established standards that govern evaluation and research. These standards define an ethical social worker as one who works in the best interests of his or her clients. This work includes expanding the knowledge base, evaluating the implementation and effectiveness of programs, and using research to improve services. See Chapter 2 for the complete NASW statement on research and evaluation.

Influence on Social Policy and Practice.   Hard data from program evaluations document the effectiveness of programs and can influence the development of policy and practice. For example, data from the evaluation of mental hospitals that indicated that these facilities were ineffective in treating mental illness played a large role in establishing deinstitutionalization policies (President's Commission on Mental Health, 1978). In addition, evidence that community-based alternatives were more effective and cost efficient also led to the adoption of community mental health services nationwide. The Program of Assertive Community Treatment (PACT) in Madison, Wisconsin, demonstrated that an intensive approach to the treatment of people with serious mental illnesses using a multidisciplinary team including case managers, a psychiatrist, nurses, social workers, and vocational specialists could provide a "hospital without walls." In addition, randomized controlled studies demonstrated that assertive community treatment and similar models of intensive case management substantially reduced the use of inpatient services, promoted continuity of outpatient care, reduced time in jail, improved family relationships, and increased residential stability for people with serious mental illnesses (Lehman, 1998; Stein & Test, 1980).

Funding.   We live in a time when evidence-based practice and accountability are rapidly increasing. Social work organizations must fund their services, whether from federal and state programs, nonprofit umbrella organizations, private foundations, or any combination thereof. Good intentions and a history of service are no longer sufficient to guarantee funding. Funders want to see evidence that the services they are financing are effective and efficient, and this evidence must be based on well-designed evaluations. New services are unlikely to be funded without an evaluation plan, and ongoing services will need evaluation data so funders can decide whether to increase or even continue funding.

One example is the Family Service Center (FSC) demonstration projects, which were initiated in 1990 to enable Head Start programs to provide a more comprehensive set of services to address low levels of literacy, lack of employability, and substance abuse among Head Start families. In order to obtain funds, FSCs were required to implement two types of evaluation activities: local evaluations by individual FSCs and a national evaluation of all projects. The national evaluation assessed the impact of the FSCs on participating families, with a particular focus on employability, substance abuse, and adult literacy. Local evaluations focused on service delivery. The national evaluation collected information from project directors and case managers about program services and implementation issues and included in-person interviews, on-site reviews, and literacy tests for families who were randomly assigned either to the FSCs or to control groups (Bernstein, Schwartz, & Levin, 2000).

Improving Programmatic Decision Making. Social work organizations must constantly make decisions about programs. Decisions might include a response to the following types of questions: Should a program be continued? Would 12 sessions be as effective as 16 sessions for an educational program? Should we hire people with a four-year degree or only MSWs? Do we need additional outreach to minority consumers of agency services? If we begin an after-school program, will community members participate? Should the community initiate a policy of arresting truant youth? Although tradition and politics generally play some role in agency decision making, program evaluation data can and should be used to promote rational decision making about programs. For this process to be conducted properly, the data must be accurate, relevant, available, and correctly interpreted and used. Unlike many research studies, program evaluation can provide continuous information to the organization about the quality and effectiveness of its services in order to promote continuous program improvement.

Promoting Efficient Services. Social work agencies are obligated to use the most effective and efficient services available to them. To meet this obligation, an organization must (a) document the cost of providing services, (b) provide evidence that it is operating in a cost-effective manner, and (c) document the benefits of its programs. Organizations that meet these goals are more likely to provide effective services, receive and maintain funding, and maintain the goodwill of the general public.

Concerns Related to Program Evaluation

In spite of the many benefits of evaluating programs, some social workers are reluctant to engage in program evaluation for a variety of reasons. Resistance to program evaluation comes from concerns or threats related to the consumers of agency services, agency workers, and the agency resources. In this section, we examine several basic concerns related to program evaluation.

Evaluation Uses Valuable Time and Resources. Social workers who oppose program evaluation argue that they do not have time to devote to evaluation because their caseloads are already too great or their waiting lists too long. Collecting data and writing reports take time and resources away from engaging in direct services. In addition, workers worry that evaluation will divert already limited funds from providing direct services to conducting research activities.

Evaluation Will Harm Clients. Another major concern of social workers is that evaluation will harm their clients, in several ways. To begin with, some workers worry that clients will perceive filling out evaluation forms and participating in other non-service-based activities as an imposition and a distraction from the actual intervention. In this way, data collection will disrupt the worker-client relationship. A related concern is that the needs of the evaluation will take priority over the needs of the people who are seeking services. For example, a research design may call for random assignment, whereas agency workers would rather assign individual clients to the intervention they think will work best for each client. Finally, some workers express concern about violating client privacy, security, and confidentiality of records when an outsider such as a consultant or a university-based entity is conducting the evaluation.

 Web Links

For more information on Argus, visit the company's Web site, which can be accessed at www.mhhe.com/krysik1.

A related issue involves protecting research participants. As we saw in Chapter 2, any research that uses federal funds or that is conducted by a university-based researcher who receives federal funds must be approved by an institutional review board (IRB). The IRB focuses on protecting human subjects from exposure to dangerous conditions, unnecessary harm, and loss of privacy. It also ensures that subjects participate with informed consent. Program evaluation often involves experimental conditions using human subjects. However, not all human service agencies must submit their proposals to an IRB. Federal regulations do not apply, for example, when a nonprofit organization is funded entirely by private donations. Nevertheless, social work ethics require the same stringent review for protecting all participants in the program evaluation. Therefore, when a program does not use an IRB, an organization may establish its own review board, or it may create a community-based board. In either case, the review board will establish policies and procedures for evaluation. It will then review evaluation proposals before services and evaluation begin. Human service agencies may also contract an outside agency with expertise in IRB on a consulting basis. For example, Argus, in Tucson, Arizona, provides independent IRB services for human service organizations.

Evaluation Will Harm Social Workers and the Organization. In addition to harming clients, evaluation has the potential to embarrass or negatively affect workers, supervisors, and administrators if negative results are made public. In addition, it can have serious political consequences. For example, evaluation data may show that one worker or unit is much more successful with cases than another. If administrators use this information in a heavy-handed way to blame, threaten, or harass the less successful worker or unit, social workers will soon distrust the evaluation process. The administration also may feel threatened by evaluation, especially one imposed from the outside. Evaluation information can highlight poor agency performance and thus threaten the agency's funding as well as its reputation in the community.

Evaluation Results Cannot Be Trusted. Political pressures and vested interests may influence who is hired to do the evaluation, what types of data are reported and not reported, which methods are used to obtain data, and how the data are interpreted. In some cases, the administration may report the program evaluation data in ways that put a positive spin on the results. At other times, when an administrator wishes to end a program, she or he may interpret data from an outside evaluator in such a way as to justify termination.

Addressing Evaluation Concerns. All of these concerns are legitimate and should be addressed with workers before an evaluation project is initiated. The evaluator should explain and emphasize the benefits of the evaluation for consumers, and the workers should receive useful information from the evaluation results. Whenever possible, social workers and other stakeholders, including clients, should have input into the evaluation process as well as access to the evaluation results by participating in an evaluation committee and sharing information with the evaluators. Workers and consumers involved in the evaluation may have greater personal investment in the evaluation when they are included in planning and implementing the study. Burdensome aspects of the evaluation should be kept to a minimum. Social workers who participate in the evaluation should be assured that service priorities will take precedence over evaluation needs, that confidentiality will be maintained, and that client rights will be protected.

Finally, the results of the evaluation should always be used to improve services and not to embarrass or intimidate agency workers. For example, administrators might look for reasons why a worker is unsuccessful. Is the worker's caseload too high? Does the worker need additional training and support? Is this a chance event outside of the worker's usual performance? Is the worker experiencing burnout? Similarly, outside evaluators such as accrediting or funding agencies must use evaluation information constructively with organizations just as with individual workers or units. In general, social workers will support efforts that they perceive as leading to an improvement in agency services, and they will undermine evaluation efforts that appear irrelevant or punitive. Evaluators should be aware of the political context in which evaluation occurs when they plan evaluation studies. Similarly, social workers should critically examine the political context of the study when they consider the results and conclusions. Case-in-Point 11.5 illustrates both design and political issues in program evaluation.

The Arizona Abstinence Only Education Program was a broadly implemented major school initiative that took place over a five-year period (1998–2003). The program served approximately 123,000 children in grades 4 through 12, most of them adolescents, in 12 of 15 Arizona counties. At the height of its implementation, the program reached as many as 175 middle and high schools, 42 detention and residential facilities, and 32 community and after-school settings. The 17 program contractors responsible for implementing the program used 14 different curricula with varying emphases. Some contractors emphasized the health benefits of abstinence, including the avoidance of sexually transmitted diseases. Others stressed refusal skills and communication, and some provided ancillary services such as youth groups and parent meetings. The program also engaged in an extensive media campaign with statewide coverage through radio, television, and nonbroadcast forms of advertising such as posters and signs on bus benches.

The Arizona Abstinence Only Education Program presented many challenges to evaluation. This Case-in-Point outlines how the external evaluator dealt with three of the challenges: diversity, primary prevention, and sensitivity.

DIVERSITY

The program was marked by diversity in target population, program delivery setting, curricula, and supplemental activities. The state believed that creating diverse programs was necessary to respond to the unique needs of local populations and settings. Although diversity was critical to the program's effectiveness, it created challenges for the evaluators. Evaluating the program as an aggregate is problematic when there is a great deal of diversity among program sites. Unless the evaluation findings are overly positive or negative, they are likely to appear average. This is the case when some sites do very well, some are in the middle, and others perform poorly. The evaluator for the program dealt with the diversity issue by designing the program evaluation to describe the operations of each contractor. The analysis was conducted and reported separately for different subgroups, including three age groups and different settings (parochial versus public schools, detention and residential youths, after-school settings, and public schools). The media campaign was evaluated separately using a statewide, randomized telephone survey.

PRIMARY PREVENTION

Measuring prevention of behavior is much more difficult than measuring its occurrence. In the case of the Arizona program, how does an evaluator measure whether children and youths are abstaining from sexual behavior? In addition to asking preteens and teens about their attitudes and intentions regarding abstinence, the evaluator also asked teens whether they had engaged in a continuum of sexual risk behaviors ranging from kissing to intercourse. Perhaps the most innovative strategy used to assess the preventive impact of the program was to match names and birth dates of participants with birth certificate data from the state Department of Vital Statistics. This strategy enabled the evaluator to calculate the number of live birth rates for female program participants and then compare these data with the rates for nonparticipants of the same age.

SENSITIVITY

Sex is a sensitive topic for parents and their children. Parents are also sensitive about research in the schools and the use of school time for nonacademic endeavors. In the early days of the program, participant recruitment was a problem because many students were not returning their signed parental consent forms. Once this problem was identified, the school administration changed the parental consent form from active consent to passive consent. In active consent, parents must sign the permission form to allow their children to participate in the program. The purpose of this procedure was to ensure that the parents understood the program. In contrast, passive permission requires parents who do *not* want their children to participate to sign the permission form. Thus, parents who do not sign the form are granting passive consent for their children to attend the program and participate in the evaluation. Switching to the passive consent process increased enrollment numbers.

Is passive permission ethical? Proponents contend that once researchers have made such good faith efforts as mailings, school meetings, sending forms home with children, and calling parents directly, passive consent is an acceptable method. Critics respond that passive consent violates the principle of informed consent because some parents may never get the information and thus have no voice in whether their children are part of an experimental program. How do you feel about passive permission?

CASE-IN-POINT 11.5

Evaluation Challenges in a Large-Scale Prevention Program
continued

 Web Links

A link to the full evaluation report can be found at www.mhhe.com/krysik1.

CONCLUSION

Social work practice exists in a political context that is strongly influenced by a marketplace mentality. The desire to be of help is not enough to ensure that programs will develop and continue. Programs that do not evaluate their services or that focus only on the number of units of service provided will not convince stakeholders that these services should be continued, no matter how efficiently they are managed. For both ethical and pragmatic reasons, it is essential that social workers present evidence of the effectiveness and benefits of their services. Systematic and research-based evaluation of social programs provides evidence that programs are needed, are operating as intended, and are producing the expected beneficial results. Program evaluation is directly linked to social work practice in that it helps focus services on outcomes for participants, improves practice through ongoing feedback about program processes, and provides evidence that workers are improving the quality of people's lives in the most cost-efficient manner.

Once the program evaluation or other research projects are designed and implemented and the data are collected and analyzed, the evaluator needs to write a report describing the process, results, and conclusions of the study. What should go in a research report and how to present the report to the intended audience are the topics in Chapter 12.

MAIN POINTS

- A program is a set of activities designed to reach specific objectives. Program evaluation is the use of research methods to answer questions related to planning, evaluating, and improving social work programs. It seeks to answer the broad question What services, provided to whom, produce what changes, for whom, under what circumstances, for how long, compared to what, at what cost?

- Types of program evaluation include evaluability assessment, needs assessment, implementation evaluation, quality improvement and program monitoring process evaluation, outcome and impact evaluation, consumer satisfaction, and cost/benefit analysis. All of these types of evaluations use scientifically based research methods and designs.

- Program evaluation requires that the program goal is consistent with the organizational mission in which the program is housed and that clear, specific, and measurable objectives are identified.

- A logic model is a program planning and evaluation tool that charts the links between social conditions, specification of goals and objectives, program activities, program outcomes, and resources or inputs.

- Program evaluation always occurs in political and organizational contexts that can help facilitate or undermine the evaluation. In reviewing or developing a program evaluation, social workers must consider who is doing the program evaluation, the reasons why an evaluation is being conducted, who stands to gain or lose from the evaluation, the ways the information is used, and who is included in development and ongoing program evaluation efforts.

- Benefits of conducting program evaluation include complying with the ethical responsibility to use the most effective methods and to provide evidence that services are effective; providing information for ongoing program improvement and promoting policy and social change; and improving the opportunities for funding needed programs. Possible negative effects of program evaluation occur when the evaluation disrupts direct services or reduces resources for services; when management uses information from the evaluation to threaten workers; and when evaluation results threaten the program's funding or reputation.

EXERCISES: PRACTICING SOCIAL WORK

1. Examine whether a substance abuse prevention program is changing attitudes and behavior among youth in the Black Feather community.

a. How will you operationalize "substance abuse" and "prevention"?

b. What measures would you use in formative evaluation to be sure the program is being delivered as intended?

c. What outcome measures would you use in your evaluation to assess the impact of the program on youth?

d. What longer-term measures can be used to assess the benefits and costs of the program?

EXERCISES: SOCIAL WORK LIBRARY

1. Read Craig, Cook, and Fraser (2004) and discuss the types of social work research that have received awards from SSWR.

2. Read Duggan (2004) and critique her approach to evaluation given the problems that led to the lack of positive findings she describes. What would you propose as the focus of the next Healthy Start program evaluation?

OTHER EXERCISES

1. Use the Internet or other sources to find information about the Scared Straight program.

   a. What outcomes measures were used to evaluate the program?

   b. From your findings, would you recommend that your community adopt the program? Why?

2. Use a search engine to find the American Evaluation Association on the Web. What resources do they offer evaluators?

3. You wish to start a Big Brother/Big Sisters mentor program at your organization.

   a. What costs will be involved in the program?

   b. What benefits might you expect?

   c. Translate some of these benefits into monetary terms.

4. Which of the following are clearly measurable objectives? Change those that are not well-written objectives to measurable outcomes objectives.

   a. Develop cultural competence.

   b. Increase the number of minority students by 10 percent.

   c. Provide housing for 30 homeless families a year for the next three years.

   d. Increase the understanding of research by MSW students.

   e. Increase the morale of staff through an awards ceremony.

   f. Place 90 percent of children with families over the next 12 months.

   g. Promote a healthy respect for the law among 10- to 12-year-old boys by September 2006.

   h. All state hospital patients are in appropriate community housing by June 30, 2007.

CHAPTER 12

Writing and Presenting Research

In the Communication Age, we must learn to extract the knowledge from the information, put it into a dynamic "digital" form, and communicate it to cause action.
—DANIEL BURRUS, TECHNOLOGY SPEAKER, FUTURIST, AND AUTHOR OF *TECHNOTRENDS*

SOCIAL WORK IS A PRACTICE PROFESSION. NOT SURPRISINGLY, then, social work research focuses on improving practice. Research accomplishes this task by testing theories of practice and human behavior, developing assessment instruments that improve practice, evaluating new and ongoing intervention programs, and providing information about social conditions that affect social policy. Research, however, is a resource-intensive process—it is costly in terms of people's time and effort. The value of doing research can be realized only when the results of studies are presented in a way that impacts social work practice. Fortunately, social work researchers have many options for sharing their research findings. Specifically, they may engage in any or all of the following activities:

- Contribute to the profession's knowledge base by publishing articles in professional journals and presenting papers at national and local conferences.

- Justify the need for policy change or new services through reports to legislators and policy makers.

- Write a grant application for funding new or existing programs.

- Educate community groups about social issues, and help secure support for services through reports in newsletters or annual reports.

- Support accountability to board members within an organization through written reports.

- Support the administration in program planning and the evaluation process through reports of process and outcomes studies.

- Document the outcomes of practice at the worker level to enhance individual practice.

Writing a research report is a creative act. Like any creative act, it requires you to put together what you know and wish to communicate with considerations about the purposes you wish to achieve and the audience to whom you will present your findings. In this chapter, we discuss how to communicate the findings of research in a way that will be best received by the intended audience. We focus on the types of research presentations that are common in social work practice, the style and format for writing and presenting research reports, and ethical and political issues to consider when you write research reports. In addition, we present evaluative criteria to help you produce your own research and critique the research of others.

By the end of this chapter, you should be able to:

- List and describe the sections of a research article.

- List and describe the sections of a research proposal.

- Explain what plagiarism is and how to avoid it.

- Describe good design elements of a research presentation.

- Critique a research report or presentation.

PUBLICATION IN PROFESSIONAL JOURNALS

The core knowledge of the social work profession is disseminated through professional journals. Social work publications can be found in a wide variety of social work and social science journals. To help social workers locate relevant publications, NASW Press publishes *An Author's Guide to Social Work Journals*, which lists approximately 200 journals of interest to social work authors (NASW, 1997). The guide provides information about the journal's mission or focus, its acceptance rate, the review process, and the procedures for submitting manuscripts for publication. Journals vary in their focus, and they generally have a fairly narrow area of interest. A journal may focus only on the outcomes of social work practice (for example, *Research on Social Work Practice*) or only on issues of technology (for example, *Journal of Technology and Human Services*). Before you submit a manuscript for publication, you should know the focus of the journal because the manuscript will be rejected if it does not match the journal's mission.

Information in journals is dynamic in that it grows and changes as publications are added to the field. One purpose of publishing in professional journals is to "get the word out" to practitioners and researchers. Thus, publishing is a strategy for informing the professional community and other interested readers about new theories or evidence to support or reject theories, new interventions, results of the evaluations of programs, and other information that increases the knowledge of the profession. Publication is a way to inform others of new developments as well as to suggest research that still needs to be done to build the knowledge base.

As both a producer and a consumer of research, you need to understand the publication process. Some journals are *refereed,* and publications undergo **blind review,** meaning that reviewers do not see any identifying information about the author(s). Exhibit 12.1 provides an overview of the review process. In other journals or special editions of some refereed journals, the reviewers know the identity of the author(s). Journals with blind review are thought to set a

---

EXHIBIT 12.1

The Publication Process

- An author writes a manuscript for publication and sends it to a journal editor.
- The editor sends the manuscript to between two and four reviewers with recognized expertise in their field. At this point, the manuscript contains no names or identifying information in order to prevent possible bias in the review (blind review).
- The reviewers provide a critique of the manuscript and make a judgment about its merit based on the author's contribution of new knowledge to the field, her or his use of appropriate methodology, and the overall writing style.
- The reviewers return the manuscript to the editor. The editor then makes a judgment based on the reviews. The judgment will usually be one of the following:
  - *Accept:* The manuscript is accepted.
  - *Accept with revisions:* The manuscript is accepted, but the author must make minor revisions before it can be published.
  - *Revise and resubmit:* The manuscript is not accepted but will be re-reviewed if the changes suggested by the reviewers are satisfactorily made.
  - *Reject:* The manuscript is not accepted for publication in the journal.
- If a manuscript is not accepted for publication, an author generally has three options: (1) make the suggested changes and resubmit the manuscript, (2) send the manuscript to a different journal with little or no change, or (3) give up on publishing the manuscript.
- If the author chooses to revise and resubmit the manuscript, the editor and/or reviewers re-review the manuscript to see if it now warrants publication. This process can occur several times.

higher standard because the identity of the author is not a factor in judging the quality of the manuscript.

You should also be aware that journals vary in their acceptance rates. Some journals accept only a small proportion of the articles that are submitted to them. For example, *Social Work* accepts approximately 15 percent of the articles submitted to it, whereas *Child and Adolescent Social Work* accepts between 40 percent and 50 percent (NASW, 1998). Authors make decisions about where to submit a manuscript for publication based on a number of factors, including the journal's mission, reputation, target audience, circulation, and acceptance rate. Authors are allowed to send a manuscript to only one journal at a time to prevent wasting the reviewers' time and to make the publication process more manageable.

The time from review to publication may be a year or even longer. Therefore, the "latest" research in journals is at least a year old. In order to reduce this time lag, some journals are publishing their work online. Online journals often use the same blind review process as print journals; however, manuscripts are transmitted electronically and are published on a Web site as soon as they are accepted. This process reduces the lag time from review to publication to only a few weeks. On the negative side, though, it limits the audience to people who have access to the Internet.

 Web Links

For an example of an online journal, visit the Web site of the Journal of Social Work Values and Ethics *at www.socialworker.com/jswve.*

Writing a Research Manuscript for Publication in a Professional Journal

A **research manuscript** describes a completed research study. Writing a research manuscript for publication in a professional journal is a matter of both substance and form. The manuscript must contribute something new and useful to the literature in a specific area. In addition, it must be written in a format that is acceptable both to the journal and to the professional community. There are several styles of formats that are appropriate for professional manuscripts. The majority of social work journals and many social science journals use the format required by the journals of the American Psychological Association (APA). **APA format** provides specific rules about the structure of the paper such as heading style, margins, spacing, and reference format (American Psychological Association, 2001). What happens when a manuscript does not follow the APA format? In some cases, the journal editor will ask the author to reformat the work into APA style. In other cases, the manuscript will be immediately rejected. Using the proper APA format (or another journal format) provides consistent expectations of format for authors and may be viewed by reviewers as a sign of the author's professionalism. Exhibit 12.2 shows two reference formats: the correct APA format and an alternative.

 Web Links

Guidelines to APA format can be found at the Web site listed at www.mhhe.com/krysik1.

The first reference is in correct APA format. The second is not. Can you find the differences?

Randall, P. (1995). Getting to adulthood: Foster youth at the crossroads. *Social Research, 62* (3), 711–730.

Randall, Paul: Getting to Adulthood: Foster Youth at the Crossroads. In: Social Research, 1995, 62 (vol. 3), p711, 19 pages;

EXHIBIT 12.2

APA Reference Format

A research manuscript traditionally has the following sections. You can use the checklists in the exhibits for critical thinking about the merits of each section of a manuscript.

The Social Work Library

See the article by Thyer (2002) for tips on how to write a manuscript for publication.

- *Title:* A descriptive title stating the theme of the research report.

- *Affiliation:* The affiliation of all authors, including university or organization of employment.

- *Abstract:* Summary of the purpose, methods, and major finding of the article.

- *Key words:* Approximately five key words describing the focus of the article. These words help researchers find the article in key word searches of bibliographic databases.

- *Introduction:* The background for the research study. The introduction states the purpose of the study and explains why the research is important. It also reviews the theory and research upon which the study is based. (See the discussion of literature review in Chapter 3.) In addition, the introduction defines the terms and variables used in the study. It leads the reader from a summary of relevant previous research to the research questions and/or hypotheses in the study to be presented. In this way the introduction serves both to educate the reader and to establish the author's credibility and expertise. Exhibit 12.3 provides checklists for the introductory sections of the manuscript.

- *Method:* As its name suggests, the method section describes the methodology used in the study so that an informed reader can judge the validity of the research. In addition, the method section should provide enough detail so that a different researcher could replicate the research in another study. Whether the design is quantitative or qualitative, this section includes the research design (for example, pretest or posttest with random assignment) as well as the rationale for using that design. It should specify the research procedures in terms of who did what, with whom, when, and where. The method section also describes the

CHECKLIST FOR EVALUATING THE POLITICS OF THE RESEARCH

❑ The author's affiliation is stated.

❑ Funding sources are acknowledged, and values are made explicit.

❑ Potential bias or conflict of interest is acknowledged.

❑ The research proposal was reviewed by an IRB or other appropriate research review.

❑ Language is free of bias, stereotypes, or other cultural insensitivity.

CHECKLIST FOR EVALUATING INTRODUCTION SECTION

❑ The purpose of the paper is stated clearly.

❑ The importance of the study is justified.

❑ There is sufficient linkage to previous literature to provide a rationale and context for the study.

❑ The literature review includes the most recent and relevant studies.

❑ Concepts and variables are clearly defined.

❑ Research questions and/or hypotheses are clearly stated.

❑ There are no ethical violations.

demographics of the sample and the population from which it was drawn as well as the sampling method. It explains which data were collected and identifies the measuring instruments or procedures that were used, with information about their source, reliability, and validity. Finally, this section describes any methodological issues that might have impacted the results of the study. For example, in a study of parent education groups, if group leaders needed to be changed halfway through the study, the methods section should report this fact. It should also point out any detail that might produce bias in the results. If the age, race, or gender of the interviewer might have affected the results, for example, this possibility should be reported. See Exhibit 12.4.

- *Results:* This section describes the major findings of the study. It generally progresses from simple to more complex findings. It includes descriptive statistics about the sample and the major variables and presents the analysis of the information, both quantitative and qualitative, that is needed to answer the research question(s) (see Chapters 8 and 9). The results section may contain tables and graphs to help summarize and clarify the results. If the study used statistical tests, the results section could indicate the types of tests and the rationale for using them. One key point to remember is that the results section should be strictly

CHECKLIST FOR EVALUATING METHOD SECTION

- ❏ The type of study is specified (qualitative, quantitative, cross-sectional, longitudinal).
- ❏ The research design is specified and appropriate for the questions or hypotheses.
- ❏ The study could be replicated based on its description.

Measurement

- ❏ Variables are clearly and logically operationalized.
- ❏ The unit of analysis is specified and logical.
- ❏ The measuring instruments or methods are specified.
  - ○ There is evidence of the reliability of the measures.
  - ○ There is evidence of the validity of the measures.
- ❏ The research procedures do not bias the measures.
- ❏ Threats to internal validity are controlled or are acknowledged.
- ❏ The study is like "real life" (external validity).

Sample

- ❏ The sample and population are specified.
  - ○ How and why the sample was selected is specified.
- ❏ The sampling procedure is specified.
- ❏ The sampling frame is specified and logical.
- ❏ The sample size is specified and is large enough for generalization and analyses.
- ❏ Information is provided about the return rate and/or attrition rate in the study.
- ❏ The sampling error is specified.
- ❏ Given the sample, the limits of generalization are specified.

Quasi Experimental and Experimental Design

- ❏ The independent and dependent variables are specified.
- ❏ The type of design is specified and logical for the purpose.
- ❏ The control or comparison group(s) is specified and justified.
  - ○ The equivalence of the groups is specified.
- ❏ The periods of measurement are specified and logical for the purpose.
- ❏ Threats to internal validity are controlled or explained (history, testing, maturation, instrumentation, statistical regression, selection, attrition).
- ❏ Issues related to a placebo effect or Hawthorne effect are explained.
- ❏ Any deception is explained and justified.

continued

EXHIBIT 12.4

Evaluating the Method Section of a Research Manuscript

EXHIBIT 12.4

Evaluating the Method Section of a Research Manuscript
continued

Survey Research

❑ The type of survey (mail, telephone, in-person, Internet) is specified.

❑ The exact questions (or where to find them) that have been asked are specified.

❑ The questions are clear and understandable by the intended respondents.

❑ Questions cover only one idea at a time.

❑ Closed questions provide all mutually exclusive categories.

❑ Categorization or coding of open-ended questions is specified and logical for the purpose.

❑ Social desirability can be ruled out as contributing to the responses.

❑ The return rate is specified and high enough to warrant generalization.

Qualitative Research

❑ The classifying or coding system for observations is specified and appropriate for the purpose.

❑ There is evidence or justification that another researcher observing the same events would classify them the same way.

❑ The impact of the researcher on the observations and coding is explained and justified.

❑ Selection of observations or interviewees is specified and justified.

❑ The impact of the researcher's own gender and cultural identity on the interpretation of what has been observed is explained.

❑ Field notes or recordings are available for review.

❑ The generalizability of the study is explained.

descriptive and factual. In other words, it should not make any attempt to interpret the meaning of the results.

- *Discussion:* This section summarizes the major findings and considers their meaning, importance, and implications. The discussion may include implications for theory development, practice, program development, education and training, policy, and further research. It may also consider the extent to which the study corroborates or contradicts the findings from previous research. Finally, it can include a description of the limitations of the study and how they might be addressed in future research. This information can be quite useful to readers. These limitations may be related to any aspect of the research method such as the lack of generalizability of the sample, limited knowledge of the validity of the measuring instruments, low return rate or high dropout rate, or the inability to collect certain data. In addition, the discussion should report any intervening variables that may have affected the study. For example, in a study of student attitudes toward alcohol use, if a drunk-driving death involving students of the school occurred just before the study, this should be reported, as it almost certainly will have influenced students' responses.

- *Conclusion:* Although not always a standard part of all manuscripts, the conclusion can be useful when the discussion is long and complex. It briefly summarizes the main findings of the study and highlights the implications of the study for practice, policy, and future research. Exhibit 12.5 provides checklists for assessing the results, discussion, and conclusion sections of the manuscript.

CHECKLIST FOR EVALUATING RESULTS SECTION

❑ Methods of data collection are specified.

❑ Statistical tests are appropriate for the type of data collected.

❑ The difference between statistical and meaningful findings is clear.

❑ All relevant analyses were performed.

❑ There are no logical flaws in the analysis and interpretation of the data.

❑ Tables and graphs summarize the results when appropriate.

❑ Tables and graphs are appropriately labeled with headings and necessary detail.

❑ The effect size (*ES*) is reported in addition to statistical significance.

❑ If qualitative data, enough examples are presented to allow the reader to understand or replicate the coding or analysis.

❑ Data are recent enough to be relevant.

❑ The results are reported as factual without interpretation.

CHECKLIST FOR EVALUATING DISCUSSION AND CONCLUSION SECTIONS

❑ There is a summary of the major findings and discussion of their significance.

❑ The conclusions are warranted by the data.

❑ How the topic adds to, modifies, replicates, or contradicts previous research is discussed.

❑ Research flaws, shortcomings, and other plausible reasons for results of the study are explained.

❑ There are implications of the results for practice and/or policy.

❑ There are specific suggestions for further research.

EXHIBIT 12.5

Evaluating the Results, Discussion, and Conclusion Sections of a Research Manuscript

- *References:* All literature and other references reviewed in the article should be cited in the format required by the journal. See the section titled "Plagiarism" later in this chapter for more information about citing references.

- *Tables and figures:* These summarize data, provide detailed information about statistical test results, and represent concepts in a graphical format. References to the tables and figures appear in the text, and the tables and figures are placed at the end of the manuscript.

As noted throughout this book, quantitative and qualitative methods are both grounded in the scientific method, and both approaches are useful for producing social work knowledge to inform practice. The checklists are helpful in analyzing both methods. Qualitative research, with its emphasis on in-depth inquiry, however, should also be evaluated by standards appropriate to that method. Glynda Hull, a professor of education at the University of California, Berkeley, in a qualitative style, offers guidelines for evaluating qualitative research in Exhibit 12.6.

EXHIBIT 12.6

Guidelines for Evaluating Qualitative Research, by Glynda Hull

WORTHY GOALS

Good qualitative research needs to serve a purpose beyond the researcher's interest in a particular phenomenon. It needs to answer a useful question or go at least part of the way toward solving or shedding light upon a significant social problem.

VIVID DESCRIPTION PLUS CONVINCING ANALYSIS

When I read qualitative research, I expect engrossing narratives and vivid descriptions. I want to come to know the people being written about and to be able to picture their families and communities. But combined with description should be convincing analysis, in which the author reveals the perspectives that inform the research and illustrate how he or she marched from particular evidence to particular conclusions.

SUFFICIENT DATA

Although length and intensity of time in the field are certainly not the sole determinants of good qualitative research, I am uneasy when researchers call their research "qualitative" or "ethnographic" and then reveal that they have spent only a few days or a week or two collecting data. I want to know that the researcher has taken the time needed to gain entry to a classroom or program or workplace, has taken the time needed to understand it in its complexity and totality, and has taken the time needed to collect sufficient data to answer the questions that were posed. All this will make findings more credible.

SUFFICIENT ACCOUNTS OF DATA AND ANALYSIS

Typically, qualitative researchers face formidable space problems in writing about their projects, which don't lend themselves to pithy summaries or representation in tables or charts, and are hampered by the page restrictions imposed in journals. Qualitative research is best described discursively and at length, so that readers can get a sense of the types of data that were collected and the ways in which those data were analyzed. Ideally, enough data should be included in a report so that a reader can examine them and compare his or her own conclusions with those of the author.

ACKNOWLEDGING DILEMMAS

Most qualitative researchers experience various dilemmas in the field whether with gaining entry to a site or establishing a relationship with participants or negotiating the extent of the study or even with some of many possible ethical problems. It is always helpful and honorable for researchers to come clean about such issues, in either the body of their paper or an appendix, to represent their research honestly and to provide helpful road maps for future field workers.

REPRESENTING OTHERS

Since at its heart qualitative research is an up close look at other lives, I am always interested in how well those other lives are represented on the page. I look for representations that are grounded, being built from actual data; that are always respectful, yet not romanticized; that reveal complex human beings rather than cartoonish stick figures; and that situate people's choices, values, and activities in a larger socio-cultural, political, and historical context.

Source: G. Hull, 2005. Used with permission.

EXHIBIT 12.6

Guidelines for Evaluating Qualitative Research, by Glynda Hull
continued

Writing a Research Proposal

A **research proposal** describes *why* a research project should be done, and it outlines the plan for *how* the research will be done. It is written for a specific purpose and often for a specific audience. The purpose and the requirements of the audience dictate the format of the proposal. Some proposals are limited to a few pages, whereas others are several hundred pages long, including supporting documentation. One purpose of a research proposal is to secure funding. Thus, the proposal may be directed to a government agency such as a federal grant program, a private agency such as United Way, or a philanthropic foundation. Another function of the proposal is to help agency board members or administrators decide whether to approve a research project within their agency. Also, when the federal government or other organization requires the researcher to obtain permission from an institutional review board (IRB) for carrying out the research, the sections of the proposal that discuss the purpose, research design, confidentiality procedures, informed consent, and qualifications of the researchers must be submitted as part of the application. Finally, writing a research proposal helps the researcher clarify in her or his mind why and how the study is to be conducted.

In writing a research proposal, the author has two primary goals. The first is to convince the audience (such as the funding agency or board) that the research is important and worth doing. To accomplish this goal, the proposal must explain the importance of the research and include a literature review that provides background about the extent and nature of the issue to be addressed. Where applicable, the proposal should also include information about pilot studies that were done in preparation for the current project. In addition, the proposal should explicitly state the benefits or outcomes of the research. These benefits can include improved social conditions, improved interventions or programs, additional information for policy development, and/or theory development. The proposal generally highlights the interests of the audience. For example, a Request for Proposals (RFP) may focus on improving substance abuse prevention for adolescents through training programs for school social workers. In this case, the proposal would need to focus on program description and evaluation rather than policy or theory, although the research may have implications for all of these areas.

The second primary goal is to convince the audience that the author possesses the expertise to conduct the research. The intended audience must believe that the author has the necessary knowledge and skills to do the proposed research. The author accomplishes this goal in part through the introduction and literature review sections, in which he or she demonstrates knowledge of the field. In addition, the author's expertise is shown through the description of the conceptualization and method of the research. Finally, authors confirm their expertise by documenting their credentials and experience. Research proposals often have a section that explicitly states the author's qualifications. This section includes educational background, current position, and previous research experience. Finally, the author's résumé often needs to be attached to the proposal. Exhibit 12.7 describes criteria for evaluating research proposals.

A research proposal generally has the following sections, although this list varies with the requirements of the funding or approving organization:

- *Abstract:* One- or two-paragraph summary of the research purpose and method.

- *Executive summary:* Brief but detailed summary of the purpose, method, benefits, and limitations of the proposed study.

EXHIBIT 12.7

Checklist for Evaluating Research Proposals

If you were deciding which research projects to fund, you might use the following criteria in evaluating research proposals for funding. Each item is rated from 1 (Unsatisfactory) to 5 (Exceptional).

Note the similarities and differences with regard to criteria used to evaluate research for publication in journals.

- ❑ The proposal recognizes needs and proposes solutions consistent with the purpose of the funding.
- ❑ There is evidence of ability to plan, arrange, and control tasks to ensure success.
- ❑ The research will make a significant contribution to the field and has clear implications for practice and/or policy.
- ❑ The study is based on good research design principles.
- ❑ The research methods fit the study questions.
- ❑ The proposal has enough flexibility to ensure success.
- ❑ The proposal addresses issues of the appropriateness and accuracy of the measures.
- ❑ The researcher has the education, knowledge, and experience to carry out the research.
- ❑ The proposal has a realistic budget, plan, and timeline.
- ❑ The researcher has sufficient resources to carry out the project.
- ❑ There is evidence of support for the project from important constituencies.
- ❑ Ethical guidelines have been addressed and followed.

- *Introduction:* Statement of the purpose and benefits of the study that includes a literature review of previous research. This section is similar to the introduction of a research manuscript for publication.

- *Method:* Description of the proposed research in terms of methodology, similar to the method section of a research manuscript for publication.

- *Data analysis:* Analysis of the research questions and/or hypotheses to be studied that specifies the data analysis that will be performed to determine the outcomes of the research. In quantitative research, the types of data that will be presented, the statistical tests to be used, and the justification for using these tests are presented. In qualitative studies, the types of analyses (such as data coding) and the justifications for these methods are specified.

- *Administrative structure:* Explanation of how the research project will be administered, including the responsibility for overall management of the project, availability of necessary resources, location of the study, and organizational context in which the study will take place. The administrative section also includes a budget, a timeline, and an organizational chart. The budget essentially describes the costs of the research project in terms of personnel, equipment, supplies, communications, stipends for subjects, consultants, travel, and any other expenses encountered by the project. Funders generally set a maximum amount they will fund for a specific project. The timeline shows in outline form the sequence of events that will take place and how long each phase of the project is expected to last. The outline should specify which activities are to take place and by what dates. Finally, the organizational chart should highlight the administrative structure of the organization conducting the research, including the lines of responsibility for managing the project.

- *References:* A list of all references used in the introduction, literature review, or other sections of the proposal. Authors should use the APA format unless they are otherwise instructed by the organization for which the report is intended.

- *Supporting documents:* A research proposal, especially one directed to a funding organization, may include letters from other organizations or important community members that support the need for the research, describe areas of collaboration, and generally endorse the project. Supporting documents may also include an organizational chart, an annual report, reports of pilot projects, and any other materials that demonstrate the need for the research and the capabilities of the researchers to accomplish their goals.

Other Research Reports

Other research reports may be written for a variety of reasons in a variety of formats, depending on the purpose of the report and the nature of the intended audience. At times, a research report will be written to summarize work on a research project because the funders require regular reports of progress every 3 months, 6 months, or 12 months. A final report to funders detailing all aspects of the project is also generally required. This report may be much longer than a research manuscript, often 100 pages or longer. Such reports should have an executive summary that describes the important results and implications of the study. See Case-in-Point 12.1 for a sample executive summary from the Casey Family Services (CFS) program that provided computers and Internet connection to foster families. The research report was 70 single-spaced pages, including graphs and tables; the executive summary was less than 3 pages. Case-in-Point 12.1 reproduces the format and main topics of the summary, leaving out some of the detailed explanations because of space considerations.

Casey Family Services (CFS) evaluated their program after one year in order to assess both its implementation and its outcomes. Based on this evaluation, recommendations were made for changes in the program and continued evaluation of the program. The research report was presented to the agency director and given to the board of directors, in part to provide information upon which to base decisions for expanding the program to other CFS divisions.

CASE-IN-POINT 12.1

Executive Summary

EXECUTIVE SUMMARY—FIRST YEAR RESULTS OF THE BUILDING SKILLS–BUILDING FUTURES (BSBF) INFORMATION TECHNOLOGY PILOT PROJECT, MARCH 2003

This project describes the pretest and posttest results of quantitative and qualitative measures of program implementation and outcomes after the first year of the program. In addition, it compares foster children in the BSBF program with a group of foster families from other CFS divisions. The results are based on 45 (82%) foster parents and 34 (69.3%) foster children in the program. A comparison group of 30 parents and 29 foster children from other divisions was also evaluated.

Successful Implementation
1. Families have received computers and initial training in successful rollout event.
2. Families have received Internet connection and Internet safety software.
3. Social workers are beginning to work with families to develop plans to enhance the technology skills of foster children. The process, however, needs further development.
4. Handbook of program policies is almost complete.
5. Policies have been developed to guide providing computers to transitioning youth, and seven youths have received computers.

Implementation Issues
1. The model has changed from a "family focused" model to a "foster child" focused model.
2. The individualized technology plan (ITP) is working effectively for only about one-third of families.
3. Community training model works for a minority of parents and children.
4. Supplementary resources and activities are being developed.

Outcomes Evaluation in Relation to Program Goals
Increase access to computers and computer skills for all children in CFS foster homes:
Mostly successfully accomplished.

1. There is improved technology access, use, and skills for the majority of parents and children in the program.
2. The program has been successful in minimizing any negative consequences associated with use of technology.
3. The majority of participants believe the BSBF program was useful in improving children's computer skills, grades, homework, ability to find information on the Internet, and interest in information technology. Improvement was moderate to high.

continued

4. Most participants experienced few if any difficulties in relation to using computers. A smaller group had concerns over receiving inappropriate material. Overall, participants' confidence in handling computer difficulties increased during the program, and very few reported serious concerns.

5. All believe the program should be continued. Based on qualitative interviews with parents, it is clear that they are genuinely appreciative of CFS's efforts to improve the technology skills of foster children. The program is good for parents' morale. The program has also increased positive interactions between parents and children around learning technology skills. The program has also increased the self-esteem and feelings of accomplishment of some foster children.

6. A minority of families (20–25%), however, are not fully engaged in the program and express low to moderate satisfaction with the program.

Assist young people as they transition from high school to jobs or college by providing them with essential computer equipment:
Appears to be successfully accomplished. Further evaluation is needed.

All eligible transition youth have computers to use for higher education. Three youths could not be reached for evaluation. The remainder are using the computer daily for schoolwork and e-mail. They are highly satisfied with the program. Criteria for eligibility to receive technology assistance at transition have been developed.

Increase the ability of foster parents to community (interact) with one another and (use) other resources (via the Internet) that are useful for them:
Partially accomplished.

1. Participants' ability to use the Internet and e-mail has increased substantially.
2. Parents' use of e-mail with CFS has also increased substantially.
3. Participants' use of the Internet for social support or to access foster family–related resources is still in the beginning stage.

Build the capacity of the CFS Division itself to serve as a resource to enhance and support the development of computer skills:
Partially accomplished.

1. CFS is seen as a source of support for securing computer upgrades and dealing with computer malfunctions.
2. Parents and social workers see project director as very helpful in all aspects of the program.
3. Technology-related newsletter was sent to families and was well received.
4. CFS has not yet begun to develop other online resources and activities (projects, Web sites, Listservs, training) to promote greater computer use by families.

CASE-IN-POINT 12.1

Executive Summary
continued

Comments and Recommendations

- Future participants should develop family commitment and basic computer skills before a computer is provided to the family.

- Development of a family-focused program requires both a "culture" and a commitment of time and resources. Current barriers perceived by social workers include workload concerns; lack of authority to monitor biological children and parents; priority given to immediate problem-focused issues rather than technology; and unclear understanding of procedures to follow.

- Community training in technology may not be an effective method for reaching the majority of families. Other models such as tutors, mentors, or training at CFS should be considered.

- Social workers should be aware that some parents do occasionally have difficulties with family arguments over computer use, children's access to pornography, and strangers trying to contact their children. Social workers should inquire about any difficulties and be trained in how to handle them.

- Some participants have benefited more than others from the program. Those with the least skills at pretest the made most improvement. Those who used the computer more frequently improve more in skills. Efforts to increase the frequency of computer use are likely to show improvement in skill levels as well.

- Given the high computer use of the comparison group, they might be described as families that are on the "technology user" side of the digital divide. The BSBF program appears to have given Bridgeport families computer use and skills similar to (but not better than) those of the comparison group. It can be argued that the BSBF program has helped Bridgeport families bridge the digital divide.

The format of the report varies depending on its audience and purpose. At times, the completed report may be written in lay terms so that the board or the general community can understand it. Research presentations in annual reports often serve this purpose. At other times, the audience may be made up of research reviewers at funding agencies that require considerable detail and statistical analyses. In any case, keeping in mind the general sections of a research manuscript—introduction, method, results, discussion, and conclusion—will serve as a useful guide to organizing the report.

Newsletters are an increasingly popular way of bringing research to the social work community. Authors can purchase templates for newsletters online, making the publishing of a newsletter relatively easy. Further, by distributing the newsletter electronically and posting it on the Web, authors can avoid printing and mailing costs. Newsletters can be organized thematically. They usually include four or five short articles written for the practice community in

Web Links

Visit www.mhhe.com/krysik1 for a list of links to online newsletters.

a specific field. The Web site for this book provides access to several online research newsletters geared to social work and its allied professions.

PRESENTING RESEARCH AT A CONFERENCE OR PROFESSIONAL MEETING

Presentations at research conferences or other professional meetings, like journal publications, are sometimes refereed and sometimes invited. There are several formats for research presentations at professional meetings: papers, poster sessions, and workshops. At times, a research presentation may report a completed research project. At other times, a conference may allow a researcher to present ideas for a project, works in progress, or a completed project that has not been formally written up. Research presentations at professional meetings may be the most cutting-edge research because the researcher often presents the study shortly after completing it rather than waiting several months for the findings to be published in a journal. On the negative side, however, conferences often accept a research presentation based on an abstract of the proposal rather than a completed manuscript. In these cases, professionals in the field may not have reviewed the entire presentation.

Unlike journal articles or research proposals, a research presentation at a professional meeting is not meant to be a one-way presentation of the project. Rather, it is intended to inform an audience as well as to provide a forum for two-way interaction involving questions and comments. As with any research paper, the presenter must take into account the knowledge level and expertise of the intended audience. The nature of the audience should determine (a) the extent to which the presenter needs to define and clarify the key concepts, (b) the appropriate level of methodological detail, and (c) the types of statistics, charts, and tables that the presenter should use.

The content of research paper presentations is similar to that of research papers and proposals. The presentation should discuss the traditional areas of introduction, method, results, and discussion in about 20 to 30 minutes, although the presenter can place more emphasis on some areas than on others depending on the focus of the conference and the interests of the audience. Research presentations vary in presentation style and format. Some presenters read their papers. Generally speaking, however, unless the paper is especially well written and of great interest to the audience, the audience is likely to tune out the speaker. Other presenters use an outline and discuss the research, often involving the audience by inviting questions and comments. Presenters increasingly use presentation software such as Microsoft PowerPoint as well as multimedia such as music, graphics, film clips, Internet sites, and videotapes. Exhibit 12.8 shows some sample slides used in a presentation at a professional conference.

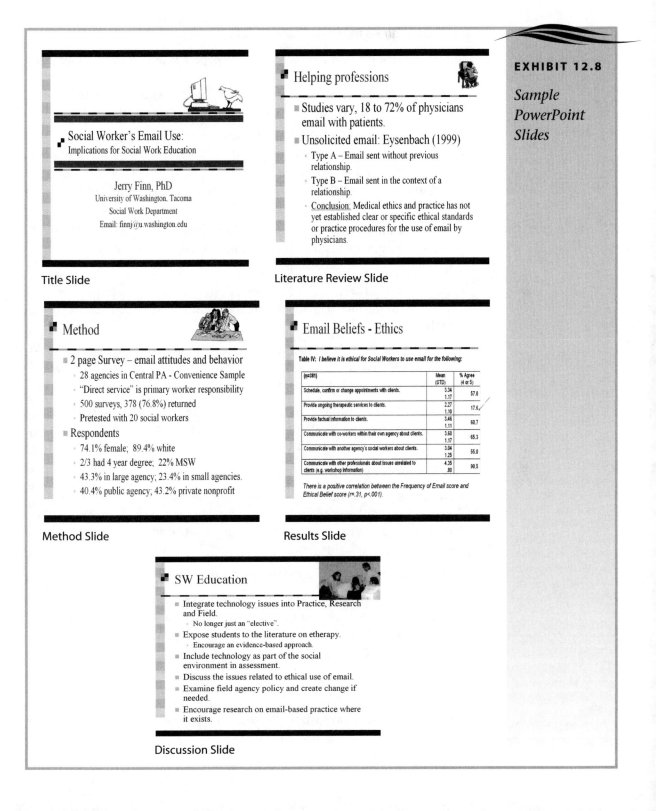

EXHIBIT 12.8

Sample PowerPoint Slides

Title Slide

Social Worker's Email Use:
Implications for Social Work Education

Jerry Finn, PhD
University of Washington, Tacoma
Social Work Department
Email: finnj@u.washington.edu

Literature Review Slide

Helping professions

- Studies vary, 18 to 72% of physicians email with patients.
- Unsolicited email: Eysenbach (1999)
  - Type A – Email sent without previous relationship.
  - Type B – Email sent in the context of a relationship.
  - Conclusion: Medical ethics and practice has not yet established clear or specific ethical standards or practice procedures for the use of email by physicians.

Method Slide

Method

- 2 page Survey – email attitudes and behavior
  - 28 agencies in Central PA - Convenience Sample
  - "Direct service" is primary worker responsibility
  - 500 surveys, 378 (76.8%) returned
  - Pretested with 20 social workers
- Respondents
  - 74.1% female; 89.4% white
  - 2/3 had 4 year degree; 22% MSW
  - 43.3% in large agency; 23.4% in small agencies.
  - 40.4% public agency; 43.2% private nonprofit

Results Slide

Email Beliefs - Ethics

Table IV: *I believe it is ethical for Social Workers to use email for the following:*

(n=381)	Mean (STD)	% Agree (4 or 5)
Schedule, confirm or change appointments with clients.	3.34 1.17	57.0
Provide ongoing therapeutic services to clients.	2.27 1.10	17.6
Provide factual information to clients.	3.46 1.11	60.7
Communicate with co-workers within their own agency about clients.	3.60 1.17	65.3
Communicate with another agency's social workers about clients.	3.04 1.25	55.0
Communicate with other professionals about issues unrelated to clients (e.g. workshop information)	4.35 .80	90.5

There is a positive correlation between the Frequency of Email score and Ethical Belief score (r=.31, p<.001).

Discussion Slide

SW Education

- Integrate technology issues into Practice, Research and Field.
  - No longer just an "elective".
- Expose students to the literature on etherapy.
  - Encourage an evidence-based approach.
- Include technology as part of the social environment in assessment.
- Discuss the issues related to ethical use of email.
- Examine field agency policy and create change if needed.
- Encourage research on email-based practice where it exists.

Tips and Guidelines for Presenting Research

The following are some pointers for presenting papers at professional conferences.

- Always have a backup of your presentation. If possible, come to the room early to make certain that the equipment is working.

- Bring hard-copy handouts of slides and other supporting printed material so that listeners do not need to take notes. Handouts also provide listeners with your name and contact information. Finally, they help the audience remember the important points of your presentation.

- If possible, move from behind a podium during your presentation in order to interact with the audience. Involve the audience by asking questions.

- Don't just read your slides or notes. It puts people to sleep. Use the slides as an outline and organizing mechanism, and freely discuss the main points.

- Be sure that people can hear you. Ask someone in the back of the room to confirm that you are speaking loudly enough before you begin your presentation. Use a microphone when necessary.

- Make certain that the entire audience can see the screen. Never block the screen yourself by standing in front of it. Do not speak facing the screen rather than your audience.

- Acknowledge good input from the audience.

- Do not get into a disagreement with audience members over research issues. Simply thank them for their thoughts or suggestions. Remember that criticism (critique) of research is part of the academic culture and should not be taken personally.

- Do not correct your co-presenter in front of the audience.

- If possible, watch a videotape of yourself doing a presentation. Check your posture, gestures, movements, and voice tone for any changes you might want to make.

Generic outline for a presentation:

- *Tell 'em what you are going to tell 'em.*
- *Tell 'em.*
- *Tell 'em what you told 'em.*

- At the end of a presentation, analyze what worked and didn't work. Keep notes for future presentations.

- Many people are nervous presenting in front of groups. It is possible to do a fine presentation when you are nervous. Nervousness usually disappears after the first few minutes.

- Avoid utterances like "uh," "um," and "mm."

- Practice, practice, practice.

- Remember to have fun!

Poster Sessions

Poster sessions are a format commonly used at professional meetings in which a number of people present their research projects at the same time. Usually poster sessions are held in a large, open space, using poster board or PowerPoint displays on computers to exhibit the highlights of research projects. Students often present their research this way. The audience moves from poster to poster, reading the material and interacting with the presenters. The following guidelines will be helpful when you are developing a poster session using poster board (Woolsey, 1989).

- Organize the material with the title at the top and the printed material placed in three or four columns. Format the printed material so that people will read it moving down the columns from left to right. Place the introduction in the upper-left corner and the conclusion in the lower-right corner. This format helps manage the flow of traffic, as people will not have to cross back and forth to read the poster.

- Try to use the 20/40/40 rule: 20 percent text, 40 percent graphics, and 40 percent open space. Do not use too much text. Graphics and tables should be the primary focus of the poster.

- Because not all people will discuss the poster with you, verbal explanation should not be necessary for people to read through or navigate the poster. Arrows may be helpful in promoting navigation.

- Use large text that can be read at a distance of six feet. Emphasize the importance of the material by varying the size of the text, printing more important material in larger sizes. Do not have large sections of small text. Use bullets.

- Include graphs and pictures with brief titles or explanations wherever possible.

- Use muted colors for the background. Bright colors are distracting. Use related colors (different shades) to distinguish among sections.

- Detail is not necessary. It can be kept for discussion with participants who visit the poster.

When using presentation software such as PowerPoint for paper presentations or poster sessions, consider the following guidelines:

- Select a format that suits the theme of your research. For example, don't use a farm scene if your research is about urban issues.

- The format should not be too busy or distracting. Use the same format for each slide.

- You should have about one slide for each minute of speaking. Leave time for questions and comments.

- Use light text with dark backgrounds for projecting slides with an overhead or computer projector. Use dark text and light backgrounds for printing.

- Limit the material on each slide. Don't let the slide look cluttered. Blank space is useful and easier on the eyes.

- Use fonts no smaller than 24 points if possible. Sans-serif fonts such as Arial or Helvetica are easier to read than serif fonts such as Times New Roman or Palatino.

- Use the 1-by-1 and 6-by-6 rules: 1 idea per page; 1 idea per line. No more than 6 words per line; no more than 6 lines per page.

- Use color to enhance organization. For example, if the first level of an outline is orange, consider printing the second level in yellow to distinguish it.

- Use graphics that relate to your presentation. They may add visual information in the form of charts or tables, or they may be used for interest value, such as a diagram or picture that relates to the information you are conveying. Many graphics are freely available on the Internet; for example, the Google search engine allows you to search for images by key words. Be very careful not to use an image that has a copyright. If you are not certain whether an image has a copyright, you can e-mail the Webmaster or contact a person listed on the Web site and ask for permission to use the image.

The Google search engine can be found at www.google.com.

You can copy an image from the Web by right-clicking on the image and then clicking **Save image as** and saving the image to your hard drive. You can also copy and paste the image directly into PowerPoint. Right-click on the image and click **Copy.** Then move to your slide in PowerPoint and click **Edit/Paste.**

- Don't use too many fancy tricks on one slide. It is distracting. Power-Point allows you to use blinking and flying text, sounds, graphics, and music, but using too many of these features will encourage the audience to focus on the technology rather than the materials being presented.

- Hard-copy handouts are great. PowerPoint can print up to six slides per page for handouts as well as notes pages with talking points that correspond to each slide for the presenter.

Workshops

Workshops are designed to actively involve the audience in learning new information or skills. A workshop may present recent research about the financial abuse of elders and teach participants about new ways to assess and intervene when they suspect financial abuse. Workshops may last from an hour and a half to three hours or longer, leaving time for the audience to practice new skills, discuss their experiences, and ask questions. Presenters often use active learning techniques such as role-playing, group discussions, and structured exercises to enhance skill development among the participants. Workshops should be developed with specific objectives to be accomplished by the end of the workshop. For example, in the elder abuse workshop, participants would be expected to meet the following objectives by the end of the workshop:

- Describe the research that suggests the extent of financial abuse of elders.

- Define financial abuse of elders, and explain the difficulties involved in operationalizing the definition.

- List and describe three types of financial abuse of elders.

- Describe the role of police, social services, and family court with regard to the financial abuse of elders.

- Conduct an assessment interview with an elder to determine whether elder abuse warrants further investigation.

Presenters should also develop an agenda that specifies the approximate time that will be allocated for each section of the workshop. In addition, they should provide participants with handouts and other materials to reinforce learning. Finally, presenters should incorporate some procedure for evaluating both content and process in their workshops. This often involves simply eliciting feedback from participants for improving the workshop the next time it is given. Exhibit 12.9 shows a sample workshop evaluation.

EXHIBIT 12.9

EXHIBIT 12.9

*Financial
Abuse of
Elders
Workshop
Evaluation*

Please answer the following questions to help us evaluate and improve the workshop in the future. Please do not write your name. All answers are confidential.

1. What did you find especially useful in the workshop?

2. What did you find *not* useful or needing change in the workshop?

3. Other comments?

4. Please rate the following on a scale from 1 (Poor) to 5 (Excellent).

	POOR				EXCELLENT
a. Overview of the research	1	2	3	4	5
b. Financial abuse video	1	2	3	4	5
c. Role-play of financial abuse interview	1	2	3	4	5
d. Group brainstorming session	1	2	3	4	5
e. Overall usefulness of the presentation	1	2	3	4	5
f. Overall presentation style of the presenter	1	2	3	4	5

PLAGIARISM

A major ethical responsibility that all researchers must respect whether they are writing or presenting research reports is to avoid plagiarism. **Plagiarize** is defined in Merriam-Webster's Collegiate Dictionary as "to steal and pass off (the ideas or words of another) as one's own: use (another's production) without crediting the source"; "to commit literary theft: present as new and original an idea or product derived from an existing source" (2005). Plagiarism is considered intellectual property theft, and theft is a serious ethical violation. All of the following actions are defined as acts of plagiarism (LaFollette, 1992; Swales & Feak, 1994).

- Intentionally using another person's words or *ideas* in your writing without properly citing them (by giving credit through referencing the material).

- Paraphrasing someone's work without giving proper credit.

- Using facts, statistics, graphs, drawings, music, or anything that is not considered common knowledge without giving proper credit through citation.

- Using someone's exact words without using quotation marks, even if you have cited the source.

- Using someone's ideas or words that you received in oral communication or by e-mail.

- "Forgetting" to cite the source of ideas or words taken directly from another person's work.

- Using another person's work because you "did not know" the rules and conventions regarding plagiarism.

Knowing what is *not* plagiarism is also useful. It is not plagiarism to write your own ideas, thoughts, experiences, observations, or research findings. In addition, you may state "common knowledge" without including a citation. For example, you may explain that George Washington was the first president of the United States without referencing it. In addition, citing sources improperly is not plagiarism; rather, it is the inappropriate use of sources (WPA, 2003). See Exhibit 12.10 for some examples of what is and is not plagiarism. A general rule for avoiding plagiarism is When in doubt, cite your source.

The Ethics and Politics of Research Reports

Research reports are written to increase knowledge and/or influence organizational or social change. They involve not only scientific considerations but also ethical and political considerations. These include Should the results be made public? If so, how and to whom will the results be distributed, and in which languages? Which data will be included, and which will be left out of a research report? What interpretation will be given to the results? Who will be given credit for authorship of the report? These decisions, and guidelines for making them, are discussed next.

EXHIBIT 12.10

Is It Plagiarism?

You read the following paragraph and wish to include it in your own work.

This study found that few foster family members currently e-mail with agency staff, and those who do, do so infrequently. Many foster parents and children expressed an interest in e-mailing with agency staff. Human service agencies will need to make decisions about the use of e-mail with foster children and their families. Should agencies encourage participants to e-mail staff? If so, how will agencies insure the privacy and security of communications? What topics should or should not be addressed through e-mail? How long should a family member be expected to wait for an answer to an e-mail? Agencies, especially those promoting the use of information technology, will need to develop specific policies and training regarding electronic communication with their clients. (Finn, Kerman, & leCornec, 2004)

Finn, J., Kerman, B., & leCornec, J. (2004). Building Skills—Building Futures: Providing information technology to foster families. *Families in Society, 85,* 165–76.

continued

EXHIBIT 12.10

Is It Plagiarism?
continued

WHAT YOU WRITE	IS IT PLAGIARISM?
In my opinion, human service agencies will need to make decisions about the use of e-mail with foster children and their families. Should agencies encourage participants to e-mail staff? If so, how will agencies insure the privacy and security of communications? What topics should or should not be addressed through e-mail? How long should a family member be expected to wait for an answer to an e-mail?	**Yes,** you used the author's exact words without giving credit, and you credit this as your opinion.
Human service agencies will need to make decisions about the use of e-mail with foster children and their families. Should agencies encourage participants to e-mail staff? If so, how will agencies insure the privacy and security of communications? (Finn, Kerman, & leCornec, 2004)	**Yes,** you gave credit but did not use quotation marks when using exact words.
If human service agencies are going to use e-mail, they will need to have policies about the use of e-mail. They will need to keep e-mail private and secure. They will also need to establish rules about when to use e-mail.	**Yes,** you paraphrased and did not give credit.
E-mail is a "ticking time bomb." Policies and procedures need to be developed before we "lose our shirts in a lawsuit."	**Yes,** the source of the quotations is not identified.
Finn, Kerman, and leCornec (2004) note that if human service agencies are going to use e-mail, they will need to have policies about the use of e-mail. They will need to keep e-mail private and secure. They will also need to establish rules about when to use e-mail.	**No,** you paraphrased and cited the reference.
If human service agencies are going to use e-mail, they will need to have policies about the use of e-mail. They will need to keep e-mail private and secure. They will also need to establish rules about when to use e-mail (Finn, Kerman).	**No,** you cited the reference incorrectly, but it is not plagiarism since you attempted to give credit.
E-mail is being used by an ever-growing number of people for both business and social reasons. The use of e-mail can be problematic at times.	**No,** this is common knowledge.
In our study of social work attitudes about e-mail, we found that almost all students are currently using e-mail, but only 18% believe that e-mail should be used for therapeutic purposes.	**No,** you are writing about your own work in your own words.

Social Work Ethics. Research reports must follow the ethical standards of the social work profession. Results must be reported truthfully and accurately. Furthermore, the report must never violate client confidentiality. No one should be identified or quoted without giving permission. In addition, the report should not reinforce stereotypes or disparage any group by presenting or interpreting the results in a biased manner.

Language. Ethics and politics are also considerations in the use of language in research reports (Scribe, 2004). Being "politically correct" is also being ethically correct. Use gender-neutral terms whenever possible—for example, *letter carrier* rather than *postman*—and avoid using *he* as an exclusive pronoun when referring to both sexes. Conversely, avoid using *she* exclusively when referring to social workers. In addition, you should strive to use terms that are ethnically and culturally sensitive to the groups under discussion. For example, the word *Indian* may be insulting to people who define themselves as Native American, American Indian, or First Nation Peoples. When you are doing research on diverse groups, consult with community members about their preferred terms of reference.

Values and Bias. With regard to creating knowledge, research may provide evidence to support or contradict a particular theory or practice method. A research report can be expected to come under attack from individuals or groups who oppose the findings for scientific or political reasons. Research related to politically divisive topics such as abortion, sex education, or gay foster parents will be especially vulnerable to political influences. Interest groups may criticize the value of the research, the methods used, the data collected, or the interpretation of the findings. Such criticisms should be anticipated. The report should address any limitations dealing with the scientific basis of the study in the discussion section. Similarly, it should acknowledge any value biases of the author that might have influenced the research. It is better to acknowledge any weaknesses of the study in a report than to have others do so publicly or in print. Keep in mind that there is no "perfect study." All studies have some limitations and are therefore open to criticism.

Organizational Issues. Organizations usually dislike surprises, especially those that may be problematic for the organization. As we saw in Chapter 11, research reports, especially those involving the evaluation of programs, have the potential to embarrass an organization or jeopardize its funding. To avoid these problems, before publishing or presenting a report, the researcher should share the results with the organization or program that has been the focus of the research. The organization and the researcher can then discuss the best ways to present the findings in a positive light. Even when the report has negative results, it can focus on the lessons learned and directions for change.

Publishing research findings can also be a political issue that requires negotiation and compromise. A research project often includes a "Memorandum of Understanding" that details the responsibilities of all parties and contains a section that discusses publication. Some organizations include a clause that specifies who "owns" the results of the research and under what circumstances the research can be published. Funders may insist that they control the decision about whether to publish the research and where to publish it as a condition of their support. In other cases, an organization may have the right to refuse publication of research for any reason (including negative findings). A researcher should be clear about the publication agreements before beginning the project. She or he should then work collaboratively with the organization concerning distribution of the results.

Authorship.   Another political issue in research reports, especially reports done by university-based researchers that are published in professional journals, is authorship. Many universities and colleges are "publish or perish" institutions. Publication can be a crucial factor in receiving tenure, promotions, and merit raises. Therefore, claiming or assigning authorship of a report is a significant issue. Regarding research publications, authorship is given to the individuals responsible for the concepts, data, and interpretation of results for the project. Authorship includes the people who do the actual writing as well as other individuals who have made substantial scientific contributions to the study. In general, the person most responsible for conceptualizing, managing, and writing the project is listed as the first author; the next most involved is second author; and so on. Being the first or second author has more status and carries more weight in faculty-related decisions about contributions to the field than does a "lower" rank. Members of a research team need to be clear on authorship before they undertake the research project. In some cases, authors may note that the work was shared equally. In such cases, authorship generally is listed alphabetically.

CONCLUSION

All researchers owe a debt to those who came before them in that current research is based on the theories and research methods previously developed by others. The practice of writing research reports, manuscripts, and newsletters and presenting research is a way of sharing information with the professional community. By doing so, others can use evidence-based practice and can build on the work already done. Human beings and social conditions are too complex for any one study to provide definitive answers to social problems. Science is a process of research, replication, and incremental knowledge development. This could not happen without formal and somewhat standardized mechanisms for sharing research studies. Writing and presenting research reports in social work is a way of becoming part of the scientific process and contributing to the generation of new knowledge for the improvement of social work practice and ultimately for the benefit of those we serve.

MAIN POINTS

- Research should be shared in order to build the knowledge base and improve practice. Presenting research through journal articles, conference presentations, reports, and newsletters requires written and oral communication skills that meet professional standards.

- A research report or manuscript generally contains the following sections: introduction, method, results, discussion, and conclusion. Manuscripts sent to journals for publication must have a specific focus and format in order to be accepted.

- Research proposals describe why a research project is needed and how the research project will be conducted. They are written in order to specify the details of the project, obtain funding for the project, and obtain permission to engage in the project. The format varies with the purpose of and audience for the proposal.

- Conference presentations often present the latest research in an area. Successful presentations require consideration of the audience and purpose of the presentation as well as practice and preparation.

- Presentation software can enhance a presentation by contributing to organization and visual appeal.

- Plagiarism involves using other people's ideas, words, and intellectual work without giving due credit through appropriate citation. Plagiarism is unethical.

- Research reports involve ethical and political as well as scientific considerations. They must be written within the values of the profession and in cooperation with all parties involved in the research. Political struggles over resources or values may affect both the content of research reports and how they are received by various interest groups.

EXERCISES: PRACTICING SOCIAL WORK

1. List the ethical and political issues involved in writing a report on the results of the Black Feather Youth Survey. How might these differ from reporting the results of any other research study?

2. Use PowerPoint to create five slides that describe the methods, results, and implications of the youth focus groups conducted with youths from the Black Feather community. The file can be found on the CD-ROM under Youth Focus Group in the Assess tab.

EXERCISES: SOCIAL WORK LIBRARY

1. Review four of the research articles from the Social Work Library. Write a list of pointers that you can use to help guide your own reporting of research. What did you like (style, organization, tables, graphics)? What would you avoid?

2. Use the checklists for evaluating research reports for judging the quality of a research report you have found at the Social Work Library.

OTHER EXERCISES

1. Discuss issues of plagiarism in the following examples:

IN YOUR RESEARCH REPORT…	DOES THIS NEED A CITATION? YES/NO	EXPLAIN YOUR ANSWER AND WHAT YOU WOULD DO.
1. You are writing your experiences using play therapy.		
2. You are writing to disagree with an editorial in the newspaper.		
3. You quote Jane Addams in the introduction of your paper.		
4. You contrast your findings with previous research findings.		
5. You state that NASW provides a *Code of Ethics* for social workers.		

continued

IN YOUR RESEARCH REPORT...	DOES THIS NEED A CITATION? YES/NO	EXPLAIN YOUR ANSWER AND WHAT YOU WOULD DO.
6. You begin your paper with an anecdote that a board member told you.		
7. You copy a message from an online self-help group and use it as an example in your paper.		
8. You use a map you found on the Internet that shows high poverty areas in the state.		
9. You want to use a famous quotation, but you can't remember who said it.		

2. You have completed a survey on the need for a youth center in your community. In which section of a research report would you put the following information?

Section: I = Introduction   M = Methods   R = Results   D = Discussion

INFORMATION	SECTION
1. The number of people interviewed.	
2. The percentage of people who would like to see sex education at the youth center.	
3. A table showing the level of support for the center by age of respondent.	
4. Data from a report of the impact of youth centers on delinquency rates in a similar community.	
5. Your thoughts about why males say they would attend the center more than females.	
6. Explanation of theories why youth become delinquent and why a center would help.	
7. An explanation of how the survey was developed.	
8. An explanation of how the needs assessment could be improved in the future.	

APPENDIX

DEGREES OF FREEDOM	PROBABILITY LEVEL		
	.10	.05	.01
1	2.706	3.841	6.635
2	4.605	5.991	9.210
3	6.251	7.815	11.345
4	7.779	9.488	13.277
5	9.236	11.070	15.086
6	10.645	12.592	16.812
7	12.017	14.067	18.475
8	13.362	15.507	20.090
9	14.684	16.919	21.666
10	15.987	18.307	23.209
11	17.275	19.675	24.725
12	18.549	21.026	26.217
13	19.812	22.362	27.688
14	21.064	23.685	29.141
15	22.307	24.996	30.578
16	23.542	26.296	32.000
17	24.769	27.587	33.409
18	25.989	28.869	34.805
19	27.204	30.144	36.191
20	28.412	31.410	37.566

TABLE A.1

Critical Values of Chi-Square

Source: Table adapted from Fisher and Yates, *Statistical Tables for Biological, Agricultural, and Medical Research* (1963, 6th ed.), London: Longman. Reprinted by permission.

TABLE A.2

Critical Values of t

df	SIGNIFICANCE LEVEL*			
	.05 / .10	.025 / .05	.01 / .02	.005 / .01
1	6.314	12.706	31.821	63.657
2	2.920	4.303	6.965	9.925
3	2.353	3.182	4.541	5.841
4	2.132	2.776	3.747	4.604
5	2.015	2.571	3.365	4.032
6	1.943	2.447	3.143	3.707
7	1.895	2.365	2.998	3.499
8	1.860	2.306	2.896	3.355
9	1.833	2.262	2.821	3.250
10	1.812	2.228	2.764	3.169
11	1.796	2.201	2.718	3.106
12	1.782	2.179	2.681	3.055
13	1.771	2.160	2.650	3.012
14	1.761	2.145	2.624	2.977
15	1.753	2.131	2.602	2.947
16	1.746	2.120	2.583	2.921
17	1.740	2.110	2.567	2.898
18	1.734	2.101	2.552	2.878
19	1.729	2.093	2.539	2.861
20	1.725	2.086	2.528	2.845
21	1.721	2.080	2.518	2.831
22	1.717	2.074	2.508	2.819
23	1.714	2.069	2.500	2.807
24	1.711	2.064	2.492	2.797
25	1.708	2.060	2.485	2.787
26	1.706	2.056	2.479	2.779
27	1.703	2.052	2.473	2.771
28	1.701	2.048	2.467	2.763
29	1.699	2.045	2.462	2.756
30	1.697	2.042	2.457	2.750
40	1.684	2.021	2.423	2.704
60	1.671	2.000	2.390	2.660
120	1.658	1.980	2.358	2.617
∞	1.645	1.960	2.326	2.576

*Use the top significance level when you have predicted a specific directional difference (a one-tailed test; e.g., Group 1 will be greater than Group 2). Use the bottom significance level when you have predicted only that Group 1 will differ from Group 2 without specifying the direction of the difference (a two-tailed test).

df	LEVEL OF SIGNIFICANCE FOR TWO-TAILED TEST*		
	.10	.05	.01
1	.988	.997	.9999
2	.900	.950	.990
3	.805	.878	.959
4	.729	.811	.917
5	.669	.754	.874
6	.622	.707	.834
7	.582	.666	.798
8	.549	.632	.765
9	.521	.602	.735
10	.497	.576	.708
11	.476	.553	.684
12	.458	.532	.661
13	.441	.514	.641
14	.426	.497	.623
15	.412	.482	.606
16	.400	.468	.590
17	.389	.456	.575
18	.378	.444	.561
19	.369	.433	.549
20	.360	.423	.537
25	.323	.381	.487
30	.296	.349	.449
35	.275	.325	.418
40	.257	.304	.393
45	.243	.288	.372
50	.231	.273	.354
60	.211	.250	.325
70	.195	.232	.303
80	.183	.217	.283
90	.173	.205	.267
100	.164	.195	.254

*The significance level is halved for a one-tailed test.

REFERENCES

Abbott, R., Barber, K. R., Taylor, D. K., & Pendel, D. (1999). Utilization of early detection services: A recruitment and screening program for African American women. *Journal of Health Care for the Poor and Underserved, 10,* 269–280.

Allen, J., & Boettcher, R. (2000). Passing a mental health levy: Lessons for the community practice professional. *Journal of Community Practice, 7,* 21–36.

American Psychological Association. (2001). *Publication manual of the American Psychological Association* (5th ed.). Washington, DC: Author.

Americans with Disabilities Act. (2004). *What is ADA: Definition of disability.* Retrieved June 5, 2005, from www.adata.org/whatsada-definition.html.

Anderson, E. (1999). *Code of the street: Decency, violence, and the moral life of the inner city.* New York: Norton.

Antonuccio, D. O., & Danton, W. G. (1995). Psychotherapy versus medication for depression: Challenging the conventional wisdom with data. *Professional Psychology: Research and Practice, 26,* 574–585.

Bane, M. J. (1997). Welfare as we might know it. *American Prospect, 30,* 47–53.

Barnes, P. M., Adams, P. F., & Powell-Griner, E. (2005). Health characteristics of the American Indian and Alaska Native adult population: United States, 1999–2003. Advance data from vital and health statistics; No 356. Hyattsville, MD: National Center for Health Statistics. Retrieved December 29, 2005, from www.cdc.gov/nchs/data/ad/ad356.pdf.

Barron-McKeagney, T., Woody, J. D., & D'Sousa, H. J. (2003). Youth mentoring: Emerging questions about effects on self-concept and school performance. *School Social Work Journal, 28,* 51–67.

Berger, T. (1964). *Little big man.* Greenwich, CT: Fawcett Publications.

Bernstein, L., Schwartz, J., & Levin, M. (2000). *Evaluation of the Head Start Family Service Center demonstration projects.* Administration on Children, Youth and Families, U.S. Department of Health and Human Services. Washington, DC.

Beverly, S. G. (2001). Material hardship in the United States: Evidence from the Survey of Income and Program Participation. *Social Work Research, 25*(3), 143–151.

Bloom, M., Fischer, J., & Orme, J. G. (2003). Evaluating practice: Guidelines for the accountable professional (4th ed.). Boston: Allyn & Bacon.

Bowman, P. J. (1983). Significant involvement and functional relevance: Challenges to survey research. *Social Work Research and Abstracts, 19,* 21–26.

Bronfenbrenner, U. (1977). Toward an experimental ecology of human development. *American Psychologist, 32,* 513–531.

Bronfenbrenner, U. (1979). *The ecology of human development: Experiment by nature and design.* Cambridge, MA: Harvard University Press.

Bronski, M. (2004). The truth about Reagan and AIDS. *Z Magazine Online, 17*(1), 1–3.

Buckner, S. (2005). Median housing values continue to rise, Census Bureau reports. Census Bureau News. Retrieved August 12, 2005, from http:www.census.gov/Press-Release/www/releases/archives/american_community_survey_acs/004974.html.

Bureau of Justice Statistics. (2003, February). *Bureau of Justice Statistics crime data brief: Intimate partner violence, 1993–2001.* Author.

Caldwell, R. A. (1992). *The costs of child abuse vs. child abuse prevention: Michigan's experience.* Lansing, MI: Michigan Children's Trust Fund. Available at www.msu.edu/user/bob/cost. html.

Campbell, D. T., & Stanley, J. C. (1963). *Experimental and quasi-experimental designs for research.* Chicago: Rand McNally.

Campbell, H. S. (1883/1970). *Prisoners of poverty: Women wage-workers, their trades and their lives.* New York: Garrett Press.

Carney, M. M., & Buttell, F. (2003). Reducing juvenile recidivism: Evaluating the wraparound service model. *Research on Social Work Practice, 13*(5), 551–568.

Casella, G., & Berger, R. L. (1990). *Statistical inference.* Belmont, CA: Duxbury Press.

Casselman, B. (1972). On the practitioner's orientation toward research. *Smith College Studies in Social Work, 42*, 211–233.

Chavkin, N. F., & Garza-Lubeck, M. (1990). Multicultural approaches to parent involvement: Research and practice. *Social Work in Education, 13*, 22–33.

Cialdini, R. B. (1993). *Influence: Science and practice* (3rd ed.). New York: Harper Collins College Publishers.

Clayton, R. R., Cattarello A. M., & Johnstone, B. M. (1996). The effectiveness of Drug Abuse Resistance Education (Project DARE): 5-year follow-up results. *Preventive-Medicine, 25*, 307–318.

Cohen, J. (1977). *Statistical power analysis for the behavioral sciences.* New York: Academic Press.

Community Health Works. (2001). *A community needs assessment of lower Manhattan following the World Trade Center attack.* New York: NYC Department of Health.

Corcoran, K., & Fischer, J. (2000). Measures for clinical practice: A sourcebook (Vols. 1 & 2, 3rd ed.). New York: Free Press.

Cowger, C. D. (1984). Statistical significance tests: Scientific ritualism or scientific method? *Social Service Review, 58*, 358–372.

Craft, J. L. (1985). *Statistics and data analysis for social workers.* Itasca, IL: F. E. Peacock.

Cross, T. L., Bazron, B. J., Dennis, K. W., & Issacs, M. R. (1989). The cultural competence continuum. In *Toward a culturally competent system of care: A monograph on effective services for minority children who are severely emotionally disturbed* (p. 13). Washington, DC: Child and Adolescent Service System Program, Technical Assistance Center, Center for Child Health and Mental Health Policy, Georgetown University Child Development Center.

CSWE. (2004). *Educational policy and accreditation standards.* Arlington, VA: Council on Social Work Education.

Cullen, F. T., Wright, J. P., & Applegate, B. K. (1996). Control in the community: The limits of reform. In A. T. Harland (Ed.), *Choosing correctional options that work: Defining the demand and evaluating the supply* (pp. 69–116). Thousand Oaks, CA: Sage.

Daro, D., McCurdy, K., Falconnier, L., & Stonjanovic, D. (2003). Sustaining new parents in home visitation services: Key participant and program factors. *Child Abuse and Neglect, 27*, 1101–1125.

Dash, L. (1994, November 2). Rosa Lee and me: What one family told me—and America—about the urban crisis. *Washington Post*, p. C1.

Dent, C. W., Galaif, J., Sussman, S., Stacy, A., Burtun, D., & Flay, B. (1993). Demographic, psychosocial, and behavioral differences in samples of actively and passively consented adolescents. *Addictive Behavior, 18*, 51–56.

DeRubeis, R. J., & Crits-Christoph, P. (1998). Empirically supported individual and group psychological treatments for adult mental disorders. *Journal of Consulting & Clinical Psychology 66*, 37–52.

Dillman, D. A. (1978). *Mail and telephone surveys: The total design method.* New York: Wiley-Interscience.

Dillman, D. A. (2000). *Mail and Internet surveys: The tailored design method* (2nd ed.). New York: Wiley.

Drumm, R. D., Pittman, S. W., & Perry, S. (2003). Social work interventions in refugee camps: An ecosystems approach. *Journal of Social Service Research, 30*(2), 67–92.

Duer Berrick, J., & Barth, R. P. (1994). Research on kinship foster care: What do we know? Where do we go from here? *Children and Youth Services Review, 16*, 1–5.

Duggan, A., Fuddy, L., Burrell, L., Higman, S. M., McFarlane, E., Windham, A., & Sia, C. (2004a). Randomized trial of a statewide home visiting program to prevent child abuse: Impact in reducing parental risk factors. *Child Abuse and Neglect, 28*, 623–643.

Duggan, A., McFarlane, E., Fuddy, L., Burrell, L., Higman, S. M., Windham, A., & Sia, C. (2004b). Randomized trial of a statewide home visiting program: Impact in preventing child abuse and neglect. *Child Abuse and Neglect, 28*, 597–622.

Ellwood, D. T. (1996). Welfare reform as I knew it: When bad things happen to good policies. *American Prospect, 26*, 22–29.

Federal Register. (2005). *Federal Poverty Level 70* (33), February 18, 8373–8375.

Fehr-Snyder, K., Nichols, J., & Slivka, J. (2004, March 18). ASU vows to fight Havasupai lawsuits. www.azcentral.com/families/education/articles/0318genes18.htm.

Fetterman, D., & Eiler, M. (2001). Empowerment evaluation and organizational learning: A path toward mainstreaming evaluation. St. Louis, MO: American Evaluation Association. Also available at www.stanford.edu/~davidf/empowermentmainstreaming.pdf.

Fetterman, D., Kaftarian, S., & Wandersman, A. (1996). *Empowerment evaluation: Knowledge and tools for self-assessment and accountability.* Thousand Oaks, CA: Sage.

Fielding, J. L., & Gilbert, N. (2002). *Understanding social statistics.* Thousand Oaks, CA: Sage.

Figueira-McDonough, J. (1993). Policy practice: The neglected side of social work intervention. *Social Work, 38*(2), 179–188.

Finckenauer, J. O. (1982). *Scared straight and the panacea phenomenon.* Englewood Cliffs, NJ: Prentice-Hall.

Finn, J. (1994). The promise of participatory research. *Journal of Progressive Human Services, 5,* 25–42.

Finn, J. (2002). MSW student perception of the ethics and efficacy of online therapy. *Journal of Social Work Education, 38,* 403–420.

Finn, J. (2004). A survey of online harassment at a university campus. *Journal of Interpersonal Violence, 19,* 468–483.

Finn, J., Kerman, B., & leCornec, J. (2003). Providing technology to foster families: First year evaluation of the Building Skills—Building Futures program. Hartford, CT: Casey Family Services.

Finn, J., Kerman, B., & leCornec, J. (2004). Building Skills—Building Futures: Providing information technology to foster families. *Families in Society, 85,* 165–176.

Fischer, G. (1991). *Supporting learning on demand with design environments.* Proceedings of the International Conference on the Learning Sciences (pp. 165–172), Evanston, IL.

Fitz-Gibbon, C. T., & Morris, L. L. (1987). *How to design a program evaluation.* Beverly Hills, CA: Sage.

Fletcher, A. C., & Hunter, A. G. (2003). Strategies for obtaining parental consent to participate in research. *Family Relations, 52*(3), 216–221.

Flexner, A. (1915). Is social work a profession? *Proceedings of the National Conference of Charities and Correction,* pp. 576–590. Chicago: The Hildmann Co.

Franklin, R. D., Gorman, B. S., Beasley, T. M., & Allison, D. B. (1996). Graphical display and visual analysis. In R. D. Franklin, D. B. Allison, & B. S. Gorman (Eds.), *Design and analysis of single-case research.* Mahwah, NJ: Erlbaum.

Freud, S. (1909/2002). *The complete psychological works of Sigmund Freud: Two case histories ("Little Hans"* and *"The Rat Man")* (Vol. 10). J. Strachey (Ed.). New York: Vintage Books.

Gibbs, L., & Gambrill, E. (2002). Evidence-based practices: Counter arguments to objections. *Research on Social Work Practice, 12,* 452–476.

Gillam, S. J., & Murray, S. A. (1996). *Needs assessment in general practice.* London: Royal College of General Practitioners.

Glennester, H. (2002). United States poverty studies and poverty measurement: The past twenty-five years. *Social Service Review, 76*(1), 83–107.

Glisson, C. (1985). In defense of statistical tests of significance. *Social Service Review, 59,* 377–386.

Goliszek, A. (2003). *In the name of science.* New York: St. Martin's Press.

Gould, S. J. (1981). *The mismeasure of man.* New York: W. W. Norton.

Graham, J. R. (2000). *MMPI-2 assessing personality and psychopathology* (3rd ed.). New York: Oxford University Press.

Green, J. (1995). Help-seeking behavior: The cultural construction of care. In J. Green (Ed.), *Cultural awareness in the human services* (pp. 51–81). Needham Heights, MA: Allyn & Bacon.

Guilford, J. P., & Fruchter, B. (1973). *Fundamental statistics in psychology and education* (5th ed.). New York: McGraw-Hill.

Harachi, T., Catalano, R. F., Hawkins, J. D. (1997). Effective recruitment for parenting programs within ethnic minority communities. *Child and Adolescent Social Work, 14,* 23–39.

Harmon M. A. (1993). Reducing the risk of drug involvement among early adolescents: An evaluation of Drug Abuse Resistance Education (DARE). College Park, MD: Center for Substance Abuse Research (CESAR), University of Maryland.

Hayes, T. J., Dwyer, F. R., Greenwalt, T. J., & Coe, N. A. (1984). A comparison of two behavioral influence techniques for improving blood donor recruitment. *Transfusion, 24,* 399–403.

Hebbeler, K. M., & Gerlach-Downie, S. G. (2002). Inside the black box of home visiting: A qualitative analysis of why intended outcomes were not achieved. *Early Childhood Research Quarterly, 17,* 28–51.

Herrenkohl, T. I., Hill, K. G., Chung, I., Guo, J., Abbott, R. D., & Hawkins, J. D. (2003). Protective factors against serious violent behavior in adolescence: A prospective study of aggressive children. *Social Work Research, 27*(3), 179–191.

Herrerias, C. (1988). Prevention of child abuse and neglect in the Hispanic community: The MADRE parent education program. *Journal of Primary Prevention, 9,* 104–119.

Hite, S. (1989). The Hite report: *Women and love: A cultural revolution in progress.* New York: Alfred A. Knopf.

Howard, M. O., McMillen, C. J., & Pollio, D. E. (2003). Teaching evidence-based practice: Toward a new paradigm for social work education. *Research on Social Work Practice, 13,* 234–259.

Hudson, W. W. (1982). *The clinical measurement package: A field manual.* Chicago: Dorsey Press.

Hudson, W. W. (1991). *MPSI technical manual.* Tempe, AZ: WALMYR.

Hudson, W. W., & Nurius, P. S. (1994). *Controversial issues in social work research.* Needham Heights, MA: Allyn & Bacon.

Hull, G. (2005). Research with words: Qualitative inquiry. National Center for the Study of Adult Learning and Literacy. Retrieved September 19, 2005, from www.ncsall.net/?id=468.

Internal Revenue Service. (2005). New law encourages tsunami relief contributions. Retrieved June 10, 2005, from www.irs.gov/newsroom/article/0,,id=133843,00.html.

Johnson, K., Noe, T., Collins, D., Strader, T., Bucholtz, G. (2000). Mobilizing church communities to prevent alcohol and other drug abuse: A model strategy and its evaluation. *Journal of Community Practice, 7,* 1–27.

Jones, J. B. (1992). *Bad blood.* New York: The Free Press.

Kazidin, A. E. (1982). Single-case research designs. New York: Oxford University Press.

Kerman, B. (2000). Foster care program needs assessment: Results of the foster parent and foster youth interview. Casey Family Services. New Haven, CT. Retrieved October 15, 2002, from www.caseyfamilyservices.org/pdfs/foster_care_assessment.pdf.

Kettner, P., Moroney, R., & Martin, L. (2002) *Designing & managing programs.* Newbury Park, CA: Sage.

Kirk, S. A., & Fischer, J. (1976). Do social workers understand research? *Journal of Education for Social Workers, 12,* 63–70.

Kirk, S. A., & Reid, W. J. (2002). *Science and social work: A critical appraisal.* New York: Columbia University Press.

Krueger, R. A., & Casey, M. A. (2000). *Focus groups: A practical guide for applied research* (3rd ed.). Thousand Oaks, CA: Sage.

Krysik, J., & LeCroy, C. W. (2002). The empirical validation of an instrument to predict risk of recidivism among juvenile offenders. *Research on Social Work Practice, 12*(1), 71–81.

Kuther, T. (2003). Medical decision-making and minors: Issues of consent and assent. *Adolescence, 38*(150), 343–358.

LaFollette, M. C. (1992). *Stealing into print: Fraud, plagiarism, and misconduct in scientific publishing.* Berkeley, CA: University of California Press.

LaFree, G., Birkbeck, C., & Wilson, N. C. (1995). *Policemen in the classroom: Albuquerque adolescents' opinions about the Drug Awareness and Resistance Education program.* Albuquerque, NM: New Mexico Criminal Justice Statistical Analysis Center.

Lamb, R., & Weinberger, L. E. (1998). Persons with severe mental illness in jails and prisons: A review. *Psychiatric Services, 49,* 483–492.

LeCroy, C. W., & Stinson, E. L. (2004). The public's perception of social work: Is it what we think it is? *Social Work, 49,* 164–174.

Lehman, A. F. (1998). Public health policy, community services, and outcomes for patients with schizophrenia. *Psychiatric Clinics of North America, 21,* 221–231.

Leventhal, J. M. (2001). The prevention of child abuse and neglect: Successfully out of the blocks. *Child Abuse and Neglect, 25,* 431–439.

Levy Zlotnik, J., Biegel, D. E., & Solt, B. E. (2002). The Institute for the Advancement of Social Work Research: Strengthening social work research in practice and policy. *Research on Social Work Practice, 12,* 318–337.

Liu, H. T. (1998, May). *Chinese elderly immigrants' utilization of human services: The case of elders from Taiwan.* Doctoral dissertation, Arizona State University, Tempe.

Lum, D. (1999). *Culturally competent practice: A framework for growth and action.* Pacific Grove, CA: Brooks/Cole.

Lynam, D. R., Milich, R., Zimmerman, R., Novak, S. P., Logan, T. K., Martin, C., Leukefeld, C., & Clayton R. (1999). Project DARE: No effects at 10-year follow-up. *Journal of Consulting and Clinical Psychology, 67,* 590–593. Available at www.apa.org/journals/features/ccp674590.pdf.

March of Dimes. (2005). Impact on business. Available at www.marchofdimes.com/prematurity/15341_15349.asp.

Maslow, A. H. (1970). *Motivation and personality* (2nd ed.). New York: Harper & Row.

McDonald Culp, A., Culp, R., Hechtner-Galvin, T., Howell, C. S., Saathoff-Wells, T., & Marr, P. (2004). First-time mothers in home visitation services utilizing child development specialists. *Infant Mental Health Journal, 25,* 1–15.

MHSIP Task Force. (1996). The MHSIP consumer-oriented mental health report card: The final report of the Mental Health Statistics Improvement Program (MHSIP) task force on a consumer-oriented mental health report card. National Mental Health Information Center. Available at www.mentalhealth.org/publications/allpubs/ MC96-60/default.asp.

Milgram, S. (1963). Behavioral study of obedience. *Journal of Abnormal and Social Psychology, 67,* 371–378.

Moore, D. (2005a, January). *The elusive truth.* Retrieved May 25, 2005, from www.gallup.com/poll/content/ default/aspx?ci=14656.

Moore, D. (2005b, April). *Telling respondents what they need to know.* Retrieved May 25, 2005, from www.gallup.com/poll/content/print.aspx?ci=15838.

Muckenhoupt, M. (2003). *Dorothea Dix: Advocate for mental health care.* New York: Oxford University Press.

Murphy, D. E. (2004, March 18). San Francisco married 4,037 same-sex pairs from 46 states. *New York Times,* p. A26.

NASW. (1997). *An author's guide to social work journals.* Washington, DC: NASW Press.

NASW. (2005). www.naswdc.org/nasw/default.asp.

National Association of Social Workers. (1999). *Code of ethics.* Revised and adopted by the Delegate Assembly of the National Association of Social Workers. Washington, DC: NASW Press.

National Cancer Institute. (2004). *Cancer nanotechnology: Going small for big advances.* (Publication No. 04-5489). Retrieved June 6, 2005, from http://otir. nci.nig.gov/brochure/pdf.

National Coalition for Homeless Veterans. (2005). Background and statistics. Retrieved October 1, 2005, from www.nchv.org/background.cfm.

Nichols-Casebolt, A., & McGrath Morris, P. (2002). Making ends meet: Private food assistance for the working poor. *Journal of Social Service Research, 28*(4), 1–22.

Norton, D. G. (1978). *The dual perspective.* New York: Council on Social Work Education.

Oakes, J. M. (2002). Risks and wrongs in social science research: An evaluator's guide to the IRB. *Evaluation Review, 26*(5), 443–479.

Office of Management and Budget. (1993). *Government performance results act.* Office of Management and Budget. Washington, DC. Retrieved September 19, 2005, from www.whitehouse.gov/omb/mgmt-gpra/gplaw2m.html#h1.

Olds, D. L., Eckenrode, J., Henderson, C. R., Kitzman, H., Powers, J., Cole, R., Sidora, K., Morris, P., Pettitt, L. M., & Luckey, D. (1997). Long-term effects of home visitation on maternal life course and child abuse and neglect. *JAMA, 278,* 637–643.

Olds, D. L., Kitzman, H., Cole, R., Robinson, J., Sidora, K., Luckey, D. W., Henderson, C. R., Jr., Hanks, C., Bondy, J., & Holmberg, J. (2004a). Effects of nurse home-visiting on maternal life course and child development: Age 6 follow-up results of a randomized trial. *Pediatrics, 114,* 1550–1559.

Olds, D. L., Robinson, J., Pettitt, L., Luckey, D. W., Holmberg, J., Ng, R. K., Isacks, K., Sheff, K., & Henderson, C. R., Jr. (2004b). Effects of home visits by paraprofessionals and by nurses: Age 4 follow-up results of a randomized trial. *Pediatrics, 114,* 1560–1568.

Padilla, A. M., & Salgado de Snyder, N. (1992). Hispanics: What the culturally informed evaluator needs to know. In M. Orlandi (Ed.), *Cultural competence for evaluators: A guide for alcohol and other drug abuse prevention practitioners working with ethnic/ racial communities.* Rockville, MD: U.S. Department of Health and Human Services.

Paris, R., & Dubus, N. (2005). Staying connected while nurturing an infant: A challenge of new motherhood. *Family Relations, 54,* 72–83.

Pence, G. E. (2000). *Classic cases in medical ethics: Accounts of cases that have shaped medical ethics, with philosophical, legal, and historical backgrounds* (3rd ed.). New York: McGraw-Hill.

Piaget, J. (1972). *The psychology of the child.* New York: Basic Books.

President's Commission on Mental Health. (1978). Report to the president from the U.S. President's Commission on Mental Health (Vol. 1). Washington, DC: Superintendent of Documents, U.S. Government Printing Office.

Proctor, E. (2001). Social work research: Asking relevant questions and answering them well. *Social Work Research, 25*(1), 3–4.

Reid, W. J., & Fortune, A. E. (1992). Research utilization in direct social work practice. In A. Grasso & I. Epstein (Eds.), *Research utilization in the social services* (pp. 97–115). New York: Haworth.

Reinharz, S. (1992). *Feminist methods in social research.* New York: Oxford.

Roe-Sepowitz, D. (2005). Indicators of self-mutilation: Youth in custody. Unpublished doctoral dissertation, Florida State University, Tallahassee.

Rosenblatt, A. (1968). The practitioner's use and evaluation of research. *Social Work, 13,* 53–59.

Rubin, A., & Babbie, E. (1997). *Research methods for social work.* (3rd ed.). Pacific Grove, CA: Brooks/Cole.

Saad, L. (2005). *Bush fails to ignite public support for reform: Social Security debate is stagnating.* Princeton, NJ: The Gallup Organization. Retrieved May 6, 2005, from www.Gallup.com/poll/content/default.aspx?ci=16153.

Saint-Exupéry, A. (1943/2000). *The little prince.* (R. Howard, Trans.). Orlando, FL: Harcourt.

Saltzburg, S. (2004). Learning that an adolescent child is gay or lesbian: The parent experience. *Social Work, 49,* 109–118.

Sarason, I. G., Sarason, B. R., Slichter, S. J., Beatty, P. G., Meyer, D. M., & Bolgiano, D. C. (1993). Increasing participation of blood donors in a bone-marrow registry. *Health Psychology, 12,* 272–276.

Scott, J. E., & Dixon, L. B. (1995). Assertive community treatment and case management for schizophrenia. *Schizophrenia Bulletin, 21,* 657–668.

Scribe, A. (2004). APA research style crib sheet. Retrieved June 15, 2005, from www.docstyles.com/apacrib.htm.

Stein, L. I., & Test, M. A. (1980). Alternative to mental hospital treatment. I. Conceptual model, treatment program, and clinical evaluation. *Archives of General Psychiatry, 37,* 392–397.

Streitfeld, D. (1988). Shere Hite and the trouble with numbers. *Chance, 1,* 26–31.

Sue, C. W., Arredondo, P., & McDavis, R. J. (1995). Multicultural counseling competencies and standards: A call to the profession, Appendix III. In J. G. Ponterotto, J. M. Casas, L. A. Suzuki, & C. M. Alexanders (Eds.), *Handbook of multicultural counseling* (pp. 626–640). Thousand Oaks, CA: Sage.

Sullivan, C. M., Rumptz, M. H., Campbell, R., Eby, K. K., & Davidson, H. W. S. (1996). Retaining participants in longitudinal community research: A comprehensive protocol. *Journal of Applied Behavioral Science, 32,* 262–276.

Swales, J., & Feak, C. B. (1994). Academic writing for graduate students. Ann Arbor, MI: University of Michigan Press.

Taylor, J. R. (1997). An introduction to error analysis (2nd ed.). Sausalito, CA: University Science Books.

Trochim, W. M. K. (2002). Types of designs. Retrieved September 10, 2004, from www.socialresearchmethods. net/kb/destypes.htm.

U.S. Census Bureau. (2002). *Technical note on same-sex unmarried partner data from the 1990 and 2000 censuses.* Retrieved June 5, 2005, from www.census.gov/population/ww.cen2000/samesex.html.

U.S. Census Bureau. (2005). *Poverty thresholds 2004.* Retrieved May 24, 2005, from www.census.gov/hhes/poverty/threshld/thresh04.html.

U.S. Social Security Administration. (2005). Child disability starter kit—Factsheet. Retrieved June 5, 2005, from www.socialsecurity.gov/disability/disability_starter_kits_child_factsheet.htm.

Viney, W., & Zorich, S. (1982). Contributions to the history of psychology XXIX: Dorothea Dix. *Psychological Reports, 50,* 211–218.

Wakefield, J. C. (1988). Psychotherapy, distributive justices, and social work. Part I. Distributive justice as a conceptual framework for social work. *Social Service Review, 62,* 187–210.

WALMYR Publishing Company, http://walmyr.com/index.html.

Webster's encyclopedic unabridged dictionary of the English language. (1989). New York: Random House.

Weinbach, R. W., & Grinnell, R. M., Jr. (2004). *Statistics for social workers.* Boston: Pearson Education.

Westerfelt, A. (2004). A qualitative investigation of adherence issues for men who are HIV positive. *Social Work, 49,* 231–239.

Woolsey, J. D. (1989). Combating poster fatigue: How to use visual grammar and analysis to effect better visual communications. *Trends in Neurosciences, 12,* 325–332.

WPA. (2003). Defining and avoiding plagiarism: The WPA statement on best practices. Council of Writing Program Administrators. Retrieved June 11, 2005, from www.ilstu.edu/~ddhesse/wpa/positions/WPAplagiarism.pdf.

Yin, R. (1994). *Case study research: Design and methods* (2nd ed.). Beverly Hills, CA: Sage.

Yllo, K. (1988). Political and methodological debates on wife abuse research. In K. Yllo & M. Bograd (Eds.), *Feminist perspectives on wife abuse* (pp. 269–281). Newbury Park, CA: Sage.

Young, C. L., & Dombrowski, M. (1990). Psychosocial influences on research subject recruitment, enrollment, and retention. *Social Work in Health Care, 14,* 43–57.

Zuckerman, D. (2000, Winter). Welfare reform in America: A clash of politics and research. *Journal of Social Issues,* 587–599.

GLOSSARY/INDEX

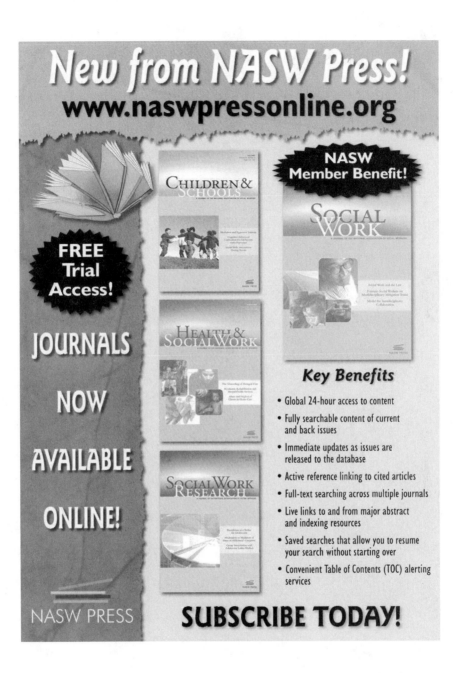